Adobe® GoLive® CS2

W9-BGM-796

Adobe® GoLive® CS2 Official JavaScript Reference

Adobe

Contents

Part 2: SDK Programmer's Reference

Preface

This book is divided into two parts. Part 1 provides an abbreviated introduction to scripting Adobe® GoLive CS2. Part 2 is a complete reference of the objects and commands in the Adobe GoLive CS2 JavaScript type library.

Advisory of previous publication

This book represents a subset of material included in the product CD for Adobe GoLive CS2. If you have the product CD, you already have access to a PDF version of this material.

About the Adobe GoLive CS2 SDK

The Software Developer's Kit (SDK) enables you to extend the behavior and user interface of Adobe GoLive CS2. Using the GoLive CS2 SDK, you can create tools tailored to your specific GoLive tasks. Using the SDK, you can create, customize, and extend most aspects of the GoLive user interface, such as:

- Menus and menu items
- Floating palettes and task-specific dialogs that include text, graphics, and controls
- Custom HTML elements, such as `<mytag>`, that can be edited in an Inspector palette
- Custom controls, that you can add as drag-and-drop items in the Objects palette
- Custom columns in the Site window

In addition, the SDK gives you programmatic options for working with Adobe GoLive CS2:

- Programmatic file and web-site resource manipulation, both local and remote
- Programmatic manipulation of the content of HTML and other markup documents
- Document parsing options for encoding, translation, localization, and non-HTML tags

The GoLive CS2 SDK defines a version of JavaScript called ExtendScript. It is very similar to the standard JavaScript, with some additional tags as described in this document. This documents generally refers simply to JavaScript and the SDK.

When the user interacts with one of your extension's user interface items, the SDK calls one or more JavaScript functions that you have created to provide the extension item's behavior. However, you don't need to be a JavaScript expert to use this SDK. If you've used HTML to create web page content, and perhaps added some interactivity to that page with JavaScript, you're already familiar with the concepts behind these extensions.

The SDK enables even inexperienced JavaScript users to create simple extensions easily with custom menus and dialogs—but it is also comprehensive and powerful. The SDK provides many JavaScript objects and methods to perform tasks on a document, on a site, in the GoLive environment, and on local and remote file systems. Nearly all of the user commands in GoLive are made available in JavaScript. Using JavaScript to automate repetitive tasks, you can, for example, edit all the documents on your site programmatically.

Because the files that define extensions use HTML syntax, you can use GoLive itself—including your own custom extensions—to create additional extensions to the GoLive design environment. In the same way that you can create JavaScript scripts to generate and manipulate HTML files, you can write JavaScript scripts to generate and manipulate GoLive extensions. Using this technique you could, for example, use JavaScript scripts to customize menu items in GoLive according to the contents of a database.

Optionally, extensions can call custom libraries written in the C and JavaScript programming languages. You can even use XML to define entirely new structured markup languages and documents to GoLive. In effect, GoLive's extensibility is unlimited.

About This Book

Part 1 of this book, the Programmer's Guide, describes how to use the SDK to add functionality and custom user interface elements to version 8.0 of Adobe GoLive CS2.

Part 2, the Programmer's Reference, provides complete reference information for the markup tags, JavaScript objects, properties, and functions, and C-language data structures and functions provided by the GoLive CS2 SDK.

This book does not document the JavaScript language nor how to use the GoLive CS2 application. For a listing of some helpful publications, see "Where to go for more information" on page 5.

Who should read this book

This book is for developers who want to extend the capabilities of Adobe GoLive using JavaScript and the special markup tags that the GoLive CS2 SDK provides. It assumes a general familiarity with the following:

- Adobe GoLive
- JavaScript
- C and C++ programming

What is in this book

Part 1 describes techniques for using the GoLive CS2 SDK to extend and customize the application. It contains the following chapters:

- Chapter 1, "Installing and Configuring the GoLive SDK," describes how to install the GoLive CS2 SDK and enable the appropriate modules.
- Chapter 2, "How to Create an Extension," describes what an extension is and what extensions can do. It provides a tutorial that creates a simple "Hello, World" extension.
- Chapter 3, "The JavaScript Environment," describes how GoLive makes JavaScript objects available to extensions and discusses other application-level considerations such as variable scoping, data sharing and communication among extensions, and timing issues.

The full Programmer's Guide on the product CD explains how to create and add menus, toolbars, windows, controls, and custom elements, and describes many tasks that can be done programmatically.

Part 2 provides detailed reference information about the markup tags and JavaScript objects that the GoLive CS2 SDK provides.

Part 2 contains the following chapters:

- Chapter 4, "Objects," describes the JavaScript objects, properties, and functions in the GoLive environment. This chapter does not describe objects that are standard parts of the JavaScript language or its Document Object Model.
- Chapter 5, "Tags," describes markup tags that the GoLive CS2 SDK supplies. You use these tags to define dialogs, palettes, controls, and custom elements your extension adds to the GoLive environment.
- Chapter 6, "Events and Event Handlers," describes optional callback functions your extension can implement to respond to events such as those generated by the user's interaction with your extension's controls.
- Chapter 7, "Defining a Syntax Scheme," describes how to write a source-code syntax scheme that a `source` control can use to check the syntax of source code you are editing in that control.

- Appendix A, "Object Palette Sort Order," provides the numeric values GoLive uses to sort icons and menu items.
- Appendix B, "Menu Names," lists the JavaScript names of existing menu items, which you can use to place new items in the menus.
- Appendix C, "Managed Layout Tags," lists the markup tags that you can manipulate without reparsing a document in Layout view.
- Appendix D, "C API for External Binary Libraries," describes data types and utility functions for creating external binary libraries that GoLive extensions can use.
- Appendix E, "Scoping in JavaScript," discusses the scoping of `name` attributes defined by extensions.

Document conventions

Typographical conventions

Monospaced font	Literal values and code, such as JavaScript code, HTML code, filenames, and pathnames.
Italics	Variables or placeholders in code. For example, in `name="`*myName*`"`, the text *myName* represents a value you are expected to supply, such as `name="Fred"`. Also indicates the first occurrence of a new term.
Sans-serif bold font	The names of GoLive UI elements (menus, menu items, and buttons). The > symbol is used as shorthand notation for navigating to menu items. For example, **Edit > Cut** refers to the **Cut** item in the **Edit** menu.

Note: Notes highlight important points that deserve extra attention.

JavaScript conventions

This book does not list properties and methods provided by the JavaScript language itself. For example, it is common for JavaScript objects to provide a `toString` method, and many of the objects the SDK supplies implement this method. However, this book does not describe such methods unless they differ from the standard JavaScript implementation.

Similarly, because most objects provided by the SDK have a `name` property, the reference does not list `name` properties explicitly.

When a JavaScript function returns a value, it is listed. When there is no return value listed, the function does not return a value.

Case sensitivity

The HTML specification specifies that attribute and element names are not case sensitive; the following HTML statements are equivalent:

```
<img ALT="graphics.tif">
<img alt="graphics.tif">
<Img Alt="graphics.tif">
```

In contrast, access to JavaScript property names is case sensitive; the following statements are not equivalent.

```
img.alt = "graphics.tif";
img.ALT = "graphics.tif";
```

In accordance with the JavaScript standard, GoLive always evaluates JavaScript property names case-sensitively. For example, GoLive does not consider `img.alt` and `img.ALT` to be equivalent. It is recommended that you adopt the convention of always using lowercase names to define HTML attributes. For example, the GoLive DOM implements the all-lowercase `bgcolor` attribute, not the mixed-case `bgColor` attribute.

Where to go for more information

This book documents the Adobe GoLive CS2 SDK only. It does not describe the full JavaScript language or the use of the GoLive CS2 application.

For instructions on how to use Adobe GoLive CS2, see GoLive Help.

For documentation of the JavaScript language or descriptions of how to use it, see any of numerous works on this subject, including the following:

JavaScript: The Definitive Guide, 4th Edition; Flanagan, D.; O'Reilly 2001; ISBN 0-596-00048-0

JavaScript Programmer's Reference; Wootton, C.; Wrox 2001; ISBN 1-861004-59-1

JavaScript Bible. 5th Edition; Goodman, D. and Morrison, M.; John Wiley and Sons 1998; ISBN 0-7645-57432

JavaScript for the World Wide Web, Fifth Edition: Visual QuickStart Guide; Negrino, Tom and Smith, Dori; Peachpit 2003; ISBN 0-321-19439-X

Adobe® GoLive® CS2

Part 1: SDK Programmer's Guide

1 Installing and Configuring the GoLive SDK

The first part of this chapter describes how to install the GoLive CS2 SDK and introduces the JavaScript environment that GoLive provides for extensions. The next part specifies the file and folder structure you must use to create an extension. This chapter concludes with an example of a simple extension that writes messages in the JavaScript Debugger window.

Installing the GoLive CS2 SDK

The GoLive CS2 SDK requires version 8.0 of Adobe GoLive CS2 and is included in the default installation. Updates to the SDK and to this documentation set are available at http://partners.adobe.com/asn.

Installing the core set of tools and sample extensions

This section describes how to install an extension in GoLive. GoLive CS2 SDK files are initially installed in a subfolder of the Adobe application folder called `Adobe GoLive SDK 8.0r1`. The extensions provided with the SDK are in the `Samples` and `Tools` folders.

Each sub-folder in the `Samples` and `Tools` folders holds a different example of an extension. It is recommended that you install the core set of sample extensions and tools, and use them to help learn about and create your own extensions.

When you have become familiar with the use of the tags, scripts, and objects these samples illustrate, you can remove any or all of them, as you prefer.

Installing the core extensions

To install an existing extension, in most cases you simply copy or move the folder to the `GoLive_dir/Modules/Extend Scripts` folder. See the Release Notes for a list of samples whose installation requires more than this; in these cases, the installation instructions are included in the extension's `Main.html` file or in the Release Notes.

➤ **The following steps make the core extensions available to GoLive:**

1. Quit GoLive if it is running.

2. Copy at least the following extension folders from the `GoLiveSDK_dir/Samples` folder to the `Adobe GoLive 8.0/Modules/Extend Scripts` folder:

- Custom Box
- KeyMap
- Markup Tree
- Menus and Dialogs
- Palettes

3. Copy the contents of the `GoLiveSDK_dir`/`Samples`/`Common` folder to the `Adobe GoLive 8.0`/`Modules`/`Extend Scripts`/`Common` folder.

4. Copy the following folders from the `GoLiveSDK_dir`/`Tools` folder to the `GoLive_dir`/`Modules`/`Extend Scripts` folder:
- Dialog Editor
- Edit Extension
- Extension Builder

5. Start GoLive.

When GoLive starts, it loads all of the extensions present in the `Extend Scripts` folder.

Uninstalling an extension

To remove an extension from GoLive, remove its folder from the `Extend Scripts` folder and restart GoLive.

You can deactivate an extension without removing it; see "Enabling and disabling modules" on page 11.

Configuring GoLive for Extension Development

Developing GoLive extensions is an iterative process that generally requires you to restart GoLive whenever you need to load a new version of the extension you are developing. JavaScript-only changes can be reloaded from the **JavaScript Debugger** without restarting GoLive.

Enabling the Extend Script module

The built-in Extend Script module must be enabled before you can load or run any extensions. The module is enabled by default. Disabling this module disables all GoLive extension capabilities, which you normally do not want to do.

➤ **If this module has become disabled, you can re-enable it as follows:**

1. Select **Edit > Preferences**.

2. In left panel of the **Preference** dialog, select **Modules**. Modules are listed on the right by folder name.

3. In the list of modules, check the Extend Script module.

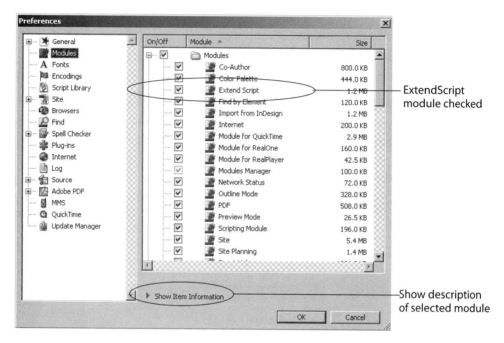

ExtendScript module checked

Show description of selected module

4. Click **OK** to confirm your changes and dismiss the Preferences panel.

5. Quit GoLive and restart it.

Enabling and disabling modules

GoLive packages much of its functionality in units known as *modules*. An extension that you develop using the SDK is simply another kind of module that GoLive can use. To add some particular new functionality to GoLive, you can install and enable the module that provides it. You can also disable or remove a module to remove its associated features and behaviors.

To turn off an extension but leave the extension in the `Extend Scripts` folder, use the **Edit > Preferences** dialog to display Modules, as shown in the figure above. In the list of modules, uncheck the modules of any extensions you want to turn off. The change takes effect when you restart GoLive.

The precise set of modules you can disable successfully depends on the features your extension or site uses—you cannot disable a module your site or your extension requires for its functionality.

Note: Do not disable the Extend Script module. If this module is not enabled, GoLive cannot load or run any extensions.

If you are not sure whether you need to enable a particular module, you can get a description of it in the Preferences dialog

➤ **Getting descriptions of modules**

1. Select **Edit > Preferences**, and in the left panel of the Preferences dialog, select **Modules**.

2. In the right pane, click to select the module to be described.

3. If **Show Item Information** appears at the bottom of the modules list, as shown in the figure above, click it to reveal the item information pane.

   A description of the selected module appears in the item information pane:

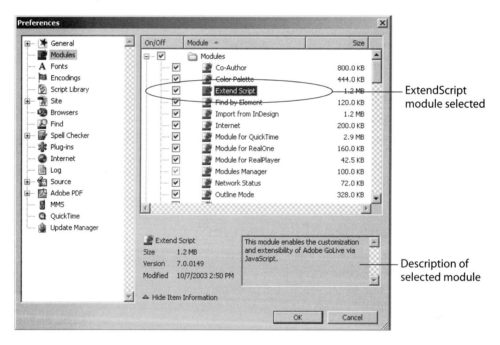

ExtendScript module selected

Description of selected module

Debugging Your Scripts

You can use either the internal GoLive JavaScript Debugger window to develop and debug your scripts, or the ExtendScript Toolkit, which is available to all Creative Suite 2 applications. To choose one or the other debugging environment, set the `internalDebugger` property (page 255) of the `settingsSDK` Object. When it is `true` (the default), the GoLive

JavaScript Debugger is active. You can use the Debugger's console to set the value to `false`, making the ExtendScript Toolkit active.

The GoLive JavaScript Debugger and ExtendScript Toolkit are described in the full written version of the reference on the Adobe GoLive CS2 CD.

These tools are complete development environments that allow you do more than just test your code—you can use them, for example, to edit documents interactively. To become familiar with the JavaScript environment in GoLive, try entering some JavaScript expressions into the Command field of a Debugger window; press ENTER to evaluate the expression. If you get a response in the output view, the command shell is ready for use; if not, see "Enabling Debug Services" in the full written version of the reference on the Adobe GoLive CS2 CD.

Error logs

All script errors are written to a log that is displayed in the Log window, which you can access through the **File >Log** command. Double click a script error entry in the log window to open the script file in the debugger and go to the error line. If an extension file contains a script tag that refers to an non-existing file, a warning is written to the log.

When a run-time error occurs in an extension script, an alert window displays the error message before the error is written to the log. Run-time errors in other scripts, such as startup scripts, are written to the log without an alert message.

2 | How to Create an Extension

Like a plug-in, an extension provides new capabilities to its host environment. With the GoLive CS2 SDK, you can use ExtendScript (Adobe's ECMAScript-compliant version of JavaScript) and HTML to create extensions that extend and customize the Adobe GoLive web-design environment.

About Adobe GoLive CS2 SDK Extensions

An extension that you create for Adobe GoLive CS2 SDK using the SDK is actually an HTML file that GoLive uses in a special way. Creating an extension is similar to creating a web page: you add tags and scripts to this file to define content. Instead of defining content for a web page, however, you use tags that define menus, dialogs, palettes, inspectors, and additional objects in the GoLive design environment. You can also create custom tags to define objects of your own.

When GoLive loads an extension, it makes the object defined in that extension available to GoLive users through the GoLive UI and through UI elements that you define.

- You can add to the GoLive menus, and create your own menus.
- You can add to GoLive windows—for example, add custom components to the Objects palette—or create your own dialogs and palettes.
- You can create custom elements, to extend the kind of markup a user can add to a page with GoLive's simple drag-and-drop technique, and customize the GoLive Inspector to make it display and modify your component's attributes.
- You can extend GoLive to integrate with other applications, web services, and more.

What can extensions do?

One of the most popular uses of an extension is the programmatic editing of files written in HTML, XML, ASP, JSP, and other markup languages.

To ease your learning curve, GoLive allows you to use familiar tools for this task. The JavaScript DOM in GoLive works just like the one in a web browser, providing programmatic access to the markup elements in an HTML file through the `markup` object. You can edit HTML files just as a browser or other HTML editor would.

The SDK can operate directly on documents in Layout view, allowing you to create extensions that automate the creation or modification of HTML pages. The SDK can also operate on documents without displaying them, enabling extensions to process batches of files rapidly.

In addition to supporting standard JavaScript DOM events, GoLive provides additional events that support the programmatic modification of documents and sites in the GoLive design environment. Responding to an event in your extension is similar to responding to one in a web page: you define an appropriately named JavaScript function within the HTML file's `<script>` element. For example, to respond to the `selection` event, you define and register a handler function for that event inside a `<script>` element in the `Main.html` file that defines the extension.

The GoLive DOM supports not just HTML, but XML (Extensible Markup Language). This ability enables GoLive to recognize other markup languages, such as those that define server-side tags, as well as the special `<jsx... >` tags that the SDK provides. As a result, you can edit an extension's `Main.html` file (or any of the other file types noted) in a GoLive document window, just like any other markup document.

GoLive CS2 SDK provides enhanced support for site-level operations, including notification of changes in the content or organization of the Site window, and programmatic selection of site assets according to criteria you specify. For example, an extension can select all files in the site that would take longer than a minute to download at 56 kbps. You can then process each selected file in some way. For example, you might compress it, downsample it, or reformat it in some way that would reduce the time required to download it.

In addition to its extended DOM and event model, the GoLive object model provides access to the GoLive application itself, which in turn makes available a host of other services and content.

The GoLive application provides access to:

- The GoLive user interface (Menus, Dialogs, Palettes, Inspectors, Site window, Document windows, Site reports, built-in localization).
- User settings, global stylesheets, preferences, shared data, other extensions.
- Custom/server tag support and special parsing behavior.
- You can create extensions that provide your own customized tags and content as icons in the Objects palette. You can also preprocess documents before the GoLive parser reads them, to deal with encoding issues or to mimic the effects of server-side code in Layout view, which is the graphical editing view in GoLive.

- Automation and macros: apply automated edits to every file in a site, or generate entire sites programmatically.
- Dynamic Content database content.
- Resources on network and WebDAV servers.

The typical extension can and does, of course, define things for itself in its own code, such as its own user interface items, custom functions, custom tags, SDK-provided tags, HTML tags, localization, source translation, and more. To accomplish this, you just add tags and functions to an extension's `Main.html` file as you might add them to a web page: tags go in the file's `<head>` and `<body>` elements, and JavaScript functions go in the file's `<script>` elements.

XML support enables even further extensibility, allowing GoLive to grow rapidly and conform easily to new standards that might emerge in the future.

Anatomy of an Extension

At its most basic, an extension consists of a `Main.html` file in a subfolder of the `Extend Scripts` folder, called the *extension folder*. The extension folder can contain other files that the extension requires, such as images. These additional files can be kept in subfolders. For example, the `Custom Box` extension's folder contains the extension's `Main.html` file, and also an `Images` subfolder that holds external `.gif` and `.jpg` image files.

The extension's `Main.html` file contains markup tags and JavaScript that define the extension. At startup time, GoLive interprets these tags and scripts to load an extension in the GoLive environment. The `Main.html` file should be an xHTML UTF-8 encoded markup document.

The extension defines objects using the GoLive SDK xHTML tags, and also defines the behavior for those objects using JavaScript code.

- The `Main.html` file defines the extension's menus, controls, inspectors, palettes, and custom tags. You can combine the special SDK tags with standard HTML tags as necessary.
- The `<jsxmodule>` tag defines the extension's name and some basic behavioral features.
- Various SDK-defined tags such as `<jsxdialog>` and `<jsxmenu>` define the extension's objects, such as windows, menus, and UI controls.
- JavaScript code contained in a `<script>` element in the `Main.html` file defines your own functions and your implementations of GoLive event-handling functions. When an event is triggered in one of your extension's objects (for example, when the user interacts with an

extension's custom menu, dialog, or palette), GoLive calls your extension's handler for that event.

Extension-building tools

The GoLive CS2 SDK includes powerful tools that make extension building easy. These tools are found in the `GoLiveSDK_dir`/Tools folder. To use them, copy them into the `GoLive_dir`/Modules/Extend Scripts folder, as described in "Installing the core set of tools and sample extensions" on page 9.

- Extension Builder

  This tool creates the skeleton code for an extension, together with the extension folder in the proper location. It opens the skeleton `Main.html` file in GoLive's Layout view, so that you can edit it to define specific objects and behavior.

  The skeleton provides the file framework, including basic HTML (such as enclosing `<html>` and `<body>` tags), and basic elements needed for an extension, such as the `<jsxmodule>` and `<script>` tags. The skeleton provides for easy automatic insertion of common objects, such as menus and windows, and provides a JavaScript script with placeholder function definitions (without body code) of the callback functions `initializeModule`, `startModule`, and `terminateModule`.

  When this tool is installed correctly, you can invoke it by choosing **Extensions > New Extension**.

- Edit Extension

  This tool complements the Extension Builder, allowing you to open and edit an extension's `Main.html` file after you first create it. Invoke it by choosing **Extensions > Edit Extension**. Together, you can use these tools to iteratively modify and test your extension, restarting GoLive as needed to load new objects.

- Dialog Editor

  This tool helps you design dialogs and add them to your extension. It adds a dialog-building tab to the Objects palette, with UI controls that you can easily drag into GoLive's Layout view of your extension's `Main.html` file.

For a step-by-step walkthrough of how to use these tools to build an extension quickly and easily, see *GoLive CS2 SDK: Getting Started*, in the `GoLive_dir`/Adobe GoLive SDK folder.

The step-by-step tutorial in this chapter (see "Creating an Extension Module" on page 20) walks you through creating an extension from scratch, to help you understand the framework and requirements that the Extension Builder tool takes care of for you.

Example Main.html File

This incomplete example shows the basic structure of the Main.html file for an extension with some typical components, such as a menu item, dialog box with UI controls, a custom element with an Inspector, and event-handling functions:

```html
<html>
   <body>
      <jsxmodule ...>
// define JavaScript event-handling functions
      <script>
         function initializeModule (){
            if confirm ("Modify...?"){
               fileGetDialog(...);}
            ...}
         function menuSignal (menuItem){
            if (menuItem.name == "myItem") {
               //do something
            }
            ...}
         ...
      </script>
// add a menu item to a GoLive menu
      <jsxmenubar>
         <jsxmenu ...>
            <jsxitem name="myItem" title="MyItem" >
         </jsxmenu>
      </jsxmenubar>
// define a dialog with UI controls
      <jsxdialog ... >
         <jsxcontrol ...>
         ...
      </jsxdialog>
// define a custom element and add it to the Objects
palette
      <jsxelement name="myTag" ...>
      <jsxepalettegroup name="myTag" ...>
      <jsxpaletteentry name="myTag" ...>
// define an Inspector for the custom element
      <jsxinspector name="myTag" ...>
         <jsxcontrol type="edit"  ...>
         ...
      </jsxinspector
   </body>
</html>
```

Creating an Extension Module

Every extension takes the form of a `Main.html` file that resides in its own uniquely named folder in the `Extend Scripts` folder. This section describes how to create the file and folder structure GoLive expects extensions to have.

To begin creating an extension, first create the *extension folder*. Create a folder with a unique name and place it in the `Adobe GoLive CS_Lang`/`Modules`/`Extend Scripts`/ folder.

In this folder, create a new file named `Main.html`. You can use any text or HTML editor to edit this file, including Adobe GoLive CS2 SDK itself.

Creating the Main.html file

The `Main.html` file contains the markup tags and JavaScript that define an extension.

➤ To create a Main.html file:

1. In GoLive, create a new page, using **File > New Document**. In the dialog, select **Favorites** and **HTML Page**, then click **OK**.

   This automatically creates and displays an HTML document with basic page elements such as `<head>` and `<body>`.

2. Switch to Source view and add a `<jsxmodule>` tag in the `<body>` element before the `<p>` start tag:

   ```
   <body>
       <jsxmodule name="My First Extension">
       <p>
       </p>
   </body>
   ```

   For more information on this tag, see "Adding the module tag" on page 22.

3. Add a `<script>` element after `<jsxmodule>`:

   ```
   <body>
       <jsxmodule name="My First Extension">
       <script>
       </script>
       <p>
       </p>
   </body>
   ```

   Typically, the `<script>` element is placed inside the `<body>` element, but you can put it inside the `<head>` element.

4. Inside the `<script>` element, add the following event handling function:

```
<script>
    function initializeModule() {

menubar["Test"].items["Item1"].addEventListener("menu
Signal",
            'function(e){Window.alert(e.target.name + "
was selected!");}')
    }
</script>
```

For more information on defining and using JavaScript functions in an extension, see "Adding event-handling functions" on page 23.

5. After the `</script>` end tag, add special SDK tags for a menu and menu item:

```
</script>
<jsxmenubar>
    <jsxmenu name="Test" title="Test menu">
        <jsxitem name="Item1" title="Item 1">
    </jsxmenu>
</jsxmenubar>
<p>
</p>
```

The file should now look like this:

```
<!DOCTYPE html PUBLIC "-//W3C//DTD HTML 4.01
Transitional//EN">
<html>
    <head>
        <meta http-equiv="content-type"
            content="text/html;charset=iso-8859-1">
        <meta name="generator" content="Adobe GoLive 7">
        <title>Welcome to Adobe GoLive 7</title>
    </head>

    <body bgcolor="#ffffff">
        <jsxmodule name="My First Extension">
        <script>
            function initializeModule() {

menubar["Test"].items["Item1"].addEventListener(
                "menuSignal", 'function(e){
                    Window.alert(e.target.name + " was
selected!");}')
            }
        </script>
        <jsxmenubar>
```

```
                    <jsxmenu name="Test" title="Test menu">
                        <jsxitem name="Item1" title="Item 1">
                    </jsxmenu>
                </jsxmenubar>
                <p>
                </p>
            </body>
        </html>
```

6. Save the document as `Main.html` in a new folder named `My First Extension` in the `Extend Scripts` folder.

7. To test your extension, restart GoLive. Select **Test menu>Item 1**. This should display the alert "`Item 1 was selected.`"

Congratulations! You have just created your first extension to GoLive. That is really all there is to creating a basic extension using the GoLive CS2 SDK.

Adding SDK Tags and JavaScript Functions to the Module

This section illustrates some development techniques by walking you through a simple extension that writes a message in the JavaScript Debugger window and displays a user alert. In this exercise, you add tags and scripts to the body of a `Main.html` file such as the one you created above.

Adding the module tag

GoLive packages much of its functionality in units known as *modules*. To add some particular new functionality to GoLive, a user can install and enable the module that provides it. A GoLive user can also disable or remove a module to remove its associated features and behaviors.

An extension that you develop using the SDK is simply another kind of module that GoLive can use. Like the built-in modules, extensions can be enabled and disabled in the Preferences dialog.

Each module must have a unique name that represents it in the global JavaScript namespace. To define the name of your extension's module, add to your extension's `Main.html` file a `<jsxmodule>` tag (page 321) that provides a `name` property:

```
// Main.html file for Hello example
<html>
    <body>
        <jsxmodule name="HelloModule" debug>
```

```
        <script>
              // functions that provide your extension's
behavior go here
              </script>
        // Tags that define your extension go here.
          </body>
       </html>
```

When GoLive loads this `Main.html` file, it creates a `module` object to represent this extension and sets the value of the object's `name` property to the `HelloModule` string. The presence of the `debug` attribute enables debugging services in the JavaScript Debugger window. Always remove the `debug` attribute from commercial versions of your extension.

The `<jsxmodule>` tag and all of its attributes are optional. If you do not supply this tag, or if this tag's `name` attribute is missing, GoLive assigns a default value to the `name` property of the `module` object it creates to represent your extension. However, it is recommended that you explicitly define your own `<jsxmodule>`'s `name` attribute so you can use it for debugging purposes.

Adding event-handling functions

The JavaScript functions that provide an extension's behavior reside within its `<script>` tags (page 323). Many of these functions are event handlers, which you register for particular event target objects. GoLive calls these functions in response to specific events, such as the GoLive user clicking something or entering text. Your extension can provide a handler to respond to a specific event in a specific object, such as the selection of a menu item or the opening of a document. When the event occurs in a target object, GoLive looks for all registered handlers for that event in that object, and if it finds one, executes it.

The *GoLive CS2 SDK Programmer's Reference* provides the names and syntax of all the event and event target objects, and describes the handlers that you can define. Most of them are optional; you only need to supply handlers for the events you need to respond to.

Module startup and termination events are handled by functions with predefined names. For example, on startup, GoLive checks all loaded modules for implementations of the `initializeModule` and `startModule` functions (page 359). If your module needs to perform any initialization, it can do it in these functions. The `initializeModule` function is called as soon as the module is loaded, and can perform any initialization that does not depend on other modules, and the `startModule` function is called after all modules are loaded. Similarly, your implementation of the

---

`terminateModule` function (page 359) can perform housekeeping tasks before GoLive unloads your extension.

The following example shows very simple implementations of the `initializeModule`, `startModule`, and `terminateModule` functions.

```
// Main.html file for Hello example
<html>
   <body>
      <jsxmodule name="HelloModule" debug>
         <script>
            // functions that provide your extension's
behavior go here
            function initializeModule() {
               writeln ("Loading the " + module.name + "
extension.");
            }
            function startModule() {
               writeln ("Starting the " + module.name +
" extension.");
            }
            function terminateModule() {
             Window.alert ("Unloading the " +
module.name + "extension.")
            }
         </script>
      // Tags that define your extension's data go here.
   </body>
</html>
```

In this example, the `initializeModule` and `startModule` functions simply display messages in the JavaScript Debugger window before the extension runs. The body of these functions consist of a `writeln` statement that uses the `name` property of the `module` object to identify the currently executing extension.

When you start GoLive and it loads this extension (along with all other extensions), the text is displayed in the Output panel in the GoLive JavaScript Debugger or in the ExtendScript Toolkit:

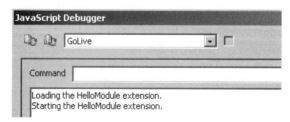

For the `terminateModule` function, you might not see such a display before GoLive quits. To make sure you see this message, the example function displays the text in a user alert like this one:

To do this, the function uses a globally available static function of the `Window` class:

```
function terminateModule() {
    Window.alert ("Unloading the " + module.name +
    "extension.")
}
```

GoLive does not unload this extension and complete the exit process until you click **OK** in the user alert dialog.

If you place this `Main.html` file in a `HelloModule` folder in the `Modules/Extend Scripts` folder and restart GoLive, you should see the loading and starting messages in the JavaScript Debugger window when GoLive restarts. When you quit GoLive, you see the alert before the application exits.

Typically, your `initializeModule` function registers the event handlers that provide behavior for your objects, and the `terminateModule` function unregisters the handlers. An extension generally provides event handlers, for example, to respond to clicks on menu items it has added, or to text entry in controls it has defined.

Summary

This short example introduces most of the concepts required to understand start using the SDK to define your own extensions. You have now seen how to:

- Create the `Main.html` file that defines an extension module.
- Add SDK tags to that file to define extension data.
- For a description of how to add tags that create menus, dialog boxes, and custom markup elements in the GoLive environment, see the full Programmer's Guide on the product CD.
  - For a complete list and description of the GoLive CS2 SDK objects, functions, and properties, see Chapter 4, "Objects," in Part 2.

- For a complete list and description of all tags that the SDK defines, see Chapter 5, "Tags," in Part 2.

- Implement and register event-handling functions for events of interest to your extension.

  - See "Handling Events" on page 34 for an introduction to the event-handling mechanism.

  - For information on show event-handling for different functional areas (for example menus and toolbars), see the full Programmer's Guide on the product CD.

  - For a complete list and description of all event and event target objects the SDK defines, see Chapter 6, "Events and Event Handlers," in Part 2.

- Use the JavaScript Debugger window to examine your extension's data and evaluate expressions within your extension's execution scope.

  Before beginning a serious extension development project, be sure to become more acquainted with the GoLive JavaScript Debugger, a fully featured, internal source debugger (see the full Programmer's Guide on the product CD).

3 | The JavaScript Environment

This chapter discusses JavaScript and ECMAScript/ExtendScript concepts and usage in GoLive, including:

- JavaScript Objects in the GoLive Environment
- Scope of Variables and Functions
- Handling Events
- Sharing Data
- Delays and Timeouts

JavaScript Objects in the GoLive Environment

GoLive provides access to data and objects in a way that JavaScript programmers will find familiar. Those new to JavaScript will discover that the GoLive environment usually provides multiple ways to access data and objects. This section describes various ways an extension's JavaScript code can access data and objects in the GoLive environment.

Objects, elements, and properties

GoLive JavaScript objects can represent parts of a document, or GoLive components:

- When GoLive loads a markup document, it generates objects to represent the markup tree of a document. Collectively, the objects that represent portions of the markup document are known as *markup objects*. Markup objects can represent HTML markup elements (as defined by a tag and its attributes), and also comments, text blocks, and other types of markup such as entities or CDATA sections.

- When GoLive loads an extension definition file (that is, the Main.html file for your extension), it creates JavaScript objects to represent the GoLive components you define, such as windows, UI controls, and menu items. For example, a `<jsxdialog>` element in your extension definition results in a window Object (page 313).

There are various ways to obtain a reference to a JavaScript object, depending on the object's type.

- You can retrieve most component objects by name from global properties, such as the `menus` and `dialogs` collections.

- Objects that represent HTML page content are available from the markup tree; you get the root object from the document Object (page 138) for the page (`document.documentElement`), and that object's properties and methods allow you to navigate the tree.

- GoLive passes relevant objects as event-object property values to event-handling functions.

For information on retrieving a particular object, see that object's description in the *GoLive CS2 SDK Programmer's Reference*.

Accessing attribute values

The attributes of an element (whether it is a document markup element or an element in your extension definition) appear as the properties of the corresponding JavaScript object. For example, the `name` attribute of the element becomes the `name` property of the object. Access to JavaScript properties is case-sensitive; that is, the `Thing` attribute creates the `Thing` property, not the `thing` property. When writing JavaScript code, observe case accordingly.

JavaScript uses the symbol `undefined` to indicate a null state. When a property exists, but no value has been explicitly set, that property has a value of `undefined`. If a property has never been defined, its state (rather than its value) is `undefined`. To test whether a property exists in JavaScript, you must test the state (not the value), by checking whether the name has a defined type; for example:

```
// correct test
if (typeof (myProperty) != undefined)
// do something
```

Do not use the following test. This tests the property's value, rather than its state, and results in a run-time error if the property does not exist:

```
// incorrect test
if (myProperty != undefined)
// if myProperty does not exist, an error occurs
```

When you must test a property's value with a case-sensitive comparison, you can use the `toLowerCase` method of the JavaScript `String` object. For example, this tests an `element` object's `tagName` property, disregarding the value's case:

```
if (currElt.tagName.toLowerCase()) ==
(tagToGet.toLowerCase())
```

For element Objects (page 156), attributes are also represented by objects, which are themselves nodes in the markup tree. Use an `element` object's getAttributeNode and setAttributeNode functions (page 157) to access the attribute object, rather than accessing the attribute directly by name, as a property of the `element` object. By using these methods, you avoid potential problems with referencing names that contain special characters, such as hyphens.

Naming objects and attributes

The value of an element's `name` attribute must follow JavaScript naming conventions. If more than one element or object uses the same name, the results of name-based object retrieval are unpredictable, so you must take care to ensure that your names are unique. One way to do this is to use a unique prefix or postfix in all of your extension's names. For example, the following element definitions begin the value of each element's `name` attribute with the letters `ADBE`.

```
<jsxmenubar> // opens definition of all menus
  <jsxmenu name="Hello" title="Hello, GoLive!"> // Hello menu
  <jsxitem name="This" title="Do Something"> // menu item
  <jsxitem name="That" title="Do Something Else" > menu item
  </jsxmenu> // closes definition of Hello menu
</jsxmenubar> // closes definition of all menus
```

When the SDK loads an extension containing these elements, it creates a `menu` object that appears in the JavaScript global `menus` collection. You can use the name to retrieve this menu from the collection:

```
var myMenu = menubar["ADBEHello"];
```

JavaScript object collections

The SDK makes commonly used objects available as the elements of array-like structures that all extensions can access. GoLive updates the contents of these structures dynamically as these objects are created and deleted.

The SDK implements many of these structures as collection Objects (page 72). This is like an array that provides access to its elements by name or index; however, collections are not actually arrays; not every collection provides numeric access to its elements, as an `array` object does.

Each of these global properties contains a collection object that GoLive updates dynamically:

Object	JavaScript Access	Contents
`boxCollection`	`boxes` global property	Read-only array of all boxes in the current document.
`controlCollection`	`controls` global property *windowObj* . `controls` property	Controls.

Object	JavaScript Access	Contents
`dialogCollection`	`dialogs` global variable	The current document's windows and dialogs that have run at least once. Read-only.
`documentCollection`	`documents` global property	Documents open in GoLive.
`history`	`document.history` property	Undo actions for the document.
`htmlStyleSetCollection`	`app.htmlStyles` property	Every HTMLStyleSet Object (page 179) in the **Window > Styles** palette.
`LinkCollection`	*boxObj*`.links` property	Links to all files that reference this box (in links) and all files this box references (out links).
`MarkupCollection`	*markupObj*`.subElements`	Immediate subelements of the *markup* object.
`MenuCollection`	`menus` global variable	All menus currently available in GoLive.
`MenuItemCollection`	`menubar[`*value*`].items` property *menuObj*`.items.`*propName*	All menu items belonging to a menu.
`PictureCollection`	`pictures` global property	All pictures accessible to this module.
`ServerInfoCollecton`	`app.server` property `website.server` property	All servers known to GoLive. All web servers for a site.
`WebsiteCollection`	`websites` global property	All web sites currently open in GoLive.

Using the global object arrays

These examples use the `menus` array to illustrate how you retrieve objects from global arrays. These arraya provide access to all of the menus and menu items added to GoLive by extensions. Most of the arrays work the same way; exceptions are noted in the Programmer's Reference, Part 2 of this book.

The following JavaScript defines a menu **Sample**, with one item, **MyItem**. The SDK creates a `menu` object named `sample` and a `menuitem` object named `item1`:

```
<jsxmenu name="sample" title="Sample" ...>
    <jsxitem name="item1" title="MyItem" ...>
</jsxmenu>
```

The following retrieves the **Sample** menu from the `menuCollection` object in the `menubar` global variable, and stores the retrieved `menu` object in the `sampleMenu` variable:

```
var sampleMenu = menubar["sample"]
```

In this case, "Sample" is the *title* of the menu, as displayed to the user, while "`sample`" is the *name* of the menu object, which you use to access it programmatically.

The following retrieves the menu item by name from the collection in the `items` property the `sample` menu:

```
menubar["sample"].items["item1"]
```

Alternatively, you can retrieve the menu item directly, using its name as a property name of the `sample` menu:

```
menubar["sample"].item1
```

GoLive also makes each menu available as a JavaScript object in the global namespace. Thus, the following simple line of JavaScript retrieves the menu item from the `sample` menu.

```
sample.item1
```

Many collections can be accessed by numeric index as well as by name. For example, if `item1` is the first menu item:

```
menubar["sample"].items[0] // 0-based index of first item
```

This is only reliable for the items, not for menus; because other extensions can also add menus, you cannot rely on the order. Some collections, like the `controls` collection, do not support numeric access at all. Most of the time, an object's unique `name` property provides the most reliable way to retrieve it.

Comparing objects

To ascertain an object's identity, you can compare the value of its `name` property to a known string, or you can compare object references directly. For example, you can test the name of a menu item in any of the following ways:

```
if (item.name == "item1") // compare object name to known
string value
if (item == menubar["sample"].items["item1"]) // compare
objects
if (item == sample.item1) // another object comparison
example
```

Updating references to objects

GoLive generates objects to represent the markup tree of a document when it loads that document. It regenerates these objects if the document changes; this is know as *reparsing* the document. If you save a reference to an object that GoLive generated as the result of interpreting a markup tag, you must update that reference any time the document containing the tag changes. For details, see the full version of the Programmer's Guide on the product CD.

Scope of Variables and Functions

You use standard JavaScript syntax to define your extension's variables and functions. When a `Main.html` file defines a "global" variable or function, GoLive actually creates the variable or function within the scope of the extension module the file defines, not in the JavaScript global namespace. It is available within the execution scope of that module. It is not available to other extensions.

The only truly global values in the GoLive JavaScript environment are those provided by system-defined global variables, such as the `app` variable and the `document` variable. These properties are available to every extension. For a complete listing and description, see Appendix E, "Scoping in JavaScript."

To demonstrate variable scope in the JavaScript Debugger window, add the following highlighted lines to the `Main.html` file that you created in Chapter 2, "How to Create an Extension," and restart GoLive.

```
// Main.html file for Hello example
<html>
  <body>
    <script>
      var myGlobal = "Hamburg, Liverpool, and London."
      function fabFour()
      {
        writeln ("The Fab Four played in " + myGlobal);
      }

      function initializeModule()
      {
        writeln ("Loading the " + module.name + " extension.");
        fabFour();
      }

      function terminateModule()
      {
       Window.alert ("Unloading the " + module.name +
"extension.")
      }
    </script>
```

```
<jsxmodule name="HelloModule" debug>
</body>
</html>
```

The new code just adds another `writeln` statement, but packages it as an extension-specific function. From within the body of this function, the `myGlobal` variable is accessible as a global variable. However, it is not accessible to any other modules.

The JavaScript Debugger shows the current scope in its module list. To set the execution scope to the `HelloModule` extension, choose its module name from the pulldown menu, as shown here.

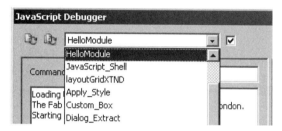

To set the global variable, type the following into the command line:

```
myGlobal = "Hartford, Hereford, and Hampshire."
```

Then run the function from the command line:

```
fabFour();
```

The function prints the changed string to the output window, using the new value of the global variable.

You might think you can access another module's variable by evaluating `module.var` or some similar JavaScript expression, but it is not that simple. You can use the common Object (page 77) to share data among extensions if necessary, although most extensions do not need to do so; see "Sharing Data" on page 37.

Releasing Memory

For optimum performance, you should release unused memory as soon as possible. You can set unneeded JavaScript variables to `null` to make them available for garbage collection.

Before it unloads your extension, GoLive calls the terminateModule (page 359) function. If you allocate any resources outside the JavaScript environment, your implementation of this function can be used to release them.

Handling Events

GoLive 8 implements a WC3-compliant event-handling mechanism. THis mechanism defines *event* objects of various types, which encapsulate information about events, and *event targets*, GoLive objects in which events can occur. The following GoLive objects act as event targets:

```
app
module
document
box
menu
menuItem
window
control
```

Each of these objects inherits the `addEventListener` function (page 373), which allows you to register a handler for a type of event that can occur in that object. When the event occurs in that object, your handler is passed a single argument, one of the Event Object Types (page 377), which encapsulates information about the event, such as where and when it occurred.

For example, a `menuSignal` event can occur in a `menuItem` object, and you can register a handler for that event that responds to the selection of a menu item that your extension added. Your handler is passed a menuEvent object (page 382).

- Your handlers for the menuSignal (page 363) and control events such as `onClick` (page 364) implement much of the UI functionality.

- Register handlers with the document Object (page 138) for document events such as `selection` and `save` (page 366).

- Register handlers with the app Object (page 53) for the `open` and `new` events (page 364), which occur when the user opens or creates a new document.

- Terminating the GoLive application generates the appterm event (page 360) in the app Object (page 53). You can register a handler for this event to do any cleanup that your extension requires.

- Other events allow more specialized responses, such as defining the appearance of a custom control when it needs to be redrawn.

For a complete list of events and the circumstances that generate them, see Chapter 6, "Events and Event Handlers."

Note: Event handling has changed significantly in this release. See "Compatibility with Previous Event Handlers" on page 395 in Part 2 of this book.

Defining and Registering Event Handlers

You must register a handler for a specific event in each event target object that should respond to that event. For example, if your extension defines two menu items, you could register a handler to respond to the menuSignal (page 363) in each of the menuItem Objects (page 225). Use the event target object's `addEventListener` function (page 373) to register for a specific event in that object.

An event handler takes a single argument, the `event` object. You can define an event handler as a separate named function, or you can define it inline during registration. Inline code can be a locally defined function that takes the event-object argument, or a simple statement.

For example, supposing that your extension adds a menu item with the name `doThisItem` to the `Hello` menu, you can register an event handler for the item in any of the following ways:

➤ **To define the handler as a separate function:**

```
//define the handler function
function doThisHandler (menuEvt) {
  Window.alert ("You chose" + menuEvt.name);
}
//register the handler for a target
function initializeModule() {
  menubar['Hello'].items['doThisItem'].addEventListener(
'menuSignal',
    doThisHandler)
}
```

➤ **To define the handler inline during registration:**

```
// register a locally-defined function
function initializeModule() {
  menubar['Hello'].items['doThisItem'].addEventListener(
'menuSignal',
    function (e) {'Window.alert ("You chose" + e.name);'})
}
—or—
// register inline source code
function initializeModule() {
  menubar['Hello'].items['doThisItem'].addEventListener(
'menuSignal',
    'Window.alert ("You chose the Do This menu item")')
}
```

It is possible to register an event handler at any time. You can, for convenience, use your extension's initialization function to register your handlers:

```
// Register event handler
function initializeModule() {

menubar['Hello'].items['doThisItem'].addEventListener(
'menuEvent',
     doThisHandler)
}
```

It is not necessary to unregister handlers on termination; the shutdown process does so automatically. To unregister a handler before termination, use the target object's removeEventListener function (page 373).

Nesting Event Handlers

When an event is generated for a child object in a hierarchy (such as a control in a tab panel in a window), GoLive goes through an event capture phase before executing the handler registered with the event trigger object, and then goes through a "bubbling" phase after executing that handler.

During the capture phase, GoLive looks for handlers for the event that are registered with ancestor objects of the target. It starts at the topmost level and runs the first handler it finds. It then runs any handler that is registered with the target object itself. After executing the target's handler, it bubbles back out through the ancestor objects, running the first registered handler that it finds on the way out.

For example, suppose a dialog window contains a panel that contains a button. A script registers an event handler function for the mouseEvent at the window object, another handler at the panel object, and a third handler at the button object (the actual target). In this case, when the user clicks the button, the handler for the topmost parent (the window object) is called first, during the capture phase, then the target button object's local handler. Finally, during the bubbling phase, GoLive calls the handler registered with the immediate parent, the panel object.

This allows you to execute multiple handlers for the same event occurrence, or to handle events at a higher level. For example, you could register a mouseEvent handler with a parent window object, instead of or in addition to handlers registered with the individual controls in the window.

If you define multiple handlers for the same event in nested objects, or use the same handler at different levels:

- Check the `eventPhase` property of the `event` object to see whether the handler has been invoked in the capture, at-target, or bubbling phase.

- Check the `currentTarget` property of the event object for the object where the currently executing handler was registered. In the capture and bubbling phase, this is an ancestor of the `target` object.

Sharing Data

You can get GoLive user preferences programmatically, and also create your own extension preferences. You can set values that persist across user sessions, or that are available to other extension only during a single session. You can also communicate with other running extensions and share data with them.

- Extension modules can use a prefs Object (page 240) to store persistent user preference data that is available to all extensions. The attribute Object (page 62) provides read-only access to a subset of GoLive's global preferences.

- The common Object (page 77) provides a place to share non-persistent data with other extensions.

- The app Object's broadcast method (page 56) allows one extension to send a message to another, and optionally receive a reply from that extension's broadcast event handler (page 360).

You cannot share or save objects, which are ephemeral. The `broadcast` method can only exchange strings with other extensions.

Persistent shared data

Extensions can create their own preference data, which persists across between user sessions and is available to all extension modules. This feature enables all extensions to share a common set of preferences and to store persistent data.

The prefs Object (page 240) in the prefs global variable (page 48) makes preference data available to all extensions. Preferences are stored as properties of this object. Create a new preference value simply by writing to a `prefs` property. For example, this creates a `myModule` preference that holds `"Version 1.0"` as its value:

```
prefs.myModule = "Version 1.0";
```

All other modules can check for the presence of this module:

```
if (prefs.myModule == "Version 1.0")...
```

When GoLive quits, it saves the `prefs` values along with all other preference data. The next time GoLive starts, it makes this data available to all modules again.

Note: You cannot save JavaScript objects as `pref` values.

Non-persistent shared data

The common Object (page 77) provides a means of sharing non-persistent string and primitive data among all currently running extensions. You cannot store objects in the `common` object.

The `common` object provides no predefined properties. Your extension can call the `common` object's `create` method to create a new namespace for shared properties in the `common` object; the namespace is then available to all extensions as a property of the `common` object.

For example, the following creates a namespace to hold properties of a particular extension, then adds a property with an assigned value:

```
common.create("myExt");
common.myExt.myProperty = myValue;
```

Communicating with other extensions

The broadcasting mechanism enables an extension to send a message to another extension requesting that it perform a task. Optionally, the called extension can return a result string.

When one extension module needs to communicate with another extension module, it calls the app Object's broadcast method (page 56). This method generates a broadcastEvent (page 378), containing the message argument. An extension that responds to messages from other extensions defines a handler for the `broadcastEvent` and registers it in the module Object (page 227).

Your handler for the `broadcastEvent` checks the `message` property, performs any tasks necessary to respond to the broadcast message, and optionally returns a result string in the `answer` property of the event object.

Use of the broadcast mechanism is entirely optional. If your extension does not need to communicate with other extensions, it need not implement a `broadcastEvent` handler.

Sending messages to other extension modules

The `broadcast` method sends its argument to the `broadcastSignal` method of any or all running extension modules.

```
broadcast (argument [, targets]);
```

This method converts the *argument* value to a string, stores the name of the calling module and the *argument* string to a `broadcastEvent` object, and generates this event in the target module or modules. The optional *targets* value is a list of modules to call, in calling order. By default, the `broadcast` method generates the event in every extension module.

Each called module's registered `broadcastEvent` handler must return a string value or `undefined`. Broadcasting terminates as soon as any extension's handler returns a value. (The handler can also store a response in the `answer` property of the event object.)

This method's result is the return value supplied by the last handler. If none of the called modules supply a return value, the `broadcast` method's return value is `undefined`.

Responding to a broadcast

To receive and respond to messages from other extensions, your extension must define a handler for the broadcast event (page 360) and register it with the `app` object. A called module's handler determines its actions according to the `message` and `sender` values in the passed broadcastEvent object (page 378). The value the handler sets in the object's `answer` property is returned as the `broadcast` method's return value. For example:

```
function handleBroadcast(bcastEvt) {
   switch (bcastEvt.message)
   {
      case thisValue:
         bcastEvt.answer=5;
      case thatValue:
         bcastEvt.answer="Yes";
      case anotherValue: {
         var myResult = myFunction();
               if (myResult)
                  bcastEvt.answer=myResult.toString()
               else
                  bcastEvt.answer="undefined";
         }
      default:
         bcastEvt.answer="undefined";
   }
}
```

```
//register handler
function initializeModule(){
   app.addEventListener( 'broadcastSignal',
handleBroadcast)
}
```

Delays and Timeouts

- GoLive has a global timer that you can use to schedule execution of your own scriptlets.

- You can set a JavaScript timeout value to avoid an infinite loop or other failure in an extension's JavaScript code that could otherwise halt GoLive indefinitely.

- You can display a progress bar or busy bar to the user while your extension performs lengthy processing tasks.

Timed tasks

You can evaluate a JavaScript expression after a specified delay. The startTimer global function accepts a scriptlet and a timeout. The scriptlet is stored internally and executed as soon as the timeout has elapsed. Optionally, the scriptlet can be scheduled for repeated execution. For example, you might schedule a script to run once per second.

The following code prints a counter in the JavaScript Output window every second:

```
counter = 0; myTimer = startTimer ("writeln (++counter)",
1000, true);
```

Note that the startTimer method's return value is required to stop this code's execution. To do so, pass this value to the stopTimer method, as the following statement does.

```
stopTimer (myTimer);
```

Setting the JavaScript timeout

You can specify the amount of time GoLive waits for JavaScript code to return control before it exits the current script unconditionally. Without this feature, an infinite loop or other failure in an extension's JavaScript code could halt GoLive indefinitely.

By default, GoLive waits forever for a JavaScript function call to complete. If you are not confident that a JavaScript function can complete its task in a reasonable amount of time, you might prefer to specify the amount of time

GoLive waits for a response. Each extension can specify its own timeout that GoLive uses to execute that extension's scripts.

To set the script execution timeout, your extension's `Main.html` file must include a `<jsxmodule>` tag (page 321) that provides a `timeout` attribute. The value of this attribute is the number of seconds GoLive waits for a script to return control before it exits the script. Values of `0` or `false` restore the default behavior of never timing out.

```
<html>
   <body>
      // give scripts ten seconds to complete before
unconditional exit
      <jsxmodule timeout=10>
         // scripts and SDK tags go here
   </body>
</html>
```

Note: An external library that calls an extension can specify a separate temporary script execution timeout for each JavaScript call.

Progress bars

To provide user feedback during lengthy operations, your extension can display a progress bar dialog or busy bar dialog. You can specify the title and the text to be shown while processing. For example:

```
app.startProgress( 'Please wait', 'Progress: 0%', false);
//show bar
app.setProgress(0,6, 'Progress: 60%');//update
periodically
```

A busy bar does not display a progress value; instead, it rotates the spiral indicator about once a second. For example:

```
app.startProgress( 'Please wait', 'Processing', true);
//busy bar
```

These are the same dialogs GoLive displays as part of its own user interface. Three methods of the app Object (page 53) make these dialogs available to extensions:

- The startProgress method (page 61) initializes and displays the progress dialog.
- The setProgress method (page 60) updates the status bar or busy bar display.
- The stopProgress method (page 61) hides the progress dialog.

As an alternative to these globally available predefined dialogs, you can define a progress-bar control in your own window.

Starting a progress or busy bar

The startProgress method has this syntax:

    app.startProgress (*title* [, *message, doBusy, seconds*])

- You must specify the string that appears in the progress window's title bar, such as "Please wait" in the examples.
- The optional *message* argument provides the initial status message displayed when the dialog opens.
- The method opens a progress bar, unless you pass true for the optional *doBusy* argument.
- The optional *seconds* argument is a number of seconds to delay before Golive displays the dialog. For example, a value of 2 means that GoLive displays the dialog only for operations that take more than 2 seconds to complete.

Updating a progress or busy bar

While the progress window is displayed, your code must update the position of the progress bar. It can optionally update the message text as well. Your code must also determine whether the user clicked the **Stop** button and act accordingly to abort the operation in progress. To perform these tasks, call the setProgress method periodically:

    setProgress (*value*, [*message*])

- The *value* argument is a value between 0 and 1 that specifies the portion of the progress bar to be drawn. For example, the value `.50` specifies that 50 percent of the progress bar is drawn to indicate a task half completed.
- The optional *message* argument is the string to display as the new status message. You can update a busy bar with a new status message; it ignores the *value* argument.

The `setProgress` method returns `false` when the user clicks **Stop** in the dialog. Your code should respond to this condition by aborting the operation that is in progress and closing the dialog. During lengthy operations, it is especially important to call the `setProgress` method regularly, so that your extension can respond quickly if the user clicks **Stop**.

When the lengthy operation is completed (or the user clicks **Stop**), call the `stopProgress` method to close the dialog.

Progress bar example

This example displays a progress bar. The `doSomeWork` function is your own code that performs the task on which you are reporting progress.

```
function progressDemo() {
    var percentDone = 0;
    var continue = true;

    app.startProgress("Progress Demo", "Starting, please
wait.", busy);

    while (continue && percentDone < 100) {

        doSomeWork(); // your own code
        percentDone += 1; // simply 1 to 100 for sample

        continue = app.setProgress(percentDone/100,
                                    'Progress: ' +
percentDone + '%';)
    }
    if (!continue) writeln ("User clicked Stop.");

    app.stopProgress();
}
```

Adobe® GoLive® CS2

Part 2: SDK Programmer's Reference

4 | Objects

This chapter describes the JavaScript objects that the SDK supplies. Some of these objects are created when GoLive interprets a `Main.html` file, while others, such as the Application object, are always available.

Global Properties and Functions

This section describes properties and methods available within the global JavaScript namespace.

Global properties

Global properties provide access to the Application object, the Module object, the Common object, and all currently available Dialogs, Palettes, Boxes, and Menus.

Various global properties provide access to collections of Dialogs, Palettes, Boxes, and Menus. A collection Object (page 72) is like an array that enables you retrieve objects by name as well as by integer index. (When two or more objects in a collection have the same `name` value, those objects cannot be retrieved by name reliably.)

Name	Type	Description
app	App	The app Object (page 53) for the GoLive application. Read-only.
boxes	Box Collection	A read-only array box Objects (page 64) for all custom boxes running in the current document. You can retrieve boxes from this array by name or by numeric index.
common	Common	The common Object (page 77) allows modules to share and exchange data. All properties of the `common` object are shared among all modules. Unlike the `prefs` object, properties are not persistent. They can hold anything except objects, which cannot be shared among extension modules.
controls	Control Collection	Deprecated in 8.0. A read-only array of control Object Types (page 78) for all controls that have run at least once in the current user session, and of dynamic controls. You can retrieve controls from this array by name.
dialogs	Window Collection	A read-only array of all window Objects (page 313) that have run at least once in the current user session. You can retrieve dialogs from this array by name or by numeric index.
document	Document	The document Object (page 138) for the current document. Read-only.

Name	Type	Description
documents	Document Collection	A read-only array of all open document Objects (page 138). Retrieve documents from this array by 0-based numeric index.
menubar	Menu Collection	A read-only array of menu Objects (page 223) for the top-level menu in the menubar, predefined or defined by any SDK module. You can retrieve menus from this array by name or by numeric index (see Appendix B, "Menu Names"). Menu items and submenus are available as properties of their parent menus. **Note:** In Mac OS®, the **GoLive** menu is not part of this collection. (Supersedes menus in 8.0)
menus	Menu Collection	Deprecated in 8.0. Use menubar instead.
module	Module	The module Object (page 227) for extension itself. Read-only.
modules	Module Collection	A read-only array of module Objects (page 227) for every loaded extension module. **Note:** Modules whose names contain spaces cannot be accessed by name, only by index.
pictures	Picture Collection	A read-only array of picture Objects (page 237) created by this module. You can retrieve pictures from this array by name or by numeric index. Picture objects created by interpreting <img> elements in this module's Main.html are available from this array immediately. A Picture object created by the createPicture function is not added to this collection until the first time it draws itself.
prefs	Preferences	The prefs Object (page 240) that gives all extension modules access to preference data. All properties of this object are persistent and have the same value for every extension module.
server	ServerInfo	The serverInfo Object (page 243) that enables extensions to request data from server information files on a Dynamic Content server. (GoLive 6 and higher)
settings	Settings	The settings Object (page 246) that provides access to GoLive settings. (GoLive 6 and higher)
website	Website	The website Object (page 296) for the active site. The active site's document does not have to be the frontmost document. The active site is the site that also shows its objects (colors, font sets, site extras) in the various palettes and menus. If you assign a website object to this property, GoLive makes that site's document frontmost.
websites	Website Collection	A collection of website Objects (page 296). Each object in the collection represents a currently open web site.

Global functions

Any JavaScript object or function can call these functions.

Function	Description
absoluteURL (relURL, baseURL, separator)	Converts a relative URL to an absolute URL using the specified base URL. Returns a string containing the converted URL value.
relURL	Relative URL to convert. If this string starts with a forward slash, it is presumed to be an absolute URL and no conversion is performed.
baseURL	URL to which this method appends the relURL value.
separator	Optional. String. The separator character used in the URL this method constructs. When not supplied, the method uses the forward slash (/) character as the separator in the new URL.
alert	Deprecated in 7.0. Use the Window Class alert static function (page 311) instead.
callCallback	Deprecated in 8.0. Site window callbacks have been replaced by standard events.
clearOutput ()	Erases the contents of the JavaScript Debugger window's output view.
command (*command*[, *input*, *skipOutput*])	Executes a command in a platform command shell. ● In Windows®, uses the command.com shell. ● In Mac OS, uses the virtual TTY terminal. Returns an object of the class ShellResult, which contains these properties: exit: The exit value of the executed process. output: The string that was sent to the standard output (stdout) of the executed process.
command	String. The command to execute, together with its parameters.
input	Optional. A string to be passed to standard input (stdin) of the executed process.
skipOutput	Optional. Boolean. When true, any output that results is not returned in the result object, which can improve performance. Default is false.

➤ **Example**

```
var res = command ('ls -l'); // in Mac OS
```

confirm	Deprecated in 7.0. Use the Window Class confirm static function (page 311) instead.

Function	Description
createPicture (*url*)	Reads a specified file to create a picture for use in an extension's drawing operation. Returns the new picture Object (page 237).
url	String. Relative or absolute URL of the file from which this function creates a picture.
disposePicture (*pic*)	Deletes a picture created by the `createPicture` method.
pic	The picture Object (page 237) to delete. When this method returns, *pic* is no longer usable.
fileGetDialog (prompt, typeList)	Presents the standard file-opening dialog for the platform on which GoLive is running. Returns the file Object (page 158) for the selected file, or `null` if the user dismissed the dialog without selecting a file.
prompt	Optional. String. A brief message to display in the file open dialog. If this string is too long, the dialog truncates it.
typeList	Optional. String. A platform-specific value indicating a list of file types to display. • In Mac OS, a comma-separated list of four-character Mac OS file types. For example, `"TEXT,APPL"` specifies that the file open dialog is to show only text files and applications. • In Windows, a semicolon-separated list of search masks. For example, `"*.jpg;*.jpeg,*.html"` specifies that the file open dialog is to show only files having names that end with one of the `.jpg`, `.jpeg`, or `.html` extensions.
filePutDialog (prompt, default, typeList)	Presents the standard file-saving dialog for the platform on which GoLive is running. Returns the file Object (page 158) for the selected file, or `null` if the user dismissed the dialog without selecting a file.
prompt	Required. A brief message to display in the file-saving dialog. If this string is too long, the dialog truncates it.

Function	Description
default	Required. A default file name to display in the file-saving dialog. This value must observe the file-naming conventions of the platform on which GoLive is running.
typeList	Optional. String. A platform-specific value indicating a list of file types to display. • In Mac OS, a comma-separated list of four-character Mac OS file types. For example, `"TEXT,APPL"` specifies that the file open dialog is to show only text files and applications. • In Windows, a semicolon-separated list of search masks. For example, `"*.jpg;*.jpeg,*.html"` specifies that the file open dialog is to show only files having names that end with one of the `.jpg`, `.jpeg`, or `.html` extensions.
folderGetDialog ([prompt])	Presents the standard folder-opening dialog for the platform on which GoLive is running. Returns the file Object (page 158) for the selected folder, or `null` if the user dismissed the dialog without selecting a folder.
prompt	Optional. String. A brief message to display to Windows users. The SDK ignores this argument in Mac OS.
prompt	Deprecated in 7.0. Use the Window Class prompt static function (page 312) instead.
registerCallback	Deprecated in 8.0. Site window callbacks have been replaced by standard events.
relativeURL (absURL, baseURL, separator)	Converts an absolute URL to a URL that is relative to the specified base URL. Returns a string containing the converted URL value.
absURL	String. Absolute URL to convert.
baseURL	String. URL used as the working directory value.
separator	Optional. String. The separator character used in the URL this method constructs. When not supplied, the method uses the forward slash (/) character as the separator in the new URL.

Function	Description
| **startTimer**<br>`(scriptlet, timeout[, repeat])` | Executes the specified JavaScript code after a specified number of milliseconds have elapsed.<br><br>Returns a number that you can pass to the stopTimer global function (page 52) to stop the repeated execution of this scriptlet.<br><br>This example updates a display item every second.<br><br>```
function myPaletteUpdate () {
   var curTime = new Date(); // Get the current
time
   // Update my palette clock...
   }
   // Call my update function, once a second,
repeatedly
   var updateScriptId =
startTimer('myPaletteUpdate()',
                          1000, true);
``` |
scriptlet	String. JavaScript expression to execute.
timeout	The number of milliseconds that must elapse before the SDK executes the scriptlet.
repeat	Optional. Pass `true` to execute the scriptlet repeatedly. Default is `false`.
stopTimer `(id)`	Stops the delayed or repeated execution of the specified scriptlet.
id	The value returned by the startTimer method (page 52) when the execution of this scriptlet was scheduled.
unregisterCallback	Deprecated in 8.0; Site window callbacks have been replaced by standard events.
write `(text)`	Writes specified text to the output view of the JavaScript Debugger palette.
text	String. The text to write.
writeln `(text)`	Writes specified text and a Linefeed character to the output view of the JavaScript Debugger palette.
text	String. The text to write.
```

app Object

Class: `JSXApplication`

The `app` object represents the GoLive application. It enables programmatic access to data and functionality that the GoLive application provides. The properties provide access to information about the environment in which the extension is running. The methods can create documents, open existing documents, display progress bars, broadcast a message string to all running extensions, and quit the GoLive application.

Note: When the GoLive application quits, it closes all open documents, prompting the user to save or discard each document's changes as necessary, and creates disk files as necessary.

Acquiring the app object

The `app` global variable makes this object available.

```
app
```

app object properties

Properties of the `app` object provide access to information about the environment in which the extension is running, such as:

- Current HTML parser preferences
- Information about the currently running GoLive application, such as its version and whether it is currently displaying a modal dialog
- Paths to commonly used folders such as the current site's folder, the system trash, the folder that holds the GoLive application, the default HTML browser application, and so on
- Shared data and user preference data provided by extensions

`appSettingsFolder`	File	The file Object (page 158) for the GoLive `Settings` folder, which holds GoLive application settings. Read-only. See also userSettingsFolder (page 56).
`asymmetricTokens`	String	A string specifying all delimiters the GoLive scanner uses with the < character to recognize asymmetric tags. By default, the string is set to `"!"`, which means that SGML-style tags, `<!tag>`, are recognized. This value reflects the setting inside the web database. The value of this property is not persistent unless the web database is saved manually. Read-only.

`clipboard`	String	The current content of the operating-system clipboard, when that content is a string. You can copy a string to the clipboard by setting this property. Read/write.
`currentFolder`	String	The path to the folder that is the current working directory. Normally, this directory is the root folder of the currently active site. Set this property to change the current working directory. Accepts a path name or a file Object (page 158) for a folder.
`defaultBrowser`	File	The file Object (page 158) for the current default HTML browser application. The value of this property is `null` when no default browser preference is specified. Read-only.
`folder`	File	The file Object (page 158) for the folder that holds the GoLive application. Read-only.
`fontsets`	FontSetCollection	The fontSetCollection Object (page 170) for all available font sets.
`htmlStyles`	HTMLStyleSet Collection	A collection of HTMLStyleSet Objects (page 179) containing those styles that appear in the **Window > HTML Styles** palette.
`imageConverter`	ImageConverter	An imageConverter Object (page 182) used for image conversion in all documents for this session.
`isModal`	Boolean	When `true`, GoLive is displaying a modal dialog. Read-only.
`osVersion`	String	The version of the operating system. Read-only.
`prefs`	GlobalPrefs	A globalPrefs Object (page 176) that provides limited access to GoLive's preferences. Read-only
`scanBrackets`	Boolean	When `true`, GoLive recognizes bracketed text, such as `[hello]`, as a tag when parsing a document. Otherwise, brackets are considered to be ordinary text. This value reflects a web setting, available interactively through the web settings dialog. The value of this property is not persistent unless the corresponding web setting is saved through the dialog.

| sdkVersion | Number | The version of the currently running GoLive SDK. Read-only. This floating-point number provides the version numbers of the GoLive application and the Extend Script module when you interpret the decimal point as a separator character. |
| | | The portion of this value appearing to the left of the decimal point is a two-digit representation of the currently running GoLive application's version number. The portion appearing to the right of the decimal point is a three-digit representation of the Extend Script module version. For version 8.0 of GoLive and release 1 of the Extend Script module, the value is `80.001`. |

The SDK release number does not necessarily match the module's version number. For example, SDK Release 4.1 supplies version 004 of the Extend Script module. For details of the configuration of a particular SDK release, see the Release Notes and Readme file that accompany the distribution. For SDK updates and new sample extensions as they become available, visit http://partners.adobe.com/asn.

server	ServerInfo Collection	A serverInfoCollection Object (page 245) containing the serverInfo Objects (page 243) for all servers known to the application.
settingsFolder	File	The file Object (page 158) for the `Modules` folder, which holds all GoLive modules. Read-only.
		For GoLive settings, see appSettingsFolder (page 53) and userSettingsFolder (page 56).
symmetricTokens	String	A string containing all delimiters which the GoLive scanner uses, together with the < character to recognize symmetric tags. By default, the string is set to `?%`, which means that `<%tags%>` and `<?tags?>` are recognized. It reflects the setting inside the web database. The value of this property is not persistent unless the web database is saved manually.
systemFolder	File	The file Object (page 158) for the folder that holds the operating system. Usually, this is the `C:\WINDOWS` or `C:\WINNT` folder in Windows. In Mac OS, this folder can have any name and it can reside on any local disk or network volume. Read-only.

tableStyles	HTMLStyleSet	An HTMLStyleSet Object (page 179) containing those styles that appear in the **Style** tab of the **Window > Table** palette.
tempFolder	File	The file Object (page 158) for the folder GoLive uses to store temporary files. Read-only.
translator	Translator	A translator Object (page 286) that allows programmatic access to a file before GoLive parsing occurs. Read-only.
trashFolder	File	The file Object (page 158) for the system Trash folder. In Windows, this object refers to the local \RECYCLED directory. In Mac OS, this object refers to the *startupDisk*:Trash folder. Read-only.
userSettingsFolder	File	The file Object (page 158) for the local folder that holds GoLive user settings. Read-only. See also appSettingsFolder (page 53).
vcs	VCSHandler Collection	A collection of VCSHandler Objects (page 292) for all defined version-control-system interfaces.
version	String	The version of the currently running GoLive application. Read only.

app object functions

Functions of the app object provide a programmatic means of performing application-level tasks, such as passing keycodes and action codes to GoLive, creating new documents or opening existing ones, opening a URL in the current browser, accessing user preferences and configuration information, broadcasting string data to all extensions, or quitting GoLive.

activate app.activate ()	Opens the current GoLive window if it is iconified or minimized, and brings it to the front of the desktop.
broadcast app.broadcast (*argument* [, *targets*])	Generates the broadcast event (page 360) in the target modules, which can register a handler for that event. The broadcastEvent argument (page 378) passed to handlers for this event pass the *argument* string in the message property. Each called module's registered handler can return a value in the object's answer property. Broadcasting terminates when any module's handler sets this value. This method's result is the answer value supplied by any called module's handler. If none of the called modules supply an answer value, this method's return value is undefined.
argument	Argument string this method passes to handlers in broadcastEvent.message (page 378). If you pass an object as this argument, it is converted to a string, and the string value is passed. Objects cannot be shared among modules.

targets	Optional. Comma-separated list of names of modules to call, in the order they are to be called. When supplied, the method generates the event only for the modules in the list. When not supplied, the event occurs in all modules.

➤ Example

A signaled module's `broadcast` event handler can set the broadcastEvent (page 378) object's `answer` value to `undefined` or a value, as shown in the following example:

```
function myBroadcastHandler(bcastEvt) {
    if (...)
        bcastEvt.answer = 5;
    else
        bcastEvt.answer = undefined;
}
```

For an example of handling this event, see the `Timer Palette` sample (called by the `Menus and Dialog` sample) included with the SDK.

createProgressLog `app.createProgressLog()`	Creates a new `progressLog` object. Returns the new progressLog Object (page 241). Before attempting to add messages to the progress log this method returns, call *progressLogObj*`.begin` (page 241) once.

createSite
`app.createSite`
  `(pathOrURL, createHomepage)`
`app.createSite`
  `(location, createHomepage)`
	Creates and returns a new website Object (page 296). Returns `null` if creation fails. (Introduced in 8.0)

pathOrURL	String. Full or partial path to the site location, specified as a URL or platform-specific path name. If you do not specify this value as a URL, this value must follow the file system conventions of the platform on which GoLive is currently running.
location	A file Object (page 158) that references the site location.
createHomepage	Optional. When `true` (the default), creates a home page at the given site location.
decodeHTML `app.decodeHTML(text[, charSet])`	Decodes the specified HTML-encoded string to plain text. Returns the plain-text string. (Introduced in 7.0)
text	The HTML-encoded string to decode.
charSet	Optional. The name of the character-encoding set to use. If not supplied, uses the encoding of the current active document. If no document is open, uses `iso-8859-1` encoding.

➤ Example

```
app.decodeHTML("&lt;img&gt;" )
```
This returns the string "`<img>`".

---

encodeHTML app.encodeHTML(*text*[, *charSet*])	Encodes a text string as HTML. Returns the HTML-encoded string. (Introduced in 7.0)
text	The HTML-encoded string to encode.
charSet	Optional. The name of the character-encoding set to use. If not supplied, uses the encoding of the current active document. If no document is open, uses iso-8859-1 encoding.

> ### ➤ Example

```
app.encodeHTML("<img>");
```
This returns the string "<img>".

getModiferState app.getModiferState()	Gets the immediate status of the modifier keys. Returns a logical OR of bit values that indicate the currently pressed modifier keys: ● 0x0001: Shift ● 0x0004: Alt ● 0x0008: Command/Control This is useful for drag-and-drop operations, where the current status of the modifier keys determines an action. You should not use this function to determine the modifier key state of an event. Events have their own key-state information and using this function will only tell you the state long after the initial event has completed, by which time the modifier may no longer be in that state.
isModulePresent	Deprecated in 6.0. Use the isOn method (page 256) of the settings.aglmodule Object (page 248).
launchHelp app.launchHelp ()	Opens the application online Help. Returns true on success. (Introduced in 7.0)
launchURL app.launchURL (*url*)	Opens the specified URL in the current browser. Returns true on success. If the current browser is not defined, this method does nothing and returns false.
url	String. The URL for the page to open.
newDocument app.newDocument() app.newDocument(*sampleFilePath*) app.newDocument(*sampleFile*)	Opens a new, empty document, optionally basing it on a template. Returns the newly created document Object (page 138), which has been added to the documents array, or null if document creation failed. When called with no argument, this is the same as choosing the **File > New** menu item.
sampleFilePath	Optional. (7.0 or later) String. Full or partial path to the file for a document to use as a template for the new document.
sampleFile	Optional. (7.0 or later) A file Object (page 158) for a document to use as a template for the new document.

openDocument `app.openDocument` (*pathOrURL* [, *encoding*])	Open the specified document. Returns the newly opened document Object (page 138), which has been added to the `documents` array, or `null` if document open failed. See also the openMarkup (page 59) method .
pathOrURL	String. Full or partial path to the file to open, specified as a URL or platform-specific path name. If you do not specify this value as a URL, this value must follow the file system conventions of the platform on which GoLive is currently running.
encoding	Optional. (6.0 or later) The name of an encoding character set. This character set overrides the default encoding that GoLive would use if the document did not contain a META tag. A META tag causes the supplied encoding to be ignored. When this argument specifies an unknown or unsupported encoding, GoLive generates an "Unsupported encoding" runtime error.
openMarkup `app.openMarkup` (*pathOrURL* [, *encoding*])	Open the specified document without displaying it in a window. Returns the newly opened document Object (page 138), which has been added to the `documents` array, or `null` if document open failed. Use this method to work with a document's markup tree without displaying the document in Layout view. Not displaying a document in Layout view saves time and memory. Also, GoLive does not reparse when Layout view is not open. To batch-process documents quickly, open them with this method rather than the openDocument method (page 59).
pathOrURL	String. Full or partial path to the file to open, specified as a URL or platform-specific path name. If you do not specify this value as a URL, this value must follow the file system conventions of the platform on which GoLive is currently running.
encoding	Optional. (6.0 or later) The name of an encoding character set. This character set overrides the default encoding that GoLive would use if the document did not contain a META tag. A META tag causes the supplied encoding to be ignored. When this argument specifies an unknown or unsupported encoding, GoLive generates an "Unsupported encoding" runtime error.
openPrefs `app.openPrefs ()`	Opens the Preferences panel. Same as choosing the **Edit > Preferences** menu item.
postKey `app.postKey (key)`	Posts a keycode to the GoLive application's input queue.
key	String. The ASCII value of the key to post or a string that begins with the character to post.
quit `app.quit ()`	Terminates the GoLive application by posting a quit message to the platform. Same as choosing the **File > Quit** menu item.

setCursor app.setCursor (*name*)	Within a mouseControl callback, changes the mouse cursor You can call this function only from within a mouseControl callback function. You can not set the cursor at any other time. You can use this, for instance, to indicate whether a custom control can accept a drop of the content being dragged. (Introduced in 7.0)
name	String. The name of the built-in mouse cursor image to display. One of arrowCopy arrowAlias arrowCopyTree hand handFloat handMove handFloatMove handCopy context pointShoot link size horizontalSize verticalSize magnifier tab default
setProgress app.setProgress (*value*[, *message*])	Updates the progress dialog. Returns true while the operation is still in progress, false if the user **Stop** in the progress dialog. While the progress bar or busy bar is displayed, call this method regularly to update the progress user interface and to determine whether the user has clicked the **Stop** button. When you call this method, GoLive automatically reparses all open documents.
value	A value between 0 and 1 that sets the progress bar's position. Busy bars ignore this parameter. A value of 1 specifies that 100% of the bar is to be drawn, and decimal values less than 1 equate to a corresponding percentage of the progress bar.
message	Optional. A status message to display in the progress dialog. Replaces the current message.

startProgress app.startProgress (*title* [, *message*, *doBusy*, *seconds*])	Displays a progress dialog with progress bar or busy bar. These are the same dialogs GoLive displays as part of its own user interface. When you call this method, GoLive automatically reparses all open documents.
title	String that appears in the dialog's title bar.
message	Optional. A status message to display in the progress dialog. Replaces the current message.
doBusy	Optional. Set to `true` to display a busy bar instead of a progress bar.
seconds	Optional. Number of seconds to wait before displaying the dialog.
stopProgress app.stopProgress()	Closes the progress window.

attribute Object

Class: JSXAttribute

This object represents an element attribute. This object includes the Node Interface (page 229), whose properties and functions allow you to traverse the node tree. It defines additional properties, but no additional functions.

(Introduced in 7.0)

Acquiring an attribute object

Get this object from an element Object (page 156), using getAttributeNode (page 157):

```
var myAttrObj = elementObj.getAttributeNode("myAttrName");
```

attribute object properties

In addition to those of the Node Interface (page 229), this object has the following properties:

name	String	The attribute name. For example, an `<img>` tag has an attribute `src`, for which the `attribute.name` value is `src`.
specified	Boolean	When `true`, the value is specified by an HTML tag attribute.
value	String	The value of the attribute, as a string.

bounds Object

Class: `Bounds`

This object encapsulates a set of bounding dimensions for an interface element (window or control), together with its position with respect to its parent window or the screen. Dimensions are measured in pixels, and a window's upper left corner is considered the origin (0,0).

(Introduced in 8.0)

Acquiring a bounds object

Get this object from a control Object Types (page 78) or window Object (page 313):

```
var myBounds = controlObj.bounds;
```

bounds object properties

This object has the following properties:

`bottom`	Number	The y-coordinate of the bottom edge of the bounding box in relation to an origin at the top left corner of the parent.
`height`	Number	The height of the bounding box in pixels.
`left`	Number	The x-coordinate of the left edge of the bounding box in relation to an origin at the top left corner of the parent. (Same as `x`.)
`right`	Number	The x-coordinate of the right edge of the bounding box in relation to an origin at the top left corner of the parent.
`top`	Number	The y-coordinate of the top edge of the bounding box in relation to an origin at the top left corner of the parent. (Same as `y`.)
`width`	Number	The width of the bounding box in pixels.
`x`	Number	The x-coordinate of the left edge of the bounding box in relation to an origin at the top left corner of the parent. (Same as `left`.)
`y`	Number	The y-coordinate of the top edge of the bounding box in relation to an origin at the top left corner of the parent. (Same as `top`.)

box Object

Class: JSXBox

A box object manages the visual representation of a custom element in Layout view.

The box object itself provides only a few convenience functions. Handlers that you register for the parseBox (page 366), drawBox (page 362), boxResized (page 360), and inspectBox (page 363) events implement the object's basic functionality. To use a box object, your extension must provide these methods, as described in Chapter 6, "Events and Event Handlers."

Acquiring box objects

GoLive creates a box object whenever the user drags a custom element's icon from the Objects palette to the Layout view of a GoLive document window, or when GoLive reads a document that contains a custom tag. GoLive does not create box objects when interpreting documents opened by the openMarkup method.

box object properties

Most of the box object's properties describe its visual representation. You can set these values to change the box's appearance in Layout view. To update the affected HTML, call methods of the markup object that the box.element property provides.

alignment	String	Gets or sets the alignment of the box. Possible values are: bottom middle top line left right absBottom absTop
bottomMargin	Number	Number of pixels by which the visible representation of the content of a container box is inset from the bottom of the box. Used only by container boxes, such as those that represent binary tags.
classid	String	The identifier that associates this box with an Inspector and a palette entry, as specified by the classid attributes of the `<jsxelement>`, `<jsxpaletteentry>` and `<jsxinspector>` elements associated with this box. In GoLive 6 or higher, set this value to activate an alternate Inspector for this box.

`document`	Document	The document Object (page 138) that contains this box.
`element`	Markup	The markup item (custom element) associated with this box. Read-only.
`height`	Number	The pixel height of the box.
`heightPercent`	Number	The percentage height of the box.
`inspector`	Window	The window Object (page 313) for the Inspector for this box, when the box is selected and an Inspector dialog is active. Otherwise `null`. Read-only.
`leftMargin`	Number	Number of pixels by which the visible representation of the content of a container box is inset from the left side of the box. Used only by container boxes, such as those that represent binary tags.
`link`	Link	When the custom element for this box refers to a file or location, the link Object (page 207) for that reference.
`links`	LinkCollection	When the custom element for this box is associated with more than one file or location, a collection of link Objects (page 207) for all files that refer to the element (*in* links) and all files the element makes reference to (*out* links).
`mouseControl`	Boolean	Optional. When `true`, the mouseControl event (page 363) is generated when you click the box, move the mouse over it, or release the mouse button over it. Default is `false`.
`name`	String	The JavaScript name of the box. Read-only.
`rightMargin`	Number	Number of pixels by which the visible representation of the content of a container box is inset from the right side of the box. Used only by container boxes, such as those that represent binary tags.
`topMargin`	Number	Number of pixels by which the visible representation of the content of a container box is inset from the top of the box. Used only by container boxes, such as those that represent binary tags.
`width`	Number	The pixel width of the box.
`widthPercent`	Number	The percentage width of the box.
`x`	Number	The x-coordinate of the top-left corner of the box in relation to an origin at the top left corner of the document. Read-only.
`y`	Number	The y-coordinate of the top-left corner of the box in relation to an origin at the top left corner of the document. Read-only.

box object functions

createLink *boxObj*.createLink ([*url*])	Creates a new link Object (page 207) and adds it to the box's links collection. Returns the link object. The Inspector windows use the createLink and removeLink functions to create or remove links in the box object in response to user interaction with urlgetter controls.
url	Optional. The URL for the new link. If not supplied, this method creates an invalid link which can be set to a valid URL at another time.
refresh *boxObj*.refresh()	Redraws the box. You can call the box object yourself to tell it to redraw itself, using this method. You might do this if, for example, the box represents a custom control that you update yourself.
removeLink *boxObj*.removeLink (*link*)	Removes the specified link from the box's links collection. The link Object (page 207) is invalid when this call returns. Inspector windows use the createLink and removeLink functions to create or remove links in the box object in response to user interaction with urlgetter controls.
link	The link Object (page 207) to remove.

changeMarkup Object

Class: JSXChangeMarkup

This object encapsulates predefined actions that change the markup of documents. Each of the predefined actions performs a particular type of transformation, according to properties that you set. The predefined actions are:

- ChangeDoctype: Changes the document type of an XML or HTML document.
- ChangeEncoding: Changes the encoding of XML or HTML document.
- ConvertMarkup: Converts between HTML and XHTML.
- RewriteSource: Rewrites the document source according to various options.

For each supported action, you can set specific properties to control the behavior; see setProperty (page 68).

To use the object, create it with one of these action names, set the properties that control how the action is performed, and pass the object to the changeMarkup (page 141) function of a document Object (page 138). For example:

```
changeEncoding = new JSXChangeMarkup("ChangeEncoding",
1);
changeEncoding.setProperty("encoding", "utf-8");
document.changeMarkup(changeEncoding);
```

(Introduced in 7.0)

Acquiring a changeMarkup object

Create a changeMarkup object using the changeMarkup Constructor (page 68).

changeMarkup object properties

| name | String | The name of the action encapsulated by this object. Pass this to the document Object's changeMarkup (page 141) function to execute the action. |
| version | Number | The version number of this action. |

changeMarkup object functions

changeMarkup Constructor new JSXChangeMarkup (*actionName*, *version*)	Creates and returns a new changeMarkup object.

actionName	The name of this action. One of:
	
	   ChangeDoctype: Changes the document type of an XML or HTML document.
	   ChangeEncoding: Changes the encoding of XML or HTML document.
	   ConvertMarkup: Converts between HTML and XHTML.
	   RewriteSource: Rewrites the document source according to various options.

version	The version number of this action.
getProperty *changeMarkupObj*.getProperty (*propName*)	Gets the value of a named property. Returns the property value as a string, or null if the property is not defined.
propName	The name of the property. Name must not be empty.
setProperty getProperty (*propName*, *value*)	Sets the value of a named property. See notes below.
propName	The name of the property.
value	The new value.

Setting properties for supported actions

The following properties can be set for the supported actions.

- When *changMarkupObj*.name="ChangeDoctype", the action changes the document type of an XML or HTML document. You can set these parameters:

propName	value	Description
doctype	PublicKey null	Sets the doctype to this public key, or when null, delete the doctype. Specify a valid key known by GoLive; for example: "-//W3C//DTD HTML 4.01//EN"
showProgress	Boolean	When true, show progress bar while performing action. Default is false.
writeSystemKey	Boolean	When true, writes the corresponding system key for the doctype (as defined by the W3C) into the doctype-declaration. For example: "http://www.w3.org/TR/html4/strict.dtd" Default is false. Affects only documents of type HTML.

- When *changMarkupObj*.name="ChangeEncoding", the action changes the encoding of XML or HTML document. You can set these parameters:

propName	value	Description
encoding	utf-8 iso-8859-1 shift-jis	The encoding to use.
reEncode	Boolean	When `true`, re-encode all encodeable text. When `false`, only change the document info (META-tag). Default is `true`.
showProgress	Boolean	When `true`, show progress bar while performing action. Default is `false`.

- When *changMarkupObj*.name="ConvertMarkup", the action converts between HTML and XHTML. You can set these parameters:.

propName	value	Description
convertToXHTML	Boolean	When `true`, convert to XHTML. When `false`, convert to HTML. In this case, all other properties except `IDToName` and `WriteFullDoctype` are ignored. Default is `false`.
IDToName	clone convert noChange	For XHTML to HTML conversion only, when no `name` attribute is present, copy (`clone`) the `id` attribute, rename (`convert`) the `id` attribute to `name`, or make no changes. Introduced in 8.0 for version 2 of this action.
nameToID	clone convert noChange	When no `id` attribute is present, copy (`clone`) the `name` attribute, rename (`convert`) the `name` attribute to `id`, or make no changes.
putSpaceBeforeSlash	Boolean	When `true` (the default), put a space before a slash.
removeMetaEncoding	Boolean	When `true`, remove the HTML `<meta>` encoding element. Default is `false`.
removeUTF8Encoding	Boolean	When `true`, remove the encoding from `<?xml...?>` statement, if it is `utf8`. Default is `false`.
removeXMLDeclaration	Boolean	When `true`, remove the `<?xml...?>` statement, if it is `utf8` or `utf16`. Default is `false`.
showProgress	Boolean	When `true`, show progress bar while performing action. Default is `false`.
wrapScriptIntoCDATA	Boolean	When `true`, wrap script into CDATA. Default is `false`.
wrapStyleIntoCDATA	Boolean	When `true`, wrap style into CDATA. Default is `false`.

propName	value	Description
writeFullDoctype	Boolean	For XHTML to HTML conversion only, when `true` (default), write the system key of the DOCTYPE, when `false`, write only the public key of the DOCTYPE.
writeXMLDeclaration	always exceptUTF never	When to write the `<?xml...?>` statement to the converted document. If the value is `exceptUTF`, writes the statement only if it is not `utf8` or `utf16`. Default is `always`. Introduced in 8.0 for version 2 of this action. Overrides `removeXMLDeclaration` if both are present.

- In `changeMarkup` version 1, when *changMarkupObj*.`name="RewriteSource"`, the action rewrites the document source according to various options. You can set these parameters:

propName	value	Description
attrCase	noChange upper lower capital	How or whether to change case of HTML attributes. Does not affect XML.
attrQuotes	noChange always nonNum necessary	How or whether to change attribute quoting.
attrSorting	noChange websettings alphabetical	How or whether to change attribute sorting. The `websettings` value uses an implicit sort order, as in 6.0.
collapseWhitespace	Boolean	When `true`, replace multiple continuous whitespace characters with a single space. Default is `false`.
cssOutput	noChange compressed compact pretty1 pretty2 pretty3 nice	How to reformat CSS source code.
cssIndent	noChange yes no	Whether to indent CSS source code.
lineBreaks	noChange mac unix win	The style of line breaks to use.
showProgress	Boolean	When `true`, show progress bar while performing action. Default is `false`.

propName	value	Description
tagCase	noChange upper lower capital	How or whether to change case of HTML elements. Does not affect XML.
useGL6Mode	Boolean	When `true`, rewrite the source according to the web settings, as in GoLive version 6.0, and ignore all other options. Default is `false`.
whitespace	noChange websettings noIndent	How and whether to indent by adding whitespace at beginning of lines. The `websettings` value indents according to the **Output** tab of the element Inspector.

collection Object

Class: `JSXCollection`

A collection object acts like an array that provides access to its elements by name. Like an array, a collection associates a set of objects or values as a logical group and provides random access to them.

Most collection objects are read-only. You do not assign objects to them yourself—the SDK updates their contents automatically as objects are created or deleted.

Collection objects are not actually arrays.

- An array places no restrictions on the type of data its elements store, while a collection object always holds the type of data indicated by its object name: a `BoxCollection` object holds box objects, a `ControlCollection` object holds control objects, and so on.

- Array members can always be accessed by numeric index. Some, but not all collections allow this.

Acquiring collection objects

You do not create collection objects yourself. The SDK creates collections when the GoLive application opens. This table describes the various collections the SDK provides, and shows how to access each of these objects in JavaScript.

Object	JavaScript Access	Contents
`BoxCollection`	boxes global variable (page 47)	All boxes in the active document. Read-only.
`ControlCollection`	window Object children property (page 313)	Controls that have run at least once in this session.
`CSSMediaList`	CSSImportRule Object (page 120) or CSSMediaRule Object media (page 122) property	Media values associated with an import or media rule, in a CSS style sheet associated with a document.
`CSSRuleCollection`	CSSStyleSheet Object (page 129) cssRules (page 130) property	Rules in a CSS style sheets associated with a document, or collected into sets in a CSSMediaRule Object (page 122). Rules can be CSSStyleRule Objects (page 127) or any of the rule subtypes.
`CSSStyleSheetCollection`	document Object styleSheets property (page 140)	The internal and external style sheets for a markup document, or the single style sheet for a style-sheet document.

Object	JavaScript Access	Contents
DialogCollection	dialogs global variable (page 47)	Dialogs that have run at least once in this session. Read-only.
DocumentCollection	documents global variable (page 48)	Documents open in GoLive.
FontSetCollection	app Object fontsets (page 54) property	All available fontSet Objects (page 169).
History	document Object history (page 139) property	Undo actions for a document.
HTMLStyleCollection	app Object htmlStyles (page 54) property	Every HTMLStyle Object (page 178) in the **Window > Styles** palette.
LinkCollection	box Object links (page 65) property	Links to all files that reference this box (in links) and all files this box references (out links).
MarkupCollection	A markup object's subElements (page 210) property	Immediate subelements of the markup object.
MarkupSettingCollection	settings.markup Object (page 252) markupSettings (page 253) property	markupSettings Object (page 217)
MarkupSettingElement Collection	markupSettings Object elements (page 217) property	markupSetting.markupSettingElement Object (page 220)
MarkupSettingEntity Collection	markupSettings Object entities (page 217) property	markupSetting.markupSettingEntity Object (page 222)
MenuCollection	menus global variable (page 48)	All menus currently available in GoLive.
MenuItemCollection	menu Object items (page 223) property	All the menu items belonging to the menu.
ModuleCollection	modules global variable (page 48)	All currently running GoLive extensions modules. **Note:** Modules whose names contain spaces cannot be accessed by name, only by index.
PictureCollection	pictures global variable (page 48)	All pictures accessible to this module.
ServerInfoCollection	server global variable (page 48), website Object server (page 297) property	All servers available to an application or web site.

Object	JavaScript Access	Contents
`VCSHandlerCollection`	app Object vcs property (page 56)	All defined version-control-system interfaces.
`WebsiteCollection`	websites global variable (page 48)	All web sites currently open in GoLive.

collection object properties

`length`	Number	The number of elements of the collection. This value is zero if the members cannot be indexed by number.

comment Object

Class: `JSXComment`

The `comment` object represents a markup comment. When you load an HTML document, GoLive generates a tree of markup objects to represent the contents. The objects have a tree structure that matches that in the source HTML. The markup objects are of various types: the element Object (page 156) for elements, the text Object (page 276) for text items, the comment Object (page 75) for comments, and the markup Object (page 215) for all other kinds of markup.

- This object includes the Node Interface (page 229), whose properties and functions allow you to traverse the node tree.
- This object includes the Markup Interface (page 209), whose properties and functions allow you to directly access document content.
- In addition, it defines some properties and functions of its own, as shown here.

(Introduced in 7.0)

Acquiring comment objects

- Create a new `comment` object using the document Object's createComment (page 142) function.
- For a markup document, the document Object's documentElement (page 138) property holds the root object of the markup tree. The page's content is represented by nodes in the tree. To retrieve the root of the markup tree for a document:

```
var tree = document.documentElement;
```

You can traverse the markup tree using the Node Interface (page 229) properties and functions of any object in the tree. In a `comment` object:

```
elementType=comment
nodeType=8
nodeName=#comment
```

comment object properties

In addition to those of the Node Interface (page 229) and Markup Interface (page 209), a `comment` object has these properties:

data	String	The text of the comment.
length	Number	Length of the text in characters.
nodeValue	String	Content of the comment.

---

comment object functions

In addition to those of the Node Interface (page 229) and Markup Interface (page 209), a `comment` object has these functions.

appendData *commentObj*.appendData(*text*)	Adds specified text at the end of the existing text in the comment. Returns `true` on success.
text The text to add.	
deleteData *commentObj*.deleteData (*offset*, *count*)	Deletes a specified number of characters from current text beginning at a specified offset from the start of text. Returns `true` on success.
offset The offset into the data at which to begin the deletion.	
count The length of data to delete.	
insertData *commentObj*.insertData(*offset*, *text*)	Inserts new text at a specified offset into the existing text. Returns `true` on success.
offset The offset into the data at which to begin the insertion.	
text The text to insert.	
replaceData *commentObj*.replaceData (*offset*, *count*, *text*)	Replaces a range of existing text with new text, beginning at a specified offset. Returns `true` on success.
offset The offset into the data at which to begin the replacement.	
count The length of data to replace.	
text The text to insert.	
substringData *commentObj*.substringData (*offset*, *count*)	Gets a substring of a specified length beginning at a specified offset. Returns a new string containing the copied characters.
offset The offset into the data.	
count The number of characters to copy.	

common Object

Class: `JSXCommon`

The `common` object provides a means of sharing non-persistent string and primitive data among all currently running extensions. It is intended for sharing preference data and the like. You cannot store objects in the `common` object.

The `common` object provides no predefined properties. An extension calls the `common` object's `create` method to create a new namespace for shared properties in the `common` object; the namespace is then available to all extensions as a property of the `common` object.

For example, the following creates a namespace to hold properties of a particular extension, then adds a property with an assigned value:

```
common.create("myExt");
common.myExt.myProperty = myValue;
```

Acquiring the common object

The `common` global property makes this object available to all Extend Script extensions.

```
common
```

common object functions

create `common.create (namespace)`	Creates a new shared property namespace in the global `common` object. Returns a reference to the data object for the namespace.
namespace	The name of a new shared property namespace.

> ### ➤ Example

The `create` method returns a reference to the namespace it creates, so you can access properties in the namespace directly:

```
var myCommon = common.create("myExt");
myCommon.myProperty = myValue;
```

Properties can hold only string or primitive values. You cannot assign any kind of object to a property of the `common` object. Because the property is itself an object, you cannot add properties directly to other properties. To create properties of properties, like `customer.first` and `customer.last`, for example, you must create the `customer` namespace, as follows:

```
var myCommon = common.create("myExt");
myCommon.create("customer");
myCommon.customer.first = "John";
myCommon.customer.last = "Perry";
writeln(common.myExt.customer.first);
writeln(common.myExt.customer.last);
```

control Object Types

Class: depends on type

This object represents a user-interface control that GoLive generates when it interprets a `<jsxcontrol>` element (page 337) in the body of a `<jsxdialog>`, `<jsxpalette>`, or `<jsxinspector>` element. The `type` attribute specifies the kind of control this element creates. The value of the `type` attribute must be one of those listed for the `<jsxcontrol>` tag (page 337).

Each type of control is an individual object type that inherits the general control properties and functions listed here. Some control types define additional properties and functions.

In 7.0, you can also create controls dynamically during a GoLive session, by calling the `add` method of a window Object (page 313) or of a panel Object (page 233). The parameters required to create each type of control are given with the description of the control type. For examples of creating these controls, see the `Dynamic UI` sample included with the GoLive CS2 SDK.

When the user interacts with a control, GoLive usually generates an event such as onClick (page 364) with that control object as the target. Controls of specific types can trigger specific events, such as onChange (page 364) when the user types into an edit control. The events and handlers are described in Chapter 6, "Events and Event Handlers."

Acquiring control objects

- When the user interacts with a control, the control object is the target of the resulting event, and is passed to the handler in the `target` property of the event object argument. For example:

```
function myClickHandler(evtObj) {
    controlObj = evtObj.target;
    ...}
```

- Get a control object by name from the collection in a window Object's `children` (page 314) property:

```
dialogs[winName].children[controlName]
```

- Get a control object by name from the array in the `children` property of a panel Object (page 233), splitpanel Object (page 271), or tabpanel Object (page 274):

```
panelObj.children[controlName]
```

general control object properties

The value of a control's `type` property defines its appearance and behavior. Some control properties are type-specific; they are not valid for all controls but only for those of certain types.

`active`	Boolean	When `true`, the control has the current keyboard focus. Read/write. (Introduced in 7.0)
`bounds`	Bounds	A bounds Object (page 63) for the size and location of this control within its parent window.
`enabled`	Boolean	When `true`, the control accepts user input as appropriate to the type, and is displayed normally. When `false`, the control does not accept input and is displayed in a special mode. Read/write.
`height, width`	—	Deprecated in 8.0. Use `bounds` and `size` instead.
`helpTip`	String	A short descriptive string that appears as a tooltip for this control. Read/write. (Introduced in 8.0)
`itemCount`	—	Deprecated in 8.0. Use `items` instead.
`items`	Array of Item and Node	The item list of a list control (`list`, `combobox`, `filelist`, or `hierarchy`) as an array of `item` control objects. To add and remove items, use the control's add (page 82) and remove (page 84) methods. To clear the list, use the removeAll (page 84) method. See Control: item Object (page 100) and Control: node Object (page 105). For other control types, this property is not present. (Introduced in 8.0)
`location`	Point	A point Object (page 239) for the position of this control within its parent window.
`multi`	Boolean	When `true`, allows selection of multiple entries in a list control, and `selection` contains an Array. For other control types, this property is not used.
`name`	String	The control's JavaScript name, as specified by the `name` attribute of the `<jsxcontrol>` element that defines this control. Read-only.
`parent`	Window Panel Control	For an `item` or `node` control, the parent list control (`list`, `combobox`, `filelist`, or `hierarchy`). For other control types, the parent of the control, a window Object (page 313) or panel Object (page 233). Read only.
`placement` `posx, posy`	—	Deprecated in 8.0. Use `bounds` and `location` instead.

selection	Array, Item, Node	Gets or sets the currently selected list item in a list control (`list`, `combobox`, `filelist`, or `hierarchy`). Each item is an `item` or `node` object. For a list box, file list, or hierarchy, if `multi=true`, an array of the item objects for all selected entries. You can set the value to a single `item` object, an array of `item` objects, or an array of `items` index values. When you set this value for a multi-selectable list, it turns on the specified selection without deselecting the other entries. Set to –1 to deselect all entries for list controls. Value is –1 for all other control types.
size	Dimension	A dimension Object (page 137) for the size of the bounding box of this control.
state	—	Deprecated in 8.0. Use `value` instead.
text	String	The text displayed in the control such as the label string of a button. For controls with editable text, contains the current text. Read/write. (Introduced in 7.0)
textselection	String	The currently selected text in controls that allow text selection. Read/write. (Introduced in 8.0)

type	String	The type of the control. One of:
		button: Pushbutton
		buttonedit: Edit field with onEnter property set to true. Optional **Enter** button, controlled by a user preference.
		colorfield: Color select field
		custom: Custom control
		checkbox: Checkbox
		combobox: Combo box (popup menu), contains item objects
		edittext: Edit field. Signals changes depending on property values for onEnter, onChange, and onNoChanged.
		editarea: Multiline edit field. Signals changes for each keystroke and loss of focus.
		filelist: A hierarchical view of files and folders, with a configurable popup list of local and remote filesystem locations.
		frame: Horizontal line, vertical line, or frame box
		hierarchy: A hierarchical view of item and node objects
		item: A selectable list item
		line: Pane separator line
		list: List box, contains item objects
		node: A list item that can contain subitems
		panel: A container with a frame that groups additional controls (see "panel Object" on page 233)
		password: Password-entry field, does not display user input
		preview: HTML browser window
		progressbar: Progress bar
		radiobutton: Radio button
		scrollbar: Scrollbar
		slider: Slider
		source: JavaScript editor with syntax checking
		splitpanel: A container with two subpanels (see "splitpanel Object" on page 271)
		statictext: Static text field
		tabpanel: A tab-grouping frame (see "tabpanel Object" on page 274)
		tree: Deprecated in 8.0. Use hierarchy or filelist instead.
		urlgetter: URL entry field.
value	Boolean	For check box and radio button controls, true if the control is selected (checked), false if it is not. For other control types, this property is not used.
		(Usage changed in 8.0. Used differently in earlier versions, generally replaced by text.)
values	—	Deprecated in 8.0. Use text, items, and textselection instead.
visible	Boolean	When true, the control is visible. When false, it is hidden. Read/write. (Introduced in 7.0)

general control object functions

These convenience functions are available for all control types. A control's most important behaviors are provided by the event-handling functions that you register for the object. The GoLive SDK calls your registered handler when the user interacts with the control. To use an interactive control object, your extension must provide an event handler, as described in Chapter 6, "Events and Event Handlers."

add *controlObj*.add (*type, text* [, *index, creationProperties*])	Adds a new item to the items array of a list control (list, combobox, filelist, or hierarchy). Creates a control object of type item or node. All other types of controls ignore this method. (Introduced in 8.0)

type	The type of the new item. One of:
	    item: For any list control, a selectable item. Creates an item object.
	    node: For a hierarchy control, an item that can contain subitems. Creates a node object.

text	The display label for the new item.
index	Optional. The 0-based index position of this item in the parent control's items list. If not specified, new items are appended to the list.

creationProperties	Optional. For hierarchy controls, an object that can contain these properties:
	    icon: The name of an image defined in extension file, to display in the item or node to the left of the text label.
	    expandIcon: The image name for an icon to indicate that the node is in its expanded state.
	    deleteable: When true, the user can delete the item or node.
	    editable: When true, the user can modify the item or node.

addItem	Deprecated in 8.0. Use the add method.
awaitDrag *controlObj*.awaitDrag ()	Reports whether the user is dragging a custom control. Returns true if the user is dragging the custom control. See the example under dispatchEvent (page 83). (Introduced in 7.0)

beginDraw *controlObj*.beginDraw()	Creates and returns a temporary draw Object (page 152) that you can call to refresh a custom control's appearance immediately in response to a change in its state. Use this method when you need to draw the appearance outside the context of the drawBox or drawControl (page 362) handler. When these drawing operations are complete, call the endDraw (page 84) method to terminate the temporary draw object. The temporary draw object this method returns is not valid after the endDraw method is called. Do not call the temporary draw object from outside the calls to the beginDraw and endDraw methods that create it and terminate it. Only one temporary draw object can exist at any time. You cannot nest calls to the beginDraw method. Never call the beginDraw method more than once before calling the endDraw method.
changeItem *controlObj*.changeItem (*index*, *newText*)	Changes the label text of an existing entry item in the items array of a list control (list, combobox, filelist, or hierarchy). All other types of controls ignore this method call. (Introduced in 7.0)
index	The 0-based index of the item to change.
newText	The new label text for the specified item.
dispatchEvent *controlObj*.dispatchEvent (*dragDropEventObj*[, *pictureObj*])	Starts a drag action. Returns true if the dragged object is received somewhere. Call this method after awaitDrag() returns true. (Introduced in 7.0)
dragDropEventObj	A dragDropEvent (page 380) object that contains all relevant information for the drag action.
pictureObj	Optional. A picture Object (page 237) to be used as the image displayed during dragging.

➤ Example

```
function mouseControl(control, x, y, state) {
    switch (state) {
        case 0: {
            if (control.awaitDrag() ) {
                var dragInfo = new JSXDragDropInfo;
                dragInfo.flavor  = "html";
                dragInfo.content = "<img src=\"\" width=\"100\"
                    height=\"100\">";
                var image = createPicture("dragImage.gif");
                var didDrop = control.dispatchEvent(dragInfo, image);
            }
        }
        break;
    }
}
```

endDraw *controlObj*.endDraw()	Terminates the drawing operation the beginDraw (page 83) method began. This method invalidates the temporary draw Object (page 152) that the beginDraw (page 83) method created.
find *controlObj*.find (*text*)	Finds and returns the item control object for the specified item if it is the items array of a list control (list, combobox, filelist, or hierarchy). All other control types ignore this method call. (Introduced in 8.0)
text	The value of the text property of the list item to find.
hide hide()	Hides the control by setting the visible property to false. (Introduced in 7.0)
refresh *controlObj*.refresh()	Redraws this control. Call this method to repaint an owner-draw custom control in response to user input.
remove *controlObj*.remove (*text*) *controlObj*.remove (*index*) *controlObj*.remove (*item*)	Removes a specified item from the items array of a list control (list, combobox, filelist, or hierarchy). All other control types ignore this method call. (Introduced in 8.0)
text	The value of the text property of the list item to remove.
index	The 0-based index of the list item to remove.
item	The item or node control object for the list item to remove.
removeAll *controlObj*.removeAll()	Removes all item entries from the items array of a list control (list, combobox, filelist, or hierarchy). All other control types ignore this method call.
removeItem	Deprecated in 8.0. Use remove() instead.
show show()	Shows the control by setting the visible property to true. (Available in 7.0, 8.0)

Control: button Object

This object represents a button control. It inherits all properties and functions of the control Object Types (page 78). (Introduced in 7.0)

Acquiring a button object

- The SDK creates a `button` object when it interprets a `<jsxcontrol>` (page 337) tag with `type="button"`. You can obtain the object by name or index from the parent window's `children` collection:

    windowObj`.children[`*controlName*`];`
    panelObj`.children[`*controlName*`];`

- To create a new `button` object dynamically, call a panel Object (page 233) or window Object's add (page 317) function with `type="button"`. Pass an object containing these optional creation parameters:

`name`	Unique JavaScript name of the control.
`helptip`	A descriptive string that appears when the mouse pointer hovers over the control.
`alignment`	An array containing the horizontal and vertical alignment string values for the control. See `<jsxcontrol>` `halign` (page 339) and `valign` (page 339) attributes. Default is `["left", "top"]`.
`icon`	The name of an image defined in the extension file, to use as an icon in the button in place of a text label.

➤ **Example**

```
myWin.add ( "button", [left, top, right, bottom],
"buttonlabel",
    { name:"myButton1", alignment:["left", "top"] } );
```

Control: checkbox Object

This object represents a checkbox control. It inherits all properties and functions of the control Object Types (page 78). (Introduced in 7.0)

Acquiring a checkbox object

- The SDK creates this object when it interprets a `<jsxcontrol>` (page 337) tag with `type="checkbox"`. You can obtain the object by name or index from the parent window's `children` collection:

  windowObj.`children[`*controlName*`]`;
  panelObj.`children[`*controlName*`]`;

- To create a new `checkbox` object dynamically, call a panel Object (page 233) or window Object's add (page 317) function with `type="checkbox"`. Pass an object containing these optional creation parameters:

`name`	Unique JavaScript name of the control.
`helptip`	A descriptive string that appears when the mouse pointer hovers over the control.
`alignment`	An array containing the horizontal and vertical alignment string values for the control. See `<jsxcontrol>` `halign` (page 339) and `valign` (page 339) attributes. Default is `["left", "top"]`.

➤ Example

```
myWin.add ( "checkbox", [left, top, right, bottom],
"mycblabel",
    { name:"myCb1", alignment:["left", "top"] } );
```

checkbox object properties

These properties apply to `checkbox` controls.

value	Boolean	For check box and radio button controls, `true` if the control is selected (checked), `false` if it is not. For other control types, this property is not used.
		(Usage changed in 8.0. Used differently in earlier versions.)

Control: colorfield Object

This object represents a color selection control. It inherits all properties and functions of the control Object Types (page 78). (Introduced in 7.0)

The `text` property reflects and sets the currently selected color. It contains a color specification, either a hexadecimal color value or a color name string as used for HTML, such as `"red"` or `"blue"`. Use the special value `"nocolor"` to indicate that no color is displayed; the control shows white with a red crossbar.

Acquiring a colorfield object

- The SDK creates this object when it interprets a `<jsxcontrol>` (page 337) tag with `type="colorfield"`. You can obtain the object by name or index from the parent window's `children` collection:

  windowObj.`children[`*controlName*`]`;
  panelObj.`children[`*controlName*`]`;

- To create a new `colorfield` object dynamically, call a panel Object (page 233) or window Object's add (page 317) function with `type="colorfield"`. Pass the hexadecimal color code string or HTML color name for the initial color in the *text* parameter. Pass an object containing these optional creation parameters:

`name`	Unique JavaScript name of the control.
`helptip`	A descriptive string that appears when the mouse pointer hovers over the control.
`alignment`	An array containing the horizontal and vertical alignment string values for the control. See `<jsxcontrol>` `halign` (page 339) and `valign` (page 339) attributes. Default is `["left", "top"]`.

> ➤ **Example**

```
myWin.add ( "colorfield", [left, top, right, bottom],
"#FF0000",
    { name:"myColorField1", alignment:["left", "top"] } );
```

Control: combobox Object

This object represents a combo box control, a current value field with a popup menu. It inherits all properties and functions of the control Object Types (page 78). (Introduced in 7.0)

Acquiring a combobox object

- The SDK creates this object when it interprets a `<jsxcontrol>` (page 337) tag with `type="combobox"` or `"popup"` You can obtain the object by name or index from the parent window's `children` collection:

    windowObj.`children[`*controlName*`]` ;
    panelObj.`children[`*controlName*`]` ;

- To create a new `combobox` object dynamically, call a panel Object (page 233) or window Object's add (page 317) function with `type="combobox"`. Pass an object containing these optional creation parameters:

`name`	Unique JavaScript name of the control.
`helptip`	A descriptive string that appears when the mouse pointer hovers over the control.
`alignment`	An array containing the horizontal and vertical alignment string values for the control. See `<jsxcontrol>` `halign` (page 339) and `valign` (page 339) attributes. Default is `["left", "top"]`.

> ➤ Example

```
myWin.add ( "combobox", [left, top, right, bottom],
   "item1,item2",
      { name:"myCombobox1", alignment:["left", "top"] });
```

To populate a `combobox` control's popup list with items, use its add (page 82) function.

combobox object properties

These properties apply to `combobox` controls.

`items`	Array of Item	The item list of a list control as an array of `item` control objects. To add and remove items, use the control's add (page 82) and remove (page 84) methods. To clear the list, use the removeAll (page 84) method.
`selection`	Item	Gets or sets the currently selected list item in a list control. Each item is a Control: item Object (page 100). Set to `-1` to deselect all entries.

combobox object functions

Use these functions to manipulate the popup list contents of `combobox` controls.

add *controlObj*.add(*type, text* [, *index, creationProperties*])	Adds a new item to the `items` array. Creates a control object of type `item`.
type	The type of the new item. Must be `item`.
text	The display label for the new item.
index	Optional. The 0-based index position of this item in the parent control's `items` list. If not specified, new items are appended to the list.
creationPropert ies	Optional. Not used for `combobox`.
changeItem	Deprecated in 8.0. To change the label of a menu item, set the `text` of the corresponding `item` object.
find *controlObj*.find (*text*)	Finds and returns the `item` control object for the specified item if it is the `items` array.
text	The value of the `text` property of the list item to find.
remove *controlObj*.remove (*text*) *controlObj*.remove (*index*) *controlObj*.remove (*item*)	Removes a specified item from the `items` array.
text	The value of the `text` property of the list item to remove.
index	The 0-based index of the list item to remove.
item	The `item` control object for the list item to remove.
removeAll *controlObj*.removeAll()	Removes all item entries from the `items` array.

Control: custom Control Object

This object represents a custom control, defined by an extension. It inherits all properties and functions the control Object Types (page 78). (Introduced in 7.0)

Acquiring a custom control object

- The SDK creates this object when it interprets a `<jsxcontrol>` (page 337) tag with `type="custom"`. You can obtain the object by name or index from the parent window's `children` collection:

  windowObj.`children`[*controlName*];
  panelObj.`children`[*controlName*];

- To create a new `custom` object dynamically, call a panel Object (page 233) or window Object's add (page 317) function with `type="custom"`. Pass an object containing these optional creation parameters:

`name`	Unique JavaScript name of the control.
`helptip`	A descriptive string that appears when the mouse pointer hovers over the control.
`alignment`	An array containing the horizontal and vertical alignment string values for the control. See `<jsxcontrol>` `halign` (page 339) and `valign` (page 339) attributes. Default is `["left", "top"]`.

> ### Example

```
myWin.add ( "custom", [left, top, right, bottom], "",
    { name:"myCustomCtl1", alignment:["left", "top"] } );
```

You must supply and register a drawBox (page 362) handler function to explicitly draw the control's appearance. Any initial value you supply in the *text* parameter is ignored.

Control: edittext Object

This object represents a text edit control. It inherits all properties and functions of the control Object Types (page 78). (Introduced in 7.0)

The `type` value of the control is `edittext`. When the SDK interprets a `<jsxcontrol>` (page 337) tag with `type="edit"`, `"editarea"`, `"buttonedit"`, or `"password"`, it creates a control with `type=edittext`, but with property values set to obtain different behaviors. The control responds (that is, fires the `onChange` event) differently depending on various factors:

- When `onNoChanged` is `true`, the control responds whether or not the text content has changed; when it is `false`, the control responds only if the content has changed.
- When `onChange` is `true`, the control responds when the user clicks outside it.
- When `onEnter` is `true` (as it is for the type `buttonedit`) the control responds when the user presses Enter, and also has an optional **Enter** button, controlled by a user preference.
- When `multiline` is `true` (as it is for the type `editarea`) the control has multiple lines, and responds to each keypress, as well as loss of focus.

Acquiring an edittext object

- The SDK creates this object when it interprets a `<jsxcontrol>` (page 337) tag with `type="edit"`, `"editarea"`, `"buttonedit"`, or `"password"`. Each value creates a control with `type=edittext`, but with property values set to obtain different behaviors. You can obtain the object by name or index from the parent window's `children` collection:

    windowObj.`children`[*controlName*];
    panelObj.`children`[*controlName*];

- To create a new `edittext` object dynamically, call a panel Object (page 233) or window Object's add function (page 317) with `type="edittext"`. Pass an object containing these optional creation parameters:

`name`	Unique JavaScript name of the control.
`helptip`	A descriptive string that appears when the mouse pointer hovers over the control.
`readonly`	When `true`, this control does not accept any keyboard input. Default is `false`.
`alignment`	An array containing the horizontal and vertical alignment string values for the control. See `<jsxcontrol>` `halign` (page 339) and `valign` (page 339) attributes. Default is `["left", "top"]`.

multiline	When `true`, allows multiple lines. When `false`, this is a single-line edit field. Default is `false`.
noecho	When `true`, this control is for password input and does not show its text value. Default is `false`.
onEnter	When `true`, GoLive calls the onChange (page 364) callback function when the edit field has the focus, the value has changed, and the user has pressed Enter. Default is `false`.
onChange	When `true`, GoLive calls the onChange (page 364) callback function when the edit field loses the focus and the value has changed. Default is `false`.
onNoChanged	When `true`, GoLive calls the onChange (page 364) callback function when the edit field value has not changed. Combine this with `onEnter` and/or `onChange`. Default is `false`.
enterOK	When `true`, and if there is an **OK** button in the window, pressing Enter in this control is the same as clicking **OK**. Default is `false`.

➤ Example

```
myWin.add ( "edittext", [left, top, right, bottom],
"Initial text",
    { name:"myEdit1", multiline:false, readonly:false,
noecho:false,
    alignment:["left", "top"], onEnter:false,
onChange:false,
    onNoChanged:false, enterOK:false} );
```

Control: filelist Object

This object represents file-selection control, a tree that displays files and folders for a selected local or remote filesystem location, and allows the user to make multiple selections.

The top of the `filelist` control contains a popup menu that allows the user to select among loaded documents and sites. The `filelist` object's `text` property contains the label for this menu.

When the user selects a location from the popup menu, the contained files and folders are displayed in the body of the control. Each file or folder is displayed using the URL string, with a checkbox to indicate its selection state. You can access the displayed `item` objects through the `filelist` object's `items` property. Each item's `selected` property reflects and controls the selection state in the parent.

Contained folders are displayed as leaf nodes (`item` objects) and cannot be opened to display additional levels of hierarchy. To display a hierarchy, use the `hierarchy` control.

The `filelist` object is a type of control, and inherits all properties and functions of the control Object Types (page 78). (Introduced in 8.0)

Acquiring a filelist object

- The SDK creates this object when it interprets a `<jsxcontrol>` (page 337) tag with `type="filelist"`. You can obtain the object by name or index from the parent window's `children` collection:

    windowObj.`children[`*controlName*`]`;
    panelObj.`children[`*controlName*`]`;

- To create a new `filelist` object dynamically, call a panel Object (page 233) or window Object's add function (page 317) with `type="filelist"`. Pass an object containing these optional creation parameters:

`name`	Unique JavaScript name of the control.
`alignment`	An array containing the horizontal and vertical alignment string values for the control. See `<jsxcontrol>` `halign` (page 339) and `valign` (page 339) attributes. Default is `["left", "top"]`.

➤ Example

```
var folders = [ app.folder, app.tempFolder,
app.settingsFolder,
        app.modulesFolder, app.userSettingsFolder,
app.appSettingsFolder];
```

```
        var filelist = myWin.add ( "filelist", [left, top,
    right, bottom]);
        for( var f=0; f<folders.length; f++ )
            filelist.add( 'item',  folders[f] );
```

filelist object properties

These properties apply to `filelist` controls.

`items`	Array of Item, Node	The item list, an array of `item` control objects. To add and remove items, use the control's add (page 82) and remove (page 84) methods. To clear the list, use the removeAll (page 84) method.
`multi`	Boolean	Always `true`, allows selection of multiple entries, and `selection` contains an array.
`selection`	Array of Item, Item	Gets or sets the currently selected file and folder items in the control. An array of the `item` objects for all selected entries.
		You can set the value to a single `item` object, an array of `item` objects, or an array of `items` index values. When you set this value, it turns on the specified selection or selections without deselecting the other entries.
		Set to `-1` to deselect all entries.
`text`	String	The label text for the control's popup menu.

filelist object functions

Use these functions to manipulate the contents of `filelist` controls.

add *controlObj*.add (*type, text* [, *index, creationProperties*])	Adds a new item to the `items` array. Creates a control object of type `item`. See example for Control: node Object (page 105).
type	The type of the new item. Must be `item`.
text	The display label for the new item.
index	Optional. The 0-based index position of this item in the parent control's `items` list. If not specified, new items are appended to the list.
creationProperties	Optional. Not used for `filelist`.
find *controlObj*.find (*text*)	Finds and returns the `item` or `node` control object for the specified item if it is the `items` array.
text	The value of the `text` property of the list item to find.

---

remove *controlObj*.remove (*text*) *controlObj*.remove (*index*) *controlObj*.remove (*item*)	Removes a specified item from the items array.
text The value of the text property of the list item to remove.	
index The 0-based index of the list item to remove.	
item The item or node control object for the list item to remove.	
removeAll *controlObj*.removeAll()	Removes all item entries from the items array.

Control: frame Object

This object represents a border or frame that can visually group other controls in a window, and can have a label or title. The frame is not a container, and is not related to other controls except by their relative positions.

The frame is a type of control, but does not signal any user events. It inherits all properties and functions of the control Object Types (page 78). (Introduced in 8.0)

Acquiring a frame object

- The SDK creates this object when it interprets a `<jsxcontrol>` tag (page 337) with `type="frame"`. In the extension's `Main.html` file, the `<jsxcontrol type= frame...>` element must precede the controls it frames. If not, the frame draws on top of the framed controls, instead of behind them.

  You can obtain the object by name or index from the parent window's `children` collection:

  windowObj`.children[`*controlName*`];`
  panelObj`.children[`*controlName*`];`

- To create a new `frame` object dynamically, call a panel Object (page 233) or window Object's add function (page 317) with `type="frame"`. Pass an object containing these optional creation parameters:

`name`	Unique JavaScript name of the control.
`alignment`	An array containing the horizontal and vertical alignment string values for the control. See `<jsxcontrol>` `halign` (page 339) and `valign` (page 339) attributes. Default is `["left", "top"]`.

> ### Example

```
myWin.add ( "frame", [left, top, right, bottom], "My
frame",
    { name:"myFrame1", alignment:["left", "top"] } );
```

Control: hierarchy Object

This object represents a tree control, which displays a list of items and subitems hierarchically. Simple list items (leaf nodes) are represented by the Control: item Object (page 100). List items that contain subitems are represented by the Control: node Object (page 105), and can be opened or closed by the user or programmatically. Nodes can be nested—that is, nodes can contain subnodes as well as simple items.

Use the `hierarchy` object's methods to add and remove items and nodes. An item or node can be displayed using label text, and an optional icon image. Using creation properties when adding an item or node, you can:

- Provide different icons to indicate the open and closed states for that item.
- Make the item deleteable, so that a user can delete it by selecting it and pressing DELETE.
- Make the item editable, so that a user can edit the text label by selecting it, then clicking again and typing new text.

The `hierarchy` object is a control type, and inherits all properties and functions of the control Object Types (page 78). The `text` property contains a title for the control, independent of the node labels. (Introduced in 8.0)

Note: This object replaces the `tree` control and treeNode, treeRoot Object (page 289), which are deprecated in 8.0.

Acquiring a hierarchy object

- The SDK creates this object when it interprets a `<jsxcontrol>` tag (page 337) g with `type="hierarchy"`. You can obtain the object by name or index from the parent window's `children` collection:

      windowObj.`children`[*controlName*] ;
      panelObj.`children`[*controlName*] ;

- To create a new `hierarchy` object dynamically, call a panel Object (page 233) or window Object's add function (page 317) with `type="hierarchy"`. Pass an object containing these optional creation parameters:

`name`	Unique JavaScript name of the control.
`alignment`	An array containing the horizontal and vertical alignment string values for the control. See `<jsxcontrol>` `halign` (page 339) and `valign` (page 339) attributes. Default is `["left", "top"]`.

➤ **Example**

```
myWin.add ( "hierarchy", [left, top, right, bottom], "My
tree",
    { name:"myTree1", alignment:["left", "top"] } );
```

To populate a `hierarchy` control with items, use its add (page 98) function.
See example for Control: node Object (page 105).

hierarchy object properties

These properties apply to `hierarchy` controls.

items	Array of Item	The item list of the control as an array of `item` and `node` control objects. To add and remove items, use the control's add (page 82) and remove (page 84) methods. To clear the list, use the removeAll (page 84) method.
multi	Boolean	When `true`, allows selection of multiple entries in the list control, and `selection` contains an array.
selection	Array of Item and Node, Item, Node	Gets or sets the currently selected list item. If `multi=true`, an array of the `item` and `node` objects for all selected entries.
		You can set the value to a single `item` or `node` object, an array of `item` or `node` objects, or an array of `items` index values. When you set this value for a multi-selectable list, it turns on the specified selection without deselecting the other entries.
		Set to `-1` to deselect all entries.

hierarchy object functions

Use these functions to manipulate the contents of `hierarchy` controls.

add *controlObj*.add(*type, text* [, *index, creationProperties*])	Adds a new item to the `items` array. Creates a control object of type `item` or `node`. See example for Control: node Object (page 105).

type	The type of the new item. One of:
	    `item`: A selectable item (leaf node). Creates an `item` object.
	    `node`: An item that can contain subitems. Creates a `node` object.

text	The display label for the new item.
index	Optional. The 0-based index position of this item in the parent control's `items` list. If not specified, new items are appended to the list.

creationProperties	Optional. An object that can contain these properties:
	`icon`: The image name for an icon to display in the item or node, to the left of the text label.
	`expandIcon`: The image name for an icon to indicate that the node is in its expanded state.
	`deleteable`: When `true`, the user can delete this item or node.
	`editable`: When `true`, the user can edit the label of this item or node.
find *controlObj*.`find` *(text)*	Finds and returns the `item` or `node` control object for the specified item if it is the `items` array.
text	The value of the `text` property of the list item to find.
remove *controlObj*.`remove` *(text)* *controlObj*.`remove` *(index)* *controlObj*.`remove` *(item)*	Removes a specified item from the `items` array.
text	The value of the `text` property of the list item to remove.
index	The 0-based index of the list item to remove.
item	The `item` or `node` control object for the list item to remove.
removeAll *controlObj*.`removeAll ()`	Removes all item entries from the `items` array.

Control: item Object

This object represents a list item in a list box, combo box, file list, or hierarchy control. Simple list items (leaf nodes) are represented by the `item` object. List items that contain subitems are represented by the Control: node Object (page 105), and can be opened or closed by the user or programmatically. Nodes can be nested—that is, nodes can contain subnodes as well as simple items.

An item or node can be displayed using label text, and an optional icon image. Different icons can be used to indicate the open and closed states of nodes. When you add items and nodes to a `hierarchy` control, you can choose to make them deleteable, so that a user can delete one by selecting it and pressing DELETE, or editable, so that the user can edit the text label by selecting it, then clicking again and typing new text.

This object inherits all properties and functions of the control Object Types (page 78). (Introduced in 8.0)

Acquiring an item object

- The SDK creates this object for each item specified when it interprets a `<jsxcontrol>` tag (page 337) with `type="listbox"`, `"combobox"`, `"filelist"` or `"hierarchy"`. You can obtain the object by name or index from the parent control's `items` collection:

    controlObj.`items` [*itemName*] ;
    controlObj.`items` [*index*] ;

- To create a new `item` object dynamically, call a list control's add function (page 82), passing the display string for the new item.

➤ Example

```
var myList = myWin.add ( "list", [left, top, right,
bottom]);
myList.add ("item", "First Choice");
myList.add ("item", "Second Choice");
```

item object properties

These properties apply only to `item` controls.

icon	String	The name of an image defined in the extension file, which appears to the left of the text string for the item. Read/write.
index	Number	The 0-based index to the item's position in the parent's `items` list. Read-only.
parent	Control	The parent list control (`list`, `combobox`, `filelist`, or `hierarchy`). Read only.

selected	Boolean	When `true`, the item is currently selected in the parent control, when `false` it is not.
text	String	The label string displayed in the item. Read/write.

item object functions

The `item` control defines these functions:

toString tostring()	Returns the index position of this item in its parent's `items` list (for compatibility with previous versions in which list items were simple strings accessed by index).
valueOf valueOf()	Returns the index position of this item in its parent's `items` list (for compatibility with previous versions in which list items were simple strings accessed by index).

Control: line Object

This object represents a line drawn in a window. It inherits all properties and functions of the control Object Types (page 78). The line's length and orientation are determined by the `size` values. If the `height` value is greater than the `width` value, the line is vertical; otherwise it is horizontal.

(Introduced in 8.0)

Acquiring a line object

- The SDK creates this object when it interprets a `<jsxcontrol>` tag (page 337) with `type="line"`. You can obtain the object by name or index from the parent window's `children` collection:

  windowObj`.children[`*controlName*`] ;`
  panelObj`.children[`*controlName*`] ;`

- To create a new `line` object dynamically, call a panel Object (page 233) or window Object's add function (page 317) with `type="line"`. Pass an object containing these optional creation parameters:

name	Unique JavaScript name of the control.
alignment	An array containing the horizontal and vertical alignment string values for the control. See `<jsxcontrol>` `halign` (page 339) and `valign` (page 339) attributes. Default is `["left", "top"]`.

➤ Example

```
var w = new Window( 'palette', 'Lines', [200,200,400,400] );
// vertical line
w.add( 'line', [10,10,10,190] );
// horizontal line
w.add( 'line', [10,10,190,10] );
```

Control: list Object

This object represents a list box control. It inherits all properties and functions of the control Object Types (page 78). (Introduced in 7.0)

Acquiring a list object

- The SDK creates this object when it interprets a `<jsxcontrol>` tag (page 337) with `type="list"`. You can obtain the object by name or index from the parent window's `children` collection:

  windowObj. `children` [*controlName*] ;
  panelObj. `children` [*controlName*] ;

- To create a new `list` object dynamically, call a panel Object (page 233) or window Object's add function (page 317) with `type="list"`. Pass an object containing these optional creation parameters:

name	Unique JavaScript name of the control.
alignment	An array containing the horizontal and vertical alignment string values for the control. See `<jsxcontrol>` `halign` (page 339) and `valign` (page 339) attributes. Default is `["left", "top"]`.
columns	Optional. An array of column title strings. To create a list box with untitled columns, pass empty strings for the number of columns. When not supplied, the list box has no columns.

➤ Example

```
myWin.add ( "list", [left, top, right, bottom],
"item1,item2",
    { name:"myList1", alignment:["left", "top"],
        columns:["title1","title2"] } );
```

This creates a list box that contains the item or items specified as initial values. To add items to the list, use the add function (page 82).

list object properties

These properties apply to `list` controls.

`items`	Array of Item	The item list of a list control as an array of `item` control objects. To add and remove items, use the control's add (page 82) and remove (page 84) methods. To clear the list, use the removeAll method (page 84).
`selection`	Array of Item, Item	Gets or sets the currently selected list item. If `multi=true`, an array of the `item` objects for all selected entries. You can set the value to a single `item` object, an array of `item` objects, or an array of `items` index values. When you set this value for a multi-selectable list box, it turns on the specified selection without deselecting the other entries. Set to −1 to deselect all entries.

list object functions

Use these functions to manipulate the contents of `list` controls.

add *controlObj*.add (*type, text* [, *index, creationProperties*])	Adds a new item to the `items` array. Creates a control object of type `item`.
type	The type of the new item. Must be `item`.
text	The display label for the new item.
index	Optional. The 0-based index position of this item in the parent control's `items` list. If not specified, new items are appended to the list.
creationProper-ties	Optional. Not used for `list`.
find *controlObj*.find (*text*)	Finds and returns the `item` control object for the specified item if it is the `items` array.
text	The value of the `text` property of the list item to find.
remove *controlObj*.remove (*text*) *controlObj*.remove (*index*) *controlObj*.remove (*item*)	Removes a specified item from the `items` array.
text	The value of the `text` property of the list item to remove.
index	The 0-based index of the list item to remove.
item	The `item` control object for the list item to remove.
removeAll *controlObj*.removeAll ()	Removes all item entries from the `items` array.

Control: node Object

This object represents a selection item that can contain subitems in a `hierarchy` control.

Simple list items (leaf nodes) are represented by the Control: item Object (page 100). List items that contain subitems are represented by the `node` object, and can be opened or closed by the user or programmatically. Nodes can be nested—that is, nodes can contain subnodes as well as simple items.

An item or node can be displayed using label text, and an optional icon image. Different icons can be used to indicate the open and closed states. When you add items and nodes to a `hierarchy` control, you can choose to make them deleteable, so that a user can delete one by selecting it and pressing DELETE, or editable, so that the user can edit the text label by selecting it, then clicking again and typing new text.

This object inherits all properties and functions of the control Object Types (page 78). (Introduced in 8.0)

Acquiring a node object

- The SDK creates this object for each node specified when it interprets a `<jsxcontrol>` tag (page 337) with `type="hierarchy"`. You can obtain the object by name or index from the parent control's `items` collection:

     controlObj.`items` [*itemName*] ;
     controlObj.`items` [*index*] ;

- To create a new `node` object dynamically, call a `hierarchy` control's add function (page 82) with the `type` "node", passing the display string for the new node.

➤ **Example**

```
var icon1= createPicture( module.folder.absurl + '/gl.png' );
var icon2= createPicture( module.folder.absurl + '/icon.png' );
var folders = [ app.folder, app.tempFolder, app.settingsFolder,
    app.modulesFolder, app.userSettingsFolder,
app.appSettingsFolder];

var hierarchy = myWin.add("hierarchy", [left, top, right,
bottom]);
for( var h=0; h<folders.length; h++ ) {
    var node = hierarchy.add( 'node', folders[h].toString(), h,
        { icon:icon1.name, expandIcon:icon2.name } )
    node.addEventListener ( 'onExpand',
        function(e) {
            if( e.target.items.length <= 0 ) {
                var f = new JSXFile( e.target.text );
                if( f.exists ) {
```

```
                var subitems = f.getContent();
                for( var s=0; s<subitems.length; s++ )
                    e.target.add( 'item', subitems[s], s,
        { icon:icon2.name } );
                    }
                }
            }
        );
    }
```

node object properties

These properties apply only to node controls.

expanded	Boolean	When true, the node is open, and the parent displays the expanded icon and this node's immediate subnodes. When false, the control is collapse, and the parent displays the standard icon and no subitems. Read/write.
icon	Picture	The name of an image defined in the extension file, which appears to the left of the text string for the node. Read/write.
index	Number	The 0-based index to the item's position in the parent's items list. Read-only.
items	Array of Item and Node	The subitem list of this node, as an array of item and node control objects. To add and remove items, use the control's add (page 82) and remove (page 84) methods. To clear the list, use the removeAll method (page 84).
parent	Control	The parent list control (list, combobox, filelist, or hierarchy). Read only.
selected	Boolean	When true, the item is currently selected in the parent control, when false it is not.
text	String	The label string displayed in the node. Read/write.

node object functions

The `node` control defines these functions:

add *controlObj*.add(*type, text* [, *index, creationProperties*])	Adds a new item to the `items` array of the `node` control. Creates a control object of type `item` or `node`.

type	The type of the new item. One of:
	   `item`: A selectable item or leaf node. Creates an `item` object.
	   `node`: A subnode that can contain additional subitems. Creates a `node` object.

text	The display text for the new item or node.
index	Optional. The 0-based index position of this item in the parent node's `items` list. If not specified, new items are appended to the list.

creationProperties	Optional. An object that can contain any of these properties:
	   `icon`: The name of an image defined in extension file, to display in the item or node to the left of the text label.
	   `expandIcon`: The image name for an icon to indicate that the node is in its expanded state.
	   `deleteable`: When `true`, the user can delete the item or node.
	   `editable`: When `true`, the user can modify the item or node.

find *controlObj*.find (*text*)	Finds and returns the `item` or `node` control object for the specified item if it is the `items` array of the parent node.
text	The value of the `text` property of the list item to find.
remove *controlObj*.remove (*text*) *controlObj*.remove (*index*) *controlObj*.remove (*item*)	Removes a specified item from the `items` array of the parent node.
text	The value of the `text` property of the list item to remove.
index	The 0-based index of the list item to remove.
item	The `item` or `node` control object for the list item to remove.
removeAll *controlObj*.removeAll()	Removes all item entries from the `items` array of the parent node.
toString tostring()	Returns the index position of this item in its parent's `items` list (for compatibility with previous versions in which list items were simple strings accessed by index).
valueOf valueOf()	Returns the index position of this item in its parent's `items` list (for compatibility with previous versions in which list items were simple strings accessed by index).

Control: preview Object

This object represents a preview control, a browser that displays HTML inside a dialog or palette window. It inherits all properties and functions of the control Object Types (page 78). In addition, it defines properties and functions of its own, that allow you to control the page display. (Introduced in 7.0)

Acquiring a preview object

- The SDK creates this object when it interprets a `<jsxcontrol>` tag (page 337) with `type="preview"`. You can obtain the object by name or index from the parent window's `children` collection:

  windowObj.`children[`*controlName*`]` ;
  panelObj.`children[`*controlName*`]` ;

- To create a new `preview` object dynamically, call a panel Object (page 233) or window Object's add function (page 317) with `type="preview"`. Pass an object containing these optional creation parameters:

`name`	Unique JavaScript name of the control.
`alignment`	An array containing the horizontal and vertical alignment string values for the control. See `<jsxcontrol>` `halign` (page 339) and `valign` (page 339) attributes. Default is `["left", "top"]`.

➤ Example

```
myWin.add ( "preview", [left, top, right, bottom], "My
page",
    { name:"myPreview1", alignment:["left", "top"] } );
```

preview object properties

busy	Boolean	When `true`, the control is in the process of loading a page.

preview object functions

goBack goBack()	Shows the previously displayed page in the history.
goForward goForward()	Goes to the next page in the history.
goHome goHome()	Goes to the browser's home page. In Mac OS, this is specified by system preferences. In Windows, it is specified by user settings in GoLive.

setFile setFile(*fileRef*)	Sets the file or URL to show in this control.
fileRef	The file to preview. Specify as a full path or URL string, or as a file Object (page 158), siteReference Object (page 260), or FTP Object (page 171).
setSource setSource(*markup*)	Sets the markup source to show in this control.
markup	A string containing HTML to display.
stop stop()	Stops loading the current page. If the control is not in the process of loading a page, does nothing.

Control: progressbar Object

This object represents a progress bar control. It inherits all properties and functions of the control Object Types (page 78). In addition, it defines properties of its own. (Introduced in 7.0)

Acquiring a progressbar object

- The SDK creates this object when it interprets a `<jsxcontrol>` tag (page 337) with `type="progressbar"`. You can obtain the object by name or index from the parent window's `children` collection:

    windowObj. `children` [*controlName*] ;
    panelObj. `children` [*controlName*] ;

- To create a new `progressbar` object dynamically, call a panel Object (page 233) or window Object's add function (page 317) with `type="progressbar"`. Pass an object containing these optional creation parameters:

name	Unique JavaScript name of the control.
helptip	A descriptive string that appears when the mouse pointer hovers over the control.
alignment	An array containing the horizontal and vertical alignment string values for the control. See `<jsxcontrol>` `halign` (page 339) and `valign` (page 339) attributes. Default is `["left", "top"]`.

➤ Example

```
myWin.add ( "progressbar", [left, top, right, bottom],
10, 0, 100,
    {name:"myBar1", readonly:false, alignment:["left",
"top"]});
```

progressbar object properties

In addition to those properties it inherits from the control Object Types (page 78), the `progressbar` object has these properties:

maxvalue	Number	The maximum value for the bar.
minvalue	Number	The minimum value for the bar.

Control: radiobutton Object

This object represents a radio-button control. It inherits all properties and functions of the control Object Types (page 78). (Introduced in 7.0)

Acquiring a radiobutton object

- The SDK creates this object when it interprets a `<jsxcontrol>` tag (page 337) with `type="radiobutton"`. You can obtain the object by name or index from the parent window's `children` collection:

  windowObj`.children[`*controlName*`]`;
  panelObj`.children[`*controlName*`]`;

- To create a new `radiobutton` object dynamically, call a panel Object (page 233) or window Object's add function (page 317) with `type="radiobutton"`. Pass an object containing these optional creation parameters:

`name`	Unique JavaScript name of the control.
`helptip`	A descriptive string that appears when the mouse pointer hovers over the control.
`groupid`	A radio button group identifier. An arbitrary string, unique within the window. All controls with the same group ID act as one radio button group.
`alignment`	An array containing the horizontal and vertical alignment string values for the control. See `<jsxcontrol>` `halign` (page 339) and `valign` (page 339) attributes. Default is `["left", "top"]`.

➤ **Example**

```
myWin.add ( "radiobutton", [left, top, right, bottom],
"choice1",
    {name:"myrb1", alignment:["left", "top"],
groupid:"myRadioGroup1" });
```

radiobutton object properties

This property applies to `radiobutton` controls.

value	Boolean	For check box and radio button controls, `true` if the control is selected (checked), `false` if it is not. For other control types, this property is not used.
		(Usage changed in 8.0. Used differently in earlier versions.)

Control: scrollbar Object

This object represents a scrollbar control. It inherits all properties and functions of the control Object Types (page 78). In addition, it defines properties of its own. (Introduced in 7.0)

Acquiring a scrollbar object

- The SDK creates this object when it interprets a `<jsxcontrol>` tag (page 337) with `type="scrollbar"`. You can obtain the object by name or index from the parent window's `children` collection:

    windowObj.`children`[*controlName*] ;
    panelObj.`children`[*controlName*] ;

- To create a new `scrollbar` object dynamically, call a panel Object (page 233) or window Object's add function (page 317) with `type="scrollbar"`. Pass an object containing these optional creation parameters:

`name`	Unique JavaScript name of the control.
`helptip`	A descriptive string that appears when the mouse pointer hovers over the control.
`alignment`	An array containing the horizontal and vertical alignment string values for the control. See `<jsxcontrol>` `halign` (page 339) and `valign` (page 339) attributes. Default is `["left", "top"]`.

➤ Example

```
myWin.add ( "scrollbar", [left, top, right, bottom], 50,
0, 100,
    {name:"scroll1", alignment:["left", "top"]});
```

If the control's width is greater than its height, the scrollbar is horizontal; otherwise, it is vertical.

scrollbar object properties

jumpdelta	Number	The amount to scroll when the user clicks in the part of the scrollbar before or behind the moveable element.
maxvalue	Number	The maximum value.
minvalue	Number	The minimum value.
stepdelta	Number	The amount to scroll when the user clicks on either of the arrow buttons.

Control: slider Object

This object represents a slider control. It inherits all properties and functions of the control Object Types (page 78). In addition, it defines properties of its own. (Introduced in 7.0)

Acquiring a slider object

- The SDK creates this object when it interprets a `<jsxcontrol>` tag (page 337) with `type="slider"`. You can obtain the object by name or index from the parent window's `children` collection:

  windowObj.`children[`*controlName*`]`;
  panelObj.`children[`*controlName*`]`;

- To create a new `slider` object dynamically, call a panel Object (page 233) or window Object's add function (page 317) with `type="slider"`. Pass an object containing these optional creation parameters:

`name`	Unique JavaScript name of the control.
`helptip`	A descriptive string that appears when the mouse pointer hovers over the control.
`alignment`	An array containing the horizontal and vertical alignment string values for the control. See `<jsxcontrol>` `halign` (page 339) and `valign` (page 339) attributes. Default is `["left", "top"]`.

➤ **Example**

```
myWin.add ( "slider", [left, top, right, bottom], 50, 0,
100,
    {name:"slider1", readonly:false, alignment:["left",
"top"]});
```

If the control's width is greater than its height, the slider is horizontal; otherwise, it is vertical.

slider object properties

`jumpdelta`	Number	The amount to move the indicator when the user clicks before or behind the moveable element.
`maxvalue`	Number	The maximum value.
`minvalue`	Number	The minimum value.
`stepdelta`	Number	The amount to move the indicator when the user clicks either of the arrow buttons.

Control: source Object

This object represents a source control, which displays and allows you to edit JavaScript source code or any other text inside a dialog or palette window. It inherits all properties and functions of the control Object Types (page 78). In addition, it defines properties of its own. (Introduced in 7.0)

This control can use a syntax scheme for marking the syntactic structure of the displayed text, if one is specified. Some syntax schemes, such as JavaScript and HTML, are provided; you can also define your own syntax schemes. For details, see Chapter 7, "Defining a Syntax Scheme."

For an example of using this object, see the `Document Source` sample provided with the SDK.

Acquiring a source object

- The SDK creates this object when it interprets a `<jsxcontrol>` tag (page 337) with `type="source"`. You can obtain the object by name or index from the parent window's `children` collection:

  windowObj.`children[`*controlName*`]` ;
  panelObj.`children[`*controlName*`]` ;

- To create a new `source` object dynamically, call a panel Object (page 233) or window Object's add function (page 317) with `type="source"`. Pass an object containing these optional creation parameters:

name	Unique JavaScript name of the control.
alignment	An array containing the horizontal and vertical alignment string values for the control. See `<jsxcontrol>` halign (page 339) and `valign` (page 339) attributes. Default is `["left", "top"]`.
readonly	When `true`, this control does not accept any keyboard input. Default is `false`.

➤ Example

```
myWin.add ( "source", [left, top, right, bottom], "My
JavaScript code",
    { name:"mySource1", readonly:false, alignment:["left",
"top"] });
```

source object properties

lineNumbers	Boolean	When `true`, show line numbers in the source code.
sourceArea	TextView	A textView Object (page 283) that contains the content being edited.

---

syntax	String	The syntax marking theme for the displayed code. One of the values that appears in the JavaScript editor's list of syntax themes. See Chapter 7, "Defining a Syntax Scheme."
wordWrap	Boolean	When `true`, wrap lines in the displayed text.

Control: statictext Object

This object represents a non-editable text control, or label. It inherits all properties and functions of the control Object Types (page 78). (Introduced in 7.0)

Acquiring a statictext object

- The SDK creates this object when it interprets a `<jsxcontrol>` tag (page 337) with `type="statictext"`. You can obtain the object by name or index from the parent window's `children` collection:

    windowObj`.children`[*controlName*]`;`
    panelObj`.children`[*controlName*]`;`

- To create a new `statictext` object dynamically, call a panel Object (page 233) or window Object's add function (page 317) with `type="statictext"`. Pass an object containing these optional creation parameters:

name	Unique JavaScript name of the control.
alignment	An array containing the horizontal and vertical alignment string values for the control. See `<jsxcontrol>` `halign` (page 339) and `valign` (page 339) attributes. Default is `["left", "top"]`.

➤ Example

```
myWin.add ( "statictext", [left, top, right, bottom],
"Label Text:",
    { name:"myStaticEdit1", alignment:["left", "top"] } );
```

Control: urlgetter Object

This object represents a URL control containing a link. It inherits all properties and functions of the control Object Types (page 78). (Introduced in 7.0)

Acquiring a urlgetter object

- The SDK creates this object when it interprets a `<jsxcontrol>` tag (page 337) with `type="urlgetter"`. You can obtain the object by name or index from the parent window's `children` collection:

  windowObj.`children[`*controlName*`]` ;
  panelObj.`children[`*controlName*`]` ;

- To create a new `urlgetter` object dynamically, call a panel Object (page 233) or window Object's add function (page 317) with `type=="urlgetter"`. Pass an object containing these optional creation parameters:

`name`	Unique JavaScript name of the control.
`helptip`	A descriptive string that appears when the mouse pointer hovers over the control.
`alignment`	An array containing the horizontal and vertical alignment string values for the control. See `<jsxcontrol>` `halign` (page 339) and `valign` (page 339) attributes. Default is `["left", "top"]`.

Example

```
myWin.add ( "urlgetter", [left, top, right, bottom],
    "http://www.adobe.com",
    { name:"myURLget1", alignment:["left", "top"] } );
```

This sets the initial display value to a URL, but does not associate the control with a link Object (page 207).

urlgetter object functions

setLink *controlObj*.`setLink` (*link*)	Sets the link used by this control. Use this function rather than setting the control's `text` property to set a displayed value that corresponds to a `link` object. Only controls of type `urlgetter` provide this method. All other control types ignore this method call.
link	A link Object (page 207) for the new link.

CSSCharsetRule Object

Class: CSSCharsetRule

This object represents a style rule of the type @charset in a CSSStyleSheet Object (page 129). It specifies a character set to be used as part of the style. For example:

```
@charset iso-8859-1;
```

Contains no functions. (Introduced in 8.0)

Acquiring a CSSCharsetRule object

- The cssRules property of the CSSStyleSheet Object (page 129) contains a collection of rules for that style sheet, which can include charset rules:

```
var myStyleSheet = docObj.styleSheets[0];
var firstRule = myStyleSheet.cssRules[0];
```

- The cssRules property of the CSSMediaRule Object (page 122) contains a collection of rules in that media set, which can include charset rules:

```
var myMediaRule = docObj.styleSheets[0].cssRules[0];
var firstRule = myMediaRule.cssRules[0];
```

CSSCharsetRule object properties

cssText	String	The entire text of the rule. Read/write.
encoding	String	The character set (charset) name.
parentRule	CSSMediaRule CSSUnknownRule	If this is part of another rule, the CSSMediaRule Object (page 122) or CSSUnknownRule Object (page 131) for the rule that contains this one.
parentStyleSheet	CSSStyleSheet	The CSSStyleSheet Object (page 129) for the style sheet that contains this rule.
type	String	The string "charset".

CSSFontFaceRule Object

Class: `CSSFontFaceRule`

This object represents a style rule of the type `@fontface` in a CSSStyleSheet Object (page 129). It specifies a font face to be used as part of the style. For example:

```
@font-face { font-family: sans-serif }
```

Contains no functions. (Introduced in 8.0)

Acquiring a CSSFontfaceRule object

- The `cssRules` property of the CSSStyleSheet Object (page 129) contains a collection of rules for that style sheet, which can include fontface rules:

```
var myStyleSheet = docObj.styleSheets[0];
var firstRule = myStyleSheet.cssRules[0];
```

- The `cssRules` property of the CSSMediaRule Object (page 122) contains a collection of rules in that media set, which can include fontface rules:

```
var myMediaRule = docObj.styleSheets[0].cssRules[0];
var firstRule = myMediaRule.cssRules[0];
```

CSSFontfaceRule object properties

`cssText`	String	The entire text of the rule. Read/write.
`parentRule`	CSSMediaRule CSSUnknownRule	If this is part of another rule, the CSSMediaRule Object (page 122) or CSSUnknownRule Object (page 131) for the rule that contains this one.
`parentStyleSheet`	CSSStyleSheet	The CSSStyleSheet Object (page 129) for the style sheet that contains this rule.
`style`	CSSStyleDeclaration	The CSSStyleDeclaration Object (page 125) that provides access to the declaration part of this rule.
`type`	String	The string `"fontface"`.

CSSImportRule Object

Class: `CSSImportRule`

This object represents a style rule of the type `@import` in a CSSStyleSheet Object (page 129). The rule references an imported style sheet; that is, another `.css` file to be included inline into the style sheet that contains this rule. For example:

```
@import
url("file:///C:/myDocuments/web-content/myStyle.css");
```

When a style sheet is imported into another (as shown by the presence of a `CSSImportRule` in that style sheet object's `ownerRule` property), you cannot use its style sheet object to modify it. To modify it, you must open the style sheet file as a separate document.

(Introduced in 8.0)

Acquiring a CSSImportRule object

- The `cssRules` property of the CSSStyleSheet Object (page 129) contains a collection of rules for that style sheet, which can include import rules:
  ```
  var myStyleSheet = docObj.styleSheets[0];
  var firstRule = myStyleSheet.cssRules[0];
  ```
- The `cssRules` property of the CSSMediaRule Object (page 122) contains a collection of rules in that media set, which can include import rules:
  ```
  var myMediaRule = docObj.styleSheets[0].cssRules[0];
  var firstRule = myMediaRule.cssRules[0];
  ```
- The `ownerRule` property of the CSSStyleSheet Object (page 129) contains an import rule object if that style sheet is imported:
  ```
  var myStyleSheet = docObj.styleSheets[0];
  var myOwner = myStyleSheet.ownerRule;
  ```

CSSImportRule object properties

`cssText`	String	The entire text of the rule. Read/write.
`href`	String	The URL of the linked style sheet that imports this one.
`media`	CSSMediaList	A collection Object (page 72) containing media type strings, as defined by the CSS standard. The list specifies media types for which this set of rules is appropriate.
`parentRule`	CSSMediaRule CSSUnknownRule	If this is part of another rule, the CSSMediaRule Object (page 122) or CSSUnknownRule Object (page 131) for the rule that contains this one.

---

parentStyleSheet	CSSStyleSheet	The CSSStyleSheet Object (page 129) for the style sheet that contains this rule.
styleSheet	CSSStyleSheet	The CSSStyleSheet Object (page 129) for the imported style sheet.
type	String	The string `"import"`.

CSSImportRule object functions

addMedium *CSSImportRuleObj*.`addMedium` (*medium*)	Adds the specified medium to the `media` list for this rule. Returns `true` on success. If this rule is itself part of an imported (linked) style sheet that is not loaded, does not add the medium and returns `false`.
medium	The name of the medium. A string.
deleteMedium *CSSImportRuleObj*.`deleteMedium` (*medium*)	Deletes the specified medium from the `media` list for this rule. Returns `true` on success. If this rule is itself part of an imported (linked) style sheet that is not loaded, does not delete the medium and returns `false`.
propertyName	The name of the medium. A string.
openDocument *CSSImportRuleObj*.`openDocument()`	Opens the referenced style sheet as a separate document and returns the document Object (page 138).

CSSMediaRule Object

Class: CSSMediaRule

This object represents a style rule of the type @media in a CSSStyleSheet Object (page 129). This rule collects other style rules into sets appropriate for specific media. For example:

```
@media screen {body {color: black; font-style: bold,
background-color: white}}
```

(Introduced in 8.0)

Acquiring a CSSMediaRule object

- The cssRules property of the CSSStyleSheet Object (page 129) contains a collection of rules for that style sheet, which can include media rules:

  ```
  var myStyleSheet = docObj.styleSheets[0];
  var firstRule = myStyleSheet.cssRules[0];
  ```

- The cssRules property of the CSSMediaRule Object (page 122) contains a collection of rules in that media set, which can include other media rules:

  ```
  var myMediaRule = docObj.styleSheets[0].cssRules[0];
  var firstRule = myMediaRule.cssRules[0];
  ```

CSSMediaRule object properties

cssRules	CSSRule Collection	A collection of the CSSStyleRule Objects (page 127, or other rule subtypes) contained in this set. Access individual rules by index.
cssText	String	The entire text of the rule. Read/write.
media	CSSMediaList	A collection Object (page 72) containing media type strings, as defined by the CSS standard. The list specifies media types for which this set of rules is appropriate.
parentRule	CSSMediaRule CSSUnknownRule	If this is part of another rule, the CSSMediaRule Object (page 122) or CSSUnknownRule Object (page 131) for the rule that contains this one.
parentStyleSheet	CSSStyleSheet	The CSSStyleSheet Object (page 129) for the style sheet that contains this rule.
type	String	The string "media".

CSSMediaRule object functions

deleteRule *CSSMediaRuleObj*.deleteRule (*index*)	Deletes the specified rule from the `cssRule` collection for this rule. Returns `true` on success.
index	The 0-based index for the rule in the `cssRule` collection.
insertRule *CSSMediaRuleObj*.insertRule (*rule*, [*insertIndex*])	Creates a CSSStyleRule Object (page 127) for the specified rule and adds it to the `cssRule` collections for this rule. Returns `true` on success.
rule	A string containing the complete text of the rule to add. For example: `myMediaRule.insertRule( 'p { background-color: red }' );`
insertIndex	Optional. The 0-based index at which to insert the rule in the `cssRule` collection. If not supplied, inserts the rule at the end of the list.

CSSPageRule Object

Class: `CSSPageRule`

This object represents a style rule of the type `@page` in a CSSStyleSheet Object (page 129). A page box is a rectangular region that contains a page area and a margin area. The keyword @page is followed by an optional page selector, then a block of declarations. The page selector specifies a set of pages to which the declarations apply: the first page, all left pages, or all right pages. The declarations specify margin and page-break properties. For example:

```
@page :left { margin-left: 4cm; margin-right: 3cm; }
```

Contains no functions. (Introduced in 8.0)

Acquiring a CSSPageRule object

- The `cssRules` property of the CSSStyleSheet Object (page 129) contains a collection of rules for that style sheet, which can include page rules:

```
var myStyleSheet = docObj.styleSheets[0];
var firstRule = myStyleSheet.cssRules[0];
```

- The `cssRules` property of the CSSMediaRule Object (page 122) contains a collection of rules in that media set, which can include page rules:

```
var myMediaRule = docObj.styleSheets[0].cssRules[0];
var firstRule = myMediaRule.cssRules[0];
```

CSSPageRule object properties

`cssText`	String	The entire text of the rule. Read/write.
`parentRule`	CSSMediaRule CSSUnknownRule	If this is part of another rule, the CSSMediaRule Object (page 122) or CSSUnknownRule Object (page 131) for the rule that contains this one.
`parentStyleSheet`	CSSStyleSheet	The CSSStyleSheet Object (page 129) for the style sheet that contains this rule.
`selectorText`	String	The text of the selector part of this rule.
`type`	String	The string `"page"`.

CSSStyleDeclaration Object

Class: `CSSStyleDeclaration`

This object represents the declaration part of a style rule in a CSSStyleRule Object (page 127). (Introduced in 8.0)

Acquiring a CSSStyleDeclaration object

The `style` property of the CSSStyleRule Object (page 127) contains the declaration object for that rule:

```
var myStyleSheet = docObj.styleSheets[0];
var myRule = myStyleSheet.cssRules[0];
var myDec = myRule.style;
```

CSSStyleDeclaration object properties

`cssText`	String	A string containing text of the declaration, a semicolon-delimited list of *property:value* pairs.
`length`	Number	The number of *property:value* pairs in this declaration.
`parentRule`	CSSStyleRule CSSImportRule CSSFontFaceRule CSSMediaRule CSSCharsetRule CSSPageRule CSSUnknownRule	The object for the rule that contains this declaration. Can be a CSSStyleRule Object (page 127), or any of the following subtypes: CSSCharsetRule Object (page 118) CSSFontFaceRule Object (page 119) CSSImportRule Object (page 120) CSSMediaRule Object (page 122) CSSPageRule Object (page 124) CSSUnknownRule Object (page 131)

CSSStyleDeclaration object functions

getPropertyPriority *CSSStyleDeclarationObj*.`getPropertyPriority` (*propertyName*)	Returns `true` if the `important` flag of the specified property is set.
propertyName The name of the property. A string.	
getPropertyValue *CSSStyleDeclarationObj*.`getPropertyValue` (*propertyName*)	Returns the value of the named property as a string.
propertyName The name of the property. A string.	

item *CSSStyleDeclarationObj*.item (index)	Returns the value of the property at the specified index as a string.
index	The 0-based index of this property in the cssText array.
removeProperty *CSSStyleDeclarationObj*.removeProperty (*propertyName*)	Removes the specified property from the rule.
propertyName	The name of the property. A string.
setProperty *CSSStyleDeclarationObj*.setProperty (*propertyName*, *propertyValue*)	Sets the value of the specified property. Creates the property if it does not yet exist, otherwise replaces the value. Returns true on success.
propertyName	The name of the property. A string.
propertyValue	The new value of the property. A string.

CSSStyleRule Object

Class: `CSSStyleRule`

This object represents a style rule in a CSSStyleSheet Object (page 129). Subtypes include:

CSSCharsetRule Object (page 118)
CSSFontFaceRule Object (page 119)
CSSImportRule Object (page 120)
CSSMediaRule Object (page 122)
CSSPageRule Object (page 124)
CSSUnknownRule Object (page 131)

A general style rule contains a selector part and a declaration part. The selector part specifies the tags to which the declared styles apply. For example:

```
H1, H2, H3 {color:blue; font-family:Arial, Helvetica}
```

Contains no functions. (Introduced in 8.0)

Acquiring a CSSStyleRule object

- The `cssRules` property of the CSSStyleSheet Object (page 129) contains a collection of rules for that style sheet, which you access by index:

```
var myStyleSheet = docObj.styleSheets[0];
var firstRule = myStyleSheet.cssRules[0];
```

- The `cssRules` property of the CSSMediaRule Object (page 122) contains a collection of rules in that media set:

```
var myMediaRule = docObj.styleSheets[0].cssRules[0];
var firstRule = myMediaRule.cssRules[0];
```

For example, the following gets and prints the types of all rules in all style sheets in a document:

```
var doc = app.openDocument( 'mydocument' );
for( var i=0; i<doc.styleSheets.length; i++) {
   for( var j=0; j<doc.styleSheets[i].cssRules.length; j++ )
{
     writeln( 'Rule type : ' +
doc.styleSheets[i].cssRules[j].type + '\t' +
        doc.styleSheets[i].cssRules[j].cssText );
}}
```

CSSStyleRule object properties

cssText	String	Read/write. The entire text of the rule, in the form *selector {declaration}*. For example:
		`"H1, H2, H3 {color:blue; font-family:Arial,`
		`Helvetica}"`

parentRule	CSSMediaRule CSSUnknownRule	If this is part of another rule, the CSSMediaRule Object (page 122) or CSSUnknownRule Object (page 131) for the rule that contains this one.
parentStyleSheet	CSSStyleSheet	The CSSStyleSheet Object (page 129) for the style sheet that contains this rule.
selectorText	String	The text of the selector part of this rule. For example: `"H1, H2, H3"`
style	CSSStyleDeclaration	The CSSStyleDeclaration Object (page 125) that provides access to the declaration part of this rule.
type	String	The string `"style"`.

CSSStyleSheet Object

Class: CSSStyleSheet

This object provides access to a CSS style sheet associated with a document. Style sheets contain rule objects of various types that describe the style rules.

Rule objects in the cssRules collection are in the same order in which those rules are defined in the style sheet. Changing the order in the collection changes the rule order in the style sheet, and thus the order in which the rules are applied to document content. Use the style sheet's deleteRule and insertRule functions to change the order.

GoLive creates the style-sheet and rule objects for an internal style sheet in a markup document only when that document is opened in Layout view. This means that for an open markup document, you can access an internal style sheet only after opening the document in Layout view.

When a markup document has an external style sheet, the style sheet itself is a .css file that you can open as a document in Adobe GoLive CS2 SDK. It is loaded as a document of type css (rather than markup). You can access the style sheet through an open markup document's styleSheets property, but it is read-only unless the style-sheet document is also open.

(Introduced in 8.0)

Acquiring a CSSStyleSheet object

- For documents of type markup and css, the styleSheets property of the document Object (page 138) contains one or more style-sheet objects.

```
var myStyleSheet = docObj.styleSheets[0];
```

- For a markup document, the property contains a collection of internal and external style sheet objects associated with the markup document.

- For a css document, this collection contains the single style sheet object for that document.

- The createCSSStyleSheet function (page 142) of the document Object (page 138) for a markup document can create a new CSSStyleSheet object for a new, empty, embedded style sheet, or a new object to represent an existing external style sheet:

```
var myStyleSheet = docObj.createCSSStyleSheet();
var myStyleSheet = docObj.createCSSStyleSheet(cssFile);
```

CSSStyleSheet object properties

`cssRules`	CSSRule Collection	A collection of rules for this style sheet. These can be CSSStyleRule Objects (page 127), or any of the following subtypes: CSSCharsetRule Object (page 118) CSSFontFaceRule Object (page 119) CSSImportRule Object (page 120) CSSMediaRule Object (page 122) CSSPageRule Object (page 124) CSSUnknownRule Object (page 131)
`ownerRule`	CSSImportRule	If this style sheet is linked by an import rule to another style sheet, contain the CSSImportRule Object (page 120) for the import rule. When present, this value indicates that a style sheet is imported into (included by) another style sheet, and cannot be modified through this style sheet object. To modify it, you must load it as a separate document using this object's openDocument function (page 121).

CSSStyleSheet object functions

`deleteRule` *CSSStyleSheetObj*.`deleteRule`(*index*)	Deletes the specified rule from the style sheet. Returns `true` on success. If this style sheet is linked to another by an import rule, does not delete the rule and returns `false`.
index	The 0-based index of the rule in the `cssRules` array.
`insertRule` *CSSStyleSheetObj*.`insertRule` (*rule*, [*insertIndex*])	Creates a CSSStyleRule Object (page 127) for the specified rule and adds it to the style sheet. Returns `true` on success. If this style sheet is linked to another by an import rule, does not add the new rule and returns `false`.
rule	A string containing the complete text of the rule to add. For example: `myStyleSheet.insertRule( 'p { background-color: red }' );`
insertIndex	Optional. The 0-based index at which to insert the rule in the `cssRules` array. If not specified, inserts the rule at the end of the array.

CSSUnknownRule Object

Class: `CSSUnknownRule`

This object represents a style rule of a type not described by the other rule classes, in a CSSStyleSheet Object (page 129). This can include rules that contain sets of other rules. (Introduced in 8.0)

Contains no functions.

Acquiring a CSSPageRule object

- The `cssRules` property of the CSSStyleSheet Object (page 129) contains a collection of rules for that style sheet, which can include unknown-type rules:

  ```
  var myStyleSheet = docObj.styleSheets[0];
  var firstRule = myStyleSheet.cssRules[0];
  ```

- The `cssRules` property of the CSSMediaRule Object (page 122) contains a collection of rules in that media set, which can include unknown-type rules:

  ```
  var myMediaRule = docObj.styleSheets[0].cssRules[0];
  var firstRule = myMediaRule.cssRules[0];
  ```

CSSPageRule object properties

`cssText`	String	The text of the rule. Read/write.
`parentRule`	CSSMediaRule CSSUnknownRule	If this is part of another rule, the CSSMediaRule Object (page 122) or CSSUnknownRule Object (page 131) for the rule that contains this one.
`parentStyleSheet`	CSSStyleSheet	The CSSStyleSheet Object (page 129) for the style sheet that contains this rule.
`type`	String	The string `"unknown"`.

DAV Object

Class: JSXDAV

This object provides access to remote data on a WebDAV server via the WebDAV protocol. Like the file Object (page 158), the DAV object refers to a virtual file or folder—that is, the remote file or folder may or may not exist. (Introduced in 7.0)

To access a WebDAV server there must be at least one DAV object connected to that server. If there are multiple DAV objects that refer to the same server with the same authorization data, you only need to connect one of the objects; all other objects are connected automatically. Similarly, when you disconnect one object, all others are disconnected automatically.

For an example of using this object, see the FTP and WebDAV sample included with the SDK.

Acquiring a DAV object

Use the DAV object constructor (page 134) to create a new DAV object:

```
var f = new JSXDAV( "http://mydav.myserver.com" );
var f = new JSXDAV( "mydav.myserver.com/myfolder/myfile.txt" );
var f = new JSXDAV( "mydav.myserver.com/myfolder/", "myname",
"mypasswrd" );
```

To create a DAV object referring to a folder on a remote file system, you must use a trailing slash to indicate that the last item in the path is a folder name and not a file name.

DAV object properties

absurl	String	The complete URL. For example: `http://mydav.myserver.com/myfolder/myfile.txt`
access	Number	Bitfield of access rights (UNIX® style): 0x0001 other execute 0x0002 other write 0x0004 other read 0x0008 group execute 0x0010 group write 0x0020 group read 0x0040 owner execute 0x0080 owner write 0x0100 owner read The object must be connected to the server to acquire this information. Read/write.
connected	Boolean	When `true`, the object is connected to the server.
creationDate	Date	A JavaScript Date object containing the platform's creation date for the file.
error	Number	Error code of last error.
exists	Boolean	When `true`, the remote file or folder exists. The object must be connected to the server to acquire this information.
host	String	The host name. For example: `http://mydav.myserver.com`
isFolder	Boolean	When `true`, the DAV object refers to a remote folder.
lastError	String	Text of last error.
lastname	String	The file or folder name.
modificationDate	Date	A JavaScript Date object containing the platform's modification date for the file.
parent	DAV	Parent file or folder of the current DAV object. The object must be connected to the server to acquire this information.
relurl	String	URL relative to the host. For example: `/myfolder/myfile.txt)`
size	Number	Size of the remote file, if it is a file. The object must be connected to the server to acquire this information.

DAV object functions

DAV object constructor new JSXDAV (*hostAndPath* [, *userName*, *password*]) new JSXDAV (*server*)	Creates a new DAV object. Returns the new DAV object for the specified server with the corresponding access permission (upon successful connection).
hostAndPath	A hostname or a hostname with a specified path to a file or folder. If the last element of the path is a folder name, it must be followed by a slash character.
userName	Optional. A user name with access permission on the server.
password	Optional. The user's password in plain text.
server	A serverInfo Object (page 243) that identifies the target file or folder.

➤ Examples

```
var f = new JSXDAV("http://mydav.myserver.com");
var f = new JSXDAV("mydav.myserver.com/myfolder/myfile.txt");
var f = new JSXDAV("mydav.myserver.com/myfolder/", "myname", "mypassword");
```

connect *DAVObj*.connect()	Establishes a connection to the server, for this object and all other DAV objects with the same authorization information. Returns true on success.
copy *DAVObj*.copy(*destFile*) *DAVObj*.copy(*absPathOrUrl*) *DAVObj*.copy(*DAV_URL*)	Copies this file or folder to the given remote or local location, if connected. Returns true on success.
destFile	An object associated with the target file or folder location. • If it is a file Object (page 158), copies this file or folder to the local destination associated with that object. • If it is an FTP Object (page 171) or DAV Object (page 132), copies this file or folder to the remote destination associated with that object.
absPathOrUrl	An absolute path or URL to the target file or folder. Must be an absolute, system-dependent path string or an absolute file URL starting with file://. In Windows, if there is no valid path given (such as "file://myfile.txt"), the file or folder is copied into the current directory.
DAV_URL	A URL to the remote target file or folder. The URL string must be either a relative URL (based on the current root folder) or an absolute URL starting with http://. This method can only copy on the same server.
createFolder *DAVObj*.createFolder(*newPath*)	Creates a new remote folder, if connected. Returns true on success.

newPath	A string defining the full path on the remote server. This can be: ● A folder name, such as `"myFolder"` ● A relative path, such as `"myFolder/mySubFolder"` ● An absolute path starting at the local root directory, such as `"/myFolder/mySubFolder"` ● A path starting with a host, such as `"http://mydav.myserver.com/rootFolder/myFolder/mySub"`
disconnect *DAVObj*.disconnect()	Disconnects this object from the server, and all other DAV objects with the same authorization information. Returns true on success.
getContent *DAVObj*.getContent ([*mask, onlyFolder*])	Creates an array of sub-files and folders if this DAV object refers to an existing folder and is connected to the server. Returns an array of DAV Objects (page 132) for each file and folder found at the DAV object's target location that matches the search criteria.
mask	Optional. The string a filename must match to be included in the result. Question marks and asterisks in this string are wildcard characters interpreted as in Windows: ● A question mark (?) represents exactly one occurrence of any character. For example, the search mask `Test?.html` retrieves folders or files named `Test1.html`, `Test2.html`, `TestN.html`, `TestX.html`, and so on. However, it would not retrieve folders or files named `Test.html` or `Test11.html`. ● An asterisk (*) represents zero or more occurrences of a single character. For example, the search mask `Test*.html` retrieves folders or files named `Test.html`, `Test1.html`, `Test11.html`, `Test111.html`, and so on. The special string `"anymask"` retrieves all files and folders in this object's folder. When not supplied, the function retrieves all files and folders in this object's folder.
onlyFolder	Optional. When true, include subfolders. Default is false.

move *DAVObj*.move(*destFile*) *DAVObj*.move(*absPathOrUrl*) *DAVObj*.move(*DAV_URL*)	Moves this file or folder to the given remote or local location, if connected. Returns `true` on success.
destFile	An object associated with the target file or folder location. ● If it is a file Object (page 158), copies this file or folder to the local destination associated with that object. ● If it is an FTP Object (page 171) or DAV Object (page 132), copies this file or folder to the remote destination associated with that object.
absPathOrUrl	An absolute path or URL to the target file or folder. Must be an absolute, system-dependent path string or an absolute file URL starting with `file://`. In Windows, if there is no valid path given (such as "`file://myfile.txt`"), the file or folder is copied into the current directory.
DAV_URL	A URL to the remote target file or folder. The URL string must be either a relative URL (based on the current root folder) or an absolute URL starting with `http://`. This method can only copy on the same server.
remove *DAVObj*.remove()	Removes the remote file or folder and sub items, if connected. Returns `true` on success.
rename *DAVObj*.rename(*newName*)	Renames the remote file or folder, if connected. Returns `true` on success.
newName	The new name for the target on the remote site. This can be a simple name, a relative or absolute path, or a path starting with a host name.

dimension Object

Class: `Dimension`

This object encapsulates a set of bounding dimensions for an interface element (window or control).

(Introduced in 8.0)

Acquiring a dimension object

Get this object from a control Object Types (page 78) or window Object (page 313), from the element's `size` property:

```
var mySize = controlObj.bounds.size;
var mySize = controlObj.size;
```

dimension object properties

This object has the following properties:

`height`	Number	The height of the element's bounding box in pixels.
`width`	Number	The width of the element's bounding box in pixels.

document Object

Class: JSXDocument

The `document` object represents an open document. The precise set of behaviors and properties a particular `document` object provides depends on whether it represents a GoLive site document, a markup document such as the HTML file that defines a web page, or some other kind of document, such as a text file.

This object includes the Node Interface (page 229), whose properties and functions allow you to traverse the node tree. In addition, it defines many properties and functions of its own, as shown here.

Acquiring document objects

The `document` global variable always holds the `document` object that represents the frontmost document window in GoLive.

```
document; // the active (frontmost) document
```

You can retrieve any document by its unique JavaScript name or by numeric index from the global `documents` array, as follows:

```
documents["mydoc.html"]; // the mydoc.html document
documents[n]; // the nth document in the collection
```

document object properties

The properties of the `document` object provide information about the current document, its elements, and the site that incorporates the page the `document` object represents. In addition to those of the Node Interface (page 229), the document object defines these properties:

dirty	Boolean	When `true`, the document has changes that need to be saved. Read/write.
documentElement	Element	When *documentObj*.`type`="markup", an element Object (page 156) that is the root of the GoLive document object model, or markup tree. Otherwise `null`. Read-only.
element	Element	Deprecated. Use `documentElement`.
encoding	String	The character encoding used for the document. Values are the same strings used by the `encoding` attribute of the `<META>` tag, such as `"iso-8859-1"` or `"shift_jis"`. Read-only.

file	File	A file Object (page 158) for the file that defines this document. If the document has not yet been saved, this value is `null`. Take care to use this object appropriately. For example, deleting or renaming the file for an open document before saving it is likely to produce adverse results.
headview	Boolean	When `true`, Layout view shows the `<head>` element.
history	History	The document.history Object (page 145) that contains the Undo/Redo history for the document. Use this object to determine the number of currently defined Undo/Redo actions and to select and go to one.
homePage	SiteReference	When *documentObj*.`type="site"`, the siteReference Object (page 260) for the home page of this document's `.site` file. Otherwise `null`. Read-only.

lineBreakMode	String	The line-break mode used in the document. One of:
		`mac`
		`unix`
		`win`
		`mixed`
		Can be set to `mac`, `unix`, or `win`. When you set the value, GoLive changes the document's line breaks to the specified mode.

links	Link Collection	A collection of link Objects (page 207) for the links contained in this document that were created with the createLink method (page 142).
mainTextArea	TextArea	When *documentObj*.`view="layout"`, the textArea Object (page 278) that manages the Layout view representation of the document's main content area. You can use this object to insert text or boxes into the document. For non-markup documents or views other than Layout, `null`.
ref	SiteReference	The siteReference Object (page 260) for the site that refers to this document.
selection	Selection	When *documentObj*.`type="markup"`, a document.selection Object (page 146). The current user selection in a markup document. This can represent a selected range of text, a set of selected elements, or the current cursor position. For non-markup documents, `null`. Read-only. Any change to the markup tree—even one that does not reparse the document—makes the current selection undefined. After the markup tree is changed or the document is reparsed, you must get a new reference to the current selection from this property.
site	SiteReference	When *documentObj*.`type="site"`, the siteReference Object (page 260) for the root of this document's site, usually a reference to a folder. Otherwise `null`. Read-only.

source	TextView	When *documentObj*.view="source", the textView Object (page 283) for the source editor, containing the entire text of the document and providing access to the selection. Otherwise null.
splitview	Boolean	When true, split-source view is open. Read/write.
styleSheets	CSSStyleSheet Collection	A collection of CSSStyleSheet Objects (page 129) associated with the document. For a css document, contains only the style sheet itself. For markup documents, contains all internal and external style sheets. ● For a markup document, you can access the internal style sheets only when the document is open in Layout view. ● External style sheets can be loaded as separate documents, with document type=css. For an open markup document with an external style sheet, you can access the style sheet through the document's styleSheets property, but it is read-only unless the style-sheet document is also open.
title	String	The document's name. This is also the name displayed to the user in the window title bar. Read-only.
type	String	The type of document this object represents. One of: markup: A markup tree site: A GoLive site document javascript: A JavaScript document css: A style-sheet document unknown: All other types of documents Read-only.
userAgentProfile	String	The browser profile of the document. When *documentObj*.view="layout", returns Adobe GoLive as the current user agent, or browser, for the document. Otherwise null.

view	String	The current view of the document. Read this value to determine the current view, or set this value to change the current view. One of:
		`layout`: Layout view
		`frame`: Frames view
		`source`: HTML Source view
		`outline`: Outline view
		`preview`: Preview view
		`unknown`: Not a layout document
		Changing a document's view causes GoLive to reparse the document.
website	Website	The website Object (page 296) for this site if this document is part of a site and the site document is open, or `null` if this is not a site document. The Site window must be open, but it need not be frontmost.

document object functions

The functions of the `document` object enable you to create an `Undo` object for the document it represents, as well as to save, close, reparse, or reformat the document this object represents. In addition to those of the Node Interface (page 229), the document object defines these functions:

changeMarkup *docObj*.`changeMarkup`(*action*)	Changes one or more property values in the document markup, or in all selected documents in the site if this is a site document.
action	The action name of a changeMarkup Object (page 67) that contains property-value pairs to propagate into the document.
clone *docObj*.`clone`()	Creates a copy of this document. Returns a new document Object (page 138). Regardless of the state of the called object, the new copy is unsaved, untitled, and not marked as changed.
close *docObj*.`close`() *docObj*.`close` (*discard*);	Closes the document. If GoLive closes the document successfully, the called `document` object is invalid when this method returns.
discard	Optional. When `true`, discards changes to the document before closing it. Available in 6.0 and later. When `false` (the default), if the document has not been saved previously, the method prompts the user for a filename, and if the document has unsaved changes, the method prompts the user to save or discard changes.

createAttribute *docObj*.createAttribute (*attrName*)	Creates and returns a new attribute Object (page 62) for the document. (Introduced in 7.0)
attrName The name for the new attribute.	
createComment *docObj*.createComment (*text*)	Creates and returns a new comment Object (page 75) with specified text. (Introduced in 7.0)
text The text contents of the new comment node.	
createCSSStyleSheet *docObj*.createCSSStyleSheet([*pathOrURL*]) *docObj*.createCSSStyleSheet([*file*]) *docObj*.createCSSStyleSheet([*doc*]) *docObj*.createCSSStyleSheet([*siteRef*])	Inserts a new, blank, embedded style sheet in the document, or a reference to the specified external style sheet. Creates the corresponding CSSStyleSheet Object (page 129) and appends it to this document's styleSheets collection (page 140). Returns true on success. (Introduced in 8.0)
pathOrURL The path or URL to an existing external style sheet for this document.	
file The file Object (page 158) for an existing external style sheet for this document.	
doc The document Object (page 138) for an existing external style sheet document (type=css).	
siteRef The siteReference Object (page 260) for an existing external style sheet for this document.	
createDocumentFragment *documentObj*.createDocumentFragment()	Creates and returns a new documentFragment Object (page 151). (Introduced in 7.0)
createElement *docObj*.createElement (*tagName*)	Creates and returns a new element Object (page 156). (Introduced in 7.0)
tagName The name of the new tag.	
createLink *docObj*.createLink(*URL*)	Creates and returns a new link Object (page 207). (Introduced in 7.0)
URL The destination of the new link.	
createPDF *docObj*.createPDF([*destFile*, *presetName*])	Creates a new PDF file from this document's content. Returns true on success. (Introduced in 8.0)
destFile Optional. The path and file name of the new PDF file, as a string or a file Object (page 158). If not specified, creates a PDF file with the same base name as the document, in the same location as the document file.	
presetName Optional. A string containing the name of a set of PDF preset options (as found in presetNames in the settings.markup Object (page 252). If not specified, uses the default presets, as found in defaultPreset in the settings.markup Object (page 252).	

createTextNode	Creates and returns a new text Object (page 276). (Introduced in 7.0)
docObj.createTextNode(*text*)	
text	The text contents of the new node.

createUndo	Creates and returns a new undo Object (page 290).
docObj.createUndo (*text*)	
text	Text to display as the name of this undo action in the **History** palette and in the **Undo** menu item.

getElementsByTagName	Creates and returns a nodeList Object (page 232) that contains all element objects with the given tag name. This function uses a case-insensitive comparison to determine whether the tag name matches the specified string. (Introduced in 7.0)
docObj.getElementsByTagName (*tagName*)	
tagName	The tag name to match.

reformat	Does everything the reparse method (page 144) does, and also formats the Source view of the document for printing. Do not call this method from within the parseBox (page 366) or undoSignal (page 367) handlers.
docObj.reformat()	

removeLink	Removes a link from the document. (Introduced in 7.0)
docObj.removeLink(*link*)	
link	The link Object (page 207) to remove.

repairActions	Regenerates JavaScript for GoLive actions on the page. Works only in Layout view. This method updates GoLive-specific JavaScript code; specifically, the code that the <csscriptdict> and <csactiondict> tags provide.
docObj.repairActions()	
	In GoLive 6 and higher, the Document object's reparse method (page 144) does not affect action code. To regenerate such code, call this method after calling the document.reparse method.

reparse *docObj*.reparse()	Generates a new markup tree for the document. After changing the source representation of a markup item, call this method to generate a new markup tree that reflects changes in the Layout view of the document. Saved references to objects representing the contents of the document, such as boxes and markup items, are invalid when this method returns. For Site documents, this method operates on every page in the site and updates the list of files the Site window displays. After adding files to a site programmatically, call this method to update the Site window. **Note:** Do not call this method from within the parseBox (page 366) or undoSignal (page 367) handlers.
save *docObj*.save()	Saves the document as a disk file. If the document has not been saved previously, this method prompts the user for a filename.
saveAs *docObj*.saveAs (*fileName*)	Saves the document as a disk file with the specified name. Returns true on success, false if the file could not be saved.
fileName	URL or platform-specific path name and file name with which to save the file.
selectElement *docObj*.selectElement (*node*)	Selects the specified element in Layout view. Returns true on success, false if the document is not in layout mode or the element does not exist.
node	The markup item to select. Any markup object.

document.history Object

This object provides access to the Undo/Redo history of the document Object (page 138).

Acquiring document.history objects

Get this object from the `history` property of a `document` object that is in Layout view:

```
document.history // when Layout view is open
```

You can access elements of the collection directly using a 0-based numeric index. The numeric index returns the name of the undo Object (page 290) for the Undo/Redo action that occupies the specified position.

document.history object properties

Properties of the `history` object provide information about the current Undo history, such as the number of actions it holds and the index of the current undo history state.

current	Number	Index position that represents the document's current state in the undo/redo history. A number between 0 and the value of the `length` property. Setting this value causes GoLive to perform all undo/redo actions necessary to adopt the document state the new index position represents.
length	Number	The number of history entries. Read-only.
maxCount	Number	The maximum count of undo/redo actions this document allows. A number between 1 and 999. Setting this property changes its value only for the current GoLive user session. The user can set this value permanently in the History palette.

document.selection Object

This object describes the current selection in a document Object (page 138). This can represent a selected range of text, a set of selected elements, or the current cursor position. This object is defined only for markup documents.

The selection takes the form of a node tree, where each node is a markup object—that is, an element Object (page 156), comment Object (page 75), or text Object (page 276). You can set the `element` property to a markup object to make its corresponding markup the current selection.

Acquiring docuement.selection objects

You can get this object from the `selection` property of a `document` object that is displayed in Layout view:

```
document.selection // when Layout view is open
```

document.selection object properties

Properties of the `selection` object provide access to the current selection in the document that provides the object.

box	Box	When the selection is an element that cannot be managed by the `layout` object (such as a custom element defined with the `<jsxelement>` tag), the box Object (page 64) that manages this element's visual representation in Layout view. Otherwise `null`. Read-only.
element	Node	The first selected element. Assign a markup object to select its corresponding markup.
length	Number	The length of the selection.
range	Range	A document.selection.range Object (page 148) that describes a range within a selection.
start	Number	Offset from the first character in the outer HTML of the selected element's source representation to the first character of the current selection.

text	String	The selected text, according to the current values of the `start` and `length` properties.
type	String	Read-only description of the kind of selection. One of: `point`: No selection. The selection reflects the position of the cursor in the document's HTML source. `part`: Part of the current markup item is selected. For example, this value would indicate a partial selection within a simple text block. `full`: The entire markup item is selected. For example, when the user clicks a `Box` object in Layout view, the SDK selects the entire markup item the box represents. `complex`: More than one markup item is selected or partially selected.

document.selection.range Object

This object describes a range in the content of a document. It is initialized from the current document selection, but retains the range information independently. When the document selection changes, the `document.selection.range` property contains a new `range` object. (Introduced in 7.0)

You can use a `range` object to modify the document selection or to modify the content inside the range. The range takes the form of a node tree, where each node is a markup object—that is, an element Object (page 156), comment Object (page 75), or text Object (page 276).

A range consists of two boundary-points corresponding to the start and the end of the range. A boundary-point's position in a document tree is characterized by a node and an offset. The node is the *container* of the boundary-point and of its position. The *offset* of the boundary-point determines its position:

- If the container is an element node, the offset is a number of child nodes from the first node.
- If the container is a text or comment node, the offset is a number of characters from the start of text.

Acquiring a range object

Get a range object from a document selection:

```
myRange = document.selection.range;
```

document.selection.range object properties

collapsed	Boolean	When `true`, the start boundary-point is equal to the end boundary-point
endContainer	Node	The end node of the range.
endOffset	Number	Character or node offset relative to the end of text or end node.
startContainer	Node	The start node of the range.
startOffset	Number	Character or node offset relative to the start of text or start node.

document.selection.range object functions

The range object functions allow you to set the endpoints that define the range, and to manipulate the element hierarchy, the selections, and the content within the range.

cloneContents *rangeObj*.cloneContents()	Copies the document contents described by this range and creates a document fragment with the copied contents. Does not delete the original document contents. Returns the documentFragment Object (page 151).
deleteContents *rangeObj*.deleteContents()	Deletes the document contents described by this range. Returns `true` on success.
extractContents *rangeObj*.extractContents()	Copies the document contents described by this range, creates a document fragment with the copied contents, and deletes the original document contents. Returns the documentFragment Object (page 151).
insertNode *rangeObj*.insertNode(*insertNode*)	Inserts a new node at the start point of the range. Returns `true` on success.
insertNode	The new node to insert. Any markup object.
selectNode *rangeObj*.selectNode(*selNode*)	Sets the range such that it includes only a specific node. Returns `true` on success.
selNode	The existing child node to be the only node included in the range. Any markup object.
selectNodeContents *rangeObj*.selectNodeContents (*selNode*)	Sets the range such that it includes only the contents of a specific node. Returns `true` on success.
selNode	The existing child node whose contents is to be included in the range. Any markup object.
setEnd *rangeObj*.setEnd (*endContainer*, *offset*)	Sets a new end point of the range. Returns `true` on success.
endContainer	The container that includes the ending point of the range. Any markup object.
offset	The character or node offset, of the ending point of the range.
setEndAfter *rangeObj*.setEndAfter(*endANode*)	Sets the end of the range to be after a specified child node of the container. Returns `true` on success.
endANode	The existing child node to end after. Any markup object.
setEndBefore *rangeObj*.setEndBefore(*endBNode*)	Sets the end of the range to be in front of a specified child node of the container. Returns `true` on success.
endBNode	The existing child node to end before. Any markup object.

setStart *rangeObj*.setStart (*startContainer*, *offset*)	Sets a new start point of the range. Returns `true` on success.
startContainer	The container that includes the starting point of the range. Any markup object.
offset	The character or node offset, of the starting point of the range.
setStartAfter *rangeObj*.setStartAfter (*startANode*)	Sets the start of the range to be after a specified child node of the container. Returns `true` on success.
startANode	The existing child node to start after. Any markup object.
setStartBefore *rangeObj*.setStartBefore (*startBNode*)	Sets the start of the range to be in front of a specified child node of the container. Returns `true` on success.
startBNode	The existing child node to start before. Any markup object.
surroundContents *rangeObj*.surroundContents (*elementNode*)	Surrounds the range with a specified node. The start tag of the element is inserted before the start point and the end tag of the element is inserted after the end point. Returns `true` on success.
elementNode	The element Object (page 156) for the new element to insert.

documentFragment Object

Class: JSXDocumentFragment

This object is a simple container for markup items and markup snippets. You can copy parts of a document's element tree into the documentFragment object. You can add, remove, or modify markup items in the fragment without any effects on an existing document. (Introduced in 7.0)

This object includes the Node Interface (page 229), whose properties and functions allow you to traverse the node tree of the document fragment's elements. It defines no additional properties or functions.

A documentFragment cannot contain another documentFragment.

Acquiring a documentFragment object

- This object is returned by a document Object's createDocumentFragment function (page 142).
- A document fragment is returned by the document.selection.range Object's cloneContents and extractContents functions (page 149).

draw Object

Class: JSXDraw

This object provides basic drawing operations for custom, owner-drawn controls. (GoLive automatically redraws all controls other than those of type custom.)

This object provides a cursor for drawing lines and text. When calling methods of the draw object, specify coordinates in the coordinate plane of the box or window that displays the object being drawn.

This object has no properties.

Acquiring draw objects

- The SDK passes a draw object as an argument to the paintEvent object (page 384) for the drawBox and drawControl events (page 362).
- The beginDraw method (page 83) of the control Object Types (page 78) also returns a draw object.

draw object functions

Functions of the draw object draw primitive graphics, text and images. Your extension's drawControl handler (page 362) can call these functions to refresh the appearance of a custom (owner-drawn) control.

drawString *drawObj*.drawString (*text*, [*charSet*])	Draws a string at the graphics cursor's current location.
text	Text string this method draws.
charSet	Optional. The name of a character-encoding set to use.
fillOval *drawObj*.fillOval (*x, y, width, height*)	Draws a filled oval in the specified location.
x	X-coordinate of the upper-left corner of the smallest rectangle that would enclose the oval to draw.
y	Y-coordinate of the upper-left corner of the smallest rectangle that would enclose the oval to draw.
width	The oval's width in pixels.
height	The oval's height in pixels.

fillRect *drawObj*.`fillRect` (*x, y, width, height*)	Draws a filled rectangle in the specified location.
`x`	X-coordinate of the upper-left corner of the rectangle to draw.
`y`	Y-coordinate of the upper-left corner of the rectangle to draw.
`width`	The rectangle's width in pixels.
`height`	The rectangle's height in pixels.
frameOval *drawObj*.`frameOval` (*x, y, width, height*)	Draws an outlined oval in the specified location.
`x`	X-coordinate of the upper-left corner of the smallest rectangle that would enclose the oval to draw.
`y`	Y-coordinate of the upper-left corner of the smallest rectangle that would enclose the oval to draw.
`width`	The oval's width in pixels.
`height`	The oval's height in pixels.
frameRect *drawObj*.`frameRect` (*x, y, width, height*)	Draws an outlined rectangle in the specified location.
`x`	X-coordinate of the upper-left corner of the rectangle to draw.
`y`	Y-coordinate of the upper-left corner of the rectangle to draw.
`width`	The rectangle's width in pixels.
`height`	The rectangle's height in pixels.

getDrawInfo
drawObj.`getDrawInfo()`
	Retrieves a pointer to a `JSADrawInfo` structure for an external function's use. You can pass this pointer to an external binary library that implements custom drawing. Returns a number that the external library function casts to a pointer.
	In Windows, the `JSADrawInfo` structure provides a `DC`. In Mac OS, this `JSADrawInfo` structure provides a `GrafPort`. The structure always provides the coordinates of the upper-left and lower-right corners that define the drawing area.
	
	`typedef struct _JSADrawInfo {`
	  `long context; // a DC (Windows) or a GrafPort (Mac OS)`
	  `long left, top; // upper left corner of rect`
	  `long right, bottom; // lower right corner of rect`
	`} JSADrawInfo;`

invertRect *drawObj*.`invertRect` (*x, y, width, height*)	Inverts the colors of the specified rectangle, producing an XOR effect. Calling this method a second time undoes the effect of the first call to this method.
`x`	X-coordinate of the upper-left corner of the rectangle to draw.

y	Y-coordinate of the upper-left corner of the rectangle to draw.
`width`	The rectangle's width in pixels.
`height`	The rectangle's height in pixels.
lineTo *drawObj*.`lineTo` (*x, y*)	Draws a line from the pen's current location to the specified position and moves the graphics cursor to the new location.
x	X-coordinate of the endpoint of the line this method draws. Also the x-coordinate of the pen's final location when this method returns.
y	Y-coordinate of the endpoint of the line this method draws. Also the y-coordinate of the pen's final location when this method returns.
moveTo *drawObj*.`moveTo` (*x, y*)	Moves the graphics cursor to the specified location.
x	X-coordinate of the pen's new location.
y	Y-coordinate of the pen's new location.
penSize *drawObj*.`penSize` (*width*)	Sets the width of the drawing pen.
width	The pen's new width in pixels.
setColor *drawObj*.`setColor` (*color*)	Sets the pen's color. Examples of valid HTML color strings are `"red"` or `"#FF0000"`. An RGB triplet value consists of three comma-separated integer values between 0 and 255. The values in the triplet specify the amount of red, green, and blue, respectively, that define the new color. For example (255, 0, 0) would light all red pixels at 100% with no green or blue pixels lit.
color	The pen's new color, expressed as an HTML color string or an RGB triplet.
stringWidth *drawObj*.`stringWidth` (*text*)	Using current font settings, returns a value specifying the width of the specified string as a number of pixels. Returns the number of pixels for the width of the text with current font settings.
text	The text this method measures.
stringHeight *drawObj*.`stringHeight` (*text*)	Calculates the height of a specified string using current font settings. Returns the number of pixels for the height of the text with current font settings.
text	The text this method measures.

textFace *drawObj*`.textFace` (*bits*)	Sets the font face GoLive uses for subsequent text output.
`bits`	Bit flags indicating the font face to use for text output, as follows: 　　1: Bold 　　2: Italic 　　4: Underlined (Mac OS only) 　　8: Outlined (Mac OS only) 　　16: Shadowed (Mac OS only) 　　32: Condensed (Mac OS only) 　　64: Extended (Mac OS only) Add these values to specify multiple faces. For example the value 3 specifies that text output is to be bolded and italicized.
textFont *drawObj*`.textFont` (*fontName*)	Sets the font GoLive uses for subsequent text output.
`fontName`	Name of the font to use for text output. For example, `"Courier"` is a valid value. Pass `"ApplicationFont"` for the font that GoLive uses to draw static text and control labels (as opposed to the system font).
textSize *drawObj*`.textSize` (*points*)	Sets the size of the font GoLive uses for subsequent text output.
`points`	Size of the font in points (1/72 inch).

element Object

Class: `JSXElement`

This object represents an individual element in an HTML document. When you load an HTML document, GoLive generates a tree of markup objects to represent the contents. The objects have a tree structure that matches that in the source HTML. The markup objects are of various types: the `element` object for elements, the text Object (page 276) for text items, the comment Object (page 75) for comments, and the markup Object (page 215) for all other kinds of markup.

- This object includes the Node Interface (page 229), whose properties and functions allow you to traverse the node tree.
- This object includes the Markup Interface (page 209), whose properties and functions allow you to directly access document content.
- This object defines additional functions, but no additional properties.

(Introduced in 7.0)

Acquiring an element object

For a markup document, the document Object's documentElement property (page 138) holds the root object of the markup tree. The page's content is represented by nodes in the tree. To retrieve the root of the markup tree for a document:

```
var tree = document.documentElement;
```

You can traverse the markup tree using the Node Interface (page 229) properties and functions of any object in the tree. In an `element` object:

```
elementType=tag
nodeType=1
nodeName=tagName
```

- Create a new element object for a specific tag using the document Object's createElement method (page 142):

  ```
  myElement = documentObj.createElement("img");
  ```

- Get a list of elements in the document for a specific tag using the document Object's getElementsByTagName method (page 143), then retrieve individual elements by index:

  ```
  elementList = documentObj.getElementsByTagName("img");
  myImg = elementList.item(0);
  ```

- The `subElements` property gets a list of all children and their children. You can use tag names as search keys to retrieve elements from this array by name.

- To retrieve any subelement by tag name, numeric index, or type, call the getSubElement method (page 212). For example, a page's visible elements are subelements of its `body` element. To retrieve a page's `<body>` subelement by tag name:

```
var bodyElt =
document.documentElement.getSubElement("body");
```

element object properties

The `element` object defines no additional properties beyond those of the Node Interface (page 229) and Markup Interface (page 209).

element object functions

In addition to those of the Node Interface (page 229) and Markup Interface (page 209), the `element` object defines these functions:

getAttributeNode *elementObj*.getAttributeNode (*attrName*)	Gets an attribute object by name. Returns the attribute Object (page 62).
attrName The name of the attribute (the value of the `name` property of the object).	
getElementsByTagName *elementObj*.getElementsByTagName (*tagName*)	Creates and returns a nodeList Object (page 232) that contains all `element` objects with the given tag name.
tagName The tag name of the elements to get.	
removeAttribute *elementObj*.removeAttribute (*attrName*)	Removes an attribute specified by name. Returns `true` on success.
attrName The name of the attribute to remove from the element.	
removeAttributeNode *elementObj*.removeAttributeNode (*attr*)	Removes and returns a specified attribute Object (page 62).
attr The attribute Object (page 62) to remove.	
setAttributeNode *elementObj*.setAttributeNode (*attr*)	Sets or replaces an attribute. Returns the inserted attribute Object (page 62).
attr The attribute Object (page 62) to insert.	

file Object

Class: `JSXFile`

This object enables extensions to create and manipulate files and folders on local file systems and HTTP servers. The methods read, write, and append to files in a manner similar to the file-streaming functions of the C-language `stdio.h` library. Other methods create files or folders, copy files, and move files.

A newly constructed `file` object simply encapsulates a path name. The existence of the object does not imply the existence of the referenced file or folder; for example, you might have created the `file` object in order to call methods that create files or folders programmatically. You must validate all `file` objects before using them:

- Check that the `file` object is neither `null` nor `undefined`.
- Check whether the `file` object represents a folder or file, as appropriate.
- If the object represents an existing folder or file, determine whether the file or folder actually exists on a disk available to the host platform.

Acquiring file objects

- Get `file` objects for file and folders at a remote location using the `getContent` function of an FTP Object (page 171) or DAV Object (page 132).
- Get `file` objects for files contained in a folder using the getFiles function (page 162) of the folder's `file` object.
- These properties of the app Object (page 53) return `file` objects for particular folders:

    app.appSettingsFolder (page 53)
    app.currentFolder (page 54)
    app.folder (page 54)
    app.settingsFolder (page 55)
    app.systemFolder (page 55)
    app.tempFolder (page 56)
    app.trashFolder (page 56)
    app.userSettingsFolder (page 56)

- To access other directories or files, use the file object constructor (page 161) to create your own `file` objects explicitly:

    ```
    new JSXFile (path)
    ```

file object properties

A `file` object always represents a file-system location. Properties of the object present this location as a URL and in platform-specific formats in Windows and Mac OS. Additional properties provide information about this file-system reference, such as whether it represents a file or a folder, and whether the referenced file or folder exists at the specified location.

`abspath`	String	The full path string to this file or folder. (Introduced in 7.0)
`absurl`	String	The full URL string for this file or folder. (Introduced in 7.0)
`alias`	String	In Mac OS: The alias name of the existing Mac OS file system alias to the file or folder. In Windows: The link to the file or folder.
`eof`	Boolean	When `true`, GoLive encountered an EOF condition during a read operation. Read-only.
`encoding`	String	The name of the document encoding character set this file uses.
`error`	Boolean	When `true`, an error was detected during a read or write operation. Read-only.
`exists`	Boolean	When `true`, the file or folder is available at the referenced location. Read-only.
`isFolder`	Boolean	When `true`, this object references a folder that is currently available to the host platform's file system. Confirms the folder's existence as well as the fact that it is not a file. Returns `false` for a file, or if the referenced folder is not available. Read-only.
`lastname`	String	The name of this file or folder. (Introduced in 7.0)
`lastError`	String	Explanatory text describing the last I/O error related to this file. You can use this property to check the result of an HTTP upload or download operation. You can set this property to any string value. To clear the current value, set this property to the empty string.

`lineBreakMode`	String	The way linebreak characters in strings are written to this file using `write` and `writeln`, and read using `read` and `readln`. One of:
		    `default`: The GoLive default style, as set in the Web Settings dialog
		    `system`: The platform style
		    `unix`: UNIX style
		    `mac`: Mac OS style
		    `win`: Windows style
		(Introduced in 7.0)

macCreator	String	In Mac OS, the referenced file's creator ID as a four-character string. The "????" value indicates that GoLive cannot determine this file's Mac OS creator code, or that GoLive is running on a Windows platform. Read-only.
macType	String	In Mac OS, the referenced file's file type as a four-character string. The "????" value indicates that GoLive cannot determine this file's Mac OS file type, or that GoLive is running on a Windows platform. Read-only.
modificationDate	Date	A JavaScript Date object containing the platform's modification date for the file.
name	String	Deprecated in 7.0. The referenced file's filename without its path. Read-only.
parent	File	The parent folder of this file or folder. or `null` for a file or folder in the root directory of the file system.
path	String	Deprecated in 7.0. The fully qualified path to the referenced file using the conventions of the current platform. Read-only.
readOnly	Boolean	Mirrors the Readonly/Locked flag of the referenced file on disk. Can be set to change the status of that flag.
ref	SiteReference	The corresponding siteReference Object (page 260), if this file or folder is part of an open site. (Introduced in 7.0)
size	Number	The file size (number of characters.) The value `0` indicates that this object represents a folder. Read-only.
url	String	Deprecated in 7.0. The path to the referenced file encoded as a fully qualified URL. Read-only.
xmp	XMP	The XMP Object (page 319) for this file's embedded XMP metadata, if this object represents a file. The value is `null` if this object represents a folder. (Introduced in 8.0) **Note:** Separate XMP files are not supported.

file object functions

Functions of the `file` object read, write, create, delete, move, copy, rename, and provide information about files or folders. The functions that create a file, read data from a file, and write data to a file are not equivalent to the user commands that perform such tasks. They are similar to functions that the C-language `stdio.h` library provides.

Note: You must validate a `file` object before calling its functions. The existence of the object does not imply the existence of the file or folder it represents.

Functions of the `file` object can fail. This object issues requests to a local or remote file system that actually manipulates the disk-based resource the object represents. Such requests may not complete. If your script depends on successful completion of a file operation, be sure to check the result of the function call.

file object constructor new JSXFile([*pathOrURL*])	Creates and returns a new file Object (page 158) that encapsulates a specified path.
pathOrURL	Optional. The pathname or URL with which the `file` object is initialized. ● Specifying a URL avoids platform-specific differences in pathname specifications. ● A pathname must observe the file system conventions of the host platform, using the appropriate delimiter character. In Windows, use a backslash (\) to separate directories, and in Mac OS, use the style specified by the `posix` property (page 255) of the settingsSDK Object (page 255). When not supplied, the function returns a `file` object that refers to the current working directory, as reported by the `app.currentFolder` property.

➤ Example

```
new JSXFile ("MySite:12/19/01:myPage.html) // Mac OS pathname w/date
```

checkUpdate *fileObj*.checkUpdate()	When this object references a GoLive component file or GoLive template file, causes all clients of this component or template to update their content if needed.
close *fileObj*.close()	Attempts to close the file, saving it to the disk if it has changed. Returns `true` if the file was closed successfully.
copy *fileObj*.copy (*newLocation*)	Copies the file or folder to a specified local or remote location. Returns `true` if the file or folder was copied successfully.
newLocation	The new file's location, specified as a partial pathname, a full pathname, or an HTTP URL, or as a file object of any of these types: file Object (page 158) FTP Object (page 171) DAV Object (page 132)
createFolder *fileObj*.createFolder()	Creates a folder at the `file` object's location. Returns `true` if the folder was created successfully.
eval *fileObj*.eval()	Opens the file if it exists and executes the JavaScript content. Returns `true` on success.

execute *fileObj*.execute(*file1*, *file2*...)	For an executable file, launches the application with the specified file or files as parameters. Returns `true` on success.
fileN	A file to pass to the application, specified as a partial pathname, a full pathname, or a local URL, or as a file Object (page 158).
forceUpdate *fileObj*.forceUpdate()	When this object references a GoLive component file or GoLive template file, updates the content of all clients that use this file.
get *fileObj*.get (*remoteURL* [, *mimeType*])	Downloads a file from a remote HTTP server to the `file` object's location. If a file already exists on disk at the exact pathname specified, this method overwrites it. Returns `true` if the file was retrieved successfully. When `false`, the *fileObj*.lastError property holds the last HTTP status code received from the remote server.
remoteURL	The remote file to download.
mimeType	Optional. This file's MIME type.
getContent *fileObj*.getContent ([*mask*, *onlyFolder*])	For a folder, gets the contents. Returns an array of file Objects (page 158) for the files and subfolders contained in this folder.
mask	Optional. The string a filename must match to be included in the result. Question marks and asterisks in this string are wildcard characters interpreted as in Windows: ● A question mark (?) represents exactly one occurrence of any character. For example, the search mask `Test?.html` retrieves folders or files named `Test1.html`, `Test2.html`, `TestN.html`, `TestX.html`, and so on. However, it would not retrieve folders or files named `Test.html` or `Test11.html`. ● An asterisk (*) represents zero or more occurrences of a single character. For example, the search mask `Test*.html` retrieves folders or files named `Test.html`, `Test1.html`, `Test11.html`, `Test111.html`, and so on. When not supplied, the function retrieves all files and folders in this object's folder.
onlyFolder	Optional. When `true`, retrieve only subfolders.
getFiles	Deprecated in 7.0. Use getContent (page 162).
loadScript *fileObj*.loadScript()	If this `file` object represents a JavaScript file, loads the script and adds it to the current extension script. The loaded script is available to the debugger. Returns `true` if the script was loaded successfully. (Introduced in 8.0)

---

move *fileObj*`.move` (*newLocation*)	Moves this `file` object's file to a specified local or remote location, and updates the object to reflect the new location. Returns `true` if the file was moved successfully. This method does not operate on folders. To move a folder, create the destination folder, move files into it, then delete the empty original folder.

      newLocation   The file's new location, specified as a partial pathname, a full pathname, or an HTTP URL, or as a file object of any of these types:

            file Object (page 158)
            FTP Object (page 171)
            DAV Object (page 132)

| **open** | Opens the `file` object's file. Returns `true` if the file was |
| *fileObj*.open ([*openMode, charSet*]) | opened successfully. |

openMode

Optional. Permissions for subsequent reading or writing operations on this file. Equivalent to open modes used by the C-language `fopen` library function.

Valid values are:

`r`: Open for reading. If the file does not exist or cannot be found, the call fails. This is the default.

`w`: Opens an empty file for writing. If the file exists, its contents are destroyed.

`a`: Open for writing at the end of the file (appending); creates the file if it does not exist.

`r+`: Opens for both reading and writing. The file must exist on disk already; this open mode does not create it.

`w+`: Opens an empty file for both reading and writing. If the file exists, this open mode overwrites it, destroying the file's previous content.

`a+`: Opens for reading and appending; creates the file if it does not exist. When a file is opened in the "a" or "a+" modes, all write operations are appended to the end of the file. You can still reposition the file pointer in this mode, but the SDK always moves it back to the end of the file before it carries out any write operation in this mode. Thus, you can't overwrite the file's existing data when you open it in this mode.

When this method opens an existing file for reading/writing in "a+" mode, it searches for a `Ctrl+Z` at the end of the file and removes it, if possible.

`t`: Open in text (translated) mode. In this mode, `Ctrl+Z` is interpreted as an end-of-file character on input, and the system attempts to replace `CRLF` sequences with linefeed characters. This is the default mode.

`b`: Open in binary (untranslated) mode. Translations involving carriage-return and linefeed characters are suppressed. May be appended to one of the other opening modes, as in this example.

```
var myDoc = fileObj.open("r+b");
```

charSet

Optional. The name of a document encoding charset. Changes the encoding of the file accordingly. When not supplied, the method attempts to detect the file's encoding. If successful, it sets *fileObj*.encoding accordingly.

openDocument *fileObj*.openDocument() *fileObj*.openDocument([*charSet*])	Opens this file in a new Document window. This is the programmatic equivalent of using the **File > Open** menu item to open an existing disk file. Returns the document Object (page 138) added to the documents global array (page 48), or `null` if an error occurred.
charSet	Optional. (6.0 or higher) The name of an encoding character set. This character set overrides the default encoding that GoLive would use if the document did not contain a META tag. The presence of a META tag in the *fileObj* document causes GoLive to ignore this argument. If the encoding is unknown or unsupported, GoLive generates an "Unsupported encoding" runtime error.
openExtDocument *fileObj*.openExtDocument()	Opens this file in an external application, according to its file type and the platform's application mapping. Returns `true` on success.
openMarkup *fileObj*.openMarkup() *fileObj*.openMarkup([*encoding*])	Reads the contents of the `file` object's file into a new document Object (page 138) without displaying it in a window. Returns the document Object (page 138) added to the documents global array (page 48), or `null` if an error occurred. Opening the document in this way enables you to modify it without causing GoLive to reparse.
encoding	Optional. (6.0 or higher) The name of an encoding character set. This character set overrides the default encoding that GoLive would use if the document did not contain a META tag. A META tag causes the supplied encoding to be ignored. If the encoding name is unknown or unsupported, GoLive generates an "Unsupported encoding" runtime error.
put *fileObj*.put (*remoteURL* [, *mimeType*])	Uploads the `file` object's file to a location on a remote HTTP server. The server must be able to fulfill HTTP PUT requests. Returns `true` if the file was uploaded successfully. When `false`, the *fileObj*.lastError property holds the last HTTP status code received from the remote server.
remoteURL	Path to the remote location in which to store the uploaded file.
mimeType	Optional. This file's MIME type.

read *fileObj*.read (*[count, charSet]*);	Reads the contents of the file from the current position forward. Returns a string containing the characters read from the file. This string never contains more than *count* characters. If the file was opened with the t *openMode* flag, translates CRLF character sequences to linefeed characters. If the file encoding is BINARY and the file was opened with the b *openMode* flag, line ending characters are not translated. Otherwise, GoLive detects the line-break mode and sets the lineBreakMode value (page 159) accordingly.
count	Optional. The number of characters to read. When not supplied, reads the entire file.
charSet	Optional. (6.0 or higher) The name of an encoding character set. This encoding overrides the file object's encoding value (page 159). If the file object has no encoding value set and this value is not supplied, uses the GoLive default encoding. If the specified encoding is unknown or unsupported, GoLive generates an "Unsupported encoding" runtime error.
readln *fileObj*.readln(*[charSet]*)	Reads one line of text from the file. Returns a string containing the characters read from the file. In binary mode, linefeeds are recognized as CR, LF, or CRLF pairs.
charSet	Optional. (6.0 or higher) The name of an encoding character set. This encoding overrides the file object's encoding value (page 159). If the file object has no encoding value set and this value is not supplied, uses the GoLive default encoding. If the specified encoding is unknown or unsupported, GoLive generates an "Unsupported encoding" runtime error.
remove *fileObj*.remove()	Deletes the file or folder. It is recommended that you prompt the user for permission to delete a file or folder. The remove method deletes the referenced file or folder immediately. It does not move the referenced file or folder to the system trash, and the deletion cannot be undone.
rename *fileObj*.rename (*newName*)	Renames the file or folder and updates the file object's name property to the new name. Returns true if the file or folder was renamed and the object updated successfully.
newName	Name to which this method sets the file object's name property. This value must not specify a path.
seek *fileObj*.seek (*pos*)	Sets the file's position cursor. Returns true if the position cursor was changed successfully.
pos	The cursor's new position, a number of characters offset from the beginning of the file. 0 specifies the beginning of the file, and *fileObj*.size specifies the end of the file.

Adobe® GoLive® CS2 Official JavaScript Reference

tell *fileObj*.tell()	Reports the current cursor position. Returns the number of characters between the beginning of file and the current position.
write *fileObj*.write (*myText1, myText2, ...*)	Writes a string to the file. Returns true if the string was written successfully. In GoLive 6 or higher, this method uses the encoder specified by the *fileObj*.encoding property.
myTextN	A comma-separated list of text strings to concatenate and write to the file.
writeln *fileObj*.writeln (*myText1,myText2, ...*)	Writes a string terminated by a linefeed character to the file. Returns true if the string was written successfully. In GoLive 6 or higher, this method uses the encoder specified by the *fileObj*.encoding property.
myTextN	A comma-separated list of text strings to concatenate and write to the file.

fontArray Object

Class: `FontArray`

A simple array of font-name strings. Contains no additional properties or methods.

Acquiring fontArray objects

Get this object from the fontSet Object's `fonts` property (page 169):

```
myFont = app.fontsets["myFontSet"].fonts["Courier"];
```

fontSet Object

Class: FontSet

Represents a font set.

Acquiring fontSet objects

Get this object by name or index from the fontSetCollection Object (page 170):

```
myFontSet = app.fontsets["MyFontSet"];
myFontSet = app.fontsets[0];
```

fontSet object properties

fonts	FontArray	The fontArray Object (page 168) containing the names of all fonts contained in this set. Read-only. Use the font set object's functions to modify this array.
name	String	The name of the font set. Read/write.

fontSet object functions

add *fontSetObj*.add (*newFontSetName*[, *insertIndex*])	Adds a new font to the set's `fonts` array. Returns `true` on success.
newFontName	String. The name of the font to add.
insertIndex	Optional. Number. The zero-based index into the `fonts` array at which to add the new font.
remove *fontSetObj*.remove (*font*)	Removes a font from the set's `fonts` array. Returns `true` on success.
font	Number or String. The index or name of the font to remove.
removeAll *fontSetObj*.removeAll()	Removes all fonts from the set's `fonts` array. Returns `true` on success.

---

fontSetCollection Object

Class: FontSetCollection

Collects all available font sets as fontSet Object (page 169) references.
Contains the collection Object (page 72) properties, and defines additional
functions for manipulating the font sets.

Acquiring fontSetCollection objects

Get this object from the app Object's fontsets property (page 54):

```
currentset = app.fontsets;
```

fontSetCollection object functions

add *fontSetCollectionObj*.add (*newFontSetName*)	Adds a new font set to the collection. Returns true on success.
newFontSetName	String. The name of the font set to add.
remove *fontSetCollectionObj*.remove (*fontSet*)	Removes a font set from the collection. Returns true on success.
fontSet	Number, String, or fontSet Object (page 169). The index, name, or object reference for the font set to remove.

FTP Object

Class: `JSXFTP`

This object provides access to remote data via the FTP protocol. Like the file Object (page 158), the `FTP` object refers to a virtual file or folder—that is, the remote file or folder may or may not exist.

To access a server, there must be at least one `FTP` object connected to that server. If there are multiple `FTP` objects that refer to the same server with the same authorization data, you only need to connect one of the objects; all other objects are connected automatically. Similarly, when you disconnect one object, all others are disconnected automatically.

For an example of using this object, see the `FTP and WebDAV` sample included with the SDK.

(Introduced in 7.0)

Acquiring an FTP object

Use the FTP object constructor (page 173) to create a new `FTP` object:

```
var f = new JSXFTP( "ftp://ftp.myserver.com" );
var f = new JSXFTP( "ftp.myserver.com/myfolder/myfile.txt" );
var f = new JSXFTP( "ftp.myserver.com/myfolder/", "myname",
"mypassword" );
```

To create an `FTP` object referring to a folder on a remote file system, you must use a trailing slash to indicate that the last item in the path is a folder name and not a file name.

FTP object properties

absurl	String	The complete URL (For example: `ftp://ftp.myserver.com/myfolder/myfile.txt`)
access	Number	A decimal number reflecting the bitfield of UNIX-style access rights: 0x0001 **other execute** 0x0002 **other write** 0x0004 **other read** 0x0008 **group execute** 0x0010 **group write** 0x0020 **group read** 0x0040 **owner execute** 0x0080 **owner write** 0x0100 **owner read** The object must be connected to the server to retrieve this information. Read/write.
connected	Boolean	When `true`, the object is connected to the server.
error	Number	Error code of last error.
exists	Boolean	When `true`, the remote file or folder exists. The object must be connected to the server to retrieve this information.
host	String	The host name (for example: `ftp://ftp.myserver.com`).
isFolder	Boolean	When `true`, the `FTP` object refers to a remote folder.
lastError	String	Text of last error.
lastname	String	The file or folder name.
modificationDate	Date	A JavaScript Date object containing the platform's modification date for the file.
parent	FTP	Parent file/folder of the current `FTP` object. The object must be connected to the server to retrieve this information.
relurl	String	URL relative to the host (for example, `/myfolder/myfile.txt`).
size	Number	Size of the remote file, if it's a file. The object must be connected to the server to retrieve this information.

FTP object functions

FTP object constructor
`new JSXFTP(`*hostAndPath*`[, `*userName*`, `*password*`])`
`new JSXFTP(`*server*`)`
	Creates and returns a new `FTP` object for the specified server with the corresponding access permission (upon successful connection).

hostAndPath	A hostname or a hostname with a specified path to a file or folder. If the last element of the path is a folder name, it must be followed by a slash character.
userName	Optional. A user name with access permission on the server.
password	Optional. The user's password in plain text.
server	A serverInfo Object (page 243) that identifies the target file or folder.

> ## Examples

```
var f = new JSXFTP( "ftp://ftp.myserver.com" );
var f = new JSXFTP( "ftp.myserver.com/myfolder/myfile.txt" );
var f = new JSXFTP( "ftp.myserver.com/myfolder", "myname", "mypassword" );
```

connect *FTPObj*`.connect()`	Establishes a connection to the server for this object and all other `FTP` objects with the same authorization information. Returns `true` on success.
copy *FTPObj*`.copy(`*destFile*`)` *FTPObj*`.copy(`*absPathOrUrl*`)` *FTPObj*`.copy(`*FTP_URL*`)`	Copies this file or folder to the given remote or local location, if connected. Returns `true` on success.
destFile	An object associated with the target file or folder location. ● If it is a file Object (page 158), copies this file or folder to the local destination associated with that object. ● If it is an FTP Object (page 171) or DAV Object (page 132), copies this file or folder to the remote destination associated with that object.
absPathOrUrl	An absolute path or URL to the target file or folder. Must be an absolute, system-dependent path string or an absolute file URL starting with `file://`. In Windows, if there is no valid path given (such as "`file://myfile.txt`"), the file or folder is copied into the current directory.
FTP_URL	An FTP URL to the remote target file or folder. The URL string must be either a relative URL (based on the current root folder) or an absolute FTP URL starting with `ftp://`. This method can only copy on the same server.

createFolder *FTPObj*.createFolder(*newPath*)	Creates a new remote folder, if connected. Returns `true` on success.

newPath	A string defining the full path on the remote server. This can be:
	• A folder name, such as `"myFolder"`
	• A relative path, such as `"myFolder/mySubFolder"`
	• An absolute path starting at the local root directory, such as `"/myFolder/mySubFolder"`
	• A path starting with a host, such as `"http://www.myserver.com/rootFolder/myFolder/mySub"`

disconnect *FTPObj*.disconnect()	Disconnects this object from the server, and all other `FTP` objects with the same authorization information. Returns `true` on success.

getContent *FTPObj*.getContent ([*mask*, *onlyFolder*])	Creates an array of sub-files and folders if this `FTP` object refers to an existing folder and is connected to the server. Returns an array of FTP Objects (page 171) for each file and folder found at the `FTP` object's target location that matches the search criteria.

mask	Optional. The string a filename must match to be included in the result. Question marks and asterisks in this string are wildcard characters interpreted as in Windows:
	• A question mark (?) represents exactly one occurrence of any character. For example, the search mask `Test?.html` retrieves folders or files named `Test1.html`, `Test2.html`, `TestN.html`, `TestX.html`, and so on. However, it would not retrieve folders or files named `Test.html` or `Test11.html`.
	• An asterisk (*) represents zero or more occurrences of a single character. For example, the search mask `Test*.html` retrieves folders or files named `Test.html`, `Test1.html`, `Test11.html`, `Test111.html`, and so on.
	The special string `"anymask"` retrieves all files and folders in this object's folder.
	When not supplied, the function retrieves all files and folders in this object's folder.

onlyFolder	Optional. When `true`, retrieve only subfolders.

move *FTPObj*.move(*destFile*) *FTPObj*.move(*path*) *FTPObj*.move(*FTP_URL*	Moves this file or folder to the given remote (*destFile* or *FTP_URL*) or local (*path*) file or folder, if connected. Returns `true` on success.
destFile	An object associated with the target file or folder location. ● If it is a file Object (page 158), copies this file or folder to the local destination associated with that object. ● If it is an FTP Object (page 171) or DAV Object (page 132), copies this file or folder to the remote destination associated with that object.
absPathOrUrl	An absolute path or URL to the target file or folder. Must be an absolute, system-dependent path string or an absolute file URL starting with `file://`. In Windows, if there is no valid path given (such as "`file://myfile.txt`"), the file or folder is copied into the current directory.
FTP_URL	An FTP URL to the remote target file or folder. The URL string must be either a relative URL (based on the current root folder) or an absolute FTP URL starting with `ftp://`. This method can only copy on the same server.
rename *FTPObj*.rename(*newName*)	Renames the remote file or folder, if connected. Returns `true` on success.
newName	The new name for the target on the remote site. This can be a simple name, a relative or absolute path, or a path starting with a host name.
remove *FTPObj*.remove()	Removes the remote file or folder and sub items, if connected. Returns `true` on success.

globalPrefs Object

This object encapsulates global application preferences. It provides read-only access to a subset of the GoLive global preferences the user can set in the **Preferences** panel. A user can access this panel through the **Edit** menu in Windows, or through the **GoLive** menu in Mac OS. Extension modules can use the `globalPrefs` object to store persistent user preference data that is available to all extensions.

The object has no functions.

Acquiring a globalPrefs object

The `app.prefs` property returns a `globalPrefs` object:

```
var myGlobalPrefs = app.prefs
```

globalPrefs object properties

`absoluteURLs`	Boolean	**Preferences > General > URL Handling > Make new links absolute** checkbox.
`defaultExt`	String	The file extension that GoLive adds to new files that are created. The default value is `html`. The user can change this default value in the **Preferences > Site > File extension** input field.
`proxyHTTP`	String	**Preferences > Internet > Use HTTP proxy > Host** input field.
`proxyPortHTTP`	String	**Preferences > Internet > Use HTTP proxy > Port** input field.
`scriptLibFolder`	String	The name of the JavaScript libraries folder that holds `.js` files. By default, this value is the site's `Generated Items` folder. The user can change this value in the **Preferences > Script Library > Folder for Script Library** input field. This property is undefined when the **Smart Objects** module is disabled. Read-only.

scriptLibName	String	The name of the site's common script library. Read-only. Default value is the `CSScriptLib.js` file. When a site window is open, default location of this file is the `Generated Items` folder in the root level of the site folder. When a site window is not open, this file is placed in a default folder:
		• GoLive CS, GoLive CS2 (Mac OS):
		`System/Preferences/Adobe/GoLive/Settings7/JScripts/` `GlobalScripts/`
		• GoLive CS, GoLive CS2 (Windows):
		`RootDrive\Documents and Settings\User\Application` `Data\Adobe\Adobe GoLive\Settings7\JScripts\GlobalScripts\`
		• GoLive 6 (Mac OS):
		`System/Preferences/Adobe/GoLive/Settings/JScripts/` `GlobalScripts/`
		• GoLive 6 (Windows):
		`RootDrive\Documents and Settings\User\Application` `Data\Adobe\Adobe GoLive\Settings\JScripts\GlobalScripts\`
		• GoLive 5:
		`Adobe GoLive 5.0/Modules/JScripts/`
useHTTPProxy	Boolean	When `true`, use an HTTP proxy.
writeGenerator	Boolean	When `true`, the `generator` meta tag is written into documents, identifying Adobe GoLive CS2 SDK as the generator.

HTMLStyle Object

Class: JSXHTMLStyle

This object encapsulates a single style in an HTMLStyleSet Object (page 179). You can read its properties to retrieve style information, and you can write to them to set style information.

This object has no functions.

Acquiring HTMLStyle objects

The htmlStyles (page 54) property of the app Object (page 53) provides an HTMLStyleSetCollection object that returns all HTMLStyleSet Objects (page 179) currently available to the GoLive application. Retrieve individual HTMLStyle objects from this collection by name, by attribute name, or by numeric index. You can then extract individual HTMLStyle objects from the HTMLStyleSet object:

        app.htmlStyles[*styleSetName*].[*styleName*]

HTMLStyle object properties

Properties of the HTMLStyle object enable you to retrieve style objects and their attributes by name.

attribute	String	Name of the style attribute
name	String	Name of the style (the element name)
value	String	Value of the attribute

➤ Example

To specify left-aligned text:

        name="div", attribute="align", value="left"

To specify bold text:

        name="b", attribute="", value=""

HTMLStyleSet Object

Class: `JSXHTMLStyleSet`

This object represents a named styleset. This styleset may appear in the **Window > Styles** palette or it may be provided by a document.

Acquiring HTMLStyleSet objects

- The htmlStyles (page 54) property of the app Object (page 53) provides an `HTMLStyleSetCollection` object that returns all HTMLStyleSet Objects (page 179) currently available to the GoLive application. These contain the styles that appear in the **Window > Styles** palette.

    ```
    app.htmlStyles[name]
    app.htmlStyles[index]
    ```

- A textArea Object's `styleSet` property (page 278) holds style information for that text block.

    ```
    textAreaObj.styleSet
    ```

HTMLStyleSet object properties

name	String	The styleset name.
paragraph	Boolean	When `true`, this styleset is for an entire paragraph.
replace	Boolean	Whether to replace or add to the current style set of a selection when this style set is applied to it. • When `true`, this style in this set replace the currently any currently applied styles. • When `false`, the styles in this set are added to the existing styles.
style	HTMLStyle	The array of HTMLStyle Objects (page 179) in this set. Read-only.

HTMLStyleSet object functions

addStyle *HTMLStyleSetObj*.`addStyle`(*styleObj*) *HTMLStyleSetObj*.`addStyle` (*elementName, attrName, attrValue*)	Adds the specified style to this styleset. Returns `true` on success.
styleObj	An HTMLStyle Object (page 178) for the style to add to the set.
elementName	Name of element that gets the new style.
attrName	Name of style attribute to add.
attrValue	Value of the named style attribute.

removeStyle
HTMLStyleSetObj.removeStyle(*index*)
HTMLStyleSetObj.removeStyle
  (*HTMLStyleObj*)
HTMLStyleSetObj.removeStyle
  (*elementName, attrName, attrValue*)
		Removes the specified style from this styleset. Returns true on success.

`index`	0-based index of the style to remove from the set.	
`HTMLStyleObj`	An HTMLStyle Object (page 178) for the style to remove from the set.	
`elementName`	Name of element from which to remove the style.	
`attrName`	Name of style attribute to remove.	
`attrValue`	Value of the named style attribute.	

setStyle		Replaces an existing style in the set with a new one. Both the existing style and the new style can be specified by index, by name, by name and attribute values, or as an object. Returns true on success.

HTMLStyleSetObj.setStyle(*existingIndex, newStyleObj*)

`existingIndex`	0-based index of the style to replace.
`newStyleObj`	An HTMLStyle Object (page 178) for the new style.

HTMLStyleSetObj.setStyle(*existingObj, newStyleObj*)

`existingObj`	The HTMLStyle Object (page 178) for the style to replace.
`newStyleObj`	An HTMLStyle Object (page 178) for the new style.

HTMLStyleSetObj.setStyle(*existingName, existingAttr, existingValue, newStyleObj*)

`existingName`	JavaScript name of style to replace.
`existingAttr`	Attribute name of style to replace.
`existingValue`	Value of the named attribute in style to replace.
`newStyleObj`	An HTMLStyle Object (page 178) for the new style.

HTMLStyleSetObj.setStyle(*existingName, existingAttr, newStyleObj*)

`existingName`	JavaScript name of style to replace.
`existingAttr`	Attribute name of style to replace.
`newStyleObj`	An HTMLStyle Object (page 178) for the new style.

HTMLStyleSetObj.setStyle(*existingName, newStyleObj*)

`existingName`	JavaScript name of style to replace.
`newStyleObj`	An HTMLStyle Object (page 178) for the new style.
`attrValue`	Value of the named style attribute.

HTMLStyleSetObj.setStyle (*existingIndex, newStyleName, newStyleAttr, newStyleValue*)

existingIndex	0-based index of the style to replace.
newName	JavaScript name of the new style.
newAttr	Attribute name of the new style.
newValue	Value of the named attribute in the new style.

HTMLStyleSetObj.setStyle (*existingObj, newStyleName, newStyleAttr, newStyleValue*)

existingObj	The HTMLStyle Object (page 178) for the style to replace.
newName	JavaScript name of the new style.
newAttr	Attribute name of the new style.
newValue	Value of the named attribute in the new style.

HTMLStyleSetObj.setStyle (*existingName, existingAttr, existingValue, newStyleName, newStyleAttr, newStyleValue*)

existingName	JavaScript name of style to replace.
existingAttr	Attribute name of style to replace.
existingValue	Value of the named attribute in style to replace.
newName	JavaScript name of the new style.
newAttr	Attribute name of the new style.
newValue	Value of the named attribute in the new style.

HTMLStyleSetObj.setStyle (*existingName, existingAttr, newStyleName, newStyleAttr, newStyleValue*)

existingName	JavaScript name of style to replace.
existingAttr	Attribute name of style to replace.
newName	JavaScript name of the new style.
newAttr	Attribute name of the new style.
newValue	Value of the named attribute in the new style.

HTMLStyleSetObj.setStyle (*existingName, newStyleName, newStyleAttr, newStyleValue*)

existingName	JavaScript name of style to replace.
newName	JavaScript name of the new style.
newAttr	Attribute name of the new style.
newValue	Value of the named attribute in the new style.

imageConverter Object

Class: `JSXImageConverter`

This object allows access to information about source images files, including PSD, SVG, EPS, PDF, AI, TIFF, and JPEG. It has methods to convert those images into formats suitable for web browsers (GIF, JPEG, PNG, WBMP), and get information about the resulting files. For an example of using this object, see the `ImageConverter` sample included with the SDK. (Introduced in 7.0)

This object has no properties.

Acquiring the imageConverter object

You can get this object from the `app` object:

```
imgConvObj = app.imageConverter;
```

imageConverter object functions

convertFile *imgConvObj*.convertFile (*sourceFile* [, *settings*, *showPDFOptionsDialog*, *showVarDialog*, *showSFWDialog*, *destFolder*, *defaultName*])	Converts and saves the given file using GoLive's SaveForWeb functionality. If the conversion and save are successful, returns the object for the created image file or folder. Otherwise returns `null`. See example below.
sourceFile	The image file, as a file path or URL string, a file Object (page 158), or a siteReference Object (page 260).
settings	Optional. An imageSettings Object (page 186) with settings for the save operation.
showPDFOptionsDialog	Optional. When `true` (the default), display the **PDF Options** dialog if the file is a PDF.
showVarsDialog	Optional. When `true` (the default), display the **Variables Settings** dialog if the file contains variables.
showSFWDialog	Optional. When `true` (the default), display the **Save For Web** dialog.
destFolder	Optional. Where the created image file (or folder in case of slices and/or rollovers) should be saved, as a file path or URL string, or as a a file Object (page 158), or a siteReference Object (page 260). When not supplied, displays a **Save** dialog.
defaultName	Optional. A name for the created file or folder. When not supplied, uses the current name with the appropriate extension; for example, when creating a GIF, `"image.png"` becomes `"image.gif"`.

convertFileToICO
imgConvObj.convertFileToICO
(*sourceFile*
  [, *settings, showPDFOptionsDialog,*
  showVarDialog, showSFWDialog,
  destFolder, defaultName])
	Converts and saves the given file as an icon (an ICO file), using GoLive's SaveForWeb functionality. If the conversion and save are successful, returns the object for the created icon file or folder. Otherwise returns null.

sourceFile	The image file, as a file path or URL string, a file Object (page 158), or a siteReference Object (page 260).
settings	Optional. An imageSettings Object (page 186) with settings for the save operation. (The save operation always uses the default icon output settings.)
showPDFOptionsDialog	Optional. When true (the default), display the **PDF Options** dialog if the file is a PDF.
showVarsDialog	Optional. When true (the default), display the **Variables Settings** dialog if the file contains variables.
showSFWDialog	Optional. When true (the default), display the **Save For Web** dialog.
destFolder	Optional. Where the created icon file (or folder in case of slices and/or rollovers) should be saved, as a file path or URL string, or as a a file Object (page 158), or a siteReference Object (page 260). When not supplied, displays a **Save** dialog.
defaultName	Optional. A name for the created file or folder. When not supplied, uses the current name with the appropriate extension; for example, "image.png" becomes "image.ico".
fileHasRollover *imgConvObj*.fileHasRollover (*sourceFile*)	Returns true if the PSD file has rollover functionality.
sourceFile	The image file, as a file path or URL string, a file Object (page 158), or a siteReference Object (page 260).
fileIsSliced *imgConvObj*.fileIsSliced(*sourceFile*)	Returns true if the PSD or SVG file contains slices.
sourceFile	The image file, as a file path or URL string, a file Object (page 158), or a siteReference Object (page 260).
getImageSize *imgConvObj*.getImageSize(*sourceFile*)	Gets the image height and width. Returns a JavaScript object with two properties, the width and height of the image, or null if the image cannot be opened by GoLive.
sourceFile	The image file, as a file path or URL string, a file Object (page 158), or a siteReference Object (page 260).

getVariables *imgConvObj*.getVariables (*sourceFile[, settings]*)	Gets variable specified in an image. If provided, the values of variables are filled from the settings. Returns an array of imageVariable Objects (page 190) for the variables that are specified in the image file.
sourceFile	The image file, as a file path or URL string, a file Object (page 158), or a siteReference Object (page 260).
settings	Optional. An imageSettings Object (page 186) containing a set of variable values.

insertSmartObject
imgConvObj.insertSmartObject
  (*sourceFile [, settings,
  showPDFOptionsDialog,
  showVarDialog, showSFWDialog,
  destFolder, defaultName]*)
	Inserts an image as a Smart Object into the current selection of the front-most HTML page, with a reference to the web-safe, optimized target file that the function creates and saves. The page must be in Layout mode and must have a selection. If the selection is not empty, the contents are replaced by the Smart Object.

sourceFile	The image file, as a file path or URL string, a file Object (page 158), or a siteReference Object (page 260).
settings	Optional. An imageSettings Object (page 186) with settings for the save operation.
showPDFOptionsDialog	Optional. When true (the default), display the **PDF Options** dialog if the file is a PDF.
showVarsDialog	Optional. When true (the default), display the **Variables Settings** dialog if the file contains variables.
showSFWDialog	Optional. When true (the default), display the **Save For Web** dialog.
destFolder	Optional. Where the created image file (or folder in case of slices and/or rollovers) should be saved, as a file path or URL string, or as a file Object (page 158), or a siteReference Object (page 260). When not supplied, displays a **Save** dialog.
defaultName	Optional. A name for the created file or folder. When not supplied, uses the current name with the appropriate extension; for example, when creating a GIF, "image.png" becomes "image.gif".

➤ Example: Converting an image file

```
function convertImage()
{
    converter = app.imageConverter;
    srcFile  = fileGetDialog("Select a source file");
    if (srcFile)
    {
        /* check for slices */
        var isSliced = converter.fileIsSliced(srcFile);
        if (isSliced)
            Window.alert("The image is sliced.");
```

```
        else
          Window.alert("The image does not contain slices.");
        /* check for variables */
        var vars     = converter.getVariables(srcFile);
        var varCount = 0;
        if (vars)
            varCount = vars.length;
        Window.alert("The image has " + varCount + " variable(s).");
        /* set all text variables to "Date() is: <current date>." */
        for (i = 0; i < varCount; i++)
        {
          var curVar = vars[i];
          if (curVar.type == "text")
            curVar.value = "Date() is: " + Date().toString() + ".";
        }
      /* create and fill settings */
      var mySettings = new JSXImageSettings;
      mySettings.setVariables(vars);
      mySettings.setGIFFormat("numColors", 128, "transparency",
true,
        "transparencyDitherAlgorithm", "diffusion");
      mySettings.matteColor = "#FFFFFF"; /* white */
      /* optimize file with the settings */
      var showPDFOptionsDialog = true;
      var showVarDialog        = false;
      var showSFWDialog        = true;

      converter.convertFile(srcFile, settings,
showPDFOptionsDialog,
        showVarDialog, showSFWDialog);
      }
}
```

imageSettings Object

Class: `JSXImageSettings`

This object holds the settings necessary for converting images using the functions of the imageConverter Object (page 182). Through this object, you have access to all the settings of the **Save For Web** dialog. For an example of using this object, see the `ImageConverter` sample included with the SDK. (Introduced in 7.0)

Acquiring the imageSettings object

You can create this object using the imageSettings Constructor (page 187):

```
var myImgSettings = new JSXImageSettings();
```

imageSettings object properties

cropRect	Rect	A rectangle to which the image should be cropped. If larger than the image, transparency is added. An array of four numeric values, [*left*, *top*, *right*, *bottom*]. The existing values can be accessed by these names; for example: `var topVal = myImgSettings.cropRect.top;`
matteColor	String	Matte color: a color string value as used in HTML, such as `"#550055"`.
outputSize	Size	The size to which the image should be rendered. A size of (0, 0) means use the image's original size. An array of two numeric values, [*width*, *height*]. The existing values can be accessed by these names; for example: `var wdVal = myImgSettings.outputSize.width;`
pageNumber	Integer	The page number of a PDF file.
pdfRotation	Integer	Rotation of a PDF file: 0, 90, 180, or 270.

resampleMethod	String	The resample method, corresponds to the setting in the **Save For Web** dialog. One of:
		
		`nearestNeighbor`
		`bilinear`
		`bicubic`
		`bicubicSmoother`
		`bicubicSharper`

scaleMode	String	The scale mode as used in SmartObjects. One of:
		
		`exactFit`
		`noBorder`
		`showAll`

suppressSlices	Boolean	When `true`, ignore slices when converting sliced files. Default is `false`.

imageSettings object functions

imageSettings Constructor `new JSXImageSettings( )`	Creates and returns a new `imageSettings` object.
getAsBase64String *imageSettingsObj*.`getAsBase64String()`	Saves the settings for reuse, as in the **Save Settings** option of the **Save For Web** dialog. Returns the `imageSettings` object as a Base64-encoded string.
getFileFormat *imageSettingsObj*.`getFileFormat()`	Gets the file format for this settings object. Returns one of `GIF`, `JPEG`, `PNG8`, `PNG24`, or `WBMP`, or `null` if no format was set.
getFileFormatOption *imageSettingsObj*.`getFileFormatOption` (*optionName*)	Gets the value of a specified format option. Returns the current value of the option, or `null` if the option was not set.
optionName	The name of the format option whose value is retrieved.
setFromBase64String *imageSettingsObj*.`setAsBase64String` (*settings*)	Restores the settings in the **Save For Web** dialog to their saved values.
settings	A base-64 encoded string containing saved settings, as returned by getAsBase64String (page 187).
setGIFFormat *imageSettingsObj*.`setGIFFormat` (*name*, *value*, ...)	Sets the output format to GIF and sets parameters for that format. Subsequent calls to this function will add parameters and not remove previously set ones. Returns `true` on success.
name	The name of the format option whose value is set.
value	The new value of the format option, of the appropriate type. For possible name-value parameter pairs, see "File Format Parameters" on page 188.
setJPEGFormat *imageSettingsObj*.`setJPEGFormat` (*name*, *value*, ...)	Sets the output format to JPEG and sets parameters for that format. Subsequent calls to this function will add parameters and not remove previously set ones. Returns `true` on success.
name	The name of the format option whose value is set.
value	The new value of the format option, of the appropriate type. For possible name-value parameter pairs, see "File Format Parameters" on page 188.

setPNG8Format *imageSettingsObj*.setPNG8Format (*name*, *value*, ...)	Sets the output format to PNG-8 and sets parameters for that format. Subsequent calls to this function will add parameters and not remove previously set ones. Returns true on success.
name	The name of the format option whose value is set.
value	The new value of the format option, of the appropriate type. For possible name-value parameter pairs, see "File Format Parameters" on page 188.
setPNG24Format *imageSettingsObj*.setPNG24Format (*name*, *value*, ...)	Sets the output format to PNG-24 and sets parameters for that format. Subsequent calls to this function will add parameters and not remove previously set ones. Returns true on success.
name	The name of the format option whose value is set.
value	The new value of the format option, of the appropriate type. For possible name-value parameter pairs, see "File Format Parameters" on page 188.
setWBMPFormat *imageSettingsObj*.setWBMPFormat (*name*, *value*, ...)	Sets the output format to WBMP and sets parameters for that format. Subsequent calls to this function will add parameters and not remove previously set ones. Returns true on success.
name	The name of the format option whose value is set.
value	The new value of the format option, of the appropriate type. For possible name-value parameter pairs, see "File Format Parameters" on page 188.
setVariables *imageSettingsObj*.setVariables (*imageVars*)	Adds PSD or SVG variable settings to this object. Returns true on success.
imageVars	An array of imageVariable Objects (page 190) for the new variable settings.

File Format Parameters

Refer to the *Adobe GoLive CS User Guide* for more complete information on what these values mean.

Name	Type	Value	Formats	Description
autoReduction	Boolean	true, false	GIF, PNG-8	auto color reduction
blurAmount	Float	0 - 2.0	JPEG	blur amount
ditherAlgorithm	String	none diffusion pattern blueNoise	GIF, PNG-8, WBMP	dither algorithm

Name	Type	Value	Formats	Description
ditherPercent	Integer	0 - 100	GIF, PNG-8, WBMP	dither percentage
embedICCProfile	Boolean	true, false	JPEG	embed ICC color profile
interlaced	Boolean	true, false	GIF, PNG-8, PNG-24	use interlacing
lossy	Boolean	true, false	GIF	lossy GIF mode
numColors	Integer	2 - 256	GIF, PNG-8	number of colors
optimized	Boolean	true, false	JPEG	use optimized JPEG
progressive	Boolean	true, false	JPEG	progressive JPEG
quality	Integer	0 - 100	JPEG	JPEG quality
reduction Algorithm	String	perceptual selective adaptive web	GIF, PNG-8	color reduction algorithm
transparency	Boolean	true false	GIF, PNG-8, PNG-24	use transparency
transparencyDitherAlgorithm	String	none diffusion pattern blueNoise	GIF, PNG-8	transparency dithering algorithm
transparencyDitherPercentage	Integer	0 - 100	GIF, PNG-8	transparency dithering percentage
webShiftPercent	Integer	0 - 100	GIF, PNG-8	color web shift percentage

imageVariable Object

Class: JSXImageVariable

This object holds the data for a variable found in a PSD or SVG file. For an example of using this object, see the `ImageConverter` sample included with the SDK. (Introduced in 7.0)

Acquiring imageVariable objects

The getVariables (page 184) method in the imageConverter Object (page 182) returns an array of `imageVariable` objects.

imageVariable object properties

name	String	Read only. The name of the variable. If no explicit text variable is defined for a PSD's topmost text layer, there is a default variable for it named `"defaultTextVariable"`.

type	String	Read only. The type of the variable. One of:
		`text`
		`visibility`

use	Boolean	When `true`, the variable is in use.
value	String or Boolean	The value of the variable. Variables of type `"text"` have string values, `"visibility"` variables have Boolean values.

➤ **Example**

```
vars
=app.imageConverter.getVariables('file://C:/Test.psd');
firstVar = vars[0];
if (firstVar.type == 'text')
    firstVar.value = 'New text';
else
    firstVar.value = false;
```

layout Object

Class: `JSXBoxLayout`

This object enables you to manipulate `box` objects, grids, tables, and other HTML elements in Layout view without reparsing. For a list of the HTML elements the `layout` object can manage, see Appendix C, "Managed Layout Tags." Elements not listed cannot be managed by a `layout` object. If your extension manipulates such objects with Layout view open, the document may be automatically reparsed and the objects regenerated.

Acquiring layout objects

Get this object from the `layout` property of any markup Object (page 215) for the HTML content of the document open in the Layout view.

   markupObj.`layout`

For example:

```
var doc = app.newDocument();
doc.view="layout";
doc.mainTextArea.insertBox("myBox");
doc.documentElement.getSubElement("myBox").layout.setAttribute
("text","www.adobe.com");
```

layout object properties

Properties of the `layout` object provide access to the objects it manages, which in turn manage various layout aspects of the element containing the `layout` object.

`grid`	Grid	A layout.grid Object (page 193) that manages the grid itself, if the containing element is a Layout Grid or a box positioned on a Layout Grid in Layout View. Otherwise `null`. Read-only.
`gridLayout`	Grid Layout	A layout.gridLayout Object (page 193) that manages the grid position of a box, if the containing element is a box positioned on a layout grid. Otherwise `null`. Read-only.
`table`	Layout Table	A layout.table Object (page 198) that manages the layout of a table, if the containing element is a `table` element. Otherwise `null`. Read-only.
`tableCell`	Table Cell	A layout.tableCell Object (page 203) that manages the layout of a cell in a table, if the containing element is a `td` or `th` element. Otherwise `null`. Read-only.

layout object functions

Functions of the `layout` object enable you to get and set attribute values in the HTML source it manages. These methods can only access attributes listed in Appendix C, "Managed Layout Tags."

getAttribute *markupObj*.layout.getAttribute(*attr*)	Gets the current value of a specified layout attribute. Returns a string containing the current value of the specified attribute (*markupObj*.layout.*attr*).
attr Name of the attribute to access.	
hasAttribute *markupObj*.layout.getAttribute(*attr*)	Returns true if *markupObj*.layout has the specified property.
attr Name of the attribute to test.	
setAttribute *markupObj*.layout.setAttribute (*attr*[, *value1*, ..., *valueN-1*, *valueN*])	Sets the value of a specified layout attribute. Returns true on success.
attr The name of the attribute whose value is set.	
value Optional. Value to which to set the attribute. The number of values to supply varies according to the attribute being set. If this argument is omitted, the method removes the attribute or its value, as appropriate. This method behaves the same way as the Inspector when the user modifies this attribute.	

layout.grid Object

Class: `JSXLayoutGrid`

This object represents a Layout Grid in Layout view. It allows your extension to edit and optimize the grid programmatically, as the user does with the Layout Grid's Inspector window and its **Optimize** command. The methods also allow your extension to add, delete, and manipulate elements in the Layout Grid.

Acquiring a layout.grid object

- You can get the `grid` object from the `document` object's `layout` object:

  `document.layout.grid`

- You can get a `grid` object from the `grid` property of any `layout` object that manages a grid or a box on a grid:

  markupObj`.layout.grid`

layout.grid object properties

`align`	String	Alignment of the layout grid. Valid values are `left`, `center`, and `right`.
`background`	String Boolean	URL of the image to display as the layout's background. When `true` or `false`, turns the display of the background image on or off.
`bgcolor`	String Number Boolean	The background color of the layout grid. A color name (such as `"red"` or `"blue"`), or a hexadecimal color value. When `true` or `false`, turns the display of the background color on or off.
`height`	Number	Height of the grid in pixels.
`width`	Number	Width of the grid in pixels.
`xGrid`	Number	Horizontal distance of grid points in pixels.
`xGridSnap`	Boolean	When `true`, the positions of boxes on the grid snap to the horizontal grid points
`xGridVisible`	Boolean	When `true`, the horizontal gridlines are visible.
`yGrid`	Number	Vertical distance of grid points in pixels.
`yGridSnap`	Boolean	When `true`, the positions of boxes on the grid snap to the vertical grid points.
`yGridVisible`	Boolean	When `true`, the vertical gridlines are visible.

layout.grid object functions

copy *markupObj*.`layout.grid.copy()`	Copies the currently selected objects to the clipboard. Returns `true` on success.
cut *markupObj*.`layout.grid.cut()`	Cuts the currently selected objects and places them on the clipboard. Returns `true` on success.

deselect
markupObj.`layout.grid.deselect`
    (*element*)
markupObj.`layout.grid.deselect`(*all*)
markupObj.`layout.grid.deselect`
    (*element, all*)
	Deselects one or all elements on the layout grid. Returns `true` on success.

`element`	The element to deselect, if it is selected.
`all`	When `true`, deselects all currently selected boxes on the layout grid.
insertBox *markupObj*.`layout.grid.insertBox` (*boxName*)	Adds a new or predefined box Object (page 64) to Layout view at the current cursor position. Returns `true` on success. To insert an element provided by the standard GoLive palettes, use one of the values shown in the table below, "Box names for predefined palette elements." (page 195)
`boxName`	JavaScript name of the box to insert. This can be: • The name of a predefined palette element, as shown below. • The `classid` value of a custom element, as given in the defining `<jsxelement>` (page 346) tag.
insertHTML *markupObj*.`layout.grid.insertHTML` (*htmlToInsert*)	Inserts a layout textbox at the current position and inserts the specified HTML source into the box. You can use this method to add a new HTML element to a document without causing GoLive to reparse. Returns `true` on success.
`htmlToInsert`	The HTML to insert.
optimize *markupObj*.`layout.grid.optimize()`	Optimizes the size of the layout grid to the dimension of all containing boxes. This is the same as clicking **Optimize** in the grid Inspector window. Returns `true` on success.
paste *markupObj*.`layout.grid.paste()`	Pastes the current clipboard contents at the current position. Returns `true` on success.

select *markupObj*`.layout.grid.select` (*element, multipleSel*)	Makes the specified element the new selection or adds the specified element to the current selection. Returns `true` on success.
`element`	The element to select. If it is a box positioned on the grid, the box is selected.
`multipleSel`	When `true`, adds this element to the current selection. When `false`, makes this element the new selection.
setCursor *markupObj*`.layout.grid.setCursor` (*x, y*)	Moves the cursor to the given grid point. Returns `true` on success.
`x`	Horizontal coordinate of the cursor's new location.
`y`	Vertical coordinate of the cursor's new location.

Box names for predefined palette elements

Basic Palette Group		Form Palette Group	
JavaScript Name	**UI Name**	**JavaScript Name**	**UI Name**
`anchor`	Anchor	`form`	Form
`applet`	Java Applet	`submit`	**Submit** button
`comment`	Comment	`reset`	**Reset** button
`floatingbox`	Floating Box	`button`	Button
`image`	Image	`inputimage`	Input image
`layoutgrid`	Layout grid	`label`	Label
`layouttextbox`	Layout Textbox	`textfield`	Text field
`linebreak`	Line break	`password`	Password field
`line`	Line	`textarea`	Text area
`marquee`	Marquee	`checkbox`	Checkbox
`plugin`	Plug-in	`radiobutton`	Radio button
`swf`	SWF Plug-in	`popup`	Popup
`quicktime`	QuickTime Plug-in	`listbox`	Listbox
`real`	Real Plug-in	`filebrowser`	File browser
`svg`	SVG Plug-in	`hidden`	Hidden

Basic Palette Group		Form Palette Group	
JavaScript Name	**UI Name**	**JavaScript Name**	**UI Name**
javascript	JavaScript	keygenerator	Key generator
spacer	Spacer	fieldset	Field set
table	Table		
w3c	W3C Object		

layout.gridLayout Object

Class: `JSXGridLayout`

This object manages the grid position of a box Object (page 64) element that is the child of a Layout Grid, specifying the position and alignment of the box in the layout grid's coordinate plane.

Acquiring layout.gridLayout objects

You can get the `gridLayout` object from the `gridLayout` property of the layout Object (page 191) for a box Object (page 64) or markup Object (page 215) element:

```
boxObj.layout.gridLayout
markupObj.layout.gridLayout
```

layout.gridLayout object properties

`halign`	String	Horizontal alignment on the grid. Values are `left`, `center`, `right`.
`height`	Number	Height of the box.
`valign`	String	Vertical alignment on the grid. Values are `top`, `center`, `bottom`.
`width`	Number	Width of the box.
`x`	Number	X position on the grid.
`y`	Number	Y position on the grid.

layout.gridLayout object functions

Functions of the `gridLayout` object change size and position of the box using grid coordinates.

`setPosition` *markupObj*`.layout.gridLayout.setPosition` (*x, y*)	Sets the position on the grid. Returns `true` on success.
x	Horizontal coordinate of the new location.
y	Vertical coordinate of the new location.
`setSize` *markupObj*`.layout.gridLayout.setSize` (*width, height*);	Sets the size of the box. Returns `true` on success.
width	New width of the box, expressed as a number of pixels.
height	New height of the box, expressed as a number of pixels.

---

layout.table Object

Class: `JSXTableLayout`

This object manipulates a `<table>` element programmatically. In addition to setting the size, number of rows/columns, and so on, methods of this object add, delete, split, or merge rows, columns, or cells.

Acquiring layout.table objects

The object is available only when the document that provides the markup Object (page 215) is displaying a `<table>` element in Layout view. You can retrieve the Table object from the `layout.table` property of the *markupObj* that manages the `<table>` element:

markupObj`.layout.table`

layout.table object properties

align	String	The alignment of the table. One of:
		　`left`
		　`right`
		　`center`

background	String Boolean	The URL of the background image. —or— When `true` or `false`, turns the background image on or off.
bgcolor	String Number Boolean	When a color name string or color number value, the background color itself. —or— When `true` or `false`, turns the background color on or off.
border	Number	Border width.
captionCell	TableCell	The caption cell. Read-only.

captionPosition	String	The position of the caption. One of:
		　`none`
		　`top`
		　`bottom`

cell	TableCellLayout Collection	Array of layout.tableCell Objects (page 203). The index is counted from left to right beginning with 0. Read-only.
cellpadding	Number	Cell padding of the table.
cellspacing	Number	Cell spacing of the table.

cellStyle	TableCellStyle Collection	An array of all the layout.tableCell.style Objects (page 205) this table uses. Cells are indexed from left to right beginning with an index of 0. Read-only.
columns	Number	Number of columns. You can set the value to change the number of columns in the table.
height	Number	Total height of the table.
rows	Number	Number of rows. You can set the value to change the number of rows in the table.
style	Table Style	The current layout.table.style Object (page 201). Read-only.
width	Number	Total width of the table.

layout.table object functions

addCurrentStyle *markupObj*.`layout.table.addCurrentStyle` (*name*)	Adds the current table style to the global `tableStyles` array using the specified JavaScript name. Returns `true` on success.
name	JavaScript name of the table style.
applyStyle *markupObj*.`layout.table.applyStyle` (*tableStyleObj*)	Applies the specified table style to this table. Returns `true` on success.
tableStyleObj	A layout.table.style Object (page 201) containing the table style to apply.
exportCellText *markupObj*.`layout.table.exportCellText` (*filePath*)	Exports the cells of the table as a tab-delimited text file at a specified location. Returns `true` on success.
filePath	Name and location of the output file, specified as a relative or fully qualified path or URL.
getCellAt *markupObj*.`layout.table.getCellAt` (*col, row*)	Gets the specified table cell from the table. Returns `true` on success.
col	Column number of the cell to retrieve. Column 0 is the first column.
row	Row number of the cell to retrieve. Row 0 is the first row.
getCellStyleAt *markupObj*.`layout.table.getCellStyleAt` (*col, row*)	Gets the style of the specified table cell from the table. Returns a layout.tableCell.style Object (page 205).
col	Column number of the cell. Column 0 is the first column.
row	Row number of the cell. Row 0 is the first row.

importCellText *markupObj*.layout.table.importCellText (*filePath*[, *separator*])	Imports text from a specified file into cells of the table. Returns true on success.
filePath	Relative or fully qualified path to the file to import.
separator	Optional. A character to be interpreted as the record-separator character. When not supplied, uses the Tab character.
insertColumnAt *markupObj*.layout.table.insertColumnAt (*pos*)	Inserts a column before the specified column. Returns true on success.
pos	Position at which to insert the new column. The first column in the table is at position 0.
insertRowAt *markupObj*.layout.table.insertRowAt (*pos*)	Inserts a row before a specified row. Returns true on success.
pos	Position at which to insert the new row. The first row in the table is at position 0.
mergeCells *markupObj*.layout.table.mergeCells (*left, top, right, bottom*)	Merges all cells that lie inside the specified rectangle. Returns true on success.
left, top	Coordinates of upper-left corner of the rectangle.
right, bottom	Coordinates of lower-right corner of the rectangle.
removeColumnAt *markupObj*.layout.table.removeColumnAt (*pos*)	Removes the specified column. Returns true on success.
pos	Position of the column to remove. The first column in the table is at position 0.
removeRowAt *markupObj*.layout.table.removeRowAt (*pos*)	Removes the specified row. Returns true on success.
pos	Position of the row to remove. The first row in the table is at position 0.
setCellStyleAt *markupObj*.layout.table.setCellStyleAt (*col, row, cellStyle*)	Sets the cell style of a specified cell in the table. Returns true on success.
col	Column number of the cell. Column 0 is the first column.
row	Row number of the cell. Row 0 is the first row.
cellStyle	A layout.tableCell.style Object (page 205) containing the new cell style.
splitCells *markupObj*.layout.table.splitCells (*x, y*)	Separates any merged cells that intersect the specified point. Returns true on success.
x, y	Coordinates of the point.

layout.table.style Object

Class: `JSXTableStyle`

This object encapsulates a `<table>` element's style information. The object provides access to the table's name, border width, cell spacing/padding, number of header rows, number of footer rows, and so on.

Acquiring layout.table.style objects

You can get style object from:

- The `style` property of the layout.table Object (page 198):

    markupObj`.layout.table.style`

- The collection in the `tableStyles` property of the app Object (page 53):

    `app.tableStyles[`*tableStyleName*`]`
    `app.tableStyles[`*n*`]`

layout.table.style object properties

`border`	Number Boolean	Table border width in pixels. —or— When `true` or `false`, switches the border on or off.
`cellpadding`	Number Boolean	Table cell padding in pixels. —or— When `true` or `false`, switches the cell padding on or off.
`cellspacing`	Number Boolean	Table cell spacing in pixels. —or— When `true` or `false`, switches the cell spacing on or off.
`name`	String	Style name.
`numFooterColumns`	Number	Number of footer columns. If this style is used for a table, the last *n* columns of the style are used once for the table and never again. All other columns of the style repeat if the real table is bigger than the style.
`numFooterRows`	Number	Number of footer rows. If this style is used for a table, the last *n* rows of the style are used once for the table and never again. All other rows of the style repeat if the real table is bigger than the style.
`numHeaderColumns`	Number	Number of header columns. If this style is used for a table, the first *n* columns of the style are used once for the table and never again. All other columns of the style repeat if the real table is bigger than the style.

numHeaderRows	Number	Number of header rows. If this style is used for a table, the first *n* rows of the style are used once for the table and never again. All other rows of the style repeat if the real table is bigger than the style.
xSize	Number	Number of columns the style affects.
ySize	Number	Number of rows the style affects.

layout.table.style object functions

getCellStyleAt *tableStyleObj*.getCellStyleAt(*col, row*)	Gets the cell style for a specified cell in a table that uses this style. Returns a layout.tableCell.style Object (page 205).
col	Column number of the cell. Column 0 is the first column.
row	Row number of the cell. Row 0 is the first row.
setCellStyleAt *tableStyleObj*.setCellStyleAt (*col, row, cellStyle*)	Sets the cell style for a specified cell in a table that uses this style. Returns true on success.
col	Column number of the cell. Column 0 is the first column.
row	Row number of the cell. Row 0 is the first row.
cellStyle	A layout.tableCell.style Object (page 205) containing the new cell style.

layout.tableCell Object

Class: `JSXTableCellLayout`

This object manages the content of a cell in a Layout Table object. It enables you to manipulate the size and style of the cell itself and to get the TextArea object that holds the cell's text content.

Acquiring layout.tableCell objects

This object is available only when the document that holds the table is displaying Layout view. Layout view provides this object as:

- The `tableCell` property of the `markup` object's Layout object

    markupObj.`layout.tableCell`

- The return value of the `getCellAt` function of the layout.table Object (page 199)

    markupObj.`layout.table.getCellAt`(*col*, *row*) (page 199)

- The `captionCell` property of the Layout Table object

    markupObj.`layout.table.captionCell`

- The `table.cell` array property of the Layout Table object, where the index is a value between 0 and

    markupObj.`layout.table.cell.length`

    markupObj.`layout.table.cell`[*index*]

layout.table Cell object properties

background	String	The URL of a background image.
bgolor	String Number	The background color name or color value.

halign	String	Horizontal alignment of text in the cell. One of:
		    left
		    center
		    right

height	Number	Height of the cell in pixels.
nowrap	Boolean	When `true`, the text of the cell does not wrap.
style	Table Cell Style	The style of the cell, a layout.tableCell.style Object (page 205).
textArea	TextArea	The textArea Object (page 278) containing the text content of the cell.

valign	String	Vertical alignment of text in the cell. One of:
		top middle bottom
width	Number	Width of the cell in pixels.

layout.tableCell object functions

applyStyle	Applies the specified table cell style to this cell.
markupObj.layout.tableCell.applyStyle (*tableCellStyleObj*)	Returns true on success.
tableCellStyleObj The layout.tableCell.style Object (page 205) containing the cell style.	

layout.tableCell.style Object

Class: JSXTableCellStyle

This object encapsulates a cell's style information. It provides information such as background color, text color, font face, and so on. In the layout.table.style Object (page 201), each table cell's style information is represented as a `layout.tableCell.style` object. The cell style affects cells in the table that uses that table style.

This object has no functions.

Acquiring layout.tableCell.style objects

- Get a cell-style object from a layout.tableCell Object's `style` property (page 203):

  markupObj`.layout.tableCell.style`

- A cell-style object is returned by the `getCellStyleAt` method of a layout.table Object (page 198) or a layout.table.style Object (page 201):

  markupObj`.layout.table.getCellStyleAt`(*col, row*)
  markupObj`.layout.table.style.getCellStyleAt`(*col, row*)

layout.tableCell.style object properties

Assign `true` or `false` to *switch on/off* use of the value in the style. The style's value is used if you set the property's value to `true`. If you set the property to `false`, GoLive does not use the style's value, regardless of the property's current value.

bgcolor	Number String Boolean	When a color name string or color number value, the background color itself. —or— When `true` or `false`, turns the style usage on or off.

fontFace	String
	Boolean
		The font face of the cell. One or more of these values:
		`plain`
		`bold`
		`italic`
		`underline`
		`strikeout`
		Multiple values are a comma-separated list.
		—or—
		When `true` or `false`, turns the style usage on or off.

fontName	String	The font names of the fontset to use.

fontSize	String Boolean	The size of the font. An absolute size, or a relative size in the form +*n* or −*n*. —or— When `true` or `false`, turns the font size usage on or off.

halign	String
	Boolean
		The horizontal alignment. One of:
		`left`
		`center`
		`right`
		`default`
		—or—
		When `true` or `false`, turns the style usage on or off.

header	Boolean	When `true`, this is a header cell.
nowrap	Boolean	When `true`, the text does not wrap.
textColor	Number String Boolean	When a color name string or color number value, the text color itself. —or— When `true` or `false`, turns the style usage on or off.

valign	String
	Boolean
		The vertical alignment. One of:
		`top`
		`center`
		`bottom`
		`default`
		—or—
		When `true` or `false`, turns the style usage on or off.

link Object

Class: `JSXLink`

This object encapsulates an active URL. GoLive creates a `link` object to represent each URL it encounters when parsing a document's source representation. Use the object to initialize a control of type `urlgetter` in an Inspector palette.

Acquiring link objects

- GoLive passes a `link` object to your linkChanged (page 363) event handler when a link changes, in the linkChangeEvent (page 382) object.
- When GoLive creates a box Object (page 64) to represent an HTML element that provides a URL, and the `link` object that encapsulates the URL is added to the collection in the `links` property of the box:

  `box.links[0]`

- To add a link to an HTML element represented by a box, use the `box` object's `createLink` method:

  `box.createLink(url)`

link object properties

Properties of the `link` object provide a URL reference and information about the referenced entity, such as whether it resides on a local disk, and transport protocols to use if it does not.

`local`	Boolean	When `true`, this link points to a file residing on a local disk; when `false`, it is remote. Read-only.
`longUrl`	String	The absolute URL to the referenced file on disk. Read-only.
`mimeType`	String	The MIME type of the file associated with this link. Read-only.
`protocol`	String	The transfer protocol used to upload or download the file associated with this link. Read-only.
`url`	String	The relative URL that this object encapsulates. Read/write.

link object functions

A `link` object's most important behaviors are provided by the linkChanged (page 363) event-handling function that you register with the document Object (page 138). To inspect a `link` object, your extension must provide this handler.

---

drawIcon *linkObj*.drawIcon (*x, y* [, *width, height*])	Draws the link's state icon at a specified location, and optionally resizes the icon. Each `link` object is associated with an icon that reflects its current state. A custom element that adds a link to the page can use this function to draw the link's icon in the custom element's graphical placeholder in Layout view. A custom element's `drawBox` method calls `box.link.drawIcon` after drawing the rest of the custom icon's placeholder. When this method draws the link's icon on top of the custom placeholder graphic, it looks as if it's part of the graphic.
x, y	Coordinates of the upper-left corner of the smallest rectangle that would enclose the icon to draw.
width, height	Optional. The icon's width and height, expressed as a number of pixels.

Markup Interface

This interface defines a set of properties and functions that are shared by the following objects:

- comment Object
- element Object
- markup Object
- text Object

These properties and functions allow you to directly access markup items in document content.

When you load an HTML document, GoLive generates a tree of markup objects to represent the contents. The objects have a tree structure that matches that in the source HTML. The markup objects are of various types: the element Object (page 156) for elements, the text Object (page 276) for text items, the comment Object (page 75) for comments, and the markup Object (page 215) for all other kinds of markup items, such as entities, notations, and CDATA sections.

Markup objects and document parsing

GoLive generates all the objects in the markup tree when it parses a document. The markup tree always reflects structural changes (for instance, when you add or delete markup objects) immediately. Other changes may be reflected in the GoLive windows, but not in the HTML source until the document is reparsed. To realize all of the changes as HTML, you must reparse the entire document. Similarly, the changed contents of the document object are not written to the disk file until the document is saved.

Reparsing a document regenerates the markup tree, and references to the markup objects are rendered obsolete. When GoLive displays a document in Layout view, GoLive might reparse the document automatically for many reasons. Every time GoLive reparses the document, your must reinitialize all of your extension's references to JavaScript objects.

If you have used the document's openMarkup method to access the markup tree, GoLive does not display the document, so Layout view cannot cause your extension to reparse the document automatically. Regardless of how you have opened a document, you can reparse it on demand by calling its reparse method.

Simply closing a document and saving changes also has the effect of reparsing it.

Note: The SDK is intended for use in Layout view. Do not use markup objects to modify HTML source programmatically while the document is in Source view. To get or set the view, use the document Object's view property (page 141).

Markup interface properties

All markup objects have these fixed properties:

`elementType`	String	The type of markup this object represents. One of: `tag`: The source text of an element of the markup tree (an element Object, page 156) `comment`: A source code comment (a comment Object, page 75) `text`: A text block (a text Object, page 276) For a markup Object (page 215), the tag type of the referenced markup: see the `<jsxelement>` (page 346) `type` attribute.
`layout`	Layout	The layout Object (page 191) that manages a supported HTML element when the document is displayed in Layout view. Otherwise, the value is `null`. Supported elements are listed in Appendix C, "Managed Layout Tags."
`subElements`	Node Collection	Read-only array of markup objects representing the subelements of this element. You can retrieve objects from this array by `tagName` values or by numeric index. If this array contains more than one element of the same name, the element returned by that name is not guaranteed.
`symmetric`	Boolean	When `true`, the end of the tag matches the beginning of the tag, as in the "`<%xxx%>`" tag.
`tagName`	String	For an element Object (page 156), the tag name of the element. For example, if this value is `"myTag"`, this `markup` object was created when the SDK interpreted a `<myTag>` element.
`tagStart`	String	For an element Object (page 156), the tag delimiter of the element tag. Typical values for this property are "" (empty string),"`<`", "`[`", "`percent`", and "`<%`".

textArea	TextArea	The textArea Object (page 278) that manages this element's text, when the document is displaying Layout view, and the `markup` object manages an HTML text element or a box Object (page 64) embedded in a text area. Otherwise, the value is `null`.
virtual	Boolean	When `true`, an element created by the Layout view that cannot be modified programmatically. The Layout view of a document may create certain markup items that are not part of the source code. By default, Layout view creates `<HTML>`, `<HEAD>`, and `<BODY>` elements whenever it opens a new HTML document. These elements are not present in the document's source text, so the `setInnerHTML` and `setOuterHTML` methods cannot modify them.

Markup interface functions

These functions manipulate the attributes and content of the source element.

deleteAttribute *markupObj*.deleteAttribute (*name*)	Deletes a specified attribute from the markup element. This method is useful for deleting attributes that have names that conflict with JavaScript naming conventions.
name Name of the attribute to delete.	
getAttribute *markupObj*.getAttribute (*name*)	Returns a string representation of the value of a specified attribute of the markup element. This method is useful for accessing attributes that have names that conflict with JavaScript naming conventions.
name Name of the attribute.	
getInnerHTML *markupObj*.getInnerHTML()	Returns a string containing the element's HTML representation, excluding the outermost tag delimiters.
getOuterHTML *markupObj*.getOuterHTML()	Returns a string containing the element's HTML representation, including the outermost tag delimiters.

getSubElement *markupObj*.getSubElement ([*tagName, index, tagType*])	Gets a subelement of the element by name, index, or type. Returns a markup object. All arguments are optional. When called with no arguments, this method returns the document's <HTML> element. When the optional *n* argument is supplied, this method returns the markup object representing the *n*th occurrence of the *<tagName>* element. This method can retrieve markup items by type. The *tagType* argument specifies the kind of markup item to retrieve. Its value corresponds to the value of the type property of the markup object GoLive creates and inserts in the DOM when it interprets a markup item. You can also think of the valid set of *tagType* values as those which correspond to valid values of the type attribute of the <jsxelement> tag. The *tagType* values "plain", "binary", and "container" retrieve HTML or XML elements. **Note:** Versions of the SDK prior to SDK 6.0r1.0 do not support the *tagType* argument to the getSubElement and getSubElementCount methods. These methods ignore the tagname actually used to mark text as a comment. The following retrieves HTML and XML comments. `markup.getSubElement ("", n, "!-");`
tagName	Optional. Tag name of the element for which this method searches. This argument is case-insensitive. For example, specifying body as this value retrieves the body element regardless of whether it is defined with a <BODY> tag or a <body> tag.
index	Optional. Number of *<tagName>* elements to skip before returning one. An index value of 0 retrieves the first *<tagName>* element found.

tagType	Optional. Type of tag to retrieve. Valid values are:
	
	    plain: simple tag
	    binary: binary tag
	    container: container tag
	    /: end tag
	    !: SGML tag
	    bracket: Lasso tag [xxx]
	    percent: tag%%
	    ssi: Server Side Includes
	    !--: comment tags
	        (not for <jsxelement>, only for getSubElement)
	    asp or '%': ASP tags <% xxxx %>
	    websiphon or <<: WebSiphon tags << xxx >>
	    ?: JSP/Processing Instructions <? *xxx* ?>

getSubElementCount	Returns the number of specified types of subelements. All arguments are optional. When no arguments are supplied, counts all subelements.

markupObj.getSubElementCount
  ([*tagName*])
markupObj.getSubElementCount
  ([*tagName, tagType*])
	Note: Versions of the SDK prior to SDK 6.0r1.0 do not support the *tagType* argument to the getSubElement and getSubElementCount methods.

tagName	Optional. Tag name of the element for which this method searches. For example, pass "img" to count the number of <img> subelements of the element the called markup object represents. When not supplied, the function counts all subelements.

tagType	Optional. (Version 6.0 or higher) Type of tag to count. Valid values are:
	    plain: simple tag
	    binary: binary tag
	    container: container tag
	    /: end tag
	    !: SGML tag
	    bracket: Lasso tag [xxx]
	    percent: tag%%
	    ssi: Server Side Includes
	    !--: comment tags
	       (not for <jsxelement>, only for getSubElement)
	    asp or '%': ASP tags <% xxxx %>
	    websiphon or <<: WebSiphon tags << xxx >>
	    ?: JSP/Processing Instructions <? *xxx* ?>

setAttribute	Sets the value of the specified attribute of the HTML element, creating the attribute if necessary. Returns true on success. This method is useful for setting attributes that have names that conflict with JavaScript naming conventions.
markupObj.setAttribute (*name, value*)	

name	Name of the attribute.
value	New value of the attribute.

> **Example**

```
//assume an html document holding an image is open in Layout view
var img = document.documentElement.getSubElement("img", i);
img.layout.setAttribute("src", "/picture1.gif");
```

setInnerHTML	Replaces the HTML text of the element without altering its surrounding tag delimiters.
markupObj.setInnerHTML (*text*)	Do not call this method from within the parseBox (page 366) or the undoSignal (page 367) handler, or from a control-interaction event handler if the control that triggered that event is displayed by an Inspector window.

text	Replacement text.

setOuterHTML *markupObj*.setOuterHTML (*text*)		Replaces the HTML text of the element, including its outermost tag delimiters. Do not call this method from within the parseBox (page 366) or the undoSignal (page 367) handler, or from the control-interaction event handler if the control that triggered that event is displayed by an Inspector window.
text	Replacement text.	
split *elementObj*.split ([*sep*])		Returns this element's inner HTML as an array of strings. This method is useful for checking the contents of custom tags.
sep	Optional. Character to interpret as separator. When not supplied, the function interprets spaces as separators. The function does not split quoted strings containing the separator character.	

markup Object

Class: `JSXMarkup`

This object represents an individual markup item in an HTML document that is not an element, text block, or comment. For example, it could represent an entity, notation, or `CDATA` section.

- This object includes the Node Interface (page 229), whose properties and functions allow you to traverse the node tree.
- This object includes the Markup Interface (page 209), whose properties and functions allow you to directly access document content.
- This object defines additional properties and functions.

Acquiring markup objects

For a markup document, the document Object's documentElement property (page 138) holds the root object of the markup tree. The page's content is represented by nodes in the tree. To retrieve the root of the markup tree for a document:

```
var tree = document.documentElement;
```

You can traverse the markup tree using the Node Interface (page 229) properties and functions of any object in the tree.

In a `markup` object, the `elementType`, `nodeType`, and `nodeName` values depend on the tag type of the referenced markup: see the `<jsxelement>` (page 346) `type` attribute.

markup object properties

In addition to the properties of the Node Interface (page 229) and Markup Interface (page 209), the attributes in an element's source representation `defines` become the properties of the corresponding object. Setting a property writes the corresponding attribute value to the element's HTML source representation. Reading a property returns the property value, or `undefined` if the attribute does not exist.

You cannot delete a property from a JavaScript object. However, you can delete the attribute that defines that property from the source representation, then regenerate the object without the property. To do so, use methods of the `markup` object to edit the element's source representation, then reparse the document to generate a new tree of `markup` objects. The new `markup` object does not have a property representing the deleted attribute.

markup object functions

In addition to the functions of the Node Interface (page 229) and Markup Interface (page 209), the `markup` object defines these functions:

removeAttribute *markupObj*.removeAttribute (*attrName*)	Removes the specified attribute. Returns `true` on success. (Introduced in 7.0)
attrName The name of the attribute to remove.	

markupSettings Object

Class: `JSXMarkupSettings`

This object gives programmatic access to web settings, as set in the **Edit > Web Settings > Markup** window. Each object encapsulates the web settings for one DTD. The properties of this object correspond to the values that you can enter or set in the Inspector for a DTD you have selected in the **Markup** tab of the Web Settings window. (Introduced in 7.0)

Note: Modifications to settings that you make with this object are not persistent. They affect only the current GoLive session.

Acquiring a markupSettings object

Get a collection of these objects from the settings.markup Object's `markupSettings` property (page 252), and retrieve the elements by 0-based index:

> `settings.markup.markupSettings` [*index*]

Get the number of objects in the collection using the `length` property:

> `settings.markup.markupSettings.length`

markupSettings object properties

`elements`	Element Collection	A collection of all markupSetting.markupSettingElement Objects (page 220) in the DTD. Access by name or by index. The `length` property contains the count of elements.
`entities`	Entity Collection	A collection of all markupSetting.markupSettingEntity Objects(page 222) in the DTD. Access by name or by index. The `length` property contains the count of entities.
`ident`	String	An internal identifier for the DTD.
`publicIdent`	String	The public identifier of the DTD.
`systemIdent`	String	The URL of the DTD.

markupSetting object functions

addElement *markupSettingObj*.`addElement` (*tagName*)	Adds a new element to this DTD. Returns `true` on success.
tagName The tag name of the element to add.	

---

markupSetting.markupSettingAttribute Object

Class: JSXMarkupSettingAttribute

This object encapsulates an attribute of an element defined by a DTD. (Introduced in 7.0)

Note: Modifications to settings that you make with this object are not persistent. They affect only the current GoLive session.

This object has no functions.

Acquiring a markupSettingAttribute object

Get a collection of attributes from the attributes property of the markupSetting.markupSettingElement Object (page 220):

```
settings.markup.markupSettings[index].elements[index].attr
ibutes[index]
```

Get the number of objects in the collection using the length property:

```
settings.markup.markupSettings[index].elements[index].attr
ibutes.length
```

markupSettingAttribute object properties

The properties of this object correspond to the values that you can enter or set in the **Basic** tab of the Inspector for a Web Settings Attribute.

comment	String	A comment for this attribute.
create	Boolean	When true, the attribute is created.
kind	String	The type of attribute. One of: required alternate optional fixed
name	String	The attribute name.

stripp	Boolean	When `true`, the attribute can be stripped.

valueType	String	The value type of the attribute. One of:
		
		`none`
		`text`
		`encoded`
		`enum`
		`color`
		`number`
		`javascript`
		`ID`
		`IDRef`
		`IDRefs`
		`entity`
		`entities`
		`nmtoken`
		`nmtokens`
		`noation`

markupSetting.markupSettingElement Object

Class: JSXMarkupSettingElement

This object encapsulates an element defined by a DTD.

Note: Modifications to settings that you make with this object are not persistent. They affect only the current GoLive session.

(Introduced in 7.0)

Acquiring a markupSettingElement object

Get a collection of element objects from the `elements` property of the markupSettings Object (page 217):

```
settings.markup.markupSettings[index].elements[index]
```

Get the number of objects in the collection using the `length` property:

```
settings.markup.markupSettings[index].elements.length
```

markupSettingElement object properties

The properties of this object correspond to the values that you can enter or set in the **Basic** and **Output** tabs of the Inspector for a Web Settings Element.

anyAttributes	Boolean	When `true`, this element can have any attribute.
attributes	MarkupSetting Attribute Collection	A collection of markupSetting.markupSettingAttribute Objects (page 218) for the attributes of this element.
comment	String	A comment for this element.

content	String	The type of content allowed in this element. One of:
		`normal`
		`space`
		`text`

endTag	String	How end tags are used for this element. One of:
		`none`
		`required`
		`optional`
		`optionalWrite`
		`attribute`

indent	Boolean	When `true`, the contents are indented.
name	String	The element name.

separationInside	String	How separation is handled inside this element. One of: none start end small medium large xlarge
separationOutside	String	How separation is handled outside this element. One of: none start end small medium large xlarge
stripp	Boolean	When `true`, the element can be stripped.
structure	String	The structure type for this element. One of: block visible invisible container break

markupSettingElement object functions

addAttribute *markupSettingElementObj*.addAttribute (*attrName*)	Adds a new attribute to this element, if it does not yet exist. Returns `true` on success.
attrName The name of the attribute to add.	

markupSetting.markupSettingEntity Object

Class: JSXMarkupSettingEntity

This object encapsulates an entity defined by a DTD. (Introduced in 7.0)

Note: Modifications to settings that you make with this object are not persistent. They affect only the current GoLive session.

This object has no functions.

Acquiring a markupSettingEntity object

Get a collection of entity objects from the `entities` property of the markupSettings Object (page 217):

```
settings.markup.markupSettings[index].entities[index]
```

Get the number of objects in the collection using the `length` property:

```
settings.markup.markupSettings[index].entities.length
```

markupSettingEntity object properties

The properties of this object correspond to the values that you can enter or set in the **Basic** and **Content** tabs of the Inspector for a Web Settings Entity.

comment	String	A comment for this entity.
content	String	The content of this entity.
name	String	The entity name.
notation	String	The **Notation** value from the Inspector for the entity.
publicIdent	String	The public identifier of the DTD.
systemIdent	String	The URL of the DTD.

menu Object

Class: JSXMenu

This object represents a GoLive menu. GoLive creates a menu object when it interprets a `<jsxmenu>` (page 325) element.

Acquiring menu objects

- You can get menu objects from the menubar (page 48) global array, by name or by 0-based index:

```
var myMenu = menubar["ADBEHello"]
var myMenu = menubar["0"]
```

The JavaScript names of all predefined menus, submenus, and menu items in the GoLive menus are provided in Appendix B, "Menu Names." You can use these names to add script-defined submenus and items in positions relative to existing items. An extension cannot redefine the behavior of a built-in menu item.

menu object properties

Properties of the menu object allow you to use its JavaScript name to retrieve it, obtain the title it displays in the GoLive menu bar, get or set the currently selected menu item, and retrieve its menu items by name or by numeric index.

items	MenuItem Collection	Read-only array of this menu's menuItem Objects (page 225). You can retrieve items from this array by 0-based numeric index or by name. When two or more objects in a collection have the same name value, those objects cannot be retrieved by name reliably.
name	String	The JavaScript name of the menu object, as specified by the name attribute of the `<jsxmenu>` tag that defines the menu. Read-only.
title	String	The title of the menu as displayed to the user. Use the ampersand character (&) to tell Windows to underline the character following the ampersand and use the Alt key with this character as a hot-key to navigate to this menu item. Use double ampersands to display an ampersand character. The property value is the title string with the ampersand characters removed. In Mac OS, the SDK ignores ampersand characters and removes them from the displayed string.

menu object functions

You can use functions of the `menu` object to add or remove menu items programmatically.

addChild
menuObj.addChild
  (*type[, name, title, insertIndex, dynamic*])
menuObj.addChild
  (*type, name, [title, dynamic*])
	Adds a new submenu or item to the menu. Returns the created menu Object (page 223) or menuItem Object (page 225).
	(Introduced in 8.0)

type	The type of child this method creates, one of the strings:
	    item
	    menu

name	Optional. JavaScript name of the menu Object (page 223) or menuItem Object (page 225) this method creates.
title	Optional. The new menu or item's display text. A value of "–" adds a separator to the menu. If not specified, the name value is used as the display text.
insertIndex	Optional. Menu item position after which this method inserts the new menu or item. When 0, the menu or item is added at the beginning of the list. The default value is -1, meaning that the new menu or item is added to the end of the list.
dynamic	Optional. For a new item, if true the created menu item is dynamic. Does nothing if specified for a new menu. Default is true.
addItem *menuObj*.addItem (*name, title* [, *before*])	Adds a new menu item before or after an existing item. Returns the created menuItem Object (page 225).
name	JavaScript name of the menuItem Object (page 225) this method creates.
title	The new menu item's display text. A value of "–" adds a separator to the menu.
before	Optional. Menu item position before which this method inserts the new menu item.
removeAll *menuObj*.removeAll ()	Removes all menu items from this menu.
removeItem *menuObj*.removeItem (*name*) *menuObj*.removeItem (*index*)	Removes the specified menu item.
name	JavaScript name of the menuItem Object (page 225) to remove.
index	0-based index of the item to remove.

menuItem Object

Class: `JSXMenuItem`

This object represents a menu item in one of the GoLive menus. GoLive creates a `menuItem` object when it interprets a `<jsxitem>` (page 326) element that is part of a `<jsxmenu>` (page 325) element. You can add menus to the menubar, and items to these menus or to the predefined menus.

You define the behavior of your menu items in the menuSignal (page 363) event handlers that you register. GoLive SDK generates this event when the user chooses any extension-defined menu item.

Acquiring menuItem objects

- When the user chooses a menu item, GoLive generates the menuSignal (page 363) event, and passes your handler a menuEvent (page 382) object. The object for the selected menu item is the target:

  ```
  var thisItem = menuEvt.target
  ```

  Your handler performs the tasks associated with the target menu item.

- The `items` property of a menu Object (page 223) holds an array of `menuItem` objects for the items in that menu. You can retrieve individual menu items from this array by name or by 0-based numeric index:

  ```
  var myFirstItem = myMenu.items["MyItem1"]
  var myFirstItem = myMenu.items[0]
  ```

The JavaScript names of all predefined menus, submenus, and menu items in the GoLive menus are provided in Appendix B, "Menu Names." You can use these names to add script-defined submenus and items in positions relative to existing items. An extension cannot redefine the behavior of a built-in menu item.

menuItem object properties

checked	Boolean	When `true`, the menu item is checked, when `false` it is not checked. Read/write. For dynamic items, can be set by the menuSetup (page 363) handler.
dynamic	—	When this valueless property is present, the SDK generates the menuSetup (page 363) event before displaying the menu item. Your registered handler sets the menu item's `enabled` or `checked` states as needed. When this property is not present, GoLive enables the menu item without placing a checkmark next to it.

---

enabled	Boolean	When `true`, the item is enabled, when `false` it is disabled. By default, menu items are enabled upon creation. The user cannot choose a disabled menu item, which is drawn in gray text. Read/write. For dynamic items, can be set by the menuSetup (page 363) handler.
menu	Menu	The menu in which this item appears. Read-only.
name	String	The JavaScript name of the menu item object, as specified by the `name` attribute of the `<jsxmenuitem>` tag that defines the menu item. Read-only.
title	String	The text this item displays in the menu. If the value of this property is a single dash, the menu item is a separator.

menuItem object functions

notify *menuItemObj*.notify ()	Generates the menuSignal (page 363) event with this object as the target, as if the user clicked this menu item.

setShortCut
menuObj.setShortCut
  (modifier, character)
	Sets a character combination for a keyboard shortcut that invokes this menu item's behavior. For example:
	  `myMenuItem.setShortCut("shift+alt", "x");`
	Returns `true` on success.

modifier	The modifier key combination for the keyboard shortcut. Values are `shift`, `control`, and `alt`. Can be the single value `control`, or any two or three values combined with a plus (+) operator. Cannot be only `alt` or only `shift`. In Mac OS, `control` maps to CMD and `alt` maps to OPT.
character	The alphabetic character for the keyboard shortcut.

module Object

Class: `JSXModule`

This object represents an individual extension module. It contains properties and functions that aid in translation and debugging.

Acquiring a module object

The SDK creates a `module` object when it interprets a `Main.html` file, regardless of whether that file provides a `<jsxmodule>` element. This object's `folder` property returns a reference to the folder that holds the `Main.html` file that the SDK interpreted to create the object.

To get the `module` object that represents the currently running extension to JavaScript callers within that module's scope, use the `module` global variable:

```
module
```

module object properties

Properties of the `module` object provide the JavaScript name of the extension module, enable debugging services, and enable dynamic localization of the module.

`callbackStack`	Array	An array of strings identifying the currently running callbacks. (Introduced in 7.0)
`debug`	Boolean	When `true`, debugging services are enabled. The SDK sets this property to `true` when any currently loaded module provides the valueless `debug` attribute in its `<jsxmodule>` (page 321) tag.
`folder`	File	A file Object (page 158) representing the folder that holds the `Main.html` file GoLive interpreted to create this module.
`info`	String	The descriptive string from the `info` attribute of the `<jsxmodule>` (page 321) tag for this module. (Introduced in 7.0)
`locale`	String	The language in which the host GoLive application is running. When set, overrides the system's locale information. This value is a country code defined by the ISO-3166-1 standard. For example, the `DE` code represents German and the `FR` code represents French. Note that the `US` code represents all dialects of English. The value is upper-case. Setting this value affects the way the `localize` method works; it does not affect the behavior of menus or dialogs.
`name`	String	This extension module's JavaScript name (the `title`) as a valid JavaScript symbol name that can be used to identify this module, for example, in an ExtendScript `import` statement.

timeout	Boolean	When `true`, the execution of JavaScript in this module terminates after the period specified in the `timeout` attribute of the `<jsxmodule>` (page 321) tag. When `false`, timeout behavior is disabled for the module.
title	String	This extension module's JavaScript name, as specified by the `name` attribute of the `<jsxmodule>` (page 321) tag the SDK interpreted to create this module.
		If the extension does not supply a `<jsxmodule>` element or does not supply a `name` attribute for this element, or if the supplied name is not a unique and valid JavaScript name, the SDK generates a unique and valid JavaScript name. Read-only.
trace	Boolean	When `true`, a trace for each callback is written to the JavaScript shell. (Introduced in 7.0)
version	String	The version string from the `version` attribute of the `<jsxmodule>` (page 321) tag for this module. (Introduced in 7.0)

module object functions

kill *moduleObj*.`kill()`	Terminates this module immediately, without processing running callbacks or calling terminateModule (page 359). (Introduced in 7.0)
localize *moduleObj*.`localize`(*message*)	Attempts to translate the specified string from the English language to the language in which GoLive is running. Returns a string containing the translated message, if found, or the original message if no translation is found.
	To translate the text, the SDK first searches for this string in the localization table that this module's `<jsxlocale>` (page 350) element provides. If the table provides a translation that fits the current language setting, this method returns the translated string. If not, this method returns the original string.
message The message to translate.	
reload *moduleObj*.`reload()`	Reloads this module's script. Does not call the initializeModule (page 359) callback. (Introduced in 7.0)
switchOff *moduleObj*.`switchOff()`	Turns this module off, as of the next application startup. (Introduced in 7.0)
terminate *moduleObj*.`terminate()`	Terminates the module. Finishes processing running callbacks, calls the terminateModule (page 359) callback, then removes this module. (Introduced in 7.0)

Node Interface

This interface defines a set of properties and functions that are shared by the following objects:

- attribute Object (page 62)
- comment Object (page 75)
- document Object (page 138)
- documentFragment Object (page 151)
- element Object (page 156)
- markup Object (page 215)
- text Object (page 276)

These properties and functions are defined according to the W3C DOM recommendations (see `http://www.w3.org/TR/2000/WD-DOM-Level-1-20000929/`). They allow you to navigate through a tree of nodes in any hierarchical arrangement of objects or elements.

Node interface properties

All properties are read-only.

childNodes	NodeList	A nodeList Object (page 232) containing the child nodes of this object.
firstChild	Node	First child node if the object has children.
lastChild	Node	Last child node if the object has children.
nextSibling	Node	The next sibling node if one exists.
nodeName	String	The node name.
nodeType	Number	The node type identifier.
nodeValue	String	The content of a text or comment element, the value of an attribute, otherwise `null`.
ownerDocument	Document	The document Object (page 138) that contains this node.
parentNode	Node	The parent node.
previousSibling	Node	The previous sibling node if one exists.

The `nodeName`, `nodeType`, and `nodeValue` properties have the following values in the following objects:

Object	nodeType	nodeName	nodeValue
attribute Object (page 62)	2	attribute name	attribute value
comment Object (page 75)	8	`#comment`	content
document Object (page 138)	9	`#document`	`null`
documentFragment Object (page 151)	11	`#document-fragment`	`null`
element Object (page 156)	1	tag name	`null`
text Object (page 276)	3	`#text`	content

In a `markup` object, these values depend on the tag type of the referenced markup: see the `<jsxelement>` (page 346) `type` attribute.

Node interface functions

appendChild *nodeObj*.`appendChild`(*newChild*)	Appends a new child at the end of the current list of children. Returns the added node object on success, otherwise returns `null`.
newChild The child node to append.	
cloneNode *nodeObj*.`cloneNode`(*deep*)	Creates a clone of this node. Returns the new object or object array, or `null` on failure.
deep If `true`, clone all subnodes.	
hasChildNodes *nodeObj*.`hasChildNodes`()	Reports whether this node has children. Returns `true` if children exist.
insertBefore *nodeObj*.`insertBefore` (*newChild*, *refChild*)	Inserts a new child before an existing child of this node. Returns the inserted node object on success, otherwise returns `null`.
newChild The child node to insert.	
refChild The existing child that identifies the location.	
removeChild *nodeObj*.`removeChild`(*child*)	Removes an existing child of this node. Returns the removed node object on success, otherwise returns `null`.
child The child node to remove.	

replaceChild	Replaces an existing child of this node. Returns the replaced
nodeObj.replaceChild (*newChild*, *oldChild*)	node object on success, otherwise returns `null`.
newChild	The child node to insert.
refChild	The existing child to replace.

nodeList Object

Class: `JSXNodeList`

A collection of elements in a markup tree. Nodes in a `nodeList` can be `markup` or `element` objects, or any of their subtypes, such as `comment` objects.

Acquiring a nodeList object

- Get a `nodeList` object from the `childNodes` property of a comment Object (page 75), text Object (page 276), or element Object (page 156).

  elementObj`.childNodes`

- Get a `nodeList` object from the document Object (page 138) or element Object's getElementsByTagName (page 143) function:

  documentObj`.getElementsByTagName ("img");`

nodeList object properties

`length`	Number	Number of nodes in the list.

nodeList object functions

`item` *nodeListObj*`.item(`*index*`)`	Returns the object at the specified position in the list. You can also access nodes in the list directly by index: *nodeListObj*`[`*index*`]`
index The 0-based position index of the desired item.	

panel Object

Class: JSXPanel

This object represents a panel within a window that frames and groups a set of controls. It can be the direct child of a window, of another panel, or of a split panel or tab panel. If it is in a tabpanel Object (page 274), it represents one tab. (Introduced in 7.0)

Like a window, a panel can contain controls. You can define the controls as part of the tag that creates the panel, or add them dynamically using the panel object's add function.

A panel object is a type of control, and inherits all properties and functions of the control Object Types (page 78).

Acquiring a panel object

- The SDK creates a panel object when it interprets a `<jsxview>` (page 332) tag that is contained in a window definition. You can obtain the object by name or index from the parent window's children collection:

      myPanel = *windowObj*.children [*panelName*] ;
      tabPanelObj.children [*panelName*] ;

- To create a new panel object dynamically, call a window Object's add (page 317) function with type="panel". Pass an object containing these optional creation parameters:

name	String	Unique JavaScript name of the panel.
alignment	Array	An array containing the horizontal and vertical alignment string values for the panel. See `<jsxcontrol>` halign (page 339) and valign (page 339) attributes. Default is ["left", "top"].
icon	Picture	The name of an image defined in the extension file, to use as the tab icon for this panel when it is in a tabpanel Object (page 274).

For example:

      myWin.add ("panel", [left, top, right, bottom],
      "initial title",
          { name:"myPanel1, alignment:["left", "top"],
      icon:"myImage1" });

- The SDK creates a panel object known as a *view resource* when it interprets a `<jsxview>` (page 332) tag that is not contained in a window definition. You can access this object by name to add it to a window dynamically:

```
myWin.add ( "panel", "viewResourceName",
    { name:"myPanel2", alignment:["left", "top"],
icon:"myImage2" } );
```

If you add a `panel` object to a tabpanel Object (page 274), it represents one tab in the tabbed window. The `alignment` value is ignored. The position of the panel is 0,0 and the size is defined by the parent `tabPanel`.

panel object properties

In addition to those of the control Object Types (page 78), the `panel` object defines this property:

`children`	Control Collection	A collection of all children in this panel—that is, all controls that are added to this panel or defined within it. Read only.

panel object functions

In addition to those of the control Object Types (page 78), the `panel` object defines this function to add child controls dynamically.

add *panelObj*.add(*type*[, *placement*, *text*, *creationParam*])	Creates and returns a new control Object Types (page 78) of the given type and adds it as a child of this container. This is identical to the window Object's add (page 317) function, except that you cannot add a `tabpanel` control.
type	The type of control to create. One of: button checkbox colorfield combobox custom edittext filelist frame hierarchy line list panel preview progressbar radiobutton scrollbar slider source statictext urlgetter Each of the control types is described under control Object Types (page 78).
placement	Optional. A read/write array containing the coordinates of the window in the form [*left*, *top*, *right*, *bottom*]. You can set this property using an JavaScript object in the form {left:value, top:value, right:value, bottom:value} or {left:value, top:value, width:value, height:value}.
text	Optional. An initial value or set of values for the control, depending on the type: • An initial text value for the new control, such as a button's text label. • Initial items for a combo box popup or list, as a comma-separated list of strings; for example "item1, item2". • The initial numeric value and minimum and maximum values for a scrollbar, slider, or progressbar; for example, 50, 0, 100.
creationParam	Optional. A JavaScript object that contains properties to set special initial values of the child element. See the individual type descriptions of the control Object Types (page 78).

---

remove	Removes a specified control from the `children` array of the panel. (Introduced in 8.0)
panelObj.`remove` (*name*) *panelObj*.`remove` (*index*) *panelObj*.`remove` (*controlObj*)	

name	The JavaScript name of the child to remove.
index	The 0-based index of the child to remove.
controlObj	The control object for the child to remove.

picture Object

Class: `JSXPicture`

This object encapsulates the properties of an image, and provides a method for drawing the image.

Acquiring a picture object

The SDK creates a `picture` object when it interprets an `<img>` element that references a graphical image file, such as a GIF or JPEG file. The SDK provides its own version of the `<img>` (page 345) tag that allows extensions to assign JavaScript names to `<img>` elements.

You can create a `picture` object explicitly using the global function createPicture (page 50), or you can use the `<img>` (page 345) tag in source and let the SDK create the object.

picture object properties

Properties of the `picture` object associate a JavaScript name with an image, and scale the picture to a specified width and height.

height	Number	The height of the picture in pixels. Setting this property causes the picture to be stretched accordingly the next time GoLive draws it.
name	String	The JavaScript name of this object, as specified by the `name` attribute of the `<img>` tag the SDK interpreted to create the object. Read-only.
width	Number	The width of the picture in pixels. Setting this property causes the picture to be stretched accordingly the next time GoLive draws it.

picture object functions

draw *pictureObj*.draw (*x*, *y* [, *width*, *height*])	Draws the image at the specified location in Layout view.
	The specified position places the picture in the coordinate plane of the container (a window Object, page 313, or panel Object, page 233) that displays the image. The origin of the coordinate system, (0,0), is the upper-left corner of the container. The coordinate value is the number of pixels by which GoLive offsets the picture's location from this origin. • Positive x values specify a location to the right of the origin, while negative values specify a location to the left of the origin. • Positive y values specify a location below the origin, while negative values specify a location above the origin.
x, *y*	The coordinates of the picture's upper-left corner.
width, *height*	Optional. The width and height in pixels for drawing the picture. Does not change the original image. If the size is different from that of the original, the drawn image is stretched or compressed to fit.

point Object

Class: `Point`

This object encapsulates the position of an interface element (window or control) relative to its parent or the screen. The upper left of a window or the screen is considered the origin (0,0).

(Introduced in 8.0)

Acquiring a points object

Get this object from a control Object Types (page 78) or window Object (page 313), from the element's `location` property:

```
var mySize = controlObj.bounds.location;
var mySize = controlObj.location;
```

dimension object properties

This object has the following properties:

x	Number	The horizontal position of the element with respect to its parent window or the screen, in pixels.
y	Number	The vertical position of the element with respect to its parent window or the screen, in pixels.

prefs Object

Class: JSXPrefs

This object represents application preferences. Extension modules can use the `prefs` object to store preference data that persists between user sessions. Because the `prefs` global property makes this object always available to all extension modules, extensions can also use it to share or exchange user preference data.

Acquiring the prefs object

You can get this object from the `prefs` global variable.

```
prefs
```

prefs object properties

Extension modules create their own preferences as properties of the `prefs` object. To create a new preference value, create a `prefs` object property.

For example, the following JavaScript code creates the `present` property that holds the "I am present" string value.

```
prefs.present = "I am present";
```

The following tests for the presence of this property and this value.

```
if (prefs.present == "I am present")
{
    // your code that uses prefs
}
```

prefs object functions

flush	Writes the current preferences to a file immediately.
prefsObj.flush ();	

progressLog Object

Class: `JSXProgressLog`

This object implements a text message buffer with stack-like capabilities. You can use it to log error messages and progress information.

Acquiring a progressLog object

You can create a `progressLog` object whenever you need one. To do so, call the app Object's createProgressLog (page 57) method:

```
app.createProgressLog()
```

Before attempting to add messages to the progress log, call *progressLogObj*.`begin` (page 241) once.

progressLog object functions

The functions of the `progressLog` object manipulate the contents of the progress log stack and specify the nesting level at which to add a new message.

addMessage *progressLogObj*.`addMessage` (*kind*, *message*[, *url*])	Adds a message string to the progress log at the stack pointer's current level.

kind	Type of icon to display. One of:
	    `error`: Error message icon.
	    `fatal`: Icon for fatal errors.
	    `info`: Icon for information.
	    `item`: Icon for a single item.
	    `warning`: Warning icon.

message	String to add to the message stack.
url	Optional. URL associated with this message, used when user double-clicks this line or displays its contextual menu.
begin *progressLogObj*.`begin`(*title*, *text*)	Initializes a progress log. Call once before calling any other `progressLog` methods.
title	Title for the Progress Log window.
text	Descriptive text in the Progress Log window.
end *progressLogObj*.`end()`	Stops using the progress log to store progress messages.
popMessage *progressLogObj*.`popMessage()`	Removes the topmost level of the progress log's message stack.

pushMessage	Adds a message string to the progress log at the top of the
progressLogObj.pushMessage	progress log's message stack and creates a new top level.
(*type*, *message* [, *url*])	

type	Type of icon to display. One of:
	error: Error message icon.
	fatal: Icon for fatal errors.
	info: Icon for information.
	item: Icon for a single item.
	warning: Warning icon.
message	String to add to the message stack.
url	Optional. URL associated with this message, used when user double-clicks this line or displays its contextual menu.

serverInfo Object

Class: JSXServerInfo

This object encapsulates information about every server used in GoLive. You can use a `serverInfo` object as a parameter when you create an FTP Object (page 171).

Note: The settings provided by this object must be determined when the FTP Object (page 171) or DAV Object (page 132) is created. You cannot set the options after object creation.

Acquiring a serverInfo object

- You can retrieve a `serverInfo` object for each server known to GoLive from the serverInfoCollection Object (page 245) in the app Object's `server` property (page 55).

- You can retrieve a `serverInfo` object for each web-publishing server of a site using the serverInfoCollection Object (page 245) in the website Object's `server` property (page 297).

  You can add servers to and remove servers from these lists.

- You can create a `serverInfo` object using the serverInfo object constructor (page 244).

serverInfo object properties

All properties are read/write.

host	String	The host name. For example: `"ftp.myserver.com"`.
iso88591	Boolean	When `true`, files are translated to ISO 88591 encoding before they are exchanged with an FTP server. Affects only Mac OS FTP connections. Default is `true` in Mac OS, `false` in Windows.
keyPassword	String	The password string for public-key authentication. Default is the empty string.
name	String	Unique name of the server data object.
passive	Boolean	When `true`, passive mode is on for FTP connections. Default determined by preferences.
password	String	The access password, in plain text.
path	String	The path on the server. For example: `"/myfolder/mysubfolder/"` For a folder on a remote file system, you must use a trailing slash to indicate that the last item in the path is a folder name and not a file name.

privateKey	File object, String	The file for the private key for public-key authentication. Can be a file Object (page 158), an absolute path string, or an absolute URL string. Default is `null`.

protocol	String	Protocol identifier. One of:
		`ftp`
		`http`
		`file`

publicKey	Boolean	When `true`, use public-key authentication. Default is `false`. Used only when `security` is `ssh` or `sftp`.
security	String	The type of connection security. One of: `none` (default) `ssl` `ssh` (FTP connections only) `sftp` (FTP connections only)
standard	Boolean	When `true`, the underlying networking framework is FTP, when `false`, it is DAV.
user	String	The user name.

serverInfo object functions

serverInfo object constructor new JSXServerInfo(*name*, *hostAndPath* [, *userName*, *password*])	Creates and returns a new `serverInfo` object. (Introduced in 7.0)
name	The JavaScript name of the `ServerInfo` object.
hostAndPath	The hostname or hostname and path for the `ServerInfo` object.
userName	Optional. The user login name on the server.
password	Optional. The user password on the server, in plain text.

➤ Examples

```
var f = new JSXServerInfo( "myServer", "ftp://ftp.myserver.com" );
var f = new JSXServerInfo( "myServer",
  "ftp.myserver.com/myfolder/myfile.txt" );
var f = new JSXServerInfo( "myServer", "ftp.myserver.com/myfolder",
  "myname", "mypassword" );
```

serverInfoCollection Object

Class: `JSXServerInfoCollection`

This object collects an array of serverInfo Objects (page 243) for all known server data in GoLive as well as for known web-publishing servers of a site. (Introduced in 7.0)

Acquiring a serverInfoCollection object

This object is available as the `server` property of either the app Object (page 53) or a website Object (page 296).

```
myServerList = app.server;
myServerList = websiteObj.server;
```

You can access objects in the collection by name, or by 0-based index:

serverInfoCollection [*"name"*]
serverInfoCollection [*index*]

serverInfoCollection object properties

`length`	Number	Number of objects in the collection.

serverInfoCollection object functions

The functions allow you to add servers to and remove them from the collection.

add *serverInfoCollectionObj* . `add` (*server*)	Adds a new server to the collection. Returns `true` on success.
`server`	The serverInfo Object (page 243) for the server to add.
remove *serverInfoCollectionObj* . `remove` (*server*)	Removes a specified server from the collection. Returns `true` on success.
`server`	The serverInfo Object (page 243) for the server to remove.

settings Object

Class: `JSXSettings`

This object provides access to a variety of settings, configurations, and user preferences in the GoLive application running the extension. You can get and set properties of this object to load and extend DTDs, user settings, registered file types, web database settings, and so on. For example, the following retrieves the `settings` CSS object, which holds style sheet information:

```
// get settings object from the settings global
var cssStyles = settings.css;
```

You can also use this object to add your own tag definitions and file types to the internal databases GoLive uses to parse documents.

This object has no functions.

Acquiring a settings object

You can get the `settings` object from the settings (page 48) global property:

```
mySettingsObj = settings;
```

settings object properties

Properties of the `settings` object provide access to browser settings, style sheet settings, and more.

`aglmodules`	SettingsAGLModule Collection	This collection contains settings.aglmodule Objects (page 248) that allow you to enable or to disable GoLive modules programmatically. Changes take effect on restart. You can access objects by name or 0-based index. **Note:** Modules whose names contain spaces cannot be accessed by name, only by index.
`css`	SettingsCSS	The settings.css Object (page 250) contains style sheet information.
`fileMappings`	SettingsFileMappings	The settings.fileMappings Object (page 251) permits the loading of additional file mappings that GoLive should recognize.
`markup`	SettingsMarkup	The settings.markup Object (page 252) allows the configuration of markup languages and text generation.

pdf	SettingPDF	The settingsPDF Object (page 254) provides access to PDF preset option collections.
sdk	SettingSDK	The settingsSDK Object (page 255) provides access to general settings for the GoLive SDK.
sdkmodules	SettingsSDKModule Collection	This collection contains settings.sdkmodule Objects (page 256) that allow you to enable or to disable GoLive SDK extensions programmatically. Changes take effect on restart. You can access objects by name or 0-based index. **Note:** Modules whose names contain spaces cannot be accessed by name, only by index.
userAgentProfiles	SettingsUAP	The settings.userAgentProfiles Object (page 258) enables you to add user agent profiles to the GoLive environment.

settings.aglmodule Object

Class: `JSXSettingAGLModulesCollection`

This object allows you to enable or to disable GoLive modules programmatically. Changes take effect on restart.

Acquiring a settings.aglmodule object

A collection of these objects is available from the settings Object's `aglmodules` property (page 246):

```
var myModArray = settings.aglmodules;
```

You can access elements of the collection by module name or by 0-based numeric index:

```
settings.aglmodules[0].switchOff() // turn off the first
module
settings.aglmodules[name].switchOff() // turn off name
module
```

Note: Modules whose names contain spaces cannot be accessed by name, only by index.

settings.aglmodules Collection object properties

`length`	Number	The number of elements in this collection. Read only.

settings.aglmodule object functions

The functions of this object allow you to check that a module is known (that is, properly loaded) and active. A module can be known, but not active. The functions also allow you to activate or inactivate a module.

isKnown `settings.aglmodules[nameOrNum].isKnown()`	Reports whether the module is known to the GoLive application. Returns `true` if the specified module has loaded successfully.
isOn `settings.aglmodules[nameOrNum].isOn()`	Returns `true` if the specified module is active.

switchOff
`settings.aglmodules[nameOrNum].switchOff`
`([keyword])`
	Deactivates the specified GoLive module. This method cannot disable the Modules Manager or extension modules. To disable extension modules, use the `switchOff` function of the settings.sdkmodule Object (page 256).

keyword	Optional. Pass $$$all$$$ to enable all GoLive modules.

---

switchOn settings.aglmodules[*nameOrNum*].switchOn ([*keyword*])	Activates the specified GoLive module. This method cannot enable the Modules Manager or extension modules. To enable extension modules, use the switchOn function of the settings.sdkmodule Object (page 256).
keyword	Optional. Pass $$$all$$$ to disable all GoLive modules.

settings.css Object

Class: `JSXSettingsCSS`

This object provides programmatic access to style sheet information. The object has no properties.

Acquiring a settings.css object

Get the object from the settings Object's `css` property (page 246):

```
var myCSSSettings= settings.css;
```

settings.css object functions

The functions allow you to modify the CSS style sheet that the application uses to render HTML by loading additional `.css` files.

loadBasic `settings.css.loadBasic(URL)`	Loads a basic CSS style sheet that the application uses to render HTML. The new style sheet is cascaded with the current one, it does not replace the current one. Returns `true` on success.
URL	URL for the style sheet file.
loadPrefs `settings.css.loadPrefs(URL)`	Loads CSS preferences from the values in the specified settings file. Returns `true` on success.

URL	URL for the style sheet settings file. The default values are specified in the file `Settings/MarkupBasics/css.pref`.
	Variables that can be set in a preferences file include:
	    `version`
	    `switch`
	    `interface`
	    `output`
	    `length`

loadSelectors `settings.css.loadSelectors(URL)`	Loads CSS selectors from the specified file. The CSS selectors are additions to a submenu in the Context Menu in the CSS Editor. Returns `true` on success.
URL	URL for the style sheet file.

settings.fileMappings Object

Class: `JSXSettingsFileMappings`

This object permits an extension to load additional file mappings that GoLive should recognize.

This object has no properties.

Acquiring a settings.fileMappings object

Get the object from the settings Object's `fileMappings` property (page 246):

```
var settings.fileMappings
```

settings.fileMappings object functions

loadMappings `settings.fileMappings.loadMappings(URL)`	Reads `.aglfmi` files from the specified folder to extend the GoLive application's file mapping information. Returns `true` on success. An `.aglfmi` file is an XML file that has the same syntax as the file mapping files that reside in the `Settings/FileMappings/` folder.
URL	URL to folder containing `.aglfmi` files.

settings.markup Object

Class: JSXSettingsMarkup

This object enables you to get and set markup-language and text-generation preferences.

Acquiring a settings.markup object

Get the object from the settings Object's `markup` property (page 246):

```
var settings.markup
```

settings.markup object properties

Properties of the object enable you to get and set preferences that govern source parsing and text generation.

`commentScripts`	String	A comma-separated list of languages in which the content of `<script></script>` are not put into "`<!--`" and "`-->`".
`foreignBinaryToken`	String	Corresponds to `app.symmetricTokens`.
`foreignStartToken`	String	Corresponds to `app.asymmetricTokens`.
`htmlAttrCase`	String	How new HTML attributes names are written to source code. Read/write. One of: upper lower capital database Only meaningful for HTML; other markup languages are presumed to be case sensitive.
`htmlElementCase`	String	How new HTML element names are written to source code. Read/write. One of: upper lower capital database Only meaningful for HTML; other markup languages are presumed to be case sensitive.
`indentAmount`	Number	Stores the number of indention characters which are written for every indention.
`indentAsciiNum`	Number	Stores the character that is used to create markup source code indention. Value is the ASCII number. Valid values ar 9 and 32.

`lineBreakMode`	String	The global line break mode of the application. Read/write. One of:
		
		 `mac`
		 `unix`
		 `win`

`markupSettings`	Markup Settings Collection	A collection of markupSettings Objects (page 217) that encapsulate web settings for all current known DTDs.

`quoteMode`	String	How new attribute values are quoted. One of:
		
		 `always`
		 `exceptNums`
		 `necessary`

`scanBrackets`	Boolean	When `true`, the characters "`[`" and "`]`" in source code are treated as braces for special elements. Old versions of the Lasso tool used this syntax. This value is the same as that of the property `app.scanBrackets`.

settings.markup object functions

These functions manipulate Adobe GoLive Markup Glue Base (`.aglmgb`) files and Adobe GoLive Markup Glue Addition (`.aglmga`) files.

- The glue base is an XML file that contains information GoLive needs to work with markup documents.

- The glue addition file is an XML file that specifies the glue it extends and the additions it defines.

Information on how to create your own glue files is not yet available. For examples, look at the `.aglmgb` and `.aglmga` files that GoLive provides.

loadGlueAdditions `settings.markup.loadGlueAdditions(URL)`	Loads markup glue additions from specified `.aglmga` files. GoLive treats these files as an addition to existing markup glues. Returns the number of glue additions loaded.
URL	URL for an additional markup glue base (`.aglmga`) file or the folder that contains one or more such files.
loadGlueBase `settings.markup.loadGlueBase(URL)`	Loads markup glue base from the specified file. You can use this method to patch existing Markup Glues. Returns the number of glue bases loaded.
URL	URL for the markup glue base (`.aglmgb`) file or the folder that contains it.

settingsPDF Object

Class: `SettingsPDF`

This object provides access to preset options for creating PDF files from documents with the document Object's createPDF (page 142) method. (Introduced in 8.0)

Acquiring a settingsSDK object

Get the object from the settings Object's `pdf` property (page 247):

```
var myPDFSetting = settings.pdf;
```

settingsPDF object properties

defaultPreset	String	The name of the currently active PDF preset options collection, used when none is specified.
presetNames	Array of String	The names of all available PDF preset option collections.

settingsSDK Object

Class: `SettingsSDK`

This object allows you to change internal settings in the GoLive CS2 SDK. (Introduced in 8.0)

Acquiring a settingsSDK object

Get the object from the settings Object's `sdk` property (page 247):

```
var mySDKSetting = settings.sdk;
```

settingsSDK object properties

`cmdDebug`	Boolean	When `true`, enables the debugger to track commands entered on the command line. Default is `false`.
`internalDebugger`	Boolean	When `true` (the default), the SDK uses the internal debugger. When `false`, it uses the ExtendScript Toolkit.
`notifyGC`	Boolean	When `true`, garbage collection operations in the JavaScript engine are reported in the debugger's output window; for example: `>> GC in myExtension` Default is `false`.
`outputFile`	File	The file Object (page 158) for the file to which output strings are written. Default is `null`.
`posix`	Boolean	When `true` (the default), the file Object (page 158) uses POSIX path strings in Mac OS, with the slash (/) delimiter. Otherwise, it uses HFS path strings with the colon (:) delimiter.
`refreshWhileResize`	Boolean	When `true`, custom controls are redrawn during a resizing of the parent window. Default is `false`.
`reparse4Attributes`	Boolean	When `false` (the default), no reparse is performed after modifying an attribute of a markup element.
`startupScriptVisible`	Boolean	When `true` (the default), the source code for startup scripts is available to the debugger.
`writeToLogWindow`	Boolean	When `true` (the default), all warnings and errors are written to the GoLive log window.

settings.sdkmodule Object

Class: JSXSettingsSDKModulesCollection

This object allows you to enable or to disable GoLive SDK extensions programmatically. Changes take effect on restart.

Acquiring a settings.sdkmodule object

A collection of these objects is available as a property of the object that the settings global variable provides.

```
var myModArray = settings.sdkmodules
```

The collection's index operator [] retrieves its elements by extension name or by numeric index:

```
settings.sdkmodules[0].switchOff() // turn off the first
module
settings.sdkmodules[name].switchOff() // turn off name
module
```

Note: Modules whose names contain spaces cannot be accessed by name, only by index.

settings.sdkmodules Collection object properties

length	Number	The number of elements in this collection. Read only.

settings.sdkmodule object functions

The functions allow you to check that an extension is known (that is, properly loaded) and active. An extension can be known, but not active. The functions also allow you to activate or inactivate an extension.

isKnown settings.sdkmodules[*nameOrNum*].isKnown()	Reports whether the specified extension module is available to the GoLive application. Returns true if the extension has loaded successfully.
isOn settings.sdkmodules[*nameOrNum*].isOn()	Reports whether the specified extension module is active. Returns true if the extension is active.
switchOff settings.sdkmodules[*nameOrNum*].switchOff ([*keyword*])	Deactivates the specified extension module.
keyword Optional. Pass $$$all$$$ to disable all extension modules.	

switchOn settings.sdkmodules[*nameOrNum*].switchOn 　([*keyword*])	Activates the specified extension module.
keyword	Optional. Pass $$$all$$$ to enable all extension modules.

settings.userAgentProfiles Object

Class: JSXSettingsUAP

This object provides access to preferences that govern the way GoLive Layout view and syntax checking models the behavior of various HTML *user agents* such as browsers or mobile Internet device displays.

A user agent specifies its preferences as an `.agluap` file that resides in the agent's own subfolder of the `GoLive/Settings/User Agent Profiles` folder. If necessary, this folder can also hold other agent-specific files, such as fonts or graphics GoLive needs to simulate the user agent's display.

Acquiring a settings userAgentProfiles object

Get the object from the settings Object's `userAgentProfiles` property (page 247):

```
var myAgtProfiles = settings.userAgentProfiles
```

settings.userAgentProfiles object properties

`defaultProfile`	String	The unique identifying name of the default User Agent Profile.

settings.userAgentProfiles object functions

The function manipulates Adobe GoLive User Agent Profile (`.agluap`) files.

`loadProfiles` `settings.userAgentProfiles.loadProfiles(URL)`	Reads the specified `.agluap` files to define new User Agent Profiles or patch existing ones. Returns the number of loaded profiles.
URL URL for the .agluap files.	

siteCollection Object

Class: `JSXSiteCollection`

This object provides iterative access to a collection of siteReference Objects (page 260) that represent the resources a particular site uses, such as files, active documents, and links. The functions facilitate batch-processing of the `siteReference` elements.

The object has no properties. You can access the collection elements directly using a 0-based numeric index, or by calling the collection's functions.

Acquiring siteCollection objects

The get methods of the siteReference Object (page 260), such as getFiles (page 265), getIncoming (page 265), and getOutgoing (page 265), return a collection of this type.

siteCollection object functions

add *siteCollectionObj*.add(*newRef*)	Adds a specified site reference to this collection. Returns `true` on success. (Introduced in 8.0)
newRef	The siteReference Object (page 260) for the file to be added to the collection.
first *siteCollectionObj*.first()	Returns the first siteReference Object (page 260) in the collection, or `null` if the collection is empty.
last *siteCollectionObj*.last()	Returns the last siteReference Object (page 260) in the collection, or `null` if the collection is empty.
next *siteCollectionObj*.next()	Returns the next siteReference Object (page 260) in the collection, or `null` if there is no next element.
prev *siteCollectionObj*.prev()	Returns the previous siteReference Object (page 260) in the collection, or `null` if there is no previous element.
remove *siteCollectionObj*.remove(*oldRef*)	Removes a specified site reference from this collection. Returns `true` on success. (Introduced in 8.0)
oldRef	The siteReference Object (page 260) for the file to be removed from the collection.

siteReference Object

Class: `JSXSiteReference`

This object encapsulates a reference to a file, a folder, or an external link such as an email address. This object provides information about the referenced resource, such as its location, file type, size, lock status, and a list of its anchors.

The object's methods get files and links of a specified type from the referenced location, which is useful for batch-processing a site's files. The methods return a siteCollection Object (page 259), which provides name-based, numeric, and iterative access to a group of `siteReference` objects.

In GoLive 6 and higher, the `siteReference` object can also store persistent string or integer data as a named value. You can use this feature to add your own properties to reference objects.

Acquiring siteReference objects

- All documents provide the ref (page 139) property, which holds a `siteReference` object representing the file for that document. This object is available only when the Site window is open and the document is part of the site.
- For a site document (a document Object, page 138, that represents an open web site):
  - Its site (page 139) property holds a `siteReference` object representing the root folder of that site:

    ```
    document.site// site's root fld when site window is
    frontmost
    ```
  - Its homePage (page 139) property holds a `siteReference` object representing the home page of the that site:

    ```
    document.homePage// site's homepage when site window
    is frontmost
    ```

    The `document` object's `site` and `homePage` properties are `null` when the site document is closed or when the object does not represent a site. For example, these properties are `null` for markup documents.
- The get methods of the `siteReference` object return iterable collections of related `siteReference` objects as the elements of a

siteCollection Object (page 259). For example, the following iterates through all files in a site's root folder:

```
refColl=website.root.getContent();
for (var ref=refColl.first();ref!=
null;ref=refColl.next()){
    writeln (ref.name);
    }
```

siteReference object properties

All properties are read-only.

propname	String	Add as strings the names of any properties you need for your Undo operation.
absurl	String	The absolute URL of the referenced file or folder.
anchors	Array	The array of anchors this file contains. Array is empty if there are no anchors on the page.
creationDate	Date	The JavaScript Date object for the creation date of the file or folder.
file	File	The file Object (page 158) for the referenced file.
fileSize	Number	The physical size of a file; 0 for folders.
isAvailableLocal	Boolean	When true, the referenced file that was downloaded from a version-control server is up-to-date—that is, there is no newer version on the server.
isCheckedOut	Boolean	When true, the file or folder is checked out in the version-control server.
isFolder	Boolean	When true, the referenced entity is a folder.
local	Boolean	When true, the referenced entity is available locally.
longUrl	String	Deprecated in 7.0. Use absURL and relURL. The absolute URL for this .site file.
mimeType	String	The MIME type of the reference
modificationDate	Date	The JavaScript Date object for the modification date of the file or folder.
name	String	The file or folder filename or URL.
prefs	Prefs	A prefs Object (page 240) you can use to store any data you need to associate with this reference. For example, you might use this object to mark the reference in some way or to associate your own values with this reference.

---

protocol	String	The file-transfer protocol (HTTP, FTP, and so on) this object's `upload` method uses to transfer the file this object represents.

publishState	String	When this reference should be published. One of:
		`never`
		`always`
		`ifused`

relurl	String	The file name if the corresponding document has been saved and the site is open. If the site is not open, the absolute URL of the referenced file or folder.
siteDoc	Document	The document Object (page 138) the `.site` file for this site. This property is `null` if the site document is not open.
status	String	The status of the reference, one of: `error`: Parsing error or other error `empty`: Empty reference `checking`: SDK is checking this reference now `invalid`: Invalid reference `ok`: The reference is valid
title	String	The document title, as specified in the `<title>` tag of the document's HTML source representation. Empty for other types.
type	String	The type of resource this object represents, one of: `html`: HTML file `folder`: Folder or directory `alias`: File or folder alias `image`: Image file `mail`: E-mail address `invalid`: Invalid reference
url	String	Deprecated in 7.0. Use `absURL` and `relURL`. The relative URL of this `.site` file.

siteReference object functions

Methods of the `siteReference` object allow you to get files, get a referenced page's incoming or outgoing links, highlight the referenced object in Layout view, and open the referenced object programmatically.

addFiles *siteReferenceObj*.`addFile`(*srcFile*) *siteReferenceObj*.`addFile`(*pathOrUrl*)	Adds a specified file to this site. Returns `true` on success. (Introduced in 7.0)
srcFile	The file Object (page 158) for the file to be added to the site.
pathOrUrl	The path or URL for the file to be added to the site.

checkIn *siteReferenceObj*.checkIn()	Checks this file into the version-control server.
checkOut *siteReferenceObj*.checkOut()	Checks this file out from the version-control server.
checkUpdate *siteReferenceObj*.checkUpdate()	When this object references a GoLive component file or GoLive template file, causes all clients of this component or template to update their content if needed.
copy *siteReferenceObj*.copy(*dest_pathOrURL*) *siteReferenceObj*.copy(*destSite*)	Copies this reference to the given path, URL, or site destination. Returns true on success. (Introduced in 7.0)
dest_pathOrURL Target path or URL.	
destSite The siteReference Object (page 260) for the target site.	
createFile *siteReferenceObj*.createFile (*URL* [, *fixDuplicateNames, show*])	Creates a generic HTML file in the specified location. Returns a new siteReference Object (page 260) for the new file, or nothing if the method could not create the file. (Introduced in 7.0)
URL Fully qualified or relative path to new file's location. Terminate this path with ".html" or another appropriate extension to avoid a warning icon in the Site window.	
fixDuplicateNames Optional. When true, append a numeric value to the end of a duplicate filename to make it unique. Default is true.	
show Optional. When true, disclose all parent folders and select the new folder in the Site window. Default is true.	

createFileFromStationery
siteReferenceObj.createFileFromStationery
  (*fileURL, stationeryURL*
  [, *fixDuplicateNames, show*])
	Uses the specified GoLive stationery file to create a HTML file at the specified location. Returns a new siteReference Object (page 260) for the new file, or nothing if the method could not create the file. (Introduced in 7.0)

fileURL Fully qualified or relative path to new file's location.	
stationaryURL Fully qualified or relative path to GoLive stationery file's location.	
fixDuplicateNames Optional. When true, append a numeric value to the end of a duplicate filename to make it unique. Default is true.	
show Optional. When true, disclose all parent folders and select the new folder in the Site window. Default is true.	

createFileFromTemplate *siteReferenceObj*.createFileFromTemplate (*fileURL, templtURL* [, *fixDuplicateNames, show*])	Uses the specified GoLive template file to create a HTML file at the specified location. Returns a new siteReference Object (page 260) for the new file, or nothing if the method could not create the file. (Introduced in 7.0)
fileURL	Relative path to new file's location.
templtURL	Fully qualified or relative path to GoLive template file's location.
fixDuplicateNames	Optional. When true, append a numeric value to the end of a duplicate filename to make it unique. Default is true.
show	Optional. When true, disclose all parent folders and select the new folder in the Site window. Default is true.
createFolder *siteReferenceObj*.createFolder(*URL* [, *fixDuplicateNames, show*])	Creates a folder in the specified location. Returns a new siteReference Object (page 260) for the new folder, or nothing if the method could not create the folder. (Introduced in 7.0)
fileURL	Location in which to create the new folder, a fully qualified or site-root relative URL.
fixDuplicateNames	Optional. When true, append a numeric value to the end of a duplicate filename to make it unique. Default is true.
show	Optional. When true, disclose all parent folders and select the new folder in the Site window. Default is true.
downloadFromServer *siteReferenceObj*.downloadFromServer()	Downloads the file represented by this siteReference object from the workgroup server.
duplicate *siteReferenceObj*.duplicate()	Duplicates the reference (as in the UI context menu of the site). Returns true on success. (Introduced in 7.0)
forceUpdate *siteReferenceObj*.forceUpdate()	When this object references a GoLive component file or GoLive template file, updates the content of all files that refer to this file. (Introduced in 7.0)
getContent *siteReferenceObj*.getContent ([*mask, onlyFolder*])	Gets a collection of files from the folder this object represents. Returns a siteReferenceCollection object containing siteReference Objects (page 260) for the found files and subfolders. (Introduced in 7.0)
mask	Optional. A mask string to filter the files selected. Only files whose names match the mask pattern are returned. The mask can contain the asterisk (*) wildcard character. The default mask is "*", which returns all files.
onlyFolder	Optional. If true, only folder names are returned. Default is false.

getFiles *siteReferenceObj*.getFiles ([*type*])	Gets an iterable collection of files from the folder this object represents, optionally filtered for type. Applies only to an open .site file. Returns A siteCollection Object (page 259).
type	Optional. One or more file types; a string composed of one or more values of the siteReference.type property, separated by any non-alpha character. For example, html+folder. When supplied, return only files that match one of the types. The mail value is not a valid argument to this function.
getIncoming *siteReferenceObj*.getIncoming ([*type*])	Gets open documents that link to this page, as siteReference objects. Returns A siteCollection Object (page 259). This method works when no Site document is open, but it retrieves links only from currently open documents. It returns a reference only if another open document refers to this page.
type	Optional. One or more file types; a string composed of one or more values of the siteReference.type property, separated by any non-alpha character. For example, html+folder. When supplied, return only files that match one of the types. The folder value is not a valid argument to this function.
getNamedLong *siteReferenceObj*.getNamedLong (*name*)	Returns the integer data stored under the specified name.
name	Name of the data to retrieve, as created by the setNamedLong (page 267) method.
getNamedString *siteReferenceObj*.getNamedString(*name*)	Returns the string data stored under the specified name.
name	Name of the data to retrieve, as created by the setNamedString (page 267) method.
getOutgoing *siteReferenceObj*.getOutgoing ([*type*])	Gets siteReference objects for pages that this page references. Returns a siteCollection Object (page 259).
type	Optional. One or more file types; a string composed of one or more values of the siteReference.type property, separated by any non-alpha character. For example, html+folder. When supplied, return only files that match one of the types. The folder value is not a valid argument to this function.

getReferencingFiles *siteReferenceObj*.getReferencingFiles ([*type*])	For a template (type="template") or a component (type="CSComponent"), creates a collection of siteReference objects for files that refer to this template or component. Returns a siteReferenceCollection object containing siteReference Objects (page 260) for the found files. (Introduced in 7.0)
type	Optional. One or more file types; a string composed of one or more values of the siteReference.type property, separated by any non-alpha character. For example, html+folder. When supplied, return only files that match one of the types. The folder value is not a valid argument to this function.
move *siteReferenceObj*.move(*dest_pathOrURL*) *siteReferenceObj*.move(*dest*)	Moves this reference to a specified destination. Returns true on success. (Introduced in 7.0)
dest_pathOrURL	The absolute path or the URL to the target destination.
destSite	The siteReference Object (page 260) for the target destination.
open *siteReferenceObj*.open()	Opens this reference in GoLive as an HTML document, returns a document object representing it, and makes that document the current document. Returns a document Object (page 138). This method is intended to open HTML documents only. Do not use this method to open other kinds of documents.
openDocument *siteReferenceObj*.openDocument()	Opens this reference in GoLive as an HTML document, returns a document Object (page 138) representing it, and makes that document the current document. (Introduced in 7.0) This method is intended to open HTML documents only. Do not use this method to open other kinds of documents.
publish *siteReferenceObj*.publish()	Publishes this file to the publishing server. (Introduced in 7.0)
remove *siteReferenceObj*.remove()	Moves this reference to the system trash or site trash, as specified by General Preferences. Returns true on success. (Introduced in 7.0)
rename *siteReferenceObj*.rename(*newName*)	Changes the internal JavaScript name for this site reference. Returns true on success. (Introduced in 7.0)
newName	The new JavaScript name for the site reference.

setNamedLong *siteReferenceObj*.setNamedLong(*name, value*)	Creates a named property in this object containing a specified long integer value. Returns `true` on success.
name Name of the property to create.	
value Value to store.	
setNamedString *siteReferenceObj*.setNamedString (*name, value*)	Creates a named property in this object containing a specified string value. Returns `true` on success.
name Name of the property to create.	
value Value to store.	
show *siteReferenceObj*.show()	Displays and highlights this reference in the Site window.
undoCheckOut *siteReferenceObj*.UndoCheckOut()	Undoes the checkout of this file from the version-control server.

socket Object

Class: `Socket`

This object lets you connect to any server on the Internet and exchange data with it using the TCP connection. It provides functions to open and close such a connection, and to read and write data over it. It can also establish a simple server, using `listen` and `poll` methods.

(Introduced in 7.0)

Acquiring a socket object

- Use the built-in `Socket` class to create a new `socket` object.

```
var myConnection = new Socket();
```

socket object properties

A `socket` object has these properties:

connected	Boolean	When `true`, the connection is active. Read-only.
eof	Boolean	When `true`, the receive buffer is empty. Read-only.
error	String	A message describing the last error. Setting the value clears any error message.
host	String	The name of the remote computer to which this object is connected, or the empty string if the connection is inactive or does not exist. Read-only.
timeout	Number	Optional. The number of seconds after which read and write operations time out. Default is 10.

socket object functions

A `socket` object has these functions.

socket object constructor `new Socket()`	Creates and returns a new `socket` object.
close *socketObj*`.close ()`	Terminates the open connection. Returns `true` on success, `false` if I/O errors occur. Deleting the connection has the same effect as closing it. However, JavaScript garbage collects the object at some unknown time, so the connection could stay open longer than you want if you do not close it explicitly.

listen *socketObj*.listen (*port* [, *encoding*])	Begins listening for incoming traffic on a specified port. Returns `true` on success. Calls to `listen` and `open` are mutually exclusive. Call one or the other, but not both.
port	The TCP/IP port number on which to listen. A number from 1 to 65535. Typically 80 for a web server, 23 for a Telnet server, and so on.
encoding	Optional. The encoding to use for the connection, such as `ASCII`, `binary`, or `UTF-8`. Default is `ASCII`.
open *socketObj*.open (*computer* [, *encoding*])	Opens a connection to a specified host for subsequent read and write operations. Returns `true` on success. Calls to `listen` and `open` are mutually exclusive. Call one or the other, but not both.

computer	The host to which to connect. The name or IP address, followed by a colon and the port number. The port number must be specified. For example:
	    `www.adobe.com:80`
	    `192.150.14.12:80`

encoding	Optional. The encoding to use for the connection, such as `ASCII`, `binary`, or `UTF-8`. Default is `ASCII`.
poll *socketObj*.poll ()	Checks a listening object for a new incoming connection. Returns the `socket` object for the connection if a connection request is detected, or `null` if none is detected. Use the returned socket object to communicate with the remote computer. After use, close the connection and delete the JavaScript object.
read *socketObj*.read ([*count*])	Reads up to a specified number of characters from the connection. Returns a string containing the characters.
count	Optional. The maximum number of characters to read. If not supplied, reads characters until the remote server closes the connection or timeout occurs.
readln *socketObj*.readln ()	Reads one line of text (up to the next linefeed character) from the connection. Recognized linefeed characters are `CR`, `LF`, `CRLF` and `LFCR` pairs. Returns a string containing the line of text.
write *socketObj*.write (*text*[, *text2*...])	Writes specified text to the connection. Returns the number of characters written.
text	One or more strings specifying the text to write. All parameters are concatenated into a single string before writing.

writeln *socketObj*.writeln (*text*[, *text2*...])	Writes specified text to the connection, appending a linefeed (LF) character. Returns the number of characters written.
text	One or more strings specifying the text to write. All parameters are concatenated into a single string before writing.

splitpanel Object

Class: `JSXSplitpanel`

This object represents a panel with two subpanels, which can be arranged vertically or horizontally. The border between the panels can be moved with the mouse.

The immediate children of a split panel must be two panel Objects (page 233). These can in turn contain additional controls. You can define the subpanels and their controls as part of the tag that creates the panel, or add them dynamically using the `splitpanel` object's `add` function.

A `splitpanel` object is a type of control, and inherits all properties and functions of the control Object Types (page 78).

(Introduced in 8.0)

Acquiring a splitpanel object

- The SDK creates a `splitpanel` object when it interprets a `<jsxsplitview>` (page 334) tag that is contained in a window definition. You can obtain the object by name or index from the parent window's `children` collection:

      myPanel = *windowObj*.children[*panelName*];
      tabPanelObj.children[*panelName*];

- To create a new `splitpanel` object dynamically, call a window Object's add (page 317) function with `type="splitpanel"`. Pass an object containing these optional creation parameters:

`name`	String	Unique JavaScript name of the panel.
`alignment`	Array	An array containing the horizontal and vertical alignment string values for the panel. See `<jsxcontrol>` halign (page 339) and valign (page 339) attributes. Default is `["left", "top"]`.

`orientation`	String	Whether the subpanels are arranged horizontally or vertically. One of:
		
		    `horizontal`: The subpanels are arranged horizontally, and the dividing line is vertical.
		    `vertical`: The subpanels are arranged vertically, and the dividing line is horizontal.

`partition`	Number	The position of the dividing line between the subpanels, as a percentage of the parent's height or width. 0 is the left or top edge, 100 is the right or bottom edge. 50 puts the line in the middle.

For example:

```
myWin.add ( "splitpanel", [left, top, right, bottom],
    "initial title",
        { name:"myPanel1, alignment:["left", "top"],
    horizontal, 50} );
```

- The SDK creates a `splitpanel` object known as a *view resource* when it interprets a `<jsxsplitview>` (page 334) tag that is not contained in a window definition. You can access this object by name to add it to a window dynamically:

```
myWin.add ( "panel", "viewResourceName",
        { name:"myPanel2", alignment:["left", "top"],
    icon:"myImage2" } );
```

If you add a `splitpanel` object to a tabpanel Object (page 274), it represents one tab in the tabbed window. The `alignment` value is ignored. The position of the panel is 0,0 and the size is defined by the parent `tabPanel`.

splitpanel object properties

In addition to those of the control Object Types (page 78), the `splitpanel` object defines this property:

children	Control Collection	A collection of all children in this panel—that is, all controls that are added to this panel or defined within it. Should contain exactly two panel Objects (page 233). The first is the left or top panel, the second is the right or bottom panel. Read only.
contentSize1 **contentSize2**	Dimension	The size of the content areas of the two subpanels. A dimension Object (page 137).
orientation	String	Whether the subpanels are arranged horizontally or vertically. One of:
		`horizontal`: The subpanels are arranged horizontally, and the dividing line is vertical.
		`vertical`: The subpanels are arranged vertically, and the dividing line is horizontal.
partition	Number	The position of the dividing line between the subpanels, as a percentage of the parent's height or width. 0 is the left or top edge, 100 is the right or bottom edge. 50 puts the line in the middle.

splitpanel object functions

In addition to those of the control Object Types (page 78), the `splitpanel` object defines this function to add `panel` controls dynamically.

add *panelObj*.add (*type*[, *text*, *creationParam*])		Creates and returns a new panel Object (page 233) as a child of this split panel. A `splitpanel` can contain only two `panel` controls as direct children.
type		The type of control to create. Must be `panel`.
text		Optional. An initial text value for the new panel. (Not used.)
creationParam		Optional. A JavaScript object that contains properties to set special initial values of the child panel.
remove *panelObj*.remove (*child*)		Removes a child panel of this split panel.
child		The panel to remove, specified by it's JavaScript name, the 0-based index in the parent's `children` array, or as a panel Object (page 233).

tabpanel Object

Class: JSXTabPanel

This object represents a tabbed window. It contains panel Objects (page 233), each of which represents one tab. The tabpanel is a type of control, and inherits all the properties and functions of the control Object Types (page 78). (Introduced in 7.0)

Acquiring a tabpanel object

- The SDK creates a tabpanel object when it interprets a `<jsxtabview>` (page 333) tag. You can obtain the object by name or index from the parent window's children collection:

  windowObj.children[*panelName*];

- To create a new tabpanel object dynamically, call a window Object's add (page 317) function with type="tabpanel". Pass an object containing these optional creation parameters:

name	String	Unique JavaScript name of the control.
alignment	Array	An array containing the horizontal and vertical alignment string values for the control. See `<jsxcontrol>` halign (page 339) and valign (page 339) attributes. Default is ["left", "top"].
contentOffset	Array	An array containing the horizontal and vertical offset values (in pixels) for the margin between the upper left corner of the panel's content area and the upper left corner of its children.

➤ Example

```
myWin.add ( "tabpanel", [left, top, right, bottom], "",
    { name:"myTabPanel1", alignment:["left", "top"],
    contentOffset: [10, 10]} );
```

tabpanel object properties

In addition to those of the control Object Types (page 78), the tabpanel object defines this property:

children	Panel Collection	A collection of all child panel Objects (page 233) of this tabpanel. Read only.
contentSize	Dimension	The size of the content area (the inner area, not counting the frame that shows the tabs). A dimension Object (page 137). (Introduced in 8.0)

tabpanel object functions

In addition to those of the control Object Types (page 78), the `tabpanel` object defines this function to add `panel` controls dynamically.

add *panelObj*.add (*type* [, *text*, *creationParam*])	Creates and returns a new panel Object (page 233) as a child of this tabbed window. Each `panel` is one tab. A `tabpanel` can contain only `panel` controls as direct children.
type	The type of control to create. Must be `panel`.
text	Optional. An initial text value for the new panel, which appears as the tab label.
creationParam	Optional. A JavaScript object that contains properties to set special initial values of the child panel.
remove *panelObj*.remove (*child*)	Removes a child panel of this tabbed window. (Introduced in 8.0)
child	The panel to remove, specified by it's JavaScript name, the 0-based index in the parent's `children` array, or as a panel Object (page 233).

text Object

Class: `JSXText`

The `text` object represents markup text. When you load an HTML document, GoLive generates a tree of markup objects to represent the contents. The objects have a tree structure that matches that in the source HTML. The markup objects are of various types: the element Object (page 156) for elements, the text Object (page 276) for text items, the comment Object (page 75) for comments, and the markup Object (page 215) for all other kinds of markup.

- This object includes the Node Interface (page 229), whose properties and functions allow you to traverse the node tree.
- This object includes the Markup Interface (page 209), whose properties and functions allow you to directly access document content.
- In addition, this object defines some properties and functions of its own, as shown here.

(Introduced in 7.0)

Acquiring text objects

For a markup document, the document Object's documentElement (page 138) property holds the root object of the markup tree. The page's content is represented by nodes in the tree. To retrieve the root of the markup tree for a document:

```
var tree = document.documentElement;
```

You can traverse the markup tree using the Node Interface (page 229) properties and functions of any object in the tree. In a `text` object:

```
elementType=text
nodeType=3
nodeName=#text
```

text object properties

In addition to those of the Node Interface (page 229) and Markup Interface (page 209), a `text` object has these properties:

data	String	The text.
length	Number	Length of the text in characters.

---

text object functions

In addition to those of the Node Interface (page 229) and Markup Interface (page 209), a `text` object has these functions.

appendData *textObj*.appendData(*text*)	Adds specified text at the end of the existing text. Returns `true` on success.
text	The text to add.
deleteData *textObj*.deleteData(*offset*, *count*)	Deletes a specified number of characters from current text beginning at a specified offset from the start of text. Returns `true` on success.
offset	The offset into the data at which to begin the deletion.
count	The length of data (number of characters) to delete.
insertData *textObj*.insertData(*offset*, *text*)	Inserts new text at a specified offset into the existing text. Returns `true` on success.
offset	The offset into the existing text.
text	The text to insert.
replaceData *textObj*.replaceData(*offset*, *count*, *text*)	Replaces a range of existing text with new text, beginning at a specified offset. Returns `true` on success.
offset	The offset at which to begin the replacement.
count	The length of data to replace.
text	The text to insert.
splitText *textObj*.splitText(*offset*)	Splits the text item at the given offset into two text items. Upon return, this object contains only the text before the offset. The method creates and returns a new text Object (page 276) containing the text after the offset.
offset	The character offset at which to split the text.
substringData *textObj*.substringData(*offset*, *count*)	Gets a substring of a specified length beginning at a specified offset. Returns a new text Object (page 276) containing the substring.
offset	The offset into the string.
count	The length of data (number of characters) to copy.

textArea Object

Class: `JSXTextArea`

This object provides access to the text components of document content in the Layout view, allowing you to set and get selection and style information. Non-text elements embedded in a selection are represented in the `text` property by a placeholder string that you can set.

Layout view always contains at least one `textArea` object. Whenever you insert text or boxes in Layout view, GoLive creates a `textArea` object to encapsulate the text. The SDK also uses the `textArea` object to represent the text content of a table cell.

Acquiring textArea objects

Get `textArea` objects in the following ways:

- The `mainTextArea` property of a document Object (page 138)

      document.mainTextArea // when document window is open

- The `textArea` property of a markup Object (page 215)

      markupObj.textArea

- The `textArea` property of a layout.tableCell Object (page 203)

      markupObj.layout.table.captionCell.textArea
      markupObj.layout.tableCell.textArea

textArea object properties

boxPlaceHolder	String	A placeholder string used to represent embedded boxes for non-text elements in the selection.
		This string can affect the `length`, and can be found by the findString (page 280) and replaceString (page 281) functions.
length	Number	Number of characters in `text`, including placeholder characters. Read-only.
selectionLength	Number	Number of selected characters. Read-only.
selectionStart	Number	Offset to the start of selection. Read-only
styleSet	HTMLStyleSet	An HTMLStyleSet Object (page 179) containing the styles that are in effect at the beginning of the current selection. The `HTMLStyleSet` name is `null`. Read-only.
text	String	The plain text of the text object. The `boxPlaceHolder` string is used to represent embedded boxes for non-text elements in the selection. Read-only.

---

textArea object functions

The functions manipulate the style of text, the content of the text, the selection of text in the area, and placement of the text cursor.

addCurrentStyle *markupObj*.textArea.addCurrentStyle (*[styleSetName]*)	Extracts the specified HTMLStyleSet Object (page 179) from the beginning of the current selection and adds it to the global list of HTML styles. Returns true on success.
styleSetName	Optional. Name of the style set to retrieve. When not supplied, adds the current style set to the global HTML style collection.
applyStyle *markupObj*.textArea.applyStyle(*styleName*) *markupObj*.textArea.applyStyle(*styleSet*) *markupObj*.textArea.applyStyle(*style*)	Applies the specified style to the text. Returns true on success. This method wraps the called textArea object's text in a style tag. The style need not be a known style. For example: textArea.applyStyle("abc def=ghi") This results in the element: <abc def="ghi">selected text</abc> Notice that the method adds quotes to attribute values in the returned text.
styleName	Name of the style to apply.
styleSet	A HTMLStyleSet Object (page 179) containing one or more styles to apply.
style	An HTMLStyle Object (page 178) for the style to apply.
copy *markupObj*.textArea.copy()	Copies the currently selected text to the clipboard. Returns true on success.
cut *markupObj*.textArea.cut()	Cuts the currently selected text, placing it on the clipboard. Returns true on success.
deapplyStyle *markupObj*.textArea.deapplyStyle(*style*)	If the specified style is present in the current selection, removes the style's effect. Returns true on success.
styleSetName	Name of the style to deapply.
deselect *markupObj*.textArea.deselect()	Deselects the text. Returns true on success.

findString
markupObj.textArea.findString
  (*searchString* [, *startPosition, ignoreCase*])
markupObj.textArea.findString
  (*regExpression*
  [, *startPosition, ignoreCase*])
		Finds a specified string in the text. Returns the character offset from the beginning of the text of the found string or expression, or -1 if the string was not found. The function overwrites the lastIndex and globalFlag standard JavaScript properties of this object.

	searchString	String to match.
	regExpression	A JavaScript regular expression to match.
	startPosition	Optional. Character offset at which to begin searching. When not supplied, the method begins searching at the beginning of the text.
	ignoreCase	Optional. When true, make case-insensitive comparisons. Default is false.

hasStyle
markupObj.textArea.hasStyle (*style*)
		Reports whether a specified style exists in the current selection. Returns one of these strings:
		  no: The style is not in the current selection.
		  partly: The style exists in the current selection, but does not terminate in the selection area.
		  full: The current selection completely contains the style.

	style	Name of the style.
insert *markupObj*.textArea.insert (*text*)		Inserts non-HTML text at the current position or replaces the current selection with the specified text. Returns true on success.
	text	Non-HTML text string to insert.
insertBox *markupObj*.textArea.insertBox (*boxName*)		Adds a box Object (page 64) with a specified name to Layout view at the current cursor position. Returns true on success. To insert a custom element, pass the value of its classid attribute. To insert an element the standard GoLive palettes provide, use one of the values listed in "Box names for predefined palette elements" on page 195. This table also indicates the name that describes this element in the GoLive user interface, as well as the palette group that provides similar elements.
	boxName	JavaScript name of the box to insert.
insertChar *markupObj*.textArea.insertChar (*aChar*)		Inserts the specified character at the current position or replaces the current selection with the specified character. Returns true on success.
	aChar	Text character to insert.

insertHTML *markupObj*.textArea.insertHTML (*text*)	Inserts the specified HTML text at the current position or replaces the current selection with *text*. Returns `true` on success.
text	Text string to insert. This string may contain any mix of HTML tags and text.
insertNewLine *markupObj*.textArea.insertNewLine ()	Ends the current paragraph and starts a new one. Returns `true` on success.
paste *markupObj*.textArea.paste ()	Pastes the current clipboard content at the current position. Returns `true` on success.
remove *markupObj*.textArea.remove ()	Removes the current selection. Returns `true` on success.
replaceString *markupObj*.textArea.replaceString (*searchString, replaceString* [, *startPosition, ignoreCase*]) *markupObj*.textArea.replaceString (*regExpression, replaceString* [, *startPosition, ignoreCase*])	Replaces specified text with the specified replacement text. Returns the character offset from the beginning of the text of the found string or expression, or -1 if the string was not found. This method overwrites the `lastIndex` and `globalFlag` standard JavaScript properties of this object.
searchString	String to match.
regExpression	A JavaScript regular expression to match.
startPosition	Optional. Character offset at which to begin searching. When not supplied, the method begins searching at the beginning of the text.
ignoreCase	Optional. When `true`, make case-insensitive comparisons. Default is `false`.
scrollToText *markupObj*.textArea.scrollToText ()	Scrolls Layout view as necessary to display the cursor's current position. Returns `true` on success.
select *markupObj*.textArea.select (*selBegin, numChars*)	Selects a specified number of characters in the text, beginning at a specified index position. Returns `true` on success.
selBegin	The index position at which the selection begins. The first character is at index position 1. For convenience, 0 also means the first character; however, the second character is still at index 2.
numChars	The number of characters to select.
selectAll *markupObj*.textArea.selectAll ()	Selects all text. Returns `true` on success.
selectParagraph *markupObj*.textArea.selectParagraph (*num*)	Selects the specified paragraph. Returns `true` on success.
num	Number of the paragraph to select. Paragraph 0 is the first paragraph.

setCursor *markupObj*.textArea.setCursor(*offset*)	Sets the cursor's position. Returns true on success.
offset	The cursor's new position, as a character offset from the beginning of text. Character 0 is the first character.
setCursorParagraph *markupObj*.textArea.setCursorParagraph (*paraNum*)	Positions the cursor just before the specified paragraph. Returns true on success.
paraNum	Number of the paragraph. Paragraph 0 is the first paragraph.

textView Object

Class: JSXTextView

This object provides access to the text selection when a document is displayed in the Source view. (Introduced in 7.0)

Acquiring textView objects

- When the document is open in Source view (that is, `document.view="source"`), get this object from the source (page 140) property of the document Object (page 138):

  ```
  var textViewObj = document.source // Current doc open
  in Source view
  ```

- When the source is displayed in a `source`-type control, get this object from the `sourceArea` property of the Control: source Object (page 114):

  sourceObj.`sourceArea`

textView object properties

length	Number	The number of characters in text.
lineCount	Number	The number of paragraphs in text.
selectionLength	Number	The number of selected characters.
selectionStart	Number	The offset from the start of text to the start of the current selection.
syntax	String	The syntax marking theme for the displayed code. One of the values that appears in the JavaScript editor's list of syntax themes.
text	String	The entire text shown in the source editor.

textView object functions

copy *textViewObj*.copy()	Copies the currently selected text to the clipboard.
cut *textViewObj*.cut()	Cuts the currently selected text, placing it on the clipboard.

findString *textViewObj*.findString (*searchStringOrExp* [, *startPosition, ignoreCase*])	Finds a specified string in the text. Returns the character offset from the beginning of the text of the found string or expression, or -1 if the string was not found. The function overwrites the lastIndex and globalFlag standard JavaScript properties of this object.
searchStringOrExp	String to match or a JavaScript regular expression to match.
startPosition	Optional. Character offset at which to begin searching. When not supplied, the method begins searching at the beginning of the text.
ignoreCase	Optional. When true, make case-insensitive comparisons. Default is false.
insert *textViewObj*.insert (*text*)	Inserts non-HTML text at the current position or replaces the current selection with the specified text.
text	Non-HTML text string to insert.
lineIndex *textViewObj*.lineIndex (*textOffset*)	Returns a line index for the line containing the specified text offset.
textOffset	A character offset from the start of text.
lineLength *textViewObj*.lineLength (*lineIndex*)	Returns the number of characters in the specified line.
lineIndex	The line index.
lineStart *textViewObj*.lineStart (*lineIndex*)	Returns the character offset from start of text for the first character in the specified line.
lineIndex	The line index.
lineText *textViewObj*.lineText (*lineIndex*)	Returns a string containing the text of the specified line.
lineIndex	The line index.
paste *textViewObj*.paste ()	Pastes the current clipboard content at the current position.
remove *textViewObj*.remove ()	Removes the current selection.

replaceString *textViewObj*.`replaceString` (*searchStringOrExp, replaceString* [, *startPosition, ignoreCase*])		Replaces specified text with the specified replacement text. Returns the character offset from the beginning of the text of the found string or expression, or -1 if the string was not found. This method overwrites the `lastIndex` and `globalFlag` standard JavaScript properties of this object.
	searchStringOrExp	String to match or a JavaScript regular expression to match.
	replaceString	String to substitute in place of found string.
	startPosition	Optional. Character offset at which to begin searching. When not supplied, the method begins searching at the beginning of the text.
	ignoreCase	Optional. When `true`, make case-insensitive comparisons. Default is `false`.
scrollToText *textViewObj*.`scrollToText`(*offset* [, *endOffset*])		Scrolls Source view as necessary to display the specified text.
	offset	The character offset from start of text to the first character of text to display.
	endOffset	Optional. The character offset of the last character of text to display.
select *textViewObj*.`select`(*offset* [, *endOffset*])		Selects the specified text.
	offset	The character offset from start of text to the first character of text to select.
	endOffset	Optional. The character offset of the last character of text to select. If not supplied, selects to the end of text.
selectAll *textViewObj*.`selectAll`()		Selects all text.
textAt *textViewObj*.`textAt` (*offset* [, *endOffset*])		Returns a string containing the specified text.
	offset	The character offset from start of text to the first character of text to return.
	endOffset	Optional. The character offset of the last character of text to return. If not supplied, returns text from *offset* to the end of text.
toString *textViewObj*.`toString`()		Returns a string containing the name of this object.

translator Object

Class: JSXTranslator

This object allows you to translate a file's source code into an HTML representation that GoLive can edit. The object gives you programmatic access to a file before GoLive parsing occurs. The methods use regular expressions to identify text to be replaced, either temporarily or permanently.

Your extension must define handlers for the translate (page 366) and inspectTranslation (page 363) events to support the document translation mechanism. Your handlers use the methods in this object.

This object has no properties.

Acquiring the translator object

GoLive creates a translator object when it interprets a <jsxtranslator> (page 352) tag in an extension's Main.html file. Get the object from the translator property of the app Object (page 53) object:

```
app.translator
```

translator object functions

You can call these methods to explicitly replace, rewrite, or translate snippets of text.

getTranslatedSnippet *translatorObj*.getTranslatedSnippet (*original, translation, urlList* [, *classID*])	Constructs translation-wrapping information for translated text. Returns a string containing the appropriately wrapped translation. This is a helper function that eases the work of constructing the correct translation-wrapping information when using replaceSnippet (page 287). Pass it the original text to be replaced, and pass the return value to replaceSnippet as the replacement text. **Note:** This function gives low-level access to the translation mechanism; it is recommended that you use the higher-level translateSnippet (page 288) method.
original	Original, pre-translation HTML source text.
translation	Your translation of *original* text.
urlList	Comma-separated list of translated text strings for URLs detected in translation. For the translator to inspect and change links, the items in this list must be in order.
classID	Optional. Class ID of the `<jsxtranslator>` element to use. When not supplied, uses the current translator.
replaceSnippet *translatorObj*.replaceSnippet (*offset, length, text*)	Replaces the source text of the current snippet at a specified offset and length with new text. Use this method to insert or remove additional HTML before letting GoLive parse the source. The function does a simple text replacement without any insertion of extra tags. Use getTranslatedSnippet (page 287) to obtain an appropriately wrapped replacement string for the text to be translated. **Note:** This function gives low-level access to the translation mechanism; it is recommended that you use the higher-level translateSnippet (page 288) method.
offset	Character offset from beginning of text at which to begin replacing characters. Index number 0 is the first character in the text buffer.
length	Number of characters to replace.
text	Replacement text string.

rewriteSnippet *translatorObj*.rewriteSnippet (*newCode, undoText*)	When the user modifies a translated snippet using your custom Inspector, the extension can use this function to rewrite the source code for the snippet. The action can be undone. After rewriting the source code as specified, the method calls the module's translate (page 366) event handler to translate the replacement code as needed.
newCode	The new `orig` value for the snippet's `<agl:translated>` tag.
undoText	The Undo operation name that appears in the **Edit > Undo** menu and History window.

translateSnippet *translatorObj*.translateSnippet (*offset, length, text* [, *urlList*])	Replaces current source text with translated text. The method inserts an `agl:translated` tag that contains the original source text in its `orig` attribute. The specified replacement *text* becomes the content of the `agl:translated` tag and is displayed by GoLive as a protected region. This tag is normally invisible; however, you can see it in the source code view in Layout mode. Switching away from Layout mode replaces the `agl:translated` tag with the original content again. The translated text is not written into a file if the translator's `direction` value is `twoway`.
offset	Character offset from beginning of text at which to begin replacing characters. Index number 0 is the first character in the text buffer.
length	Number of characters to replace.
text	Replacement text string.
urlList	Optional. A comma-separated list of translated text strings for URLs detected in translation. Use this if the untranslated snippet contains URLs that you want to translate. For the translator to inspect and change links, the items in this list must be in order.

➤ Example

This illustrates the replacement of the tag `<mytag>` with the text "Mock Content":

```
<agl:translated classid="myTagID" orig="%3cmytag%3e">
  Mock Content
</agl:translated>
```

treeNode, treeRoot Object

Class: `JSXTreeNode`, `JSXTreeRoot`

Deprecated in 8.0. In place of `tree` controls, use `hierarchy` or `filelist` controls, which contain `node` objects. See Control: node Object (page 105).

undo Object

Class: `JSXUndo`

This object encapsulates information needed to undo or redo an editing operation on a custom element.

GoLive provides built-in undo support for dropping and resizing the box for a custom element in the Layout view. The user can undo or redo such operations by choosing the **Undo** or **Redo** item from the **Edit** menu. To undo any other operations involving your custom element, you must implement code that provides such behavior.

You can add undo support for any operation that does not cause GoLive to reparse. To undo an operation, you use a saved value, such as a name, to retrieve a previously changed `markup` object. Reparsing the document discards the `markup` object the saved value represents. Thus, any operation that reparses the document cannot be undone.

Even if your particular extension does not cause Layout view to reparse the document, the user or another extension may cause a reparse.

Acquiring undo objects

- In the body of the method that performs an operation to be undone, use the document Object's createUndo (page 143) method to create an `undo` object, initialize it by adding properties, and return it to GoLive by calling its `submit` method:

```
var undo = document.createUndo ("operationName")
```

- The SDK generates the undoSignal (page 367) event the whenever the user issues the command to do, undo, or redo an operation. It passes an undoEvent (page 388) object to the handler, with the `undo` object in the `undo` property:

```
var undoObj = undoEvt.undo
```

undo object properties

The `undo` object provides no properties of its own. You can add as its properties any data your extension requires to perform an operation or reverse its effects. Add properties to the `undo` object by declaring and assigning them, as in this example:

```
// create empty Undo object
var undo = document.createUndo ("operationName")
// add properties
undo.myProperty = myValue;
undo.myOtherProerty = myOtherValue;
```

```
undo.myThirdProp = yetAnotherValue;
// submit the undo object to GoLive
undo.submit();
```

When you have finished adding properties to the undo object, pass it to GoLive by calling the object's submit method.

undo object functions

The undo object provides only one function of its own: the submit method, which passes an initialized undo object to GoLive. You must provide the behaviors by implementing and undoSignal (page 367) event-handling function that the GoLive SDK calls as needed to process undo actions.

submit *undoObj*.submit()	Returns an initialized undo object to GoLive. GoLive adds this object to the document's History list and immediately passes the undo object to the undoSignal (page 367) handler with an action code of 1, to specify that undoSignal is to perform the operation for the first time.

VCSHandler Object

Class: VCSHandler

A handler associated with a script-defined panel in the Site window that implements an interface to a version-control system. The panel is defined by an element of the <jsxvcs> (page 357) tag that defines this handler. The panel appears in the Site Settings dialog and in the site-creation wizard.

This object is the target of all version-control-system events; see Event names (page 360) and Event Object Types (page 377). (Introduced in 8.0)

Acquiring VCSHandler objects

- The vcs (page 56) property of the app Object (page 53) contains a collection of VCSHandler objects for all version-control-system interfaces defined in the system.
- Create a new VCSHandler object using the <jsxvcs> (page 357) tag. This element contains a <jsxview> (page 332) element that defines the associated tab panel.

VCSHandler object properties

name	String	The unique name of the handler.
panel	Panel	The panel Object (page 233) for the tab panel associated with this handler in the Site window.
title	String	The display name that identifies this panel and handler in the Site Settings dialog and in the site-creation wizard.

VCSRevisionInfo Object

Stores file revision information for a version-control-system interface. (Introduced in 8.0)

Acquiring VCSRevisionInfo objects

An array of VCSRevisionInfo objects is returned in the revisions property of a VCSRevisionEvent (page 393) object, which is passed to handlers for the vcsFolderContent (page 367) and vcsRevisions (page 368) events. Your handler for this event must create these objects as needed for your own VCSHandler Object (page 292), using the constructor.

- For the vcsFolderContent (page 367) event, the revisions array should contain a VCSRevisionInfo object for each file found in the given folder. In this case, set only the url (page 295) property.

      example

- For the vcsRevisions (page 368) event, the revisions array should contains a VCSRevisionInfo object for each existing revision of the requested file. In this context, do not set the url (page 295) property.

      example

VCSRevisionInfo object properties

comment	String	A comment describing the revision.
lockedUser	String	The name of the user who locked the file.
lockStatus	String	The file's locking or check-out status. One of: none: File is not locked. localCheckedOut: File is checked out by a local user. serverCheckedOut: File is checked out by someone else.
revision	String	The revision's unique identifier.
syncStatus	String	The synchronization state of the file. One of: match: The file exists both locally and on the server and both files are identical. localOnly: The file exists only locally. localNewer: The file exists locally and on the server, but the local file is newer. serverNewer: The file exists locally and on the server, but the remote file is newer. serverOnly: The file exists only on the server. serverDeleted: The file was deleted on the server. conflict: An unresolvable conflict exists between the local and the remote file.

timestamp	Date	The date and time of the revision.
url	String	The absolute URL of the file, where the triggering event was vcsFolderContent (page 367).
user	String	The current user's user name.

VCSRevisionInfo object constructor

VCSRevisionInfo object constructor new VCSRevisionInfo (*url*, *revisionNo*, *user*, *comment*, *time*)	Creates and returns a new VCSRevisionInfo object.
url	The absolute URL of the file. A string.
revisionNo	The revision's unique identifier. A string.
user	The current user's user name. A string.
comment	A comment describing the revision. A string.
time	The date and time of the revision. A JavaScript Date object.

VCSSettings Object

Provides access to the current settings of the version-control system. (Introduced in 8.0)

Acquiring VCSSetting objects

A settings object is returned in the `settings` property of any VCS `Event` object. See Event Object Types (page 377).

VCSSettings object properties

url	String	Read/write. The URL of the version-control system server.
user	String	Read/write. The current user's user name.
password	String	Read/write. The current user's password.
any property name	String Number Boolean	Read/write. Any custom settings for a custom VCS handler.

website Object

Class: `JSXWebsite`

This object enables you to manipulate a web site that is currently open in the GoLive design environment. The corresponding Site window must be open, although it need not be frontmost. You can use this object and its methods to:

- Clean up a site
- Create new pages and folders in a site
- Rescan a site
- Get and set selections in site window
- Add custom columns to the site window
- Export a site

Acquiring website objects

- Create a new object using the app Object's createSite (page 57) method (Introduced in 8.0):

  ```
  mySiteObj = app.createSite("C:/mydir/mysite");
  ```

- Global properties (page 47) provide access to `website` objects:

  ```
  website
  websites[number]
  ```

- The `website` property (*not* the `site` property) of a document Object (page 138) provides a `website` object if a web site uses the document:

  ```
  document.website
  documentObj.website
  ```

These examples both retrieve the same `website` object, which provides access to the currently active site:

```
var theActiveSite = website;
theActiveSite = document.website;
```

website object properties

`cleanupSettings`	CleanupSettings	A website.cleanupSettings Object (page 304) that contains cleanup settings, passed as an argument to the `website.cleanup` method.
`currentServer`	ServerInfo	A serverInfo Object (page 243) for the currently active web publishing server. (Introduced in 7.0)
`currentUserName`	String	The current workgroup user name. (Introduced in 7.0)

dataFolder	SiteReference	The siteReference Object (page 260) for the web-data directory of the site. Read-only. (Introduced in 8.0)
document	Document	The document Object (page 138) that represents the site.
exportSettings	ExportSiteSettings	A website.exportSettings Object (page 306) that contains export settings, passed as an argument to the website.exportSiteSettings method.
homePage	SiteReference	The siteReference Object (page 260) for the home page of the site. Assigning a value makes the referenced page into the new home page.
isLocalSite	Boolean	When true, This is a local site. When false, it is a workgroup site. (Introduced in 7.0)
isOnline	Boolean	When true, the site is currently connected to a workgroup server. (Introduced in 7.0)
isWorkgroupSite	Boolean	When true, this is a workgroup site. When false, it is a local site. (Introduced in 7.0)
root	SiteReference	The siteReference Object (page 260) for the web-content directory of the site. Read-only.
server	ServerInfo Collection	A serverInfoCollection Object (page 245) containing serverInfo Objects (page 243) for the web-publishing servers available to this site. (Introduced in 7.0)
settings	SiteSettings	A website.siteSettings Object (page 308) that contains the various settings objects. (Introduced in 7.0)
settingsFolder	SiteReference	The siteReference Object (page 260) for the web-settings directory of the site. Read-only. (Introduced in 8.0)
siteFolder	SiteReference	The siteReference Object (page 260) for the absolute root directory of the site. Read-only. (Introduced in 8.0)
sitename	String	The name of the site without the .site extension. Read-only.

website object functions

Methods of the website object manipulate files, selections, and custom column content in an open site window. In general, actions performed through this object can be undone and redone. To undo or redo the most recent site-window change, call the website object's undo or redo method.

addColumn *websiteObj*.addColumn (*name* [, *width, alignment*])	Adds a column to the GoLive Site Files tab. Returns the identifier number of the new column, or -1 if it could not create the column. The custom column this method creates calls the function that your extension has registered for the onFileTabContentCallback (page 365) event to retrieve its content. If the user selects this column, GoLive calls the function registered for the onFileTabCompareCallback (page 365) event to sort its data.
name	Label to display at the top of the new column.
width	Optional. Width of the column in pixels. Range 50 to 320. Default is 50.

alignment	Optional. Alignment of the column's content. One of:
	    left
	    right
	    center
	Default is left.

addFile
websiteObj.addFile (*srcFile*,
  destRef)
websiteObj.addFile (*pathOrUrl*,
  destRef)
	Adds a file or contents of a folder to the site. Returns true on success. (Introduced in 7.0)

srcFile	The file Object (page 158) for the file to be added to the site. If it represents a folder, all contained files and folders are added recursively.
pathOrUrl	The path or URL for the file to be added to the site. Can be absolute or relative to the site location.
destRef	The siteReference Object (page 260) for the target site.

addPrefColumn
websiteObj.addPrefColumn
  (*name, prefName*
  [, *width, alignment*])
	Adds a column to the GoLive Site Files tab that shows a specified property of a siteReference object. Returns the identifier number of the new column, or -1 if it could not create the column. This method is usually faster than the addColumn (page 298) method, because it does not call back into your JavaScript code.

name	Label to display at the top of the new column.
prefName	The name of the property whose value is displayed as the column content.
width	Optional. Width of the column in pixels. Range 50 to 320. Default is 50.

alignment	Optional. Alignment of the column's content. One of:
	    left
	    right
	    center
	Default is left.

canRedo *websiteObj*.canRedo()	Returns true if the last Undo operation in this site can be reversed.

canUndo *websiteObj*.canUndo()	Returns `true` if the last operation in this site can be undone.
cleanup *websiteObj*.cleanup ([*cleanupSettings*])	Cleans up the site using specified settings. Equivalent to choosing the **Site > Cleanup Site** menu item in GoLive 6 or higher. Returns `true` on success.
cleanupSettings	A website.cleanupSettings Object (page 304) that encapsulates the settings. When not supplied, the method uses the site's preference settings.

> ## ➤ Example

This code allows all site cleanup behaviors to default, except for the display of lists of items the `cleanup` method added or removed:

```
// don't display add/remove lists
website.cleanupSettings.showRemoveList = false;
website.cleanupSettings.showAddList = false;
website.siteSettings(website.cleanupSettings);
```

createFile *websiteObj*.createFile(*URL* [, *fixDuplicateNames, show*])	Creates a generic empty text file in the specified location. Returns the siteReference Object (page 260) for the new file, or nothing if it could not create the file.
URL	Fully qualified or site-root relative path to new file's location. Terminate this path with ".html" or another appropriate extension to avoid a warning icon in the Site window.
fixDuplicateNames	Optional. When `true` (the default), append a numeric value to the end of a duplicate filename to make it unique.
show	Optional. When `true` (the default), disclose all parent folders and select the new folder in the Site window.
createFileFromStationery *websiteObj*.createFileFromStationery (*fileURL, stationeryURL* [, *fixDuplicateNames, show*])	Uses a GoLive stationary file to create a new HTML file at the specified location. Returns the siteReference Object (page 260) for the new file, or nothing if it could not create the file.
fileURL	Fully qualified or site-root relative path to new file's location.
stationeryURL	Fully qualified or site-root relative path to the GoLive stationary file's location.
fixDuplicateNames	Optional. When `true` (the default), append a numeric value to the end of a duplicate filename to make it unique.
show	Optional. When `true` (the default), disclose all parent folders and select the new folder in the Site window.

createFileFromTemplate *websiteObj*.createFileFromTemplate (*fileURL, temptlURL* [, *fixDuplicateNames, show*])	Uses a GoLive template file to create a new HTML file at the specified location. Returns the siteReference Object (page 260) for the new file, or nothing if it could not create the file.
fileURL	Fully qualified or site-root relative path to new file's location.
templURL	Fully qualified or site-root relative path to the GoLive template file's location.
fixDuplicateNames	Optional. When `true` (the default), append a numeric value to the end of a duplicate filename to make it unique.
show	Optional. When `true` (the default), disclose all parent folders and select the new folder in the Site window.
createFolder *websiteObj*.createFolder (*URL* [, *fixDuplicateNames, show*])	Creates a folder in the *URL* location. Optionally, appends a numeric suffix to duplicate folder names or displays the new folder and its ancestors in the Site window. Returns the siteReference Object (page 260) for the new folder, or nothing if it could not create the folder.
URL	Location in which to create the new folder, specified as a fully qualified or site-root relative URL.
fixDuplicateNames	Optional. When `true` (the default), append a numeric value to the end of a duplicate filename to make it unique.
show	Optional. When `true` (the default), disclose all parent folders and select the new folder in the Site window.
deselectAllFiles *websiteObj*.deselectAllFiles()	Deselects all files in the Files tab of the Site window. Returns `true` on success.
exportSite *websiteObj*.exportSite (*folderURL* [, *exportSettings*])	Exports this web site using specified settings. Returns `true` on success.
URL	Folder in which to place the exported site, specified as a fully qualified URL.
exportSettings	Optional. A website.exportSettings Object (page 306) that encapsulates the settings. When not supplied, the method uses the site's preference settings.

➤ Example

The following exports the site with all options allowed to default, except the site structure option:

```
var mySettings = website.exportSettings;
mySettings.siteStructure = siteStructure.FLAT;
website.exportSite(mySettings);
```

The following exports the site with all options allowed to default, except the show dialog option:

```
var mySettings = new JSXExportSiteSettings();
mySettings.showDialog = false;
website.exportSite(mySettings);
```

getSelectedExtrasFiles *websiteObj*.getSelectedExtrasFiles()	Get all selected files in the Extra tab of the Site window. Returns a SiteCollection object containing siteReference Objects (page 260) for all selected files. (Introduced in 7.0)
getSelectedFiles *websiteObj*.getSelectedFiles()	Gets an iterable collection of all selected files in the Files tab of the Site window. Returns a siteCollection Object (page 259) object containing siteReference Objects (page 260) for all selected files.
insertColumn *websiteObj*.insertColumn(*name* [, *index, width, alignment*])	Creates a custom column in the Files tab of the Site window. Returns the identifier number of the new column, or -1 if it could not create the column. The custom column this method creates calls the function that your extension has registered for the onFileTabContentCallback (page 365) event to retrieve its content. If the user selects this column, GoLive calls the function registered for the onFileTabCompareCallback (page 365) event to sort its data.
name	Label to display at the top of the new column.
index	Optional. Position at which to insert the new column. Valid value range from 1 (insert after the first, or Name column) to the number of columns. Default is 1.
width	Optional. Width of the column in pixels. Range 50 to 320. Default is 50.

alignment	Optional. Alignment of the column's content. One of:
	    left
	    right
	    center
	Default is left.

insertPrefColumn
websiteObj.insertPrefColumn
  (*name, prefName*
   [, *index, width, alignment*])
	Inserts a new column in the Files tab of the Site window, at a specified position, that displays the value of the specified property of a `siteReference` object. Returns the identifier number of the new column, or -1 if it could not create the column.
	
	This method is usually faster than the insertColumn (page 301) method, because it does not call back into your JavaScript code.

name	Label to display at the top of the new column.
prefName	The name of the property whose value is displayed as the column content.
index	Optional. Position at which to insert the new column. Valid value range from 1 (insert after the first, or Name column) to the number of columns. Default is 1.
width	Optional. Width of the column in pixels. Range 50 to 320. Default is 50.

alignment	Optional. Alignment of the column's content. One of:
	    left
	    right
	    center
	Default is left.

publish *websiteObj*.publish(*allFiles*)	Publishes this site on the current active publish server. Returns `true` on success. (Introduced in 7.0)
allFiles	When `true`, publish all files of the site, otherwise only modified files.
redo *websiteObj*.redo()	Reverses the effects of the most recent *websiteObj*.undo method. Returns `true` on success.

refreshFileView
websiteObj.refreshFileView()
websiteObj.refreshFileView
  (*siteReference*)
websiteObj.refreshFileView
  (*siteCollection*)
websiteObj.refreshFileView
  (*URL1* [, *URL2, ... , URLn*])
	Updates folders or lists of folders in the Files tab of the Site window. Returns `true` on success.
	
	This method rescans the specified folder for single-user sites and gets the actual data from the server for workgroup sites. It rescans the root if called without any arguments. If your extension creates new files, the Site window may not display them until after you call this method.

siteReference	A siteReference Object (page 260) for a specific file to update.
siteCollection	A siteCollection Object (page 259) containing siteReference Objects (page 260) for a group of files to update
URL	One or more site-root relative paths to specific files to update.

removeColumn *websiteObj*.removeColumn (*name*) *websiteObj*.removeColumn (*columnID*)	Removes the specified column from the Files tab of the Site window. This method only removes custom columns added by the SDK. It cannot remove columns built into the Site window. After removing the column, GoLive calls the onFileTabColumnIDCallback (page 365) method. If your extension creates more than one custom column, you must implement this method, which updates your extension's references to the column IDs of the remaining columns.
name	JavaScript name of column to remove.
columnID	Column identifier of the column to remove, as returned by the addColumn (page 298) method that created the custom column.
selectAllFiles *websiteObj*.selectAllFiles ()	Selects all files in the Files tab of the Site window. Returns true on success.

selectFiles
websiteObj.selectFiles
  (*fileRef1 [, fileRef2, ... , fileRefn]*)
websiteObj.selectFiles
  (*SiteCollection*)
websiteObj.selectFiles
  (*URL* [, *URL2, ... , URLn*])
	Selects the specified files in the Files tab of the Site window. Returns a siteCollection Object (page 259) object containing siteReference Objects (page 260) for all selected files.

siteReference	A file Object or siteReference Object (page 260) for a specific file to select.
siteCollection	A siteCollection Object (page 259) containing siteReference Objects (page 260) for a group of files to select.
URL	One or more site-root relative paths to specific files to select.
undo *websiteObj*.undo ()	Undoes the most recent change to the Site window. Returns true on success.

website.cleanupSettings Object

Class: JSXCleanupSiteSettings

This object encapsulates web site cleanup options. Configure the object with property values that enable or disable specific options, then pass the object to the website Object's cleanup (page 299) function.

Upon its creation, the properties of this object hold the current cleanup settings, as determined by site preference. To configure the object, you need only set the values of properties you want to alter, and allow the others to retain their default values.

Acquiring a cleanupSettings objects

Get this object directly from the website Object's cleanupSettings property, or indirectly from the website Object's settings.cleanupSettings property (page 296):

websiteObj.cleanupSettings
websiteObj.settings.cleanupSettings
documentObj.website.cleanupSettings;

website.cleanupSettings object properties

The properties correspond to options in the GoLive Cleanup Site Options dialog.

Property	Default Value	Description
addColors	true	When true, adds to the site's color prefs (page 261) any color the site uses.
addExternals	true	When true, copies external files into the site folder and updates links to reference the local copies.
addFiles	true	When true, adds to the site window all files present in the site folder.
addFontsets	true	When true, adds to the site's fontset prefs (page 261) any fontset the site uses.
removeColors	false	When true, clears the site's color prefs (page 261).
removeExternals	false	When true, removes references to files outside the site folder.
removeFiles	false	When true, removes files the site does not reference.
removeFontsets	false	When true, clears the site's fontset prefs (page 261).
rescanRoot	true	When true, rescans the site's root folder before cleaning up the site.

Property	Default Value	Description
showAddList	true	When true, displays a list in which the user confirms or denies the addition of new files to the site.
showRemoveList	true	When true, displays a list in which the user confirms or denies file deletions before they occur.

website.exportSettings Object

Class: `JSXExportSiteSettings`

This object encapsulates web site export options. Configure the object with property values that enable or disable specific options, then pass the object to the website Object's exportSite (page 300) function.

Upon its creation, the properties of this object hold the current export settings, as determined by site preference. To configure the object, you need only set the values of properties you want to alter, and allow the others to retain their default values.

Acquiring an exportSettings object

- You can construct a new `exportSettings` object whenever you need one:

  ```
  new JSXExportSiteSettings; // new operator
  JSXExportSiteSettings(); // constructor function
  ```

- Get this object directly from the website Object's `exportSettings` property, or indirectly from the website Object's `settings.exportSettings` property (page 296):

  ```
  websiteObj.exportSettings
  websiteObj.settings.exportSettings
  documentObj.website.exportSettings;
  ```

website.exportSettings object properties

The properties correspond to options in the GoLive Export Site Options dialog.

`flattenScriptLib`	Boolean	Default is `false`.
`honorPublishGroups`	Boolean	Default is `true`.
`honorPublishPages`	Boolean	Default is `true`.
`mediaFolder`	String	Fully qualified URL to folder that is to contain exported media. Used only when `siteStructure` is `SPLITPAGESANDMEDIA`. Default is the current site prefs (page 261) value.
`orphanFilesFolder`	String	current Site `prefs` value
`pagesFolder`	String	Fully qualified URL to folder that is to contain exported pages. Used only when `siteStructure` is `SPLITPAGESANDMEDIA`. Default is the current site prefs (page 261) value.

publishOnlyReferenced	Boolean	Default is `true`.
publishOrphanFiles	Boolean	Default is `false`.
showDialog	Boolean	Default is `true`.
siteStructure	String	How the exported items are to be organized at the destination. One of: `siteStructure.SITE`: Site structure is defined by a GoLive `.site` file. This is the default. `siteStructure.SPLITPAGESANDMEDIA`: Site retrieves pages and media from designated folders outside of the site folder. `siteStructure.FLAT`: No structure. All contents of site reside in one folder.
stripComments	Boolean	Default is `false`.
stripGoLiveTags	Boolean	Default is `false`.
stripSpaces	Boolean	`false`

➤ **Example**

This shows how to export the pages and media to separate destinations:

```
// specify pages separate from media
var mySettings = website.exportSettings;
mySettings.siteStructure =
"siteStructure.SPLITPAGESANDMEDIA";
mySettings.pagesFolder = "mydisc/mysite/mypages/"
mySettings.mediaFolder = "mydisc/mysite/mymedia/"
website.exportSite(mySettings);
```

website.siteSettings Object

Class: JSXSiteSettings

This object provides access to local site settings. It has no functions.

Acquiring a website.siteSettings object

Get this object from the settings property of the website Object (page 296):

```
website.settings
```

website.siteSettings object properties

cleanupSettings	CleanupSettings	A website.cleanupSettings Object (page 304) that encapsulates the cleanup settings.
exportSettings	ExportSetting	A website.exportSettings Object (page 306) that encapsulates the export settings.
urlHandling	URLSettings	A website.URLsettings Object (page 309) that encapsulates settings for URL handling.

website.URLsettings Object

Class: JSXSettingsURL

This object provides access to global and local site URL-handling settings, as in the **Site > Settings > URL Handling** dialog. It has no functions. (Introduced in 7.0)

Acquiring a website.URLsettings object

Get this object indirectly from the website Object's `settings.urlHandling` property (page 296):

```
websiteObj.settings.urlHandling
documentObj.website.settings.urlHandling;
```

website.URLSettings object properties

The properties correspond to settings in the **Site > Settings > URL Handling** dialog.

addMailto	Boolean	When `true`, automatically add `"mailto:"` to Addresses.
cgiParameters	String	When `cutAfterCGIParameters` is true, the CGI parameters to cut after.
checkCaseSensitive	Boolean	When `true`, make URLs case sensitive.
cutAfterCGIParameter	Boolean	When `true`, cut URLs after the specified `cgiParameters`.
hexEncode	Boolean	When `true`, use hexadecimal URL encoding.
makeNewAbsolute	Boolean	When `true`, make new links absolute.
utf8Encode	Boolean	When `true`, use UTF8 URL encoding.

Window Class

Class: `JSXWindow`

In addition to the constructor that creates new `window` objects, the `JSXWindow` class provides static functions that you can use without creating a `window` object. In some cases, these functions replace global functions in earlier releases. It is recommended that you replace your use of the corresponding global functions with the new static `Window` object functions.

Window object constructor

new JSXWindow(*type*, *title*, *placement*, *creationProperties*)	Creates and returns a new window Object (page 313).

type	The type of window. One of:
	    `dialog`
	    `palette`
	Note: You cannot create a window of type `document`, `inspector`, or `debugger`, but you can access windows of these types using the find (page 312) method.

title	The title that appears in the window title bar or at the bottom left of an inspector window.
placement	An array containing the coordinates of the window in the form [*left*, *top*, *right*, *bottom*]. You can set this using an JavaScript object in the form `{left:value, top:value, right:value, bottom:value}` or `{left:value, top:value, width:value, height:value}`.

creationProperties	Optional. An object that can contain these properties:
	    `name`: A unique JavaScript name for the window.
	    `resize`: When `true` and the type is `dialog`, the window can be resized. (`palette` windows are always resizeable.)
	    `minsize`: An array [*minWidth*, *minHeight*] that sets the minimum size for a resizeable window.

Window class static functions

alert JSXWindow.alert *(text)*	Displays a specified string in a user alert box that provides an **OK** button. Hides the dialog when the user clicks the button. The alert dialog is not intended for lengthy messages. It resizes to some extent to fit the given text, but can truncate text that is too long. **Note:** In 7.0 and higher, use this function instead of the global alert (page 49) function.

text   A brief message to display to the user.

This method displays a modal dialog such as this:

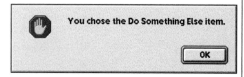

confirm JSXWindow.confirm *(text)*	Displays a specified string in a modal dialog box that provides **Yes** (default) and **No** buttons. Hides the dialog when the user clicks a button. Returns `true` if the user clicked **Yes** to dismiss the dialog, `false` if the user clicked **No**. Although this dialog displays more text than the `alert` and `prompt` methods do, it still truncates strings that are too long to fit in the dialog. **Note:** In 7.0 and higher, use this function instead of the global confirm (page 49) function.

text   A brief message to display to the user.

This method displays a modal dialog such as this:

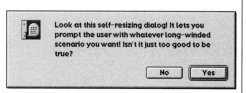

find JSXWindow.find (*type, identifier*)	Finds an existing window of a specified type. Returns a window Object (page 313). To get the SDK-defined JavaScript Debugger window: <pre>debuggerWin = Window.find("debugger", "sdk");</pre>

type	The type of window. One of:
	<pre>debugger
	dialog
	document
	inspector
	palette</pre>

identifier	An identifier for a specific window. The form depends on the type: ● `debugger`: The identifier for the SDK-defined JavaScript Debugger window is "`sdk`". ● `dialog`: A dialog name defined in any running extension. ● `document`: The full or relative path or filename for the document file. For a new document, use "`untitled.html`". You can use a fragment of the path. For example, for an existing document at "`/Volumes/myVol/myDoc.html`" you can use "`myDoc.html`". ● `inspector`: An inspector name defined in any running extension, the name of an application inspector, or `current` to get the current active inspector. ● `palette`: A palette name defined in any running extension, or the title string or name of any palette window (including application palettes). Note that title strings are localized.
prompt JSXWindow.prompt (*prompt, default*)	Displays a modal dialog that returns the user's text input. Hides the dialog when the user clicks a button. Returns the string containing the text the user entered in the input field before clicking **OK**. Returns `null` if the user clicks **Cancel**. **Note:** In 7.0 and higher, use this function instead of the global prompt (page 51) function.
text	A brief message to display to users, usually to provide instructions on the text input that is needed.
default	A default prompt string that the user can select by clicking **OK**.

This method displays a modal dialog such as this:

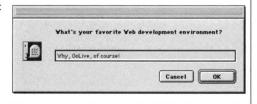

window Object

Class: JSXWindow

The window object provides access to dialogs, palettes, inspectors, and document windows, and to the SDK-defined JavaScript Debugger window. (Introduced in 7.0)

Note: This object supersedes the deprecated dialog object in 7.0.

GoLive creates a window object when it interprets a <jsxdialog> (page 330), <jsxpalette> (page 331), <jsxinspector> (page 348), or <jsxtoolbar> (page 327) element.

- A window defined with the <jsxdialog> tag is displayed by calling show, which does not return until the user dismisses the window. This type of window is called a *modal dialog*. Other windows do not respond to user input while the dialog is visible.

- A window defined with the <jsxpalette> or <jsxinspector> tags is displayed modelessly. It always exists, but can be shown or hidden. Although both <jsxpalette> and <jsxinspector> windows are floating palette windows, they are displayed and hidden differently.

- A window defined with the <jsxtoolbar> tag is displayed as part of GoLive's main toolbar. It is visible by default, but can be shown or hidden. In Windows, it can be undocked and displayed as a separate window. A toolbar window cannot be accessed through the Window.find method, and cannot be created programmatically, but it is in the dialogs (page 47) list, and can be accessed by name.

The objects in the dialogs[] array represent windows that have run at least once. For a dialog-type window, the SDK adds the window's JavaScript representation to the global dialogs array the first time the show method displays the window. The window object is not present in this array until the show method has displayed it at least once.

When the user dismisses the dialog, the SDK hides it but does not terminate the window object. Thus, you can retrieve from the dialogs[] array any dialog that has run at least once, even if the user has already dismissed it. The window's controls retain the values they had when the user dismissed the dialog. If you do not want to display these values, you must reinitialize them before displaying the window again.

Accessing a window object

- Use the Window object constructor (page 310) to create a new `window` object.

```
var w = new Window
   ("palette","Testpalette",[100,100,260,250]);
```

- Get a collection of windows from the dialogs (page 47) global property.
- Use the static find (page 312) method of the built-in Window Class (page 310) to find an existing `window` object (except toolbar windows).

```
var debuggerWin = Window.find("debugger", "sdk");
var tester = Window.find("palette", "Testpalette");
```

window object properties

box	Box	The box Object (page 64) being inspected by this active Inspector window. This property is `null` for all other windows, and when this Inspector window is inactive. Read-only.
bounds	Bounds	A bounds Object (page 63) for the size and location of this window's content area within the window. (Introduced in 8.0)
children	Control Collection	A collection of all children if this window, that is all controls that are added to this window. Read only.
collapsed	Boolean	When `true`, this palette window is docked under another palette window and collapsed. Applies only to palettes. Read/write. (Introduced in 8.0)
controls	—	Deprecated in 8.0. Use `children` instead.
enabled	Boolean	When `true`, this window can accept user input, and its children can do so if they are individually enabled. When `false`, neither the window nor any of its children can accept user input.
focus	Control	The control object that currently has the input focus. Assigning a control object to this property sets the input focus to that control, if possible.
frame	—	Deprecated in 8.0. Use `frameBounds` instead.
frameBounds	Bounds	A bounds Object (page 63) for the size and location of this window's frame. (Introduced in 8.0) Inspectors have all 0 dimensions when they are inactive. You cannot set the bounds of an `inspector` window.
frameLocation	Point	A point Object (page 239) for the position of this window's frame in parent or screen coordinates. (Introduced in 8.0)
frameSize	Dimension	A dimension Object (page 137) for the size of the window's frame. (Introduced in 8.0)

location	Point	A point Object (page 239) for the position of this window's content area. (Introduced in 8.0)
name	String	The window's JavaScript name. Read-only.
placement	—	Deprecated in 8.0. Use `frameBounds` instead.
size	Dimension	A dimension Object (page 137) for the size of the window's content area. (Introduced in 8.0)
stashed	Boolean	When `true`, this palette window is stashed -- that is, docked to a screen or window edge. Applies only to palettes. Read/write. (Introduced in 8.0)
stashPosition	String	Where this palette window is stashed (docked). One of: `left`: Docked at the left edge of the parent window or screen. `right`: Docked at the right edge of the parent window or screen. `none`: Not docked. Applies only to palettes. Read/write. (Introduced in 8.0)
text	String	The title of this window. For inspectors, it is the label shown in the left-bottom corner of the inspector window. Read/write.
title	—	Deprecated in 8.0. Use `text` instead.

type	String	The type of the window. One of:
		`debugger`
		`dialog`
		`document`
		`inspector`
		`palette`
		`toolbar`

visible	Boolean	When `true`, the window is visible. ● Set to `true` or `false` to show or hide a palette window. ● Read-only for dialogs and Inspector windows. The value of this property does not indicate whether the dialog is within the boundaries of the screen.

window object properties: debugger window

These properties are defined only in the SDK-defined JavaScript Debugger window. They control the display orientation of the various parts of the window. To obtain this window, use the static find (page 312) method of the built-in Window Class (page 310):

```
debuggerWin = Window.find( "debugger", "sdk" );
```

debuggerOrientation	String	Within the Debugger frame, the display orientation of Source panel with respect to the Info panel (containing the Stack and Variables views). One of: `horizontal`: Display Source panel to the left of Info panel. `vertical`: Display Source frame above Info panel.
infoOrientation	String	Within the Info panel, the display orientation of Stack view with respect to the Variables view. One of: `horizontal`: Display Stack view to the left of Variables view. `vertical`: Display Stack view above Variables view.
shellOrientation	String	The display orientation of the JavaScript Shell frame with respect to the Full Debugger frame. One of: `horizontal`: Display Shell frame to the left of Debugger frame. `vertical`: Display Shell frame above Debugger frame.

window object functions

add *windowObj*.add(*type*[, *placement*, *text*, *creationParam*])	Creates and returns a new control Object Types (page 78) of the given type and adds it as a child of this window.

type	The type of control to create. One of:
	
	`button`
	`checkbox`
	`colorfield`
	`combobox`
	`custom`
	`edittext`
	`filelist`
	`frame`
	`hierarchy`
	`line`
	`list`
	`panel`
	`preview`
	`progressbar`
	`radiobutton`
	`scrollbar`
	`slider`
	`source`
	`splitpanel`
	`statictext`
	`tabpanel`
	`urlgetter`
	
	Each of the control types is described under control Object Types (page 78).

placement	Optional. A read/write array containing the coordinates of the window in the form [*left,top,right,bottom*]. You can set this property using an JavaScript object in the form `{left:value, top:value, right:value, bottom:value}` or `{left:value, top:value, width:value, height:value}`
text	Optional. An initial value or set of values for the control, depending on the type: ● An initial text value for the new control, such as a button's text label. ● Initial items for a combo box popup or list, as a comma-separated list of strings; for example `"item1,item2"`. ● The initial numeric value and minimum and maximum values for a scrollbar, slider, or progressbar; for example, `50, 0, 100`.
creationParam	Optional. A JavaScript object that contains properties to set special initial values of the child element. See the individual type descriptions of the control Object Types (page 78), panel Object (page 233), splitpanel Object (page 271), and tabpanel Object (page 274).
center *windowObj*.center()	Centers the window on the screen.

close *windowObj*.close([*retValue*])	Closes the window.
retValue	Optional. A number to return from the add (page 317) or runModal (page 318) function that opened the window.
createMenu *paletteObj*.createMenu()	Creates and returns a new menu Object (page 223) for a flyout menu for this palette window, or the existing object if the menu already exists. Ignored for a dialog window.
exitModal	Deprecated in 8.0. Use hide instead.
hide *windowObj*.hide(*n*)	Hides the window. For a dialog, call this function from the onClick (page 364) event handler for a button that dismisses the dialog, passing a number to be returned by the show call that opened the window.
n	Optional. A value to return from the currently executing show function call. Typically, this value indicates whether the user confirmed, canceled, or made some other choice in a dialog. It is up to your callback implementation to interpret the value.
remove *windowObj*.remove (*name*) *windowObj*.remove (*index*) *windowObj*.remove (*controlObj*)	Removes a specified control from the children array of the window. (Introduced in 8.0)
name	The JavaScript name of the child to remove.
index	The 0-based index of the child to remove.
controlObj	The control object for the child to remove.
runModal	Deprecated in 8.0. Use show instead.
show *windowObj*.show()	Shows the window. For a dialog, does not return until the window is closed by a call to hide, then returns a number passed from the hide call, which can be used to indicate how the window was closed. For other windows, it is 0.
showArea *windowObj*.showArea(*area, onOff*)	For the debugger window only, shows or hides one of the panels.

area	The panel to show or hide. One of:
	    shell
	    debugger
	    stack
	    watch

onOff	When true, show the specified panel. When false, hide it.

XMP Object

Class: JSXXMP

This object provides access to embedded XMP metadata for a file. It provides function to access, set, and delete properties in the metadata.

(Introduced in 8.0)

Acquiring the XMP object

The xmp property of a file Object (page 158) contains the XMP object for the metadata for the corresponding file.

```
var myFile = fileGetDialog();
var xmp = myFile.xmp;
```

XMP object properties

existingNameSpaces	Array	An array of all namespace names used in the file's XMP metadata. Read-only.
nameSpace	String	The current namespace name. Default is: http://ns.adobe.com/xap/1.0/ You can add a namespace by setting this to one that does not exist.
property_name	String	You can access each property of the current namespace through a property of the same name.

XMP object functions

deleteProperty XMPObj.deleteProperty(propertyName)	Deletes the specified property in the current namespace. Returns true on success.
propertyName	The name of the property in the current namespace.
dump XMPObj.dump()	Writes all XMP metadata into the JavaScript Debugger output.
getPropertyValue XMPObj.getPropertyValue(propertyName)	Gets the value of the specified property in the current namespace. Returns a string for a single-valued property, or an array for a multi-valued property.
propertyName	The name of the property in the current namespace.

setPropertyValue *XMPObj*.setPropertyValue (*propertyName*, *propertyValue*)	Sets the value of the specified property in the current namespace. Creates the property if it does not yet exist, otherwise replaces the value. Returns the new value.
propertyName	The name of the property in the current namespace.
propertyValue	The new value of the property. A string for a single-valued property, or an array of strings for a multi-valued property.

5 | Tags

This chapter contains reference descriptions of all xHTML markup tags the GoLive CS2 SDK provides. GoLive interprets these tags to create the JavaScript objects described in Chapter 4, "Objects."

Extensions

An extension or module contains code defined in scripts within its `Main.html` file, and object defined by GoLive XML elements within that file.

GoLive always creates a module Object (page 227) when it loads an extension's `Main.html` file, even if the extension does not define a `<jsxmodule>` (page 321) element. If it exists, this tag's attributes activate debug mode, automatic localization of JavaScript strings, and a specified JavaScript execution timeout for this extension's `module` object only.

Normally, all files in the `GoLive_dir`/`Modules/Extend Scripts/Common` subfolder are loaded with all extensions. The `<jsxexclude>` (page 322) element allows an extension to prevent a JavaScript file found in the `Common` folder from being loaded into the extension.

Scripts are defined by the standard JavaScript `<script>` (page 323) element. Normally, scripts reside inside the `<body>` element, but you can place them inside an optional `<head>` element.

jsxmodule

Sets this extension module's JavaScript name and activates optional features.

Syntax
```
<jsxmodule name="moduleName" timeout="seconds"
locale="countryCode" debug>
```

Attributes

name	Optional. Specifies this module's JavaScript name. In the JavaScript name space, the `module.name` expression evaluates to this value. If the `<jsxmodule>` tag is missing or if it supplies no `name` attribute, GoLive supplies a default `module.name` value which is the name of the folder that holds the extension's `Main.html` file.
debug	Optional. When any module supplies this attribute, the full JavaScript Debugger window is enabled and active for all modules.

`timeout`	Optional. The number of seconds the JavaScript engine waits for a response from the currently running JavaScript code. If this amount of time elapses without a response from the currently running JavaScript code, GoLive generates a timeout runtime error, stops waiting for a response, and exits the script. You can disable this behavior by setting *moduleObj*.`timeout` to `false`. By default, the GoLive engine waits indefinitely for JavaScript code to return. Your module can specify the amount of time GoLive waits for its JavaScript code to return by setting this attribute's value to a number of seconds between `0` and `9999`. (9999 seconds is 2 hours, 46 minutes 39 seconds.) Setting this attribute to `0` seconds or `false` causes GoLive to wait indefinitely for this module's code to return. GoLive always waits indefinitely for its calls to your Events and Event Handlers (page 359) to return, regardless of whether you have specified a timeout value. The code that sets the global default timeout value runs once when GoLive initializes all the modules in the `Extend Scripts` folder at startup time.
`locale`	A temporary locale used to translate the module's strings for testing purposes. Within the scope of this module, this value overrides the locale ID that GoLive uses. Valid values are two-letter ISO-3166-1 country codes as used for top-level Internet domains, such as `DE` for Germany or `IT` for Italy. The `US` country code represents all versions of English. Valid codes are those representing the Roman-language subset of all codes the ISO-3166-1 standard defines. You can disable all of the module's automatic translation features by setting `NONE` as this attribute's value; however, this feature is intended for development and testing purposes only. Do not use this feature to disable automatic localization in commercial extensions.
`info`	An information string that describes the extension. It is visible from the User Interface by selecting **Edit > Preferences > Modules >** *module* **> Show Item Information**. The string is localized like other strings. You only need to make a matching entry in the locale table.
`version`	A string value that identifies the version number of the extension. It is visible from the User Interface by selecting **Edit > Preferences > Modules >** *module* **> Show Item Information**

jsxexclude

Designates a JavaScript file in the `Common` subfolder that should not be loaded and executed as part of this extension.

Syntax

```
<jsxexclude src="relativeURL" />
```

Attributes

`src`	URL for the path to the JavaScript file to exclude from this extension. The URL is relative to: *GoLive_dir*/Modules/Extend Scripts/Common

script

Wraps your extension's JavaScript code in the `<script>` tag set.

Syntax
```
<script [src="localURLOnly"] > JavaScriptCode </script>
```

Attributes

src	Optional. Relative URL for the path to an external JavaScript file on the local file system. This attribute does not support URLs to remote files. The URL is relative to the `Main.html` file that contains this `<script>` tag.

Notes

Typically, the `Main.html` file defines all of an extension's code, and the `src` attribute is not needed. When used in a `Main.html` file, a `<script>` element that provides a `src` attribute value cannot provide any other content. For example:

```
<script src="myScript.js"></script>
<script>
   initializeModule() {
      }
   parseBox() {
      }
</script>
```

When using the `src` attribute in a `Main.html` file, note the following differences from the JavaScript 1.1 standard for Web browser use of this attribute:

- Included files must reside on the local file system. A URL reference to a file residing on a remote server is not a valid `src` attribute value.

- JavaScript code appearing between the `<script>` and `</script>` tags in the `Main.html` file executes after code provided by the `src` attribute. JavaScript in the `Main.html` file overwrites same-named entities defined by the external file.

Note: A GoLive 5 extension's `Main.html` file was restricted to exactly one set of `<script></script>` tags; in GoLive 6 and later, the `Main.html` file can hold multiple `<script>` tags.

Menus and Toolbars

Use the following tags to create menus and toolbars:

- One `<jsxmenubar>` (page 324) binary tag per `Main.html` file surrounds all the other tags that add menus to the GoLive menu bar.

- The `<jsxmenu>` (page 325) tag defines a custom menu that appears to the left of the **Window** menu in the GoLive menu bar. This tag creates a menu Object (page 223).

- The `<jsxitem>` (page 326) tag defines a custom menu item that appears in a custom menu. This tag creates a menuItem Object (page 225).

The menu Object (page 223) for each predefined and script-defined menu is available by name as an element of the menubar (page 48) global array. Each menu item is accessible through its parent `menu` object. The JavaScript names of all predefined menus, submenus, and menu items in the GoLive menus are provided in Appendix B, "Menu Names." You can use these names to add script-defined submenus and items in positions relative to existing items; however, an extension cannot redefine the behavior of a built-in menu item.

When GoLive is about to display a menu item, it generates the menuSetup (page 363) event with that item as the target. Your registered handler for this event can enable or disable the item and set or clear its check mark.

When the user chooses a menu item, GoLive generates the menuSignal (page 363) event with that item as the target. Your registered handler for this event provides the item's behavior.

- The `<jsxtoolbar>` (page 327) tag defines a new toolbar that appears within the main GoLive toolbar.

Each toolbar you create is represented by a window Object (page 313) with `type="toolbar"`. Like any other window, it contains controls. For a toolbar, these are typically buttons with icons. When a user interacts with a toolbar control, GoLive generates the appropriate interact event (such as onClick, page 364) with that control as the target. Your registered handler for this event provides the control's behavior.

jsxmenubar

This tag wraps all of the tags that define an extension's custom menus and custom menu items. The `<jsxmenubar>` tag wraps the GoLive menu bar. An extension's source code must not contain more than one `<jsxmenubar></jsxmenubar>` tag set.

Syntax

```
<jsxmenubar>
    <!-- <jsxmenu> element goes here. -->
</jsxmenubar>
```

The `<jsxmenubar>` tag has no attributes.

jsxmenu

This tag creates a custom menu that appears in the GoLive menu bar. The binary `<jsxmenu>` tag wraps one or more `<jsxitem>` tags, which define individual menu items. This tag creates a menu Object (page 223).

A `<jsxmenu>` element must be contained by a `<jsxmenubar>` element. Only one `<jsxmenubar>` element is allowed per module, so all of the extension module's `<jsxmenu>` elements must be contained by this `<jsxmenubar>` element.

Syntax

```
<jsxmenu name="name" title="Menu text"
        location="relativePlacement"
lname="existingMenuOrItem">
    <!-- <jsxitem> elements go here -->
</jsxmenu>
```

Attributes

name	The JavaScript name of the menu. This name appears in the JavaScript global namespace and in the `menubar` global array.
	• If it is one of the predefined menu names, the new menu is added as a submenu of that menu. Predefined menu names are:
	`file`
	`edit`
	• If it is not one of the predefined menu names, the new menu is added at the top level of the GoLive menu bar.
	If this value duplicates the name attribute of any other `<jsxmenu>` element in any other module, this element's menu items are appended to the previously defined menu.
title	The menu's title in the GoLive menu bar or in the parent menu.

location	Optional. Where in the parent menu to insert this submenu. One of:
	`before`: Before the item specified by `lname`.
	`after`: After the item specified by `lname`
	`start`: At the top of the parent menu
	`end`: At the bottom of the parent menu
lname	Optional. When `location` is `"before"` or `"after"`, the JavaScript name of an existing menu item. See Appendix B, "Menu Names."

jsxitem

This tag defines a single menu item inside a menu. This tag creates a menuItem Object (page 225).

Syntax

```
<jsxitem name="objectName" title="menuItemText" dynamic
        location="relativePlacement"
lname="existingMenuItem">
```

Attributes

name	The JavaScript name of the menu item. This name appears as a property of this menu item's enclosing menu Object (page 223) and as an element of that object's items (page 223) array.
title	The menu item's text as it appears in the menu. Set this attribute's value to a single dash (`"-"`) creates a menu separator item.
dynamic	When this attribute is present, GoLive passes this menu item to its extension's `menuSetup` method before displaying it. The `menuSetup` method sets the item's checked and enabled states. Menu items that do not include this attribute do not generate calls to the `menuSetup` method.
location	Optional. Where in the parent menu to insert this item. One of:
	`before`: Before the item specified by `lname`.
	`after`: After the item specified by `lname`.
	`start`: At the top of the parent menu.
	`end`: At the bottom of the parent menu.
lname	Optional. When `location` is `"before"` or `"after"`, the JavaScript name of an existing menu item. See Appendix B, "Menu Names."

Notes

A menuItem Object (page 225) is accessible both as a property of its menu Object (page 223) and as an element of that object's items (page 223) array.

For example, if the `myItem` menu item appears in the `myMenu` custom menu, the `myMenu.myItem` expression provides access to this menu item in JavaScript.

You can also retrieve the item using its name as the index into the `myMenu` object's `items` array. For example, if the `<jsxitem>` element definition supplies `Fred` as the value of its name attribute, you could retrieve it by that name:

```
var menuItemHolder = myMenu.items ["Fred"];
```

Custom menu examples

The following markup defines a menu item to be placed in the submenu **New** of the **Site** menu, following the first separator. The menu item initializes itself dynamically—its checked state changes each time the user chooses it. Selecting the menu item opens an alert window that displays the menu item text.

```
<jsxmenubar>
    <jsxmenu name="site">
        <jsxmenu name="SiNw">
            <jsxitem name="myItem" title="My Item"
location="after"
                lname="dsi4"/>
        </jsxmenu>
    </jsxmenu>
</jsxmenubar>

<script>
    initializeModule() {
        app.addEventListener( "menuSetup",
menuSetupHandler );
        app.addEventListener( "menuSignal", menuClicked );
    }
    menuSetupHandler( evObj ) {
        if (evObj.target.name == "myItem" )
            item.checked = !item.checked;
    }
    menuClicked( evObj ) {
        if (evObj..target.name == "myItem")
            alert ("Selected: " + item.title);
    }
</script>
```

jsxtoolbar

This tag defines a toolbar. New toolbars are automatically added to the toolbar section of the **Window** menu, and are visible by default as part of GoLive's main toolbar. This tag creates a a window Object (page 313) with `type="toolbar"`.

Syntax

```
<jsxtoolbar name="objectName" title="toolbarTitle"
width="numPixels">
   <jsxcontrol type="button" picture="icon" ... />
   ...
</jsxtoolbar>
```

Attributes

name	The JavaScript name of the window Object (page 313) for this toolbar.
title	The toolbar's title string, which appears in the toolbar section of the **Window** menu. In Windows, if you undock the toolbar, this string appears as the window title.
width	The width in pixels of the toolbar.

Notes

Each toolbar you create is represented by a window Object (page 313). Like any other window, it contains controls. For a toolbar these are typically (but not necessarily) buttons with icons. The controls are placed relative to the parent's position; the toolbar should be wide enough to accommodate all controls and spacing.

In Windows, the user can undock the toolbar (drag it away from the main toolbar) and display it as a separate window with the specified title.

Toolbar window objects cannot be accessed through the Window.find method, but they are in the dialogs (page 47) list, and can be accessed by name. The window object's visible property controls whether the toolbar is shown.

Example

```
<jsxtoolbar name="myToolbar" title="My Toolbar" width="55">
   <jsxcontrol height="20" name="tbbutton1" picture="icon1"
     posx="2" posy="2" type="button" value="" width="24" />
   <jsxcontrol height="20" name="tbbutton2" picture="icon2"
     posx="28" posy="2" type="button" value="" width="24" />
</jsxtoolbar>
```

Dialogs and Palettes

There are three tags you can use to create different kinds of windows:

- The `<jsxdialog>` (page 330) tag defines a modal dialog window. This dialog requires a response before it allows the user to continue.

- The `<jsxpalette>` (page 331) tag defines a palette window, also known as a modeless dialog window. This window does not require a response. Its name appears in the GoLive **Windows** menu. You can display or hide the window interactively or programmatically.

- The `<jsxinspector>` (page 348) tag creates a special-purpose palette used to implement the Inspector for a custom tag the `<jsxelement>` (page 346) tag defines. The SDK activates this palette automatically when the custom element is the selected element in a GoLive document window. Because an Inspector is always associated with a `<jsxelement>` element, information on using the `<jsxinspector>` tag is in "Objects Palette Icons and Customized Content" on page 342.

The dialog, palette, or Inspector is the container for a collection of `<jsxcontrol>` (page 337) elements that provide the rest of the dialog's user interface.

When GoLive interprets one of these elements, it creates a `dialog` object to represent it. The `name` attribute defines the JavaScript name of the `dialog` object. You can retrieve a `dialog` object by name from the dialogs (page 47) global array:

```
var myWin = dialogs["objectName"];
```

The `dialog` object also appears as a property of the global namespace. You can retrieve a `dialog` object by name directly from the JavaScript global namespace:

```
var myWin = objectName;
```

Control Containers

Dialogs and palettes can group controls by defining them within a container element. When GoLive interprets one of these elements, it creates a type of control object to represent it. However, these containers do not have any user-interface behavior.

- The `<jsxview>` (page 332) tag defines a simple rectangular frame (a panel) to contain user-interface controls or other subpanels.

- The `<jsxtabview>` (page 333) tag defines a tabbed frame, like that of a palette. It can contain only subpanels; it cannot directly contain user-interface controls.

- The `<jsxsplitview>` (page 334) tag defines a split frame that contains exactly two subpanels; it cannot directly contain user-interface controls.

jsxdialog

The `<jsxdialog>` tag defines a modal dialog window that acts as a container element for the tags and attributes that define the dialog's content. The content of a dialog is a form that GoLive implements as a table. The `<jsxdialog>` tag wraps this form. This tag creates a window Object (page 313) with `type="dialog"`.

Syntax

```
<jsxdialog name="objectName" title="Title Of Dialog"
width="numPixels"
    height="numPixels" [resize]>
    <!-- <jsxcontrol> elements here -->
</jsxdialog>
```

Attributes

name	The dialog's name in the global JavaScript namespace. For reliable name-based access, this value must be unique in the universe of all currently running extensions.
title	The title of the dialog window.
width	The width in pixels. If you use a layout grid to design the dialog in GoLive, the SDK embeds a `<table>` tag that overrides this value.
height	The height in pixels. If you use a layout grid to design the dialog in GoLive, the SDK embeds a `<table>` tag that overrides this value.
resize	Optional. No value. If supplied, the dialog is interactively resizeable.

Notes

You can place buttons, checkboxes, static text, and other controls in the dialog by adding `<jsxcontrol>` elements to the body of the `<jsxdialog>` element definition.

The `runModal` method of the window Object (page 313) causes it to execute as a modal dialog—it requires a response before allowing the user to proceed. There are two ways to create a button that closes the dialog window:

- Name the button one of the special names `dialogok`, `dialogcancel`, or `dialogother`. When the user clicks a button having one of these names, the `runModal` method closes the dialog and returns a numeric value corresponding to the name of the button.

- Call the `exitModal` method from the `controlSignal` method that handles that button's events. Pass as the `exitModal` method's argument a value the `runModal` method is to return as the reason the dialog closed.

jsxpalette

The `<jsxpalette>` tag creates a modeless dialog, also known as a floating window or palette window. The palette's title appears in the **Window** menu. The upper right corner of the palette window provides an optional pull-down menu. This tag creates a window Object (page 313) with `type="palette"`.

Syntax

```
<jsxpalette name="objectName" title="Title Of Palette"
    width="numPixels" height="numPixels" winmenu="true|false">
    <!-- <jsxcontrol> elements that define palette content -->
    <!-- <jsxmenu> and <jsxitem> elements that define palette
    menu -->
</jsxpalette>
```

Attributes

name	The palette's name in the global JavaScript namespace. For reliable name-based access, this value must be unique among all currently running extensions.
title	The title of the palette window. This text also appears in the **Window** menu.
width	The palette's width in pixels.
height	The palette's height in pixels.
winmenu	Optional. When `false`, this window does not appear in the Window menu. Default is `true`. (Introduced in 8.0)

Notes

When GoLive interprets a `<jsxpalette>` element, it creates a palette-type window Object (page 313). The element can contain menu elements to define the popup menu, and control elements to define user-interface controls in the window.

The object has a `visible` property, which you can set to show or hide the palette window; however, there is no corresponding `visible` attribute in the `<jsxpalette>` element. By default, GoLive displays your palette window the first time it loads the extension that provides the `<jsxpalette>` tag. In subsequent user sessions, GoLive displays or hides the palette according to whether it was displayed or hidden at the end of the previous GoLive user session.

---

jsxview

A `<jsxview>` element defines a panel, a simple a rectangular area which can contain controls or other panels. A panel can be contained in a dialog, palette, or inspector window, or in a tab panel or split panel. This tag creates a panel Object (page 233).

Syntax

```
<jsxview name="JSName" title="panelTitle"
width="numPixels"
        height="numPixels" posx="numPixels",
posy="numPixels"
        picture="iconName" resource="resourceName">
  <!-- Control definitions here -->
</jsxview>
```

Attributes

name	The panel's name in the global JavaScript namespace. For reliable name-based access, this value must be unique among all currently running extensions.
title	The title of the panel. If this panel is the child of a tab panel, this string appears in the tab.
width	The width in pixels.
height	The height in pixels.
posx	The x-coordinate of the upper-left corner of the panel in the parent. The window origin is the upper left corner. Positive values are to the right of the origin, negative values to the left.
posy	The y-coordinate of the upper-left corner of the control in the parent. The window origin is the upper left corner. Positive values are to below the origin, negative values above.
picture	When the panel is used as a tab in a `<tabview>` element, the icon to use in the tab in place of the `title` string.
resource	The name of an independently defined panel resource to reuse.

Notes

You can define a panel directly inside a dialog, or palette:

```
<jsxdialog ...>
  <jsxview ...>
      <jsxcontrol ...>
      </jsxcontrol>
  </jsxview>
</jsxdialog>
```

You can also define a panel outside a window, as a *panel resource*. A panel resource defines a reusable group of controls. One resource definition can be reused in a number of windows. For a panel resource, omit the position parameters:

```
<jsxview name="resourceName" title="resourceTitle"
width="numPixels"
        height="numPixels">
   <!-- Control definitions here -->
</jsxview>
```

After it is defined, you can include a resource in a window, specifying it by name and setting the position. For example:

```
<jsxdialog name="UIResourceTest" title="UI Resource
Test"
      width="" height="">
   <jsxview resource="myResView" name="Test View"
posx="10" posy="10">
</jsxdialog>
```

The panel is included in the window along with all of its controls.

jsxtabview

The `<jsxtabview>` tag creates a tabbed window. A tab panel cannot contain controls directly; it can contain only panels. Each panel is displayed as a tab within the container. This tag creates a tabpanel Object (page 274).

You can define the panels with their controls directly inside the tab panel element or you can use panel resources. A `<jsxtabview>` must be contained in a window definition, such as a `<jsxdialog>` element.

Syntax

```
<jsxtabview name="JSName" title="panelTitle"
width="numPixels"
        height="numPixels" posx="numPixels"
posy="numPixels"
            offsetx="numPixels" offsety ="numPixels">
   <!-- Panel definitions here -->
</jsxtabview>
```

Attributes

name	The panel's name in the global JavaScript namespace. For reliable name-based access, this value must be unique among all currently running extensions.
title	The title of the panel.
width	The width in pixels.
height	The height in pixels.

posx	The x-coordinate of the upper-left corner of the panel in the parent. The window origin is the upper left corner. Positive values are to the right of the origin, negative values to the left.
posy	The y-coordinate of the upper-left corner of the control in the parent. The window origin is the upper left corner. Positive values are to below the origin, negative values above.
offsetx	The horizontal offset value (in pixels) for the margin between the upper left corner of the panel's content area and the upper left corner of its children.
offsety	The vertical offset value (in pixels) for the margin between the upper left corner of the panel's content area and the upper left corner of its children.

Notes

Because each panel is a tab, you need not specify its position within the container. However, you can give `picture` attribute for the panel, which specifies an icon to use in the tab. For example:

```
<jsxtabview name="mytabpanel" posx="10" posy="9"
width="235" height="136">
    <jsxview resource="tabpanel1" name="tabpanel1"
height="84" width="201"
           picture="imagename">
    <jsxview resource="tabpanel2" name="tabpanel2"
height="84" width="201">
        <jsxview resource="tabpanel3" name="tabpanel3"
height="84" width="201">
    </jsxtabview>
```

jsxsplitview

A `<jsxsplitview>` element defines a a panel with two subpanels, which can be arranged vertically or horizontally. The border between the panels can be moved with the mouse. A split panel can be contained in a dialog, palette, or inspector window, or in another panel. This tag creates a splitpanel Object (page 271).

(Introduced in 8.0)

Syntax

```
</jsxsplitview>
    <jsxsplitview name="JSName" posx="numPixels"
    posy="numPixels"
                    width="numPixels" height="numPixels"
                    halign="alignOption"
    valign="alignOption"
                    orientation="horizontal|vertical"
                    partition="percentage">
        <jsxview ...>
```

```
        <!-- Control definitions here -->
    </jsxview>
    <jsxview ...>
        <!-- Control definitions here -->
    </jsxview>
</jsxsplitview>
```

Attributes

`name`	The panel's name in the global JavaScript namespace. For reliable name-based access, this value must be unique among all currently running extensions.
`posx`	The x-coordinate of the upper-left corner of the panel in the parent. The window origin is the upper left corner. Positive values are to the right of the origin, negative values to the left.
`posy`	The y-coordinate of the upper-left corner of the panel in the parent. The window origin is the upper left corner. Positive values are to below the origin, negative values above.
`width`	The width in pixels.
`height`	The height in pixels.
`halign`	The horizontal alignment of the panel when the size of the window changes. One of: `left`: Pin the left edge, do not move or resize `center`: Pin the center, change the X position by half of window resize delta `right`: Pin the right edge, change the X position by window resize delta `scale`: Resize to maintain relative width
`valign`	The vertical alignment of the panel when the size of the window changes. One of: `top`: Pin the top edge, do not move or resize `center`: Pin the center, change the Y position by half of window resize delta `bottom`: Pin the bottom edge, change the X position by window resize delta `scale`: Resize to maintain relative height
`orientation`	Whether the subpanels are arranged horizontally or vertically. One of: `horizontal`: The subpanels are arranged horizontally, and the dividing line is vertical. `vertical`: The subpanels are arranged vertically, and the dividing line is horizontal.
`partition`	The position of the dividing line between the subpanels, as a percentage of the parent's height or width. 0 is the left or top edge, 100 is the right or bottom edge. 50 puts the line in the middle.

jsxlayoutline

The `<jsxlayoutline>` tag defines a demarcation line in a window that determines the autolayout behavior of that window when the UI strings are localized. Include this tag in any window or view element to enable autolayout.

Syntax

```
<jsxlayoutline x="horizPos" y="vertPos"
length="numPixels"
        direction="true|false">
```

Attributes

x	The x-coordinate of the origin of the demarcation line. The window origin is the upper left corner. Positive values are to the right of the origin, negative values to the left.
y	The y-coordinate of the origin of the demarcation line. The window origin is the upper left corner. Positive values are to below the origin, negative values above.
length	The length in pixels of the demarcation line. The line extends down from the x, y position.
direction	When false (the default), controls to the left of the demarcation line change size, and those on the right change position. When true, this is reversed: controls on the right change size, and those on the left change position.

Notes

When GoLive translates UI strings to the local language, the length of the string can change. This can affect the appearance of your control layout. Include the <jsxlayoutline> (page 335) tag in a window definition to take advantage of the autolayout feature. When this feature is enabled, GoLive automatically adjusts the sizes and locations of controls in the window to allow for different string lengths in different languages. It can resize static text fields to grow or shrink with changes in language, and move controls to allow for other controls that have changed size.

The attribute values define a vertical line in the window. The line is not displayed in GoLive; it determines which controls should change size, and which should change position. The controls on one side of the line (by default, the left) change size to allow for localized strings, and the controls on the other side change position to accommodate the changes in the first group.

(Introduced in 7.0)

Controls

The `<jsxcontrol>` tag (page 337) creates the controls in a dialog, palette, or Inspector. This tag creates a control Object Types (page 78).

When a user interacts with a control, GoLive generates the appropriate interaction event (such as onClick, page 364) with that control object as the target. Your registered handler for this event provides the control's behavior.

jsxcontrol

The `<jsxcontrol>` tag (page 337) creates a variety of controls that appear as the content of dialogs. Its attribute values define the control's type, its initial position, and its alignment behavior.

Syntax

```
<jsxcontrol type="typeOfControl" name="JSName"
value="initialText"
   helpTip="help_string" posx="numixels"
posy="numPixels"
   width="numPixels" height="numPixels"
   halign="alignOption" valign="alignOption"
   group="groupID"
   onChange="true|false" onNoChanged="true|false"
   onEnter="true|false" enterOK="true|false" >
   <!--- <jsxlistcolumn> elements go here -->
   <!--- <jsxparam> elements go here -->
</jsxcontrol>
```

Attributes

`type`	The type of control this element defines. One of: `button`: Pushbutton `buttonedit`: An `edit` control with the `onEnter` property set to `true`. Has an optional **Enter** button, controlled by a user preference. `color`: Color select field `colorfield`: Color select field `combobox`: Edit field with popup menu `custom`: Custom control `checkbox`: Checkbox `check`: Checkbox `edit`: Edit field that signals a change depending on property values for `onEnter`, `onChange`, and `onNoChanged`. `editarea`: Multiline edit field that signals a change for each keystroke and loss of focus. `filelist`: A tree control that displays a file and folder hierarchy. `frame`: Horizontal line, vertical line, or frame box. `hierarchy`: A tree control whose nodes can contain subnodes. Nodes be opened and closed, edited, and deleted. `line`: Separator line `list`: List box `listbox`: List box `password`: Password-entry field `popup`: Edit field with popup menu (same as `combobox`) `preview`: HTML browser window `progressbar`: Progress bar `radio`: Radio button `radiobutton`: Radio button `scrollbar`: Scrollbar `slider`: Slider `source`: JavaScript editor with syntax checking `static`: Static text field `statictext`: Static text field `urlgetter`: URL entry field
`name`	The JavaScript name of the control. The control appears under this name as a property of the dialog or palette that contains it. For example, the JavaScript expression `myDialog.myControl` returns the control named `myControl` that is contained by the dialog container named `myDialog`. You can also use the control's `name` value to retrieve it from the `children` array of its parent. Each control's name must be unique among all controls that share the same dialog container. Controls that do not share the same dialog container can use non-unique names. For example, a `<jsxcontrol>` element having the name `myButton` can be used in multiple dialog containers without causing namespace clashes. However, two controls having the name `myButton` cannot appear in the same dialog or palette. **Note:** When a control's name is not unique among all currently running extensions, the control cannot be retrieved reliably by name from the global `controls` array.

value	The control's initial text. Corresponds to the `text` property of the control object, and is used in various ways in different control types.
	For `combobox` and `list` controls this value is a comma-separated list of items to display. A dash creates a menu item separator. For example, `<jsxcontrol type=popup value= "Red, - , Blue" ... >` creates a list in which a separator appears between the `Red` and `Blue` list items.
	Note: You can initialize the display of a `urlgetter` control by assigning a URL as its `value`, but this does not associate the control with a `link` object for that URL. To associate the control with a link Object (page 207), call the setLink (page 117) function.
helpTip	A short descriptive string that appears as a tooltip for certain types of controls. (Introduced in 8.0)
posx posy	The x- and y-coordinates of the upper-left corner of the control in the parent. The upper-left corner of a window or control is the origin (0,0). Values greater than 0 are to the right and down, values less than 0 are to the left and up.
	When the user drops the control on a table grid in layout mode, GoLive updates these attributes.
height width	The control's height and width in pixels.
	For a `line`, `slider`, `progressbar`, or `scrollbar`, if the `height` value is greater than the `width` value, the control is vertical; otherwise it is horizontal.
	A `frame` is drawn as a horizontal line when the `height` attribute is omitted, and a vertical line when the `width` attribute is omitted. When both attributes are supplied, it is a box.
halign	The horizontal alignment of the control when the size of the window changes. One of:

	`left`: Pin the left edge, do not move or resize
	    `center`: Pin the center, change the X position by half of window resize delta
	    `right`: Pin the right edge, change the X position by window resize delta
	    `scale`: Resize to maintain relative width

valign	The vertical alignment of the control when the size of the window changes. One of:
	    `top`: Pin the top edge, do not move or resize
	    `center`: Pin the center, change the Y position by half of window resize delta
	    `bottom`: Pin the bottom edge, change the X position by window resize delta
	    `scale`: Resize to maintain relative height

group	For `radiobutton` only. The group ID for radio buttons. An arbitrary string value, unique within the window. All buttons with the same group ID act as a set of radio buttons, where selecting one deselects all others in the group. When this attribute is not present for a button, that button is not affected by other buttons.
onChange	For `edit` control only. When `true`, GoLive generates the onChange (page 364) event with this control as the target when the edit field has the focus, the value has changed, and the user has pressed ENTER. Default is `false`.

---

onNoChanged	For `edit` control only. When `true`, GoLive generates the onChange (page 364) event with this control as the target when the edit field value has not changed. Combine this with `onEnter` and/or `onChange`. Default is `false`.
onEnter	For `edit` control only. When `true`, GoLive generates the onChange (page 364) event with this control as the target when the edit field has the focus, the value has changed, and the user has pressed ENTER. Default is `false`.
enterOK	For `edit` control only. When `true`, and if there is an OK button in the window, pressing ENTER in this control is the same as clicking OK. Default is `false`.

Notes

Controls dropped on a layout grid are implemented as table elements. Such controls ignore the `width` and `height` attributes their enclosing dialog specifies. Instead, they use the table's `width` and `height` attributes as the size of their enclosing container.

jsxlistcolumn

To define a column in a `list` control, enclose `<jsxlistcolumn>` elements in the `<jsxcontrol>` element. Each element defines one column.

Syntax
```
<jsxlistcolumn [title="titleString"]
value="value1,value2, ... valuen">
```

Attributes

title	Optional. The title of this column.
value	A comma-separated list of the list items in this column.

jsxparam

To initialize the numeric limits of the `scrollbar`, `slider`, and `progressbar` controls, enclose `<jsxparam>` elements in the `<jsxcontrol>` element.

Syntax
```
<jsxparam name="paramName" value="num">
```

Attributes

name	The parameter being initialized. One of:
	`min`: The minimum value.
	`max`: The maximum value.
	`steps`: For a `slider` control, the number of tick marks.
	`line`: For a `scrollbar` control, the number of pixels to move to scroll one line.
	`page`: For a `scrollbar` control, the number of pixels to move to scroll one page.
value	The initial numeric value of the named parameter.

Objects Palette Icons and Customized Content

The Objects palette holds icons the user can drag to Layout view to add predefined content to the page. This predefined content is known as a *palette entry*.

You can use the following tags to install a custom palette entry in the Objects palette:

- The `<jsxpaletteentry>` (page 344) tag defines the palette entry itself:
  - It provides the content this palette entry adds to the page. This content can consist of any combination of standard HTML tags, SDK-defined tags, custom tags defined by the `<jsxelement>` tag, and associated attribute values.
  - It supplies the drag-and-drop icon that represents this content in the Objects palette.

    Use the `<img>` tag to supply palette icons and the placeholder graphic that represents a custom element in Layout view. The SDK-provided version of this tag provides a `name` attribute that the standard HTML version of the tag does not provide. This additional attribute enables your extension's JavaScript code to retrieve and manipulate `<img>` elements by name.

- The `<jsxelement>` (page 346) tag defines the name of a custom markup tag to associate with the palette entry's content. For example, you can use this tag to define your own `<mytag>` tag. An associated `<jsxpaletteentry>` element provides content that the `<mytag>` tag adds to the page. The name of a custom tag must consist of lowercase characters only.

- The `<jsxinspector>` (page 348) tag creates the Inspector window used to interact with the content the palette entry adds to the page.

- The `<jsxpalettegroup>` (page 343) tag specifies the Objects palette tab that is to hold the palette entry's drag-and-drop icon. This tag can create a new, named tab in the Objects palette or it can specify the use of any existing tab except the Custom tab. Optionally, this tag can supply a custom icon to display on the tab itself.

GoLive uses the `classid` attributes of the `<jsxelement>`, `<jsxpaletteentry>`, `<jsxinspector>`, and `<jsxpalettegroup>` tags to associate the palette entry with a custom tag and an Inspector window. All of the tags that define a palette entry must specify the same `classid` attribute value.

jsxpalettegroup

The `<jsxpalettegroup>` tag specifies the Objects palette tab that holds a group of palette entries. This tag can define a new tab in the Objects palette or select any existing tab except the Custom tab. Optional attributes specify the tab's label text, icon, and location with respect to other tabs in the Objects palette.

Syntax

```
<jsxpalettegroup name="objectName" display="tabName"
tabOrder="anInteger"
      order=anInteger picture="tabIcon" >
  <!-- <jsxpaletteentry> elements -->
</jsxpalettegroup>
```

Attributes

name	The JavaScript name of this palette group. Case-sensitive. Can be your unique identifier or one of five predefined values. Specifying a unique value creates a new tab in the Objects palette. Specifying a predefined name installs this palette group in one of the built-in Objects palette tabs. The predefined names are:
	Basic: Basic elements (images, plug-ins, scripts, and so on)
	Forms: Form elements
	Project: Site elements
	CSObjects: Smart objects
	Head: Header elements
	Frames: Frame elements
	You cannot add items to the Custom or Library tab of the Objects palette.
display	The text that identifies this palette group and its tab in the UI. Appears in the Palette menu of the Objects palette, and in the status bar of the Objects palette when the mouse cursor pauses over this palette group's tab.
	This value is ignored for the predefined tab names.
taborder	A number for the position of this new tab among all tabs appearing in the Objects palette. Higher values place the tab further to the right.
	This value is ignored for the predefined tab names.
	For the tab order values of built-in tabs, see Appendix A, "Object Palette Sort Order."

order	A number for the position of this palette group's entries among all entries in the Objects palette's built-in tabs. Higher values place the entry further to the right. The highest valid value is 32767.
	This value is used only to add palette entries to one of the built-in tabs, such as the Basic tab. When you add palette entries to your own tab, this value is ignored. GoLive adds entries to a custom palette in the order the extension's source code defines them. To rearrange the icons in your own palette, reorder their definitions.
	You use the same approach to add your icon group to a built in tab: if the value of your palette entry's `order` attribute is less than that used by a built-in icon group, GoLive places your icon group to the left of that icon group.
	For the order values of built-in tabs, see Appendix A, "Object Palette Sort Order."
picture	The JavaScript name of the `<img>` element that provides the tab's icon. GoLive automatically scales this image to 12x12 pixels when it installs the palette group's icon.
	This value is ignored for the predefined tab names.

jsxpaletteentry

The `<jsxpaletteentry>` tag defines a palette entry within a palette group. The body of this element defines the HTML content this palette entry adds to the page when the user drags the palette entry's icon from the Objects palette to Layout view.

Syntax

```
<jsxpaletteentry display="DescriptionOfTag"
classid="uniqueIdemtifier"
        picture="paletteIcon" hilitepicture="paletteIcon"
head="true|false" >
   <!-- HTMLContentOfCustomTagHere -->
</jsxpaletteentry>
```

Attributes

display	The name that appears in the lower-left corner of the Objects palette when the mouse pointer pauses over this palette entry.
classid	The class name of the markup item. This value must match the `classid` attribute of the `<jsxelement>` this `<jsxpaletteentry>` installs in the Objects palette, and that of the `<jsxinspector>` window. An individual `classid` value must be unique among all currently running extensions, and must be used by one extension only.
picture	The JavaScript name of the `<img>` element for the icon that is displayed in the palette. GoLive automatically scales this picture to 24x24 pixels when it installs the palette entry.

hilitepicture	Optional. The JavaScript name of the `<img>` element for the highlight icon that is displayed in the palette when this entry is selected. GoLive automatically scales this picture to 24x 24 pixels when it installs the palette entry.
head	When supplied as a valueless attribute or when `true`, this palette entry is added to the `<head>` when dragged to a page. When not supplied or when `false`, it is added to the body at the current position in the document content.

Notes

Your `<jsxpaletteentry>` element replaces the `<HTMLContentOfCustomTagHere>` placeholder with the exact HTML content your palette entry is to insert into the GoLive document. This content can consist of any combination of HTML, SDK-defined tags, and custom tags defined by the `<jsxelement>` tag.

The `<jsxelement>` tag defines only the name of a custom tag. The default attributes the custom tag provides, as well as their values, are defined by the `<jsxpaletteentry>` element having the same `classid` attribute value. If the `<jsxelement>` tag that defines the custom tag name specifies `width` and `height` attributes, GoLive uses them to set the size of the box Object (page 64) it creates to represent a palette entry dropped into Layout view.

img

GoLive provides its own version of the familiar `<img>` tag. In addition to providing a `name` attribute, this tag provides attributes that support platform-specific paths to the image source file.

Syntax

```
<img name="JavaScriptName" macsrc="urlOrPathname"
winsrc="urlOrPathname">
```

Attributes

name	The JavaScript name of the markup item GoLive generates when it parses this tag and its attributes.
src	The URL of the source image file. To provide platform-specific pathnames, specify `winsrc` and `macsrc` attributes instead of a `src` attribute.
macsrc	The URL of the image source file in Mac OS.
winsrc	The URL of the image source file in Windows.

---

jsxelement

This tag defines the name of a custom markup tag. The attributes specify characteristics of the box Object (page 64) that provides this element's visual representation in Layout view.

Syntax

```
<jsxelement tagName="nameOfCustomTag"
classid="jsxpaletteentryID"
    type="typeOfTag" glue="mkupLang"
leftMargin="numPixels"
    rightMargin="numPixels" topMargin="numPixels"
    bottomMargin="numPixels" invisible
fixedWidth="numPixels"
    fixedHeight="numPixels" >
</jsxelement>
```

Attributes

tagName	The name of the tag that this element defines. Valid values are composed of lowercase characters only.
classid	Unique identifier associated with the tag. This value must match the classid attribute of the `<jsxpaletteentry>` and `<jsxinspector>` tags associated with the custom tag this `<jsxelement>` tag defines. An individual classid value must be unique among all currently running extensions, and must be used by one extension only.
	Note: Do not confuse this tag's attributes with those of the custom tag it defines. The `<jsxelement>` tag defines ONLY the custom tag's name. The custom tag's attributes and any other content it adds to the page are defined by the `<jsxpaletteentry>` (page 344) element that has the same classid.

`type`	The tag type. One of:
	
	    `binary`: A binary tag that can contain any HTML code. The code is not displayed and your extension must draw and maintain this box's visual representation in Layout view.
	
	    `container`: A binary tag that can contain any HTML code. The code is displayed inside this box, which must provide adequate margins. The `drawBox` function must draw within these margins. Drawing that occurs outside the margins is not displayed on the screen. By default, container boxes cannot be resized.
	
	    `head`: A custom element to be included in the `<head>` section.
	
	    `plain`: A standard tag that draws a placeholder graphic in Layout view.
	
	    `ssi`: A server-side include; a comment that begins with a pound sign (#).
	
	    `bracket`: A tag delimited by straight brackets; [*tagName*], where *tagname* is the value of this element's `tagName` attribute.
	
	    `percent`: A tag delimited by double percent (%%) signs.
	
	    `""` (the empty string): A standard HTML tag. No characters after the left angle bracket (<) are part of the tag delimiter.
	
	    `!--`: A comment open tag; the `<!--` tag that begins a standard HTML comment.
	
	    `!`: An SGML tag; the `<!`*chars*`>` SGML tag, where *chars* is the value of this element's `tagName` attribute.

`glue`	Optional. A string specifying the markup language environment in which this custom tag overloads the standard one. For example, you could use this attribute to define a custom `img` tag that GoLive uses only for source written in a particular markup language, such as WML or XML. When not present, defining your own version of an existing tag replaces that tag everywhere.
`leftMargin`	The left margin of the generated container box.
`rightMargin`	The right margin of the generated container box.
`topMargin`	The top margin of the generated container box.
`bottomMargin`	The bottom margin of the generated container box.
`invisible`	When true, this is an invisible element. By default, Layout view displays placeholder graphics that represent invisible elements such as Actions or a Layout Grid. You can toggle the visibility of the placeholders with the **View > Hide/Show Invisible Items** menu item.
`fixedwidth`	Optional. If present, the box cannot be resized horizontally. Can be specified with or without a value, which denotes the width of the box. By default, container boxes cannot be resized.
`fixedheight`	Optional. If present, the box cannot be resized vertically. Can be specified with or without a value, which denotes the height of the box. By default, container boxes cannot be resized.

jsxinspector

This tag defines the Inspector window for the box Object (page 64) that GoLive creates when the user drops a palette entry into Layout view. This tag creates a window Object (page 313) with `type="inspector"`.

Syntax

```
<jsxinspector name="objectName" title="nameInWindowMenu"
        classid="yourUniqueID" width="anInteger"
height="anInteger"
        minwidth="numPixels" minheight="numPixels" >
    <!-- <jsxcontrol> elements go here -->
</jsxinspector>
```

Attributes

name	The JavaScript name of the Inspector window. This name appears in the `dialogs` global array.
title	The title of the Inspector dialog.
classid	An identifier that associates a custom element with its Inspector. This value must match the `classid` attributes of the `<jsxpaletteentry>` and `<jsxelement>` tags that define the custom element to inspect. An individual `classid` value must be unique among all currently running extensions, and must be used by one extension only.
minwidth	Minimum width of the Inspector window in pixels. GoLive 6 and higher.
minheight	Minimum height of the Inspector window in pixels. GoLive 6 and higher.

Notes

An Inspector is a special kind of dialog or window; its attributes, structure, and behavior are the same as those of the `<jsxdialog>` (page 330) tag. All Inspectors use the same window, so you can ignore the `<table>` tag that usually defines a dialog's window size. (The Inspector lays out its controls on a grid—controls dropped on a layout grid are implemented as table elements.)

When a custom box is selected, GoLive activates the Inspector window having the same `classid` value as the selected box. Before displaying the window, GoLive calls your inspectBox (page 363) handler, with the selected box as the target. Your handler initializes the elements of the Inspector window to display the current data.

When the user manipulates controls in the Inspector, GoLive calls the control-interaction event handler just as it would for any other dialog, with the control that changed as the target. Your handler alters the corresponding elements of the box as well as the HTML representation of its code to reflect a new value returned by the control that changed.

The value of the `<jsxinspector>` tag's `name` attribute appears as a property of the JavaScript global namespace and as an element of the global `dialogs` (page 47) array.

In GoLive 6 and higher, a `box` object can have multiple Inspectors. To create more than one Inspector, define additional Inspectors with alternate *classid* attributes:

```
<jsxinspector name="insp1" title="one"
classid="myclass">
  . . .
</jsxinspector>
<jsxinspector name="insp2" title="two"
classid="alternate">
  . . .
</jsxinspector>
```

At runtime, you can specify which Inspector a box is to use by setting its `classid` property. For example, the following specifies that the `myBox` object is to use the Inspector created from the `<jsxinspector classid=` `"alternate"` `...>` element:

```
var myBox = boxes[0]; box.classid = "alternate";
```

Language Localization

Localization translates UI strings into the local language of the computer running GoLive (or the language set by the module Object's `locale` property, page 227). The `<jsxlocale>` (page 350) tag supplies or points to an HTML table that maps English-language versions of an extension module's strings to their localized counterparts. The SDK uses this table to replace English-language strings with localized versions when GoLive loads the extension module. The SDK automatically replaces value strings that are embedded within window and control definition tags with localized versions, so that menu items and such are localized. To enable the dynamic localization of strings that are arguments to JavaScript methods, replace them explicitly with calls to the module Object's `localize` method (page 227):

```
module.localize("EnglishStringToLocalize");
```

jsxlocale

This tag contains or points to a table that defines localized versions of the strings an extension displays in the GoLive user interface. The tag can include the table itself as content, or point to a table defined in another file, or both.

Syntax

```
<jsxlocale src="pathToFolder/filename.html">
    // include inline localization table here
</jsxlocale>
```

Attributes

src	Optional. The location of a `.html` file containing a localization table. An absolute path, or a relative path with respect to the location of this `Main.html` file.

Notes

Typically, the `Main.html` file for the extension includes a `<jsxlocale>` tag with a `src` attribute that points to the external localization table, but does not include the localization table itself as content. Parsing large tables slows extension initialization; an external localization table file avoids this. Each included file can also include a `src` attribute to create a chain of documents.

The SDK always checks for localization tables in the `Common` folder, in addition to any tables that you supply explicitly in a particular module using this tag. You can store localization tables in the `Common` folder to make them available to all modules.

The table must present localization data in the following format:

- The topmost item in each column is a two-letter country code identifying the language in which the rest of the column's entries are written. Valid codes are those for the roman-character language subset of all codes the ISO-3166-1 standard defines.

- The leftmost item in each row is an English-language string to be localized. This string must appear in the table exactly as it appears in the extension's source code. The remaining cells in each row hold localized versions of the string in the leftmost cell.

If you display a localization table, it looks something like this:

US	DE	NO
Are you sure?	Sind Sie sich sicher?	Er du sikker?
Search	Suchen	Start søk

Example Localization Table

```
<jsxlocale>
<table>
<tr>
<th>US</th>
<th>DE</th>
<th>FR</th>
<th>JP</th>
<th>ES</th>
<th>IT</th>
<th>NL</th>
<th>SV</th>
<th>DA</th>
</tr>
<tr>
<td>Cancel</td>
<td>Abbrechen</td>
<td>Annuler</td>
<td>ÉLÉÉÉìÉZÉã</td>
<td>Cancelar</td>
<td>Annulla</td>
<td>Annuleren</td>
<td>Avbryt</td>
<td>AnnullÈr</td>
</tr>
</table>
```

Document Source Translation

A source translator preprocesses source files before GoLive parses them, replacing any strings in any way you choose. The `<jsxtranslator>` (page 352) tag creates a translator Object (page 286). This object, together with callback functions you provide, translates strings during the preprocessing phase. You can use a source translator to, for example:

- Translate a source file's syntax into a format GoLive can parse, such as XML or HTML.
- Mimic the behavior of server-side includes or other dynamic content in Layout view when a live server or database connection is not present.

jsxtranslator

The `<jsxtranslator>` tag defines a translator Object (page 286). A translator preprocesses source code to translate it as defined by your extension. It contains `<param>` (page 353) subelements that define the types of files to be processed, and the regular expressions in those files to be replaced.

Syntax

```
<jsxtranslator classid="uniqueIdentifier"
direction="oneway|twoway"
      haslinks="yes|no" blend="yes|no" >
  <!--- <param> elements go here -->
</jsxtranslator>
```

Attributes

classid	An identifier that associates this translator element with its Inspector. This Inspector allows you to modify your source code just like any other Inspector. This `classid` value must be unique among all currently running extensions, and must be used by one extension only.
direction	Whether translation is permanent or temporary. One of: • `twoway`: Display translated page content Layout view without changing source code permanently. Use this option to simulate server-side replacement. • `oneway`: Translate the page content permanently while still preserving the untranslated snippets in special elements. Translators of this style can mimic code generators.
haslinks	Optional. When `yes`, use this translator when reparsing files to translate links, such as server-side includes. When `no` (the default), this translator does not translate links. Note that translating links can be time-intensive.
blend	Optional. When `yes` (the default), the translated region has a color applied in Layout view. When `no`, use document's original color values in the translated region.

Example

This defines a translator element that acts on all `.html` or `.htm` files that contain the `"<time>"` Unicode source string.

```
<jsxtranslator classid="timeClass" direction="twoway">
    <param name="extension" value="html">
    <param name="extension" value="htm">
    <param name="expression" value="<time">
</jsxtranslator>
```

This translator provides the `haslinks=yes` attribute, indicating that GoLive is to use this translator to process links when it reparses the source document. It acts on all `.html` or `.htm` files that contain the `"#include"` Unicode source string.

```
<!-- translates SSI includes in .html and .htm files -->
<jsxtranslator classid="SSIinclude" direction="twoway"
haslinks="yes">
    <param name="extension" value="html">
    <param name="extension" value="htm">
    <param name="expression" value="#include">
</jsxtranslator>
```

param

The `param` tag specifies a file type or a regular expression that can be processed by the translator that contains it. To create a translator that processes multiple expressions in multiple filetypes, define multiple `<param>` subelements in the enclosing `<jsxtranslator>` (page 352) element.

Syntax

```
<param name="extension" value= filenameExtension>
<param name="expression" value= regExp>
```

Attributes

name	Whether this element describes a filetype or a regular expression. One of: extension expression
value	When `name` ="extension", the filename extension for files this translator can process. When `name` ="expression", a regular expression to be found in files this translator can process.

Example

The following sample code defines a translator element that acts on all
`.html` or `.htm` files that contain the `"<time"` Unicode source string.

```
<jsxtranslator classid="timeClass" direction="twoway">
   <param name="extension" value="html">
   <param name="extension" value="htm">
   <param name="expression" value="<time">
</jsxtranslator>
```

Markup Language Generator

Your component can contains source files in any MIME type, as long as you register a generator for that MIME type. If you link a component object to a file of a MIME type for which a generator exists, that generator is listed in the Generator popup of the component's Inspector. When the user selects a generator, GoLive triggers the generateMarkupForURL (page 362) event. Your handler must process the component before including it in your GoLive page.

You define generator callback functions for a specific MIME type, and register the generator by including the `<jsxmlgenerator>` tag in your extension.

(Introduced in 7.0)

jsxmlgenerator

The `<jsxmlgenerator>` tag registers a generator that converts a specific MIME type to HTML.

Syntax
```
<jsxmlgenerator mimetype="MIMEtype" internalname="iName"
uiname="uName"
    settings="yes|no">
</jsxmlgenerator>
```

Attributes

mimetype	The MIME type that this generator can translate to HTML.
internalname	The internal name of this generator. This identifies the generator in the MLGenerateEvent (page 383) object, in case you have more than one `<jsxmlgenerator>` in your extension's Main.htm.
uiname	The name for this generator that appears in the component Inspector.
settings	When yes, the generator can be configured on a per-component-instance basis, and the **Settings** button in the component Inspector is enabled. When the user clicks it, GoLive calls your inspectMarkupForURL (page 363) handler, passing a MLGenerateEvent (page 383).

Example
```
<jsxmlgenerator mimetype="text/csv" internalname="csv"
uiname="csv"
    settings="yes">
</jsxmlgenerator>
```

A sample extension can be found in the `MLGenerator` extension in the `Samples` folder. This sample converts standard CSV format files into HTML tables.

Version Control System Interface

You can implement an interface to a version-control system by creating a VCSHandler Object (page 292).

jsxvcs

The `<jsxvcs>` tag creates a VCSHandler Object (page 292). When an extension creates a version-control-system handler, that system appears as a choice in the Site Settings dialog and the site-creation wizard. The contained `jsxview` (page 332) element defines a panel Object (page 233) that is added to the Settings dialog when the user enables version control for a site and chooses this version-control system.

An extension creates a handler and panel to provide configuration settings needed for a specific version control system. The controls generate user interface events, and your handlers for these events can store user choices so that your version-control event handlers can access them as needed in order to interact with the version control system. The target object of all version-control events for your version control system is this VCSHandler Object (page 292). You can choose to store user choices in this object.

For details of the version-control event types and objects, see "Event names" on page 360 and "Event Object Types" on page 377.

Syntax

```
<jsxvcs name="unique_name" title="display_name"
features="feature_list">
   <jsxview ...>
       ...UI controls...
   </jsxview>
</jsxvcs>
```

Attributes

name	The unique name of this handler. This name is added to the drop-down list of available version-control systems.

`title`	The name for this handler that appears on the tab of the associated panel in the Site window, when the user chooses this handler from the drop-down list.
`features`	A list containing any of the following values, with any separating character: `foldercontent`: When present, the handler can explore folder content in the version-control depot, in response to the vcsFolderContent (page 367) event. When not present, that event is not generated. `users`: When present, the handler can retrieve user information in response to the vcsUsers (page 369) and vcsUserData (page 369) events. When not present, those events are not generated. `emptyfolder`: When present, the handler can create and handle empty folders in the version-control depot. `restoredeleted`: When present, the handler can find and restore deleted files in response to the vcsDeletedFiles (page 367) and vcsRestore (page 368) events. When not present, those events are not generated.

Example

```
<jsxvcs name="myVCSHandler" title="My VCS Handler"
           features="foldercontent users emptyfolder">
<jsxview ...>
</jsxview>
</jsxvcs>
```

6 | Events and Event Handlers

This chapter describes the event-handling mechanism that Adobe GoLive CS2 SDK (version 8.0) uses when system or user events occur, such as a change in the state of a control or document. Your extension can define event-handling functions to respond to given events as needed, and register those functions with the objects in which the events might occur. You need not implement event-handling functions for features your extension does not use. For example, if your extension does not provide a custom control, it need not register any event-handling functions with that object.

Note: Event handling has changed significantly in release 8.0. See "Compatibility with Previous Event Handlers" on page 395.

Initialization and Termination Handlers

GoLive looks for and calls these global functions when your extension is loaded or unloaded. Your extension can provide implementations to perform initialization and cleanup for your own module, and register them like any other event handlers; see "Registering event handlers" on page 369. Each such handler is passed a moduleEvent (page 383) object, and the target of the event is the module Object (page 227) for your module.

(All calls available in 5.0, 6.0, 7.0, 8.0)

Function	Description
`initializeModule`	Called after the module has been loaded.Your implementation of this function performs extension-specific startup tasks, such as initializing your extension's global variables, registering callbacks to respond to system events and other initialization functions that *do not* depend upon other extensions or the GoLive UI.
`startModule`	Called after the GoLive UI and extension modules have completed initialization. Your implementation of this function initializes your module's UI and module-to-module communication.
`terminateModule`	Called before the module is being unloaded. Your implementation of this function performs extension-specific shutdown tasks such as releasing saved references to JavaScript objects, disconnecting from a database, or in the case of extensions that use external C++ libraries, deallocating memory reserved by external library functions.

Event Handling

In GoLive 8, each type of object in which an event can occur is considered an *event target*, and has methods that allow you to register handlers for events that occur in that object. Event targets are existing system and UI objects such as documents, windows, and controls, which inherit additional event-registration functionality from the EventTarget Class (page 373).

Information about events is encapsulated by *event objects*; GoLive passes an event object as the single argument to any handlers that are registered for an event. Event objects are of specific types, which correspond to specific events. The event objects inherit most of their functionality from the Event Class (page 376), which defines basic properties such as where and when the event occurred. Most Event Object Types (page 377) define additional properties for specific categories of events, such as mouse events, menu events, and document events.

Event names

The following events are generated in GoLive 8.0:

Event name	Description
`activate`	Target is the document Object (page 138). Generated when a document becomes the active document (is brought to the front). Handlers are passed the documentEvent (page 380) object.
`appterm`	Target is the app Object (page 53). Generated when the GoLive application terminates, or if any application terminates that was launched with a file Object's execute (page 162) function. Handlers are passed the systemEvent (page 387) object.
`boxResized`	Target is a box Object (page 64). Generated when the user resizes or repositions a custom box in the Layout view. Handlers are passed the boxEvent (page 377) object.
`broadcast`	Target is a module Object (page 227). When one extension module needs to communicate with another extension module, it calls the app Object's broadcast (page 56) function, which generates this event for all modules (or for specified modules only). The broadcasting mechanism enables an extension to send a message to another extension requesting that it perform a task. An extension that needs to respond to messages from other extensions must register a handler for this event. Handlers are passed the broadcastEvent (page 378) object.

Event name	Description
`btReceive`	Target is the app Object (page 53). Generated when GoLive CS2 receives an interapplication message from another Adobe Creative Suite 2 application. Your handler is executed before the global `BridgeTalk.onReceive` message-handling method. For complete documentation of interapplication communication and the `bridgeTalk` message object, see the *Bridge JavaScript Reference*, available with Adobe Creative Suite 2. Handlers are passed the BridgeTalkEvent (page 377) object.
`close`	Target is the document Object (page 138). Generated when a document is closed. Handlers are passed the documentEvent (page 380) object.
`cmImageBox`	Target is the app Object (page 53). Generated for interactions with the context menu for images in the Layout view. Handlers are passed the contextMenuEvent (page 378) object.
`cmLayout`	Target is the app Object (page 53). Generated for interactions with the context menu for the Layout view. Handlers are passed the contextMenuEvent (page 378) object.
`cmLayoutSubDoc`	Target is the app Object (page 53). Generated for interactions with the **Document** submenu of the context menu for the Layout view. Handlers are passed the contextMenuEvent (page 378) object.
`cmLayoutSubView`	Target is the app Object (page 53). Generated for interactions with the **View** submenu of the context menu for the Layout view. Handlers are passed the contextMenuEvent (page 378) object.
`cmSiteSectionPDF`	Target is the app Object (page 53). Generated for interactions with the **Create PDF** section of the context menu for files listed in the Site window. Handlers are passed the contextMenuEvent (page 378) object.
`cmSiteSectionPublish`	Target is the app Object (page 53). Generated for interactions with the **Publish Server** section of the context menu for the Site window. Handlers are passed the contextMenuEvent (page 378) object.
`cmSiteSectionLinks`	Target is the app Object (page 53). Generated for interactions with the **Show In & Out Links** section of the context menu for files listed in the Site window. Handlers are passed the contextMenuEvent (page 378) object.
`cmSiteSubLinks`	Target is the app Object (page 53). Generated for interactions with the **Update Files Dependent On** submenu of the context menu for the Site window. Handlers are passed the contextMenuEvent (page 378) object.

Event name	Description
cmSiteSubNew	Target is the app Object (page 53). Generated for interactions with the **New** submenu of the context menu for the Site window. Handlers are passed the contextMenuEvent (page 378) object.
cmSiteSubOpen	Target is the app Object (page 53). Generated for interactions with the **Open** submenu of the context menu for files listed in the Site window. Handlers are passed the contextMenuEvent (page 378) object.
cmSiteSubPublish	Target is the app Object (page 53). Generated for interactions with the **Publish Server** submenu of the context menu for the Site window. Handlers are passed the contextMenuEvent (page 378) object.
cmSiteSubSettings	Target is the app Object (page 53).Generated for interactions with the **Settings** submenu of the context menu for the Site window. Handlers are passed the contextMenuEvent (page 378) object.
cmSource	Target is the app Object (page 53). Generated for interactions with the context menu for the Source view. Handlers are passed the contextMenuEvent (page 378) object.
cmTextSelection	Target is the app Object (page 53). Generated for interactions with the context menu for a text selection in the Layout view. Handlers are passed the contextMenuEvent (page 378) object.
deactivate	Target is the document Object (page 138). Generated when a document ceases to be the active document (another document is brought to the front). Handlers are passed the documentEvent (page 380) object.
dragControl	Target is a custom control Object Types (page 78). Generated when something is dragged over a custom control. Handlers are passed the dragDropEvent (page 380) object.
drawBox	Target is a box Object (page 64). Generated when a custom box needs to be redrawn in Layout view. Handlers are passed the paintEvent (page 384) object.
drawControl	Target is a custom control Object Types (page 78). Generated when a custom control needs to be redrawn in a dialog or palette. Handlers are passed the paintEvent (page 384) object.
generateMarkupForURL	Target is the app Object (page 53). If you link a component object to a file of a MIME type for which a Markup Language Generator (page 355) exists, that generator is listed in the Generator popup of the component's Inspector. When the user selects the generator, GoLive triggers this event. Handlers are passed the MLGenerateEvent (page 383) object.

Event name	Description
inspectBox	Target is the box Object (page 64). Generated when GoLive needs to display the Inspector for a custom box defined by an extension. The handler should set the initial values for the Inspector's controls. Handlers are passed the inspectEvent (page 381) object.
inspectMarkupForURL	Target is the app Object (page 53). When the `<jsxmlgenerator>` (page 355) tag has `"settings=yes"`, the **Settings...** button in the component Inspector is enabled. When the user clicks it, GoLive triggers this event. Handlers are passed the MLGenerateEvent (page 383) object.
inspector	Target is the app Object (page 53). Generated for any change in an Inspector. Handlers are passed the applicationEvent (page 377) object.
inspectTranslation	Target is the app Object (page 53). Generated when the protected region that displays translated replacement text is activated. Handlers are passed the inspectTranslationEvent (page 381) object.
leaveview	Target is the document Object (page 138). Generated when a document view is closed. Handlers are passed the documentEvent (page 380) object.
linkChanged	Target is a document Object (page 138). Generated when a link changes; for example, when a user interacts with a point-and-shoot link in Site view, or with a `urlgetter` control in an Inspector window. Handlers are passed the linkChangeEvent (page 382) object.
menuSetup	Target is a menu Object (page 223). Generated before displaying a dynamically initialized menu item (a `<jsxitem>` element that provides the valueless `dynamic` attribute.) Handlers are passed the menuEvent (page 382) object.
menuSignal	Target is a menuItem Object (page 225). Generated when the user chooses a menu item. Handlers are passed the menuEvent (page 382) object.
mouseControl	Target is a box Object (page 64) or custom control Object Types (page 78). Generated for these mouse-related events: ● Moving the cursor ● Moving the cursor into, out of, or over a control or box in Layout view ● Clicking or releasing a button Handlers are passed the mouseEvent (page 384) object.

Event name	Description
new **opened**	Target is the app Object (page 53). Generated when a new document is created or an existing document is opened. Handlers are passed the documentEvent (page 380) object.

onChange	Target is a control Object Types (page 78), one of these types:
	
	`edittext`
	`urlgetter`
	`source`
	`scrollbar`
	`slider`
	`item` *in* `list, combobox, hierarchy, filelist`
	`node` *in* `hierarchy, filelist`
	
	Generated when an editing change occurs in the control. You can control the exact circumstance with the `onChange`, `onEnter`, and `onNoChanged` creation parameters of the control; see `<jsxcontrol>` (page 337) tag and Control: edittext Object (page 91).
	Handlers are passed the UIEvent (page 388) object.

onClick	Target is a control Object Types (page 78), one of these types:
	
	`button`
	`checkbox`
	`radiobutton`
	`colorfield`
	`list`
	`combobox`
	`filelist`
	`hierarchy`
	`item` *in* `hierarchy`
	`node` *in* `hierarchy`
	
	Generated when the control is clicked.
	Handlers are passed the UIEvent (page 388) object.

onClose	Target is a window Object (page 313). Generated when the window is closed. Handlers are passed the UIEvent (page 388) object.
onCollapse	Target is a control Object Types (page 78) of type `node` in a `hierarchy` control. Generated when the user collapses (closes) the node to hide its children. Handlers are passed the UIEvent (page 388) object.
onExpand	Target is a control Object Types (page 78) of type `node` in a `hierarchy` control. Generated when the user expands (opens) the node to display its children. Handlers are passed the UIEvent (page 388) object.
onFileSelectionChange	Target is a website Object (page 296). Generated when the file selection changes in the Files tab of the Site window. Handlers are passed the siteTabsEvent (page 386) object.

Event name	Description
onFileTabColumnIDCallback	Target is a website Object (page 296). Generated when the user removes a custom column from the Site window at run time. Handlers are passed the siteTabsEvent (page 386) object.
onFileTabCompareCallback	Target is a website Object (page 296). Generated when a custom column needs to compare two objects, such as when the user clicks the title to sort the contents according to the cell values. Handlers are passed the siteTabsEvent (page 386) object.
onFileTabContentCallback	Target is a website Object (page 296). Generated when a custom column requests its content, which happens when the user selects the Tab containing the column. Handlers are passed the siteTabsEvent (page 386) object.
onMove	Target is a window Object (page 313). Generated when the window is moved. Handlers are passed the UIEvent (page 388) object.
onResize	Target is a window Object (page 313). Generated when the window is resized. Handlers are passed the UIEvent (page 388) object.
onShow	Target is a window Object (page 313) or panel Object (page 233). Generated when the window is opened, or when the pane becomes the frontmost panel in a window or in its `tabpanel` parent. Handlers are passed the UIEvent (page 388) object.
onWebsiteClose	Target is the app Object (page 53). Generated when the user closes a web site in the Site window. Handlers are passed the siteEvent (page 385) object.
onWebsiteOpen	Target is the app Object (page 53). Generated when the user opens a web site in the Site window. Handlers are passed the siteEvent (page 385) object.
onWebsiteSwitch	Target is the app Object (page 53). Generated when the user switches web sites in the Site window. Handlers are passed the siteEvent (page 385) object.

Event name	Description
`parseBox`	Target is a document Object (page 138). GoLive generates this event when: • The document that contains the tag is opened in Layout view. • The user switches to the document window's Layout view from some other view. • The user or JavaScript code changes a non-SDK element of the document while Layout view is active. (A non-SDK element is one that uses any markup tag not defined by the SDK.) • The document's `reparse` function is called when Layout view is active. This event does not occur when Layout view is not active, nor when GoLive parses an HTML tag managed by a `layout` object. You can avoid generating this event by adding your custom element to the page as a subelement of a layout.grid Object (page 193). Handlers are passed the boxEvent (page 377) object.
`preview`	Target is the document Object (page 138). Generated when a document is previewed. Handlers are passed the documentEvent (page 380) object.
`previewNavigate`	Target is a `preview`-type control Object Types (page 78). Generated when the user navigates to a new page in the control. Handlers are passed the UIEvent (page 388) object.
`publishSite`	Target is a website Object (page 296). Generated when files are about to be uploaded to the site. Handlers are passed the publishEvent (page 385) object.
`save`	Target is the document Object (page 138). Generated when a document is saved, before the document is written out. Handlers are passed the documentEvent (page 380) object.
`saved`	Target is the document Object (page 138). Generated when a document is saved, after the document is written out. Handlers are passed the documentEvent (page 380) object.
`selection`	Target is the document Object (page 138). Generated when the selection changes in an open document. Handlers are passed the documentEvent (page 380) object.
`translate`	Target is the app Object (page 53). Generated when the translator detects a match with its defined file types and one of its regular expressions. Your handler performs the translation of the found text to HTML. Handlers are passed the translateEvent (page 387) object.

Event name	Description
translationLinkChanged	Target is the app Object (page 53). Generated when a link changes within translated text, to report the change to the document-translation mechanism. Handlers are passed the translatedLinkChangeEvent (page 387) object.
undoSignal	Target is a module Object (page 227). Generated when the user issues the command to do, undo, or redo a task. Handlers are passed the undoEvent (page 388) object.
vcsAdd	Target is a VCSHandler Object (page 292). Generated when the user adds a file to a version-control system. Handlers are passed the VCSCheckInEvent (page 389) object.
vcsCheckIn	Target is a VCSHandler Object (page 292). Generated when the user checks in a file to a version-control system. Handlers are passed the VCSCheckInEvent (page 389) object.
vcsCheckOut	Target is a VCSHandler Object (page 292). Generated when the user checks out a file from a version-control system. Handlers are passed the VCSCheckOutEvent (page 390) object.
vcsCheckSettings	Target is a VCSHandler Object (page 292). Generated when the user is creating a new site document for a version-control system, whenever the site-creation wizard needs to determine whether the **Next** button should be enabled or disabled. The handler should set the result property of the event object to true to enable the button. Handlers are passed the VCSWizardEvent (page 395) object.
vcsCopy	Target is a VCSHandler Object (page 292). Generated when the user copies a file that is controlled by a version-control system to a temporary local file. Handlers are passed the VCSCopyEvent (page 390) object.
vcsDeletedFiles	Target is a VCSHandler Object (page 292). Generated when the user retrieves deleted files from a version-control server. Handlers are passed the VCSDeletedEvent (page 390) object.
vcsFolderContent	Target is a VCSHandler Object (page 292). Generated when the user requests the contents of a folder in the version-control system. This event is only generated when the creation of the handler includes the foldercontent feature; see the jsxvcs (page 357) tag. Handlers are passed the VCSRevisionEvent (page 393) object.
vcsHeadRev	Target is a VCSHandler Object (page 292). Generated when the user retrieves the head revision or opens an older revision of a file that is controlled by a version-control system. Handlers are passed the VCSGetHeadEvent (page 391) object.

Event name	Description
vcsInitializePanel	Target is a VCSHandler Object (page 292). Generated when the user selects your version control system in the Site Settings dialog or Version Control wizard. Your handler can initialize the custom panel associated with your script-defined VCSHandler Object (page 292). Handlers are passed the VCSPanelEvent (page 393) object.
vcsLogin **vcsLogout**	Target is a VCSHandler Object (page 292). Generated when the user logs in or out of a version-control system. The login handler can log in to the version-control-system server and set up any required data. Handlers are passed the VCSAuthEvent (page 389) object.
vcsNew	Target is a VCSHandler Object (page 292). Generated when the user creates a new site for a version-control system, or mounts an existing site. When mounting an existing site, the handler should download the files for that site. Handlers are passed the VCSNewEvent (page 392) object.
vcsRemove	Target is a VCSHandler Object (page 292). Generated when the user removes a file that is controlled by a version-control system. Handlers are passed the VCSMoveEvent (page 392) object.
vcsRename	Target is a VCSHandler Object (page 292). Generated when the user renames a file that is controlled by a version-control system. Handlers are passed the VCSMoveEvent (page 392) object.
vcsResetRev	Target is a VCSHandler Object (page 292). Generated when the user requests that a specific revision of a file controlled by a version-control system be considered the new head revision. Handlers are passed the VCSGetRefEvent (page 391) object.
vcsRestore	Target is a VCSHandler Object (page 292). Generated when the user restores to the version-control server a deleted version of a file or files. Handlers are passed the VCSCheckOutEvent (page 390) object.
vcsRev	Target is a VCSHandler Object (page 292). Generated when the user requests a specific revision of a file controlled by a version-control system. Handlers are passed the VCSGetRefEvent (page 391) object.
vcsRevert	Target is a VCSHandler Object (page 292). Generated when the user reverts the version of a file that is controlled by a version-control system. This action discards local changes and undoes the previous checkout operation. Handlers are passed the VCSCheckOutEvent (page 390) object.
vcsRevisions	Target is a VCSHandler Object (page 292). Generated when the user requests all revisions of a file from the version-control system. Handlers are passed the VCSRevisionEvent (page 393) object.

Event name	Description
vcsStatus	Target is a VCSHandler Object (page 292). Generated when GoLive retrieves the current status of a file. This occurs, for example, when a user tries to edit a file that is not checked out, or if the user requests synchronization. Handlers are passed the VCSStatusEvent (page 394) object.
vcsTerminatePanel	Target is a VCSHandler Object (page 292). Generated when the user deselects your version control system in the Site Settings dialog or Version Control wizard. Your handler can clean up structures that support the custom panel associated with your script-defined VCSHandler Object (page 292). Handlers are passed the VCSPanelEvent (page 393) object.
vcsUserData	Target is a VCSHandler Object (page 292). Generated when the user requests the names of all users connected to a version-control system. Your handler retrieves the user names. Handlers are passed the VCSUserDataEvent (page 394) object.
vcsUsers	Target is a VCSHandler Object (page 292). Generated when the user requests additional information for a given user of the version-control system. Your handler retrieves the information. Handlers are passed the VCSUsersEvent (page 395) object.
view	Target is the document Object (page 138). Generated when a document view is opened. Handlers are passed the documentEvent (page 380) object.

Registering event handlers

A script can register an event-handler function for a specific event and event target, by calling the event target's addEventListener (page 373) function. You can register:

- The name of a handler function defined in the extension that takes one argument, the event object. For example:

```
myMenuItem.addEventListener( 'menuSignal', myFunction );
```

- A locally defined handler function that takes one argument, the event object. For example:

```
myMenuItem.addEventListener( 'menuSignal',
    'function(e){/*handler code*/}');
```

- A string containing arbitrary JavaScript source code to be executed when the event occurs. For example:

```
myMenuItem.addEventListener( 'menuSignal',
    'for( var i=0; i<100; i++ ) writeln(i);' );
```

The handler or registered code statement is executed when the specified event occurs in the target. A script can programmatically simulate an event by calling an event target's `dispatchEvent` function.

You can remove a handler that has been previously registered by calling the event target's `removeEventListener` function. The parameters you pass to this function must be identical to those passed to the `addEventListener` call that registered the handler. Typically, an extension would register all event handlers in the initializeModule (page 359) function, and unregister them in the terminateModule (page 359) function; however, unregistering handlers on termination is not required.

You can register for an event in a parent or ancestor object of the actual target; see the following section.

How registered event-handlers are called

When an event occurs in a target, all handlers that have been registered for that event and target are called. Multiple event handlers can be registered for the same event in different targets, even in targets of the same type. For example, if there is a dialog with two checkboxes, you might want to register an `onClick` handler for each `checkbox` object. You would do this, for example, if each checkbox reacts differently to the click.

You can also register events for child objects with a parent object. If both checkboxes should react the same way to a mouse click, they require the same handler. In this case, you can register the handler with the parent window or container instead. When the `onClick` event occurs in either child control, the handler registered for the parent window is called.

You can combine these two techniques, so that more than one action occurs in response to the event. That is, you can register a general event handler with the parent, and register a different, more specific handler for the same event with the child object that is the actual target.

The rules for how multiple event handlers are called depend on three phases of event propagation, as follows:

- Capture phase

  When an event occurs in an object hierarchy, it is *captured* by the topmost ancestor object at which a handler is registered (the window, for example). If no handler is registered for the topmost ancestor, GoLive looks for a handler for the next ancestor (the tabbed pane, for example), on down through the hierarchy to the direct parent of actual target. When GoLive finds a handler registered for any ancestor of the target, it executes that handler then proceeds to the next phase.

- At-target phase

  GoLive calls any handlers that are registered with the actual target object.

- Bubble phase

  The event *bubbles* back out through the hierarchy; GoLive again looks for handlers registered for the event with ancestor objects, starting with the immediate parent, and working back up the hierarchy to the topmost ancestor. When GoLive finds a handler, it executes it and the event propagation is complete.

For example, suppose a dialog window contains a panel which contains a button. A script registers an event handler function for the mouseEvent at the window object, another handler at the panel object, and a third handler at the button object (the actual target).

When the user clicks the button, the window object's handler is called first (during the capture phase), then the button object's handler (during the at-target phase). Finally, GoLive calls the handler registered with the panel object (during the bubble phase).

If you register a handler at an ancestor object of the actual event target, you can specify the third argument to the addEventListener (page 373) function, so that the ancestor's handler responds only in the capture phase, not in the bubbling phase. For example, the following menu-item click handler, registered with the parent menu object, responds only in the capture phase:

```
myMenu.addEventListener("menuSignal", handleAllItems,
true);
```

This value is false by default, so if it is not supplied, the handler can respond only in the bubbling phase when the object's descendent is the target, or when the object is itself the target of the event (the at-target phase).

To distinguish which of multiple registered handlers is being executed at any given time, the event object provides the eventPhase property, and the currentTarget property, which In the capture and bubbling phases contains the ancestor of the target object at which the currently executing handler was registered.

You can capture any event at the level of the app Object (page 53), which is the root ancestor of all other objects. The following figure generally illustrates the object hierarchy for event targets:

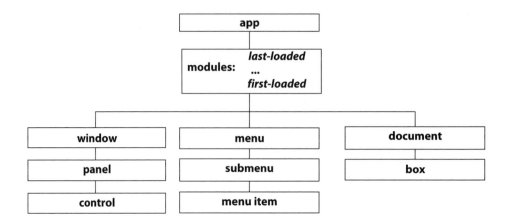

EventTarget Class

An event target is a JavaScript object where events can occur. Event handler functions can be registered for specific targets. The following GoLive objects act as event targets:

app Object (page 53)
module Object (page 227)
document Object (page 138)
box Object (page 64)
menu Object (page 223)
menuItem Object (page 225)
window Object (page 313)
panel Object (page 233)
control Object Types (page 78)

Event objects inherit from the `EventTarget` class the following functions for registering event handlers and simulating event occurrences:

addEventListener
addEventListener
  (*eventType*, *handlerFunction*
  [, *capture*])
	Registers an event-handling function to be called when a specified event occurs in this target. Returns `true` on success.

eventType	The event name. This is one of the events listed in Event names (page 360), or the name of an event created by a script using `new JSXEvent`, for use with the dispatchEvent (page 374) function (see "Constructing event objects" on page 374).
handlerFunction	The function to register for the specified event in this target. This can be the name of a function defined in the extension, a locally defined handler function, or a string containing JavaScript source code to be executed when the event occurs. A handler function takes one argument, the `event` object.
capture	Optional. When `true`, the handler is called only in the capturing phase of the event propagation. Default is `false`, meaning that the handler is called in the bubbling phase if this object is an ancestor of the target, or in the at-target phase if this object is itself the target.

removeEventListener
removeEventListener
  (*eventType*, *handlerFunction*
  [, *capture*])
	Unregisters an event-handling function for a specified event. Returns `true` if this handler was previously registered for this event.
	
	All arguments must be identical to those that were used to register the event handler.

eventType	The event name.
handlerFunction	The function or code that was registered for the specified event in this target.
capture	Optional. Whether the handler was to respond only in the capture phase.

dispatchEvent dispatchEvent (*obj* [,*data*])	Simulates the occurrence of an event in this target. A script can create an event object for a specific event and pass it to this method to start the event propagation for the event (see "Constructing event objects" on page 374). Returns `true` if the default action of the event should be canceled.
obj	An `event` object.
data	Optional. Data to pass to the event handler, of the type appropriate to the type of event object. For example, a `dragControl` event expects an `image` object.

Constructing event objects

You can construct event objects and send them to a target object's dispatchEvent (page 374) function to simulate a user action. The constructors for all events except the dragDropEvent (page 380) have the same syntax.

Basic event constructor

```
new [xxx]Event(eventName, capture, bubble, isCancelable)
```

eventName	String	The event name.
capture	Bool	When `true`, the event should be triggered in ancestors of the target object during the capture phase.
bubble	Bool	When `true`, the event should be triggered in ancestors of the target object during the bubbling phase.
isCancelable	Bool	When `true`, the event can be canceled.

➤ **Examples**

```
var myMenuSigEvt = new JSXMenuEvent( myMenuItem,
'menuSignal',
        false, false, false );
var myEvt = new Event( myTargetObject, 'myEventName',
        true, false, true );
```

dragDrop event constructor

```
new JSXDragDropEvent(flavor, content, capture, charSet,
baseURL)
```

flavor	String	The type of drag content. One of: `html`: The content is HTML source. `files`: The content contains "\n"-separated absolute file URLs. `colors`: The content contains "\n"-separated HTML colors.
content	String	The content being dragged.
charSet	String	The character set (charset name) used for encoding the drag content.
baseURL	String	The base URL for any relative URLs in the HTML content.

Event Class

An event object is passed to an event-handler callback function. There is a specialized event object for each event type. The specialized objects inherit these properties and functions from the `Event` class.

Event class properties

bubbles	Bool	When `true`, the event supports the bubbling phase.
cancelable	Bool	When `true`, the handler can call this object's preventDefault (page 376) method to cancel the default action of the event.
captures	Bool	When `true`, the event supports the capturing phase.
currentTarget	EventTarget	The event-target object where the currently executing handler was registered. This could be an ancestor of the target object, if the handler is invoked during the capture or bubbling phase.

eventPhase	String	Current event propagation phase. One of:
		`capture`
		`target`
		`bubble`

target	EventTarget	The event-target object where the event occurred.
timeStamp	Date	Time the event was initiated. A JavaScript DateTime object.
type	String	The name of the event that occurred. This is one of the events listed in Event names (page 360), or the name of an event created by a script using `new JSXEvent`, for use with the dispatchEvent (page 374) function (see "Constructing event objects" on page 374).

Event object functions

preventDefault preventDefault()	Cancels the default action of this event, if this event is cancelable (that is, `cancelable=true`). Returns `true` if the action is successfully canceled.
stopPropagation stopPropagation()	Stops event propagation after executing the current handler. Returns `true`.

Event Object Types

Subclasses of the `Event` class represent specific events. Event objects can be of the following types, presented here in alphabetical order, with additional properties defined for the type.

applicationEvent

Passed to handlers for the inspector (page 363) event. Your handler implements your module's response to changes in an Inspector that your module provides.

Defines no additional properties.

boxEvent

Passed to handlers for the boxResized (page 360) and parseBox (page 366) events. The handler can initialize the box, redraw the box, or resize the box. Your handler should avoid operations that cause GoLive to reparse the document. Calling `setInnerHTML`, `setOuterHTML`, `document.reparse` or `document.reformat` from within this handler results in a runtime error.

In addition to the properties and functions of the `Event` class, defines these properties:

`box`	The box Object (page 64) that is associated with the event target. (For a parsing events, the target is a `document` object. For resize events, the box is the target.)
`height`	The height of the box in pixels.
`reason`	The reason for a parsing event. One of: 2: Box was repositioned. 3: Custom element dropped from Objects palette or pasted from clipboard.
`width`	The width of the box in pixels.

BridgeTalkEvent

Passed to handlers for the btReceive (page 361) event. Your handler implements your module's response to interapplication messages received from other Adobe Creative Suite 2 applications; it is executed before the global `BridgeTalk.onReceive` message-handling method. If your handler cancels the event, the global method is not called.

A message typically contains an ExtendScript script, and your handler typically evaluates this script, and stores the result of evaluation in the `response` property of the event object. If the original message contains an `onResult` callback, the interapplication messaging framework automatically returns the value of `response` to the sender.

For complete documentation of interapplication communication and the `bridgeTalk` message object, see the *Bridge JavaScript Reference*, available with Adobe Creative Suite 2.

In addition to the properties and functions of the `Event` class, defines these properties:

message	The `bridgeTalk` message object that was received. Typically contains an ExtendScript script encapsulated in a string in the `body` property.
response	Read/write. A string containing a result, typically the result of evaluating the script contained in the message's `body` property.

broadcastEvent

Passed to handlers for the broadcast (page 360) event. Your handler performs any tasks necessary to respond to the broadcast message, and, optionally, returns a result string. Use of the broadcast mechanism is entirely optional. If your extension does not need to communicate with other extensions, it need not implement a handler for this event.

In addition to the properties and functions of the `Event` class, defines these properties:

answer	Read/write. Data of any type that can be set in response to the broadcast message.
message	The broadcasted message.
sender	The module Object (page 227) that sent the broadcast.

contextMenuEvent

Passed to handlers for the context menu events (see page 361 and page 362):

cmImageBox
cmLayout
cmLayoutSubDoc
cmLayoutSubView
cmSiteSectionPDF
cmSiteSectionPublish
cmSiteSectionLinks
cmSiteSubLinks
cmSiteSubNew
cmSiteSubOpen
cmSiteSubPublish

cmSiteSubSettings
cmSource
cmTextSelection

Register your event handler with the app Object (page 53). The event that occurred is found in the `type` property, and depends on which context menu or submenu the user interacted with. Various kinds of user interaction can generate the event; they are distinguished by the `action` value. The `target` of the event is the `app` object, but the `menu` property contains the `menu` or `menuItem` object associated with the triggering action; for example, the menu item that the user selected.

The handler performs the appropriate action depending on the specific `action` type:

- The `extend` action allows you to add new submenus and menu items to a context menu when GoLive first creates it.
- The `setup` and `signal` types correspond to the menuSetup and menuSignal events (page 363) for non-context menus.
  - The `setup` action allows you to enable or disable items before a context menu opens.
  - The `signal` action handler defines a menu item's behavior.
- The `open` and `close` actions allow you to handle submenu events.

In addition to the properties and functions of the `Event` class, defines these properties:

action	The specific action that triggered the event in the context menu. One of:
	`close`: A submenu was closed.
	`extend`: The context menu or submenu has been set up; the script can add submenus or menu items to it.
	`open`: A submenu was opened.
	`setup`: The context menu or submenu is about to open; the script can set the enabled state of items.
	`signal`: A menu item was clicked.
menu	The menu Object (page 223) or menuItem Object (page 225) associated with the event, depending on the `action` type:
	`close`: The menu Object for the submenu that was closed.
	`extend`: The menu Object for the context menu or submenu that has been set up.
	`open`: The menu Object for the submenu that was opened.
	`setup`: The menu Object for the context menu or submenu that is about to open.
	`signal`: The menuItem Object for the item that was clicked.

documentEvent

Passed to handlers for these events:

activate (page 360)
close (page 361)
deactivate (page 362)
leaveview (page 363)
new (on `app` object) (page 364)
opened (on `app` object) (page 364)
preview (page 366)
save (page 366)
saved (page 366)
selection (page 366)
view (page 369)

The event that occurred is found in the `type` property. Your handler responds to the user interaction as required.

In addition to the properties and functions of the `Event` class, defines these properties:

`document`	The document Object (page 138) that is affected. (For types `new` and `opened`, the target is the app Object (page 53). For other types, this is the same as the `target`.)
`preview`	Read/write. When `type=preview`, the file Object (page 158) or siteReference Object (page 260) for a file that should be opened in a browser window. Preview events are cancelable; that is, your handler can call the event object's preventDefault (page 376) method to cancel the default behavior.

dragDropEvent

Passed to handlers for the dragControl (page 362) event. Your handler can, for example, change the mouse icon to indicate whether a control is capable of accepting the dragged object, or change the content of what is dropped. This type of event is cancelable; that is, your handler can call the event object's preventDefault (page 376) method to cancel the default behavior.

In addition to the properties and functions of the `Event` class, defines these properties:

`baseURL`	Read/write. Base URL for any relative URLs in the HTML content.
`content`	Read/write. The content being dragged.
`dropTarget`	The target of a drag-and-drop action, a custom control. See Control: custom Control Object (page 90).
`encoding`	Read/write. The character set (charset name) used for encoding the drag content.

Adobe® GoLive® CS2 Official JavaScript Reference

flavor	Read/write. The type of drag content. One of:
	`html`: The content is HTML source.
	`files`: The content contains "\n"-separated absolute file URLs.
	`colors`: The content contains "\n"-separated HTML colors.
handle	Read/write. When `true`, the target can accept a drag-and-drop action when the state property is `check`.
state	State of the drag-drop operation, based on the mouse position. One of:
	`check`: When the drag enters or moves over the drop target, GoLive checks the `handle` property to determine if the target can handle the content.
	`enter`: The drag is at its first position after entering a drop target.
	`continue`: The drag is moving over the drag target.
	`exit`: The drag is at its first position after leaving the drag target.
	`drop`: The drag has just been dropped onto the drop target.
type	The specific type of event that occurred. One of:
	`dragControl`: A drag was initiated in a custom control.
	`drop`: A drop occurred in a document.
x	Horizontal position of the drag, in the coordinate system of the window containing the target control.
	If the target is a document, this value is not a position, but provides information about the drop target, depending on the view:
	layout view—selection offset
	head view—index of head item
	source view—selection offset
	frame view—0
	outline view—0
y	Vertical position of the drag, in the coordinate system of the window containing the target control.
	If the target is a document, this value is always 0.

inspectEvent

Passed to handlers for the inspectBox (page 363) event. In addition to the properties and functions of the `Event` class, defines these properties:

inspector	The window Object (page 313) for the Inspector that is associated with the event target (a `box` object).

inspectTranslationEvent

Passed to handlers for the inspectTranslation (page 363) event. Your handler uses data it extracts from the specified source to initialize the Inspector. Implement a handler for this event if you define an Inspector for your replaced code. The handler can use `app.translator.rewriteSnippet` to change the original code.

Note: If your translator reports URLs, your use of `urlgetter` controls in the Inspector must differ from the use in custom boxes:

- You cannot choose a random name for the `urlgetter` control. Instead you must name it "link0" for the first link you report during translation, "link1" for the second, and so on.

- Your translatedLinkChangeEvent (page 387) handler responds to changes in the `urlgetter`. Your inspectEvent (page 381) handler should handle all of your Inspector's other controls as it normally would.

In addition to the properties and functions of the `Event` class, defines these properties:

`inspector`	The window Object (page 313) for the Inspector that is associated with the event target (the `app` object).
`source`	A Unicode string containing the original untranslated code of one translation instance (not the whole document).

linkChangeEvent

Passed to handlers for the linkChanged (page 363) event. Your handler updates your extension's JavaScript references to the link. In addition to the properties and functions of the `Event` class, defines these properties:

`link`	An array of link Objects (page 207) for the links that have changed.

menuEvent

Passed to handlers for the menuSetup (page 363) and menuSignal (page 363) events. The event that occurred is found in the `type` property. Your handler initializes the menu or implements the behavior of menu items that your extension provides.

- Your menuSetup (page 363) handler sets a dynamic menu item's check mark or disables the menu item, by setting the `enabled` and `checked` properties of the menu item object. GoLive then displays the menu and its items as specified by the current values of these properties.

- Your menuSignal (page 363) handler responds to the user's choice of any menu item your extension provides.

You can register your handler with the parent menu Object (page 223) and access individual items through the `items` property, or register the handler directly with the menuItem Object (page 225).

Defines no additional properties or functions.

MLGenerateEvent

Passed to handlers for the generateMarkupForURL (page 362) and inspectMarkupForURL (page 363) events. This object encapsulates information about a Markup Language Generator (page 355) that converts a specific MIME type to HTML. The event that occurred is found in the `type` property.

- Your generateMarkupForURL (page 362) handler processes the selected component before including it in your GoLive page. It should return HTML in the form of a regular component (that is, it must contain a `<body>` element). It can interpret the `settings` string in any way you want. The handler must set the generated HTML component (`outSource`) and modified settings string (`outSettings`) in the passed event object.
- Your inspectMarkupForURL (page 363) handler determines the new settings and sets the `OutSettings` string in the event object.

In addition to the properties and functions of the `Event` class, defines these properties:

context	The context of the call. Currently, the only valid value is `component`.
generatorName	Internal name of the generator (in case you have more than one `<jsxmlgenerator>` in your extension's `Main.htm`).
isTest	When `true`, run the generator in test mode for debugging.
outSource	Read/write. The handler must set this value to the HTML component it creates.
outSettings	Read/write. The handler must set this to the settings value it creates. These settings are displayed subsequently in the Inspector's Settings popup.
settings	A settings string in an extension-defined format, stored with the component. When the event is generated, this contains the current settings, as set in the Inspector's Settings popup. Your handler can use this string as desired to configure one component instance.
url	The URL of the linked source file to be translated to HTML.

moduleEvent

Passed to handler for the initializeModule (page 359), startModule (page 359), and terminateModule (page 359) events. Currently defines no additional properties.

mouseEvent

Passed to handlers for the mouseControl (page 363) event. Your handler implements the response to mouse activity in a custom control. The object encapsulates information about triggering event, including the type of mouse event that occurred, whether keys were depressed together with the mouse action, the position of the mouse cursor at the time of the action, and whether the action was part of a drag-and-drop operation.

In addition to the properties and functions of the `Event` class, defines these properties:

`altKey`	When `true`, the ALT key was pressed at the time of the event.
`button`	Which mouse button was pressed at the time of the event. Supports only the value 1, indicating the left button. (Use `mode` for further information.)
`clientX`	Horizontal position of the mouse pointer relative to the upper-left corner of the event target.
`clientY`	Vertical position of the mouse pointer relative to the upper-left corner of the event target.
`ctrlKey`	When `true`, the CTRL key was pressed at the time of the event.
`dragBox`	Read/write. Used only when target is a box Object (page 64). When `true`, the box can be dragged.
`mode`	The mouse action that occurred. One of: 0 - left button was pressed 1 - pointer was moved while the left button was pressed (drag) 2 – button was released 3 – pointer moved over control while button was not pressed (Introduced in 7.0) (4, 5 - unused) 6 – pointer entered the control (Introduced in 7.0) 7 – pointer left the control (Introduced in 7.0)
`relatedTarget`	Identifies a secondary target for certain event types: For `mouseover`, the target the pointer exited. For `mouseout`, the target the pointer entered.
`screenX`	Horizontal position of the mouse pointer relative to the screen.
`screenY`	Vertical position of the mouse pointer relative to the screen.
`shiftKey`	When `true`, the **Shift** key was pressed at the time of the event.

paintEvent

Passed to handlers for the drawBox (page 362) and drawControl (page 362) events. The handler updates the appearance of the box or custom control.

The handler must not call any functions other than drawing functions. Attempting to reparse the document or to download a file causes a run-time error.

In addition to the properties and functions of the `Event` class, defines these properties:

draw	The draw Object (page 152) used to accomplish the drawing operation that updates the appearance of the box or custom control that is the event target.

publishEvent

Passed to handlers for the publishSite (page 366) event. The handler can take any action with respect to the files to be uploaded, including changing the list of files or canceling the upload operation.

In addition to the properties and functions of the `Event` class, defines these properties:

references	The siteCollection Object (page 259) containing the files to be uploaded.

siteEvent

Passed to handlers for site events in the Site window (page 365):

onWebsiteClose
onWebsiteOpen
onWebsiteSwitch

The event that occurred is found in the `type` property. Your handler can perform any task you need to perform before the Site window closes, opens, or switches to a new web site.

When your handler executes, the site being closed has not yet closed; it is still available from the collection in the global website (page 48) property. Similarly, the newly opened site, or the new site to which the window is switching, are also available in the global collection, as well as in this object.

In addition to the properties and functions of the `Event` class, defines these properties:

site	The website Object (page 296) associated with the event.

siteTabsEvent

Passed to handlers for selection and custom-column events in the Files tab of the Site window:

onFileSelectionChange (page 364)
onFileTabColumnIDCallback (page 365)
onFileTabCompareCallback (page 365)
onFileTabContentCallback (page 365)

The event that occurred is found in the `type` property.

- Your handler for onFileSelectionChange (page 364) performs any task you need to perform when the file selection in the Files tab of the Site window changes.

- Your handler for onFileTabColumnIDCallback (page 365) updates the column ID values of custom columns that remain in the Site window after a custom column is removed. (It is not needed if there is only one custom column.) It is called once for each remaining custom column.

- Your handler for onFileTabCompareCallback (page 365) is called repeatedly, with each of pair of cell values, until the contents of the column are sorted. Your handler compares the two siteReference Objects (page 260) to determine which should come before the other.

- Your handler for onFileTabContentCallback (page 365) determines what should be displayed in your custom column, and returns the string in the `content` property.

Note: To update custom content without using an event handler, you can associate a column with a named property of a siteReference Object (page 260). Create the named property using the `siteReference` function setNamedString (page 267) or setNamedLong (page 267), then pass the property's name when you create the custom column using the website Object's addPrefColumn (page 298) or insertPrefColumn (page 302) function.

In addition to the properties and functions of the `Event` class, defines these properties:

`changedId`	Read/write. Your onFileTabColumnIDCallback (page 365) handler sets this to the column identifier number to be used for this custom column after a custom column was removed. The custom column will be referenced by this value from now on.

`compare`	Read/write. Your onFileTabCompareCallback (page 365) handler sets this to an integer value that indicates the result of your comparison:
	
	`-1: ref < compareRef`
	` 0: ref = compareRef`
	` 1: ref > compareRef`

---

compareRef	The siteReference Object (page 260) for the row being compared to the current row.
content	Read/write. Your onFileTabContentCallback (page 365) handler sets this to a string, which GoLive displays in the id column of the target site's Site window.
id	Column identifier number for the current, as returned by the addColumn (page 298) or insertColumn (page 301) function of the website Object (page 296). If a column is being removed, this is the ID the current column had before the removal.
ref	The siteReference Object (page 260) for the current row.

systemEvent

Passed to handlers for the appterm (page 360) event. The handler should perform any cleanup needed when the GoLive application terminates.

In addition to the properties and functions of the Event class, defines these properties:

process	The file Object (page 158) for a system process. For the appterm event, the application that terminated.
type	One of: appterm: The application terminated.

translatedLinkChangeEvent

Passed to handlers for the translationLinkChanged (page 367) event. Your handler updates your extension's JavaScript references to this link. (Not that these are text links, not link objects.)

In addition to the properties and functions of the Event class, defines these properties:

index	The link to change, specified as an index into the total number of links in the text to be translated. Index position 0 holds the first link in the text.
source	The original untranslated code string for the link.
url	The URL to which the handler sets the link it translates.

translateEvent

Passed to handlers for the translate (page 366) events. Your handler performs the translation of text to HTML.

You must implement a handler to support automatic document translation. Your handler must detect the document parts that need translation, and translate them by calling the function `app.translator.translateSnippet`.

In some cases, this function only receives the original code instead of the entire source; for example, when the original source is changed by a call to `rewriteSnippet`. Because `rewriteSnippet` only changes the original code, it calls `translate` afterwards to give the extension a chance to update the replacement code according to the changes to the original code.

In addition to the properties and functions of the `Event` class, defines these properties:

`documentUrl`	The URL of the document.
`siteUrl`	The URL of the site.
`source`	A Unicode string containing the entire document.

UIEvent

Passed to handler for these events:

> onChange (page 364)
> onClick (page 364)
> onClose (page 364)
> onCollapse (page 364)
> onExpand (page 364)
> onMove (page 365)
> onResize (page 365)
> onShow (page 365)
> previewNavigate (page 366)

The event that occurred is found in the `type` property. Handlers respond to the user's action as needed.

In addition to the properties and functions of the `Event` class, defines these properties:

`url`	The URL string (for the previewNavigate, page 366, event only). This type of event is cancelable; that is, your handler can call the event object's preventDefault (page 376) method to cancel the default behavior.

undoEvent

Passed to handlers for the undoSignal (page 367) events. Your handler implements the do, undo, and redo operations.

In addition to the properties and functions of the `Event` class, defines these properties:

action	Action code indicating whether this function should do the operation for the first time, undo the operation, or redo the operation. Values are: 0: Do. Called as soon as the object is submitted. 1: Undo 2: Redo
undo	The undo Object (page 290) associated with this action, that encapsulates data required to do, undo, and redo the task.

VCSAuthEvent

Passed to handlers for the vcsLogin and vcsLogout events (page 368). Your handler implements the login and logout operations for your script-defined VCSHandler Object (page 292).

In addition to the properties and functions of the `Event` class, defines these properties:

result	Read/write. A string containing the result of the operation. Default is "ok". To notify the version-control system of an error, your handler can set this to an error message.
settings	A VCSSettings Object (page 295) containing the version-control settings for this operation.

VCSCheckInEvent

Passed to handlers for the vcsAdd and vcsCheckIn events (page 367). Your handler implements the add and checkin operations for your script-defined VCSHandler Object (page 292).

In addition to the properties and functions of the `Event` class, defines these properties:

comment	A string containing a checkin comment.
references	A siteCollection Object (page 259) containing the siteReference Objects (page 260) for files affected by this operation.
result	Read/write. A string containing the result of the operation. Default is "ok". To notify the version-control system of an error, your handler can set this to an error message.
settings	A VCSSettings Object (page 295) containing the version-control settings for this operation.
site	A website Object (page 296) for the site being operated on.

VCSCheckOutEvent

Passed to handlers for the vcsCheckOut (page 367), vcsRevert (page 368), and vcsRestore (page 368) events. Your handler implements the checkout, revert, and restore operations for your script-defined VCSHandler Object (page 292).

In addition to the properties and functions of the `Event` class, defines these properties:

references	A siteCollection Object (page 259) containing the siteReference Objects (page 260) for files affected by this operation.
result	Read/write. A string containing the result of the operation. Default is "ok". To notify the version-control system of an error, your handler can set this to an error message.
settings	A VCSSettings Object (page 295) containing the version-control settings for this operation.
site	A website Object (page 296) for the site being operated on.

VCSCopyEvent

Passed to handlers for the vcsCopy (page 367) event. Your handler implements the copy operation for your script-defined VCSHandler Object (page 292). In addition to the properties and functions of the `Event` class, defines these properties:

destination	A file Object (page 158) for the local destination file of the copy operation.
references	A siteCollection Object (page 259) containing the siteReference Objects (page 260) for sites affected by this operation.
result	Read/write. A string containing the result of the operation. Default is "ok". To notify the version-control system of an error, your handler can set this to an error message.
settings	A VCSSettings Object (page 295) containing the version-control settings for this operation.
revNumber	A string containing the revision identifier of the file being copied.
site	A website Object (page 296) for the site being operated on.

VCSDeletedEvent

Passed to handlers for the vcsDeletedFiles (page 367) event. Your handler implements the deleted file retrieval operation for your script-defined

VCSHandler Object (page 292). In addition to the properties and functions of the `Event` class, defines these properties:

deleted	Read/write. An initially empty array that the handler fills with instances of VCSRevisionInfo Objects (page 293) for the retrieved files.
result	Read/write. A string containing the result of the operation. Default is "ok". To notify the version-control system of an error, your handler can set this to an error message.
settings	A VCSSettings Object (page 295) containing the version-control settings for this operation.
site	A website Object (page 296) for the site being operated on.

VCSGetHeadEvent

Passed to handlers for the vcsHeadRev (page 367) event. Your handler implements the file revision retrieval for your script-defined VCSHandler Object (page 292).

In addition to the properties and functions of the `Event` class, defines these properties:

references	A siteCollection Object (page 259) containing the siteReference Objects (page 260) for files affected by this operation.
result	Read/write. A string containing the result of the operation. Default is "ok". To notify the version-control system of an error, your handler can set this to an error message.
settings	A VCSSettings Object (page 295) containing the version-control settings for this operation.
site	A website Object (page 296) for the site being operated on.

VCSGetRefEvent

Passed to handlers for the vcsRev and vcsResetRev events (page 368). Your handler implements the download operation for your script-defined VCSHandler Object (page 292).

In addition to the properties and functions of the `Event` class, defines these properties:

references	A siteCollection Object (page 259) containing the siteReference Objects (page 260) for files affected by this operation.
result	Read/write. A string containing the result of the operation. Default is "ok". To notify the version-control system of an error, your handler can set this to an error message.

---

revNumber	A string containing the revision identifier for the requested revision.
settings	A VCSSettings Object (page 295) containing the version-control settings for this operation.
site	A website Object (page 296) for the site being operated on.

VCSMoveEvent

Passed to handlers for the vcsRemove (page 368) and vcsRename (page 368) events. Your handler implements the removal or renaming operation for your script-defined VCSHandler Object (page 292).

In addition to the properties and functions of the Event class, defines these properties:

destination	A siteReference Object (page 260) for the remote destination file of the move operation.
references	A siteCollection Object (page 259) containing the siteReference Objects (page 260) for files affected by this operation.
result	Read/write. A string containing the result of the operation. Default is "ok". To notify the version-control system of an error, your handler can set this to an error message.
settings	A VCSSettings Object (page 295) containing the version-control settings for this operation.
site	A website Object (page 296) for the site being operated on.

VCSNewEvent

Passed to handlers for the vcsNew (page 368) event. Your handler can download files for an existing site that is being mounted, or implement the site-creation operation for your script-defined VCSHandler Object (page 292).

In addition to the properties and functions of the Event class, defines these properties:

creationType	The string new if the user is creating a new version-control-system site, or mount if the user is mounting an existing site.
result	Read/write. A string containing the result of the operation. Default is "ok". To notify the version-control system of an error, your handler can set this to an error message.

settings	A VCSSettings Object (page 295) containing the version-control settings for this operation.
url	A string containing the URL of the root folder for the site being mounted or created.

VCSPanelEvent

Passed to handlers for the vcsInitializePanel (page 368) and vcsTerminatePanel (page 369) events. Your handler should initialize and clean up after a custom Site-window panel associated with your script-defined VCSHandler Object (page 292).

In addition to the properties and functions of the `Event` class, defines this property:

settings	A VCSSettings Object (page 295) containing the version-control settings for this operation.

VCSRevisionEvent

Passed to handlers for the vcsFolderContent (page 367) and vcsRevisions (page 368) events. for your script-defined VCSHandler Object (page 292). Your handler implements the file download for your script-defined VCSHandler Object (page 292).

- For the vcsFolderContent (page 367) event, the `revisions` property contains a VCSRevisionInfo Object (page 293) for each file found in the given folder. Only the url (page 295) property is of interest in this context.

- For the vcsRevisions (page 368) event, the `revisions` property contains a VCSRevisionInfo Object (page 293) for each existing revision of the requested file. In this context, the url (page 295) property is not useful.

In addition to the properties and functions of the `Event` class, defines these properties:

references	A siteCollection Object (page 259) containing the siteReference Objects (page 260) for files affected by this operation.
result	Read/write. A string containing the result of the operation. Default is "ok". To notify the version-control system of an error, your handler can set this to an error message.
revisions	An array of VCSRevisionInfo Objects (page 293) containing revision information for returned files.

settings	A VCSSettings Object (page 295) containing the version-control settings for this operation.
site	A website Object (page 296) for the site being operated on.

VCSStatusEvent

Passed to handlers for the vcsStatus (page 369) event.

In addition to the properties and functions of the `Event` class, defines these properties:

references	A siteCollection Object (page 259) containing the siteReference Objects (page 260) for files affected by this operation.
result	Read/write. A string containing the result of the operation. Default is "ok". To notify the version-control system of an error, your handler can set this to an error message.
settings	A VCSSettings Object (page 295) containing the version-control settings for this operation.
site	A website Object (page 296) for the site being operated on.
status	Read/write. An array of VCSRevisionInfo Objects (page 293) containing status information for returned files. The handler should create and add an instance for each file, setting its `syncStatus`, `lockStatus`, and optional `lockedUser` properties appropriately.

VCSUserDataEvent

Passed to handlers for the vcsUserData (page 369) event. Your handler can set the property values with additional information it retrieves for the user identified in the `user` property.

In addition to the properties and functions of the `Event` class, defines these properties:

comment	Read/write. A string containing a comment about the user.
email	Read/write. A string containing the user's email address.
realName	Read/write. A string containing the user's real name.
result	Read/write. A string containing the result of the operation. Default is "ok". To notify the version-control system of an error, your handler can set this to an error message.
settings	A VCSSettings Object (page 295) containing the version-control settings for this operation.

site	A website Object (page 296) for the site being operated on.
user	Read/write. A string containing the user's username, for whom additional information has been requested.

VCSUsersEvent

Passed to handlers for the vcsUsers (page 369) event. Your handler implements the retrieval of user names of all users connected to the version-control system.

In addition to the properties and functions of the Event class, defines these properties:

result	Read/write. A string containing the result of the operation. Default is "ok". To notify the version-control system of an error, your handler can set this to an error message.
settings	A VCSSettings Object (page 295) containing the version-control settings for this operation.
site	A website Object (page 296) for the site being operated on.
users	Read/write. An initially empty array that your handler fills with strings containing the retrieved user names.

VCSWizardEvent

Passed to handlers for the vcsCheckSettings (page 367) event. When the user is setting up a new site document for a version-control system, your handler determines whether the current site-creation wizard page is finished for your script-defined VCSHandler Object (page 292).

In addition to the properties and functions of the Event class, defines these properties:

result	Read/write. Set to true to enable the **Next** button in the wizard's current page, or to false to disable the **Next** button.
settings	A VCSSettings Object (page 295) containing the version-control settings for this operation.

Compatibility with Previous Event Handlers

In previous GoLive versions (up to GoLive 7.0) all events were handled by predefined global callback functions. For example, a click on a button was handled by the global callback function controlSignal. Extensions could provide implementations of these functions to respond to events as needed,

---

with the callback function itself determining which specific object and action triggered the event.

This method is still supported, but the new event model allows your script to respond to more specific events, and to define handlers for specific events in individual objects.

Many of the old-model callback names correspond directly with new-model event names, and can be replaced by handlers for those events. Some do not; for example:

- `controlSignal` is replaced by the various individual control-interaction events:

  onClick (page 364)
  onClose (page 364)
  onChange (page 364)
  onMove (page 365)
  onResize (page 365)
  onShow (page 365)
  previewNavigate (page 366)

- `docSignal` is replaced by events that correspond more-or-less to the previous types:

  activate (page 360)
  close (page 361)
  deactivate (page 362)
  leaveview (page 363)
  new (on `app` object) (page 364)
  opened (on `app` object) (page 364)
  preview (page 366)
  save (page 366)
  saved (page 366)
  selection (page 366)
  view (page 369)

- `moduleSignal` is replaced by the inspector (page 363) event.

- `appSignal` is replaced by the appterm (page 360) event.

The previous event callback mechanism still works. If your extension defines one of the named callbacks, GoLive executes that callback when the corresponding event is triggered, passing the same argument list that was defined for the callback in GoLive 7.0 and earlier.

Similarly, the Site window callbacks (which worked differently from the general event callbacks) have been updated so that events in the Site window are now handled in the same way as other events. However, you can still register callback handlers in the previous way (using the `registerCallback` function), and those handlers will still work.

Event Summary

The following table shows all of the events that can occur in GoLive. For each event, the columns show:

- The type of event object that is passed to handler functions for this type of event
- The target objects in which the event can occur
- Whether the event supports calls during the capture and bubbling phases of event propagation
- Whether the event can be canceled using the event object's preventDefault (page 376) method
- Whether the event is global. Global events fire in all extensions, not just in the extension where the event occurs

Event name	Event object	Targets	capture	bubble	cancel	global
initializeModule startModule terminateModule	moduleEvent	module	X	X		
new opened	documentEvent	app	X	X		X
close view leaveview save saved activate deactivate preview	documentEvent	document	X	X		X
selection	documentEvent	document				X
drop	dragDropEvent	document	X		X	X
dragControl	dragDropEvent	customControl	X			X
undoSignal	undoEvent	module	X	X		
linkChanged	linkChangeEvent	document	X	X		X
translationLinkChanged	translatedLinkChangeEvent	app	X			
translate	translateEvent	app	X			
appterm	systemEvent	app				X
inspector	applicationEvent	app				X
inspectBox	inspectEvent	box	X	X		
inspectTranslation	inspectTranslationEvent	app	X	X		

Event name	Event object	Targets	capture	bubble	cancel	global
parseBox	boxEvent	document	X	X		
boxResized	boxEvent	box	X	X		
drawBox	paintEvent	box	X	X		
broadcast	broadcastEvent	module	X	X		X
drawControl	paintEvent	customControl	X	X		
mouseControl	mouseEvent	customControl, box	X	X		X
menuSetup menuSignal	menuEvent	menuItem	X	X		
generateMarkupForURL inspectMarkupForURL	MLGenerateEvent	app	X	X		X
onClick	UIEvent	control: button checkbox radiobutton colorfield list combobox	X	X		
onChange	UIEvent	control: edittext urlgetter source scrollbar slider	X	X		
onShow onClose onMove onResize	UIEvent	window	X	X		
previewNavigate	UIEvent	control: preview	X	X	X	
onExpand onCollapse	UIEvent	control: listitem	X	X		
cmImageBox cmTextSelection cmLayout cmLayoutSubDoc cmLayoutSubView cmSiteSectionPublish cmSiteSectionSettings cmSiteSectionLinks cmSiteSubNew cmSiteSubOpen cmSource	contextMenuEvent	app				

Event name	Event object	Targets	capture	bubble	cancel	global
onWebsiteOpen onWebsiteClose onWebsiteSwitch	siteEvent	app				X
onFileSelectionChange onFilesTabContentCallback onFilesTabCompareCallback onFilesTabColumnIDCallback	siteTabsEvent	website	X	X		X
publishSite	publishEvent	website	X	X	X	X
btReceive	bridgeTalkEvent	app	X	X	X	X
vcsInitializePanel vcsTerminatePanel	VCSPanelEvent	VCSHandler	X	X		
vcsCheckSettings	VCSWizardEvent	VCSHandler	X	X		
vcsNew	VCSNewEvent	VCSHandler	X	X		
vcsLogin vcsLogout	VCSAuthEvent	VCSHandler	X	X		
vcsHeadRev	VCSGetHeadEvent	VCSHandler	X	X		
vcsRev vcsResetRev	VCSGetRefEvent	VCSHandler	X	X		
vcsStatus	VCSStatusEvent	VCSHandler	X	X		
vcsCheckOut vcsRevert	VCSCheckOutEvent	VCSHandler	X	X		
vcsCheckIn vcsAdd	VCSCheckInEvent	VCSHandler	X	X		
vcsRemove vcsRename	VCSMoveEvent	VCSHandler	X	X		
vcsFolderContent vcsRevisions	VCSRevisionEvent	VCSHandler	X	X		
vcsCopy	VCSCopyEvent	VCSHandler	X	X		

7 | Defining a Syntax Scheme

This chapter describes how to write a source-code syntax scheme that the GoLive JavaScript source editor can use to check and mark the syntax of source code you are editing in that control. This editor is used in every JavaScript source editor: the Source document pane, the split pane view, the JavaScript Debugger Source view, and in `source`-type control Object Types (page 78).

GoLive provides predefined syntax marking schemes for various standard syntaxes:

```
html
javascript
php
css
```

In addition, the SDK provides some dynamic syntax schemes in the file `Default.syntax` in the `Settings/Code` folder. You can extend the definitions in this file, or create an entirely new syntax scheme, saving it in a file with the `.syntax` extension in the same folder. When GoLive starts up, it gets syntax schemes from all `*.syntax` files in the `Settings/Code` folder.

The editor uses all available schemes in determining how to mark its displayed text.

Syntax Scheme Tags

The structure of a syntax scheme is defined in XML. You use XML tags as described here to define the behavior of your own syntax scheme for a particular piece of code. The examples for each tag are taken from the complete "Example Syntax Scheme" on page 407.

syntax

The root element is defined by the `<syntax>` tag, which contains all definitions for the scheme. The following attributes are defined in the `<syntax>` element:

name	String	The syntax scheme name. Provide this name in the `source` control object's `syntax` property to use this scheme.
mime-type	String	The mime-type of the code for this scheme.
extensions	String	The file extensions of the code for this scheme.

scriptlanguage	String	The language attribute in a script element with this scheme
charsequence endsequence	String	A sequence of characters where the syntax scheme begins in an HTML file, and the sequence of characters where it ends.

You must set least one of these attributes besides the `name` to declare the context for this scheme.

➤ **Example**

```
<syntax name="My3D" extensions="m3d">
```

This defines the name of the scheme as `My3D` and specifies the file extension of affected code files as `.m3d`.

exampletext

The `<syntax>` element must contain an `<exampletext>` element. The contents of this element is displayed (using the defined display styles) in the Preferences dialog for Source. To preserve the white space, enclose the `<exampletext>` element in a CDATA section.

➤ **Example**

This is the example text for the Example Syntax Scheme (page 407):

```
<exampletext><![CDATA[
#my format
begin
    variable: origin1 values: [0,3,4]
    variable: orign2 values: [2,7,3]
end
]]></exampletext>
```

splittable

The `<syntax>` element contains one or more `<splittable>` elements. The element contains a set of characters that the editor uses to logically segment the code. The element has a `type` attribute:

type	String	How code can be split at these characters. One of: `left`: Split code only on the left side of these characters. `right`: Split code only on the right side of these characters. `both`: Split code on both sides of these characters.

The splitting characters are typically separator characters such as commas or colons, and delimiters, such as quote or brace characters, that enclose a logical entity. The special values SPC and TAB specify the space and tab characters. You can specify any ASCII character with `ASCxxx`, using the decimal ASCII value.

Note: You must define delimiter characters as splittable in order to define an entity with those delimiters to be marked with a distinctive style; see the `<entity>` (page 404) tag.

Splitting each line into logical segments makes it easier for you, and for the GoLive syntax checker, to find locations where the syntax context changes. The segments are used both for parsing and for display; when there is more code to display than fits on a line or in the window, the editor can split it before or after the characters specified here.

➤ Example

This defines the splitting characters for the Example Syntax Scheme (page 407):

```
<splittable type="both">SPCTAB[]:#"</splittable>
```

By defining more than one `<splittable>` element you can create finer distinctions, resulting in more segments and less redundant checking:

```
<splittable type="both">SPCTAB:"</splittable>
<splittable type="left">[#"</splittable>
<splittable type="right">]</splittable>
```

keyset

The `<syntax>` element contains one or more `<keyset>` elements that define the appearance of a piece of code. A `<keyset>` element must be defined before any `<entity>` element that uses it. The attributes are:

name	String	The keyset name. This appears in the source preferences in the **Themes** tab, and is the value of the `keyset` attribute of an `<entity>` tag.
bold	Boolean	When `true`, mark with a bold font.
italic	Boolean	When `true`, mark with italic font.
underline	Boolean	When `true`, mark with underline.
fontsize	Number	Mark with a font of this size.
color	String	Mark with this color. A color name or hexadecimal RGB identifier.

All attributes except name are optional, but you must set at least one to declare the style for this keyset.

➤ Example

In the Example Syntax Scheme (page 407), these elements define appearances that combine font styles and colors, and specify the colors using hexadecimal RGB values:

```
<keyset name="Comment" bold="false" italic="true"
underline="false"
    color="#990000"/>
<keyset name="NumberArray" bold="true" italic="false"
underline="false"
    color="#009999"/>
```

These keysets specify colors using color names, and shows how they are used in subsequent `<entity>` elements:

```
<keyset name="commentappearance" color="red" />
<keyset name="keywordappearance" color="blue" />
<entity name="commentrange" startseq="/*" endseq="*/"
parent="root"
    keyset="commentappearance"/>
<entity name="BLUEKEYWORD" parent="root"
keyset="keywordappearance"/>
```

entity

The `<syntax>` element contains one or more `<entity>` elements that define a `range` or a `keyword` for your syntax scheme, as specified by the `type` attribute. The attributes are:

name	String	For a keyword, the name of the keyword. For a range, a descriptive name.

type	String	The type of entity defined. One of:
		`range`
		`keyword`

keyset	Keyset	The name of the `<keyset>` element that defines the appearance for this entity. Must be defined earlier in the scheme definition.
parent	Entity	The name of an `<entity>` element for a range within which this element must be nested. • For a range, the delimiting characters only identify this entity if they are found within the parent range. • For a keyword, the name only identifies this entity if found within the parent range. The value `root` means that the entity is not nested.

---

startseq endseq	String	For a range, the sequences of characters that start and end the range. Special values for endseq are: ● linebreak: Range ends before the next line break. ● whitespace: Range ends before the next space or tab character.
completion	String	For a keyword, if this attribute is present, the keyword is shown in the completion popup in the source control. If it has a value, that text is inserted for completion. Use the % character in the completion string to define the final cursor position in the text.

➤ Examples

This defines a range that identifies C-style commented text:

```
<entity name="comment" type="range" startseq="/*"
endseq="*/" />
```

This defines a nested range, where the commentSpecial entity must be contained in a comment entity. The special comment is delimited by the # character:

```
<entity name= "comment" type="range" startseq="/*"
endseq="*/"
   parent="root"/>
<entity name= "commentSpecial" type="range" startseq="#"
endseq="#"
   parent="comment" />
```

In the Example Syntax Scheme (page 407), these elements define different appearances for comments, keywords and number arrays.

The cr range starts with # and ends with the next line break. It uses the appearance defined by the Comment keyset:

```
<entity type="range" name="cr" keyset="Comment"
startseq="#"
   endseq="linebreak" parent="root"/>
```

The ar range is delimited by square braces, [], and uses the appearance defined by the NumberArray keyset:

```
<entity type="range" name="ar" keyset="NumberArray"
startseq="["
   endseq="]" parent="root" />
```

These elements define the keywords, which use the appearance defined by the Keywords keyset:

```
<entity type="keyword" name="begin" keyset="Keywords"
parent="root" />
<entity type="keyword" name="end" keyset="Keywords"
parent="root" />
```

```
<entity type="keyword" name="variable" keyset="Keywords"
parent="root"
    completion=": %name%"/>
<entity type="keyword" name="values" keyset="Keywords"
parent="root"
    completion=": [%]" />
```

smartselect

The optional `<smartselect>` element defines an entity that can be selected by a double click. The attributes are:

startseq endseq	String	The sequences of characters that start and end the selectable element. Special values for `endseq` are: <ul><li>`linebreak`: Range ends before the next line break.</li><li>`whitespace`: Range ends before the next space or tab character.</li></ul>
inner	Boolean	When `true`, double-click selects only the text between the delimiters. When `false`, the delimiters are also included in the selection.
nested	Boolean	When `true`, the delimiter characters themselves can appear nested within the selection.

Example:

```
<smartselect startseq="[" endseq="]" inner="true"
nested="true" />
```

functionkey

The optional `<functionkey>` element defines how function names can be extracted from the code for the "Navigate through code" popup list, indicated by the [] icon in the Source view. The attributes are:

name	String	The function identifier. The word that appears after this string in the source code is considered to be the function name, and appears in the popup list of functions.
parent	Entity	The parent entity of the function definition, or `root` if the function-definition entity is not nested.

➤ Example

```
<functionkey name="fnDeclare" parent="root"/>
```

balancebrackets

The optional `<balancebrackets>` element enables automatic bracket balancing and defines the closing bracket characters. It has one attribute:

brackets	String	The characters to be considered as closing brackets for automatic balancing.

➤ **Example**

```
<balancebrackets brackets=">]})" />
```

Example Syntax Scheme

The following source code text has a comment that starts with #, some keywords (`begin`, `end`, `variable`, `values`) and a special color for the number arrays. Each of these elements is marked distinctively by color and font style.

```
#my format
begin
    variable: origin1 values: [0,3,4]
    variable: origin2 values: [2,7,3]
end
```

The syntax scheme definition for this marking style looks like this:

```
<syntax name="my3d" extensions="m3d">

<exampletext><![CDATA[
#my format
begin
    variable: origin1 values: [0,3,4]
    variable: origin2 values: [2,7,3]
end
]]></exampletext>

<splittable type="both">SPCTAB[]:#"</splittable>

<keyset name="Comment" bold="false" italic="true"
underline="false"
    color="#990000"/>
<keyset name="Keywords" bold="true" italic="false"
underline="false"
    color="#000099"/>
<keyset name="NumberArray" bold="true" italic="false"
underline="false"
    color="#009999"/>
```

```
<entity type="range" name="cr" keyset="Comment"
startseq="#"
   endseq="linebreak" parent="root" />
<entity type="range" name="ar" keyset="NumberArray"
startseq="[" endseq="]"
    parent="root" />
<entity type="keyword" name="begin" keyset="Keywords"
parent="root" />
<entity type="keyword" name="end" keyset="Keywords"
parent="root" />
<entity type="keyword" name="variable" keyset="Keywords"
parent="root"
   completion=": %name%"/>
<entity type="keyword" name="values" keyset="Keywords"
parent="root"
   completion=": [%]"/>

</syntax>
```

8 | ExtendScript Tools and Features

ExtendScript is Adobe's extended implementation of JavaScript, and is used by all Adobe Creative Suite 2 applications that provide a scripting interface. In addition to implementing the JavaScript language according to the W3C specification, ExtendScript provides certain additional features and utilities.

- For help in developing, debugging, and testing scripts, ExtendScript provides:
  - The ExtendScript Toolkit (page 409), an interactive development and testing environment for ExtendScript.
  - A global debugging object, the Dollar ($) Object (page 424).
  - A reporting utility for ExtendScript elements, the ExtendScript Reflection Interface (page 428).
- In addition, ExtendScript provides these tools and features:
  - A localization utility for providing user-interface string values in different languages. See "Localizing ExtendScript Strings" on page 431.
  - Global functions for displaying short messages in dialog boxes. See "User Notification Helper Functions" on page 435.
  - An object type for specifying measurement values together with their units. See "Specifying Measurement Values" on page 438.
  - Tools for combining scripts, such as a `#include` directive, and `import` and `export` statements. See "Modular Programming Support" on page 443.
  - Support for extending or overriding math and logical operator behavior on a class-by-class basis. See "Operator Overloading" on page 446.
- ExtendScript provides a common scripting environment for all Adobe Creative Suite 2 applications, and allows interapplication communication through scripts.
  - To identify specific Adobe Creative Suite 2 applications, scripts must use Application and Namespace Specifiers (page 451).
  - Applications can run scripts automatically on startup. See "Script Locations and Checking Application Installation" on page 453.

The ExtendScript Toolkit

The ExtendScript Toolkit provides an interactive development and testing environment for ExtendScript in all Adobe Creative Suite 2 applications. The

Toolkit includes a full-featured, syntax-highlighting editor with Unicode capabilities and multiple undo/redo support. The Toolkit allows you to:

- Single-step through JavaScripts inside a CS2 application.
- Inspect all data for a running script.
- Set and execute breakpoints.

The Toolkit is the default editor for ExtendScript files, which use the extension .jsx. You can use the Toolkit to edit or debug scripts in JS or JSX files.

When you double-click a JSX file in the platform's windowing environment, the script runs in the Toolkit, unless it specifies a particular target application using the #target directive. For more information, see "Selecting a debugging target" on page 412 and "Preprocessor directives" on page 443.

Configuring the Toolkit window

The ExtendScript Toolkit initially appears with a default arrangement of panes, containing a default configuration of tabs. You can adjust the relative sizes of the panes by dragging the separators up or down, or right or left. You can regroup the tabs. To move a tab, drag the label into another pane.

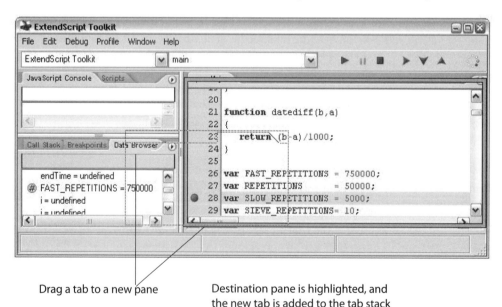

Drag a tab to a new pane

Destination pane is highlighted, and the new tab is added to the tab stack

If you drag a tab so that the entire destination pane is highlighted, it becomes another stacked tab in that pane. If you drag a tab to the top or bottom of a pane (so that only the top or bottom bar of the destination pane is highlighted), that pane splits to show the tabs in a tiled format.

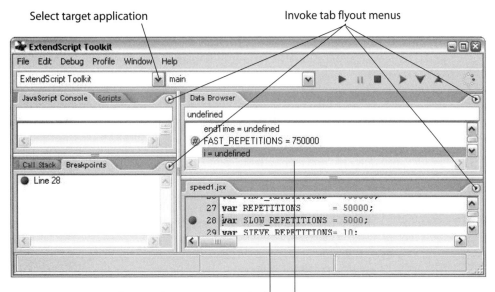

Select target application   Invoke tab flyout menus

Split pane shows Browser and Editor tabs

Each tab has a flyout menu, accessed through the triangle icon in the upper right corner. The same menu is available as a context menu, which you invoke with a right-click in the tab. This menu always includes a **Hide Pane** command to hide that pane. Use the **Window** menu to show a hidden pane, or to bring it to the front.

The Editor, which has a tab for each script, has an additional context menu for debugging, which appears when you right-click in the line numbers area.

The Toolkit saves the current layout when you exit, and restores it at the next startup. It also saves and restores the open documents, the current positions within the documents, and any breakpoints that have been set.

- If you do not want to restore all settings on startup, hold SHIFT while the Toolkit loads to restore default settings. This reconnects to the last application and engine that was selected.

- If you want to restore the layout settings on startup, but not load the previously open documents, choose **Start with a clean workspace** in the Preferences dialog.

Selecting a debugging target

The Toolkit can debug multiple applications at one time. If you have more than one Adobe Creative Suite 2 application installed, use the drop-down list at the upper left under the menu bar to select the target application. All installed applications that use ExtendScript are shown in this list. If you select an application that is not running, the Toolkit prompts for permission to run it.

All available engines in the selected target application are shown in a drop-down list to the right of the application list, with an icon that shows the current debugging status of that engine. A target application can have more than one ExtendScript engine, and more than one engine can be *active*, although only one is *current*. An active engine is one that is currently executing code, is halted at a breakpoint, or, having executed all scripts, is waiting to receive events. An icon by each engine name indicates whether it is *running*, *halted*, or *waiting* for input:

running

halted

waiting

The current engine is the one whose data and state is displayed in the Toolkit's panes. If an application has only one engine, its engine becomes current when you select the application as the target. If there is more than one engine available in the target application, you can select an engine in the list to make it current.

When you open the Toolkit, it attempts to reconnect to the same target and engine that was set last time it closed. If that target application is not running, the Toolkit prompts for permission to launch it. If permission is refused, the Toolkit itself becomes the target application.

If the target application that you select is not running, the Toolkit prompts for permission and launches the application. Similarly, if you run a script that specifies a target application that is not running (using the `#target` directive), the Toolkit prompts for permission to launch it. If the application is running but not selected as the current target, the Toolkit prompts you to switch to it.

If you select an application that cannot be debugged in the Toolkit (such as Adobe Help), an error dialog reports that the Toolkit cannot connect to the selected application.

The ExtendScript Toolkit is the default editor for JSX files. If you double-click a JSX file in a file browser, the Toolkit looks for a `#target` directive in the file and launches that application to run the script; however, it first checks for syntax errors in the script. If any are found, the Toolkit displays the error in a message box and quits silently, rather than launching the target application. For example:

Selecting scripts

The Scripts tab offers a list of debuggable scripts for the target application, which can be JS or JSX files or (for some applications) HTML files that contain embedded scripts.

Select a script in this tab to load it and display its contents in the editor pane, where you can modify it, save it, or run it within the target application.

Tracking data

The Data Browser tab is your window into the JavaScript engine. This tab displays all live data defined in the current context, as a list of variables with their current values. If execution has stopped at a breakpoint, it shows variables that have been defined using `var` in the current function, and the function arguments. To show variables defined in the global or calling scope, use the call stack to change the context (see "The call stack" on page 415).

You can use the Data Browser to examine and set variable values.

- Click a variable name to show its current value in the edit field at the top of the tab.

- To change the value, enter a new value and press ENTER. If a variable is read-only, the edit field is disabled.

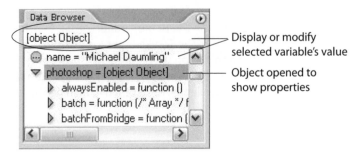

Display or modify selected variable's value

Object opened to show properties

The flyout menu for this tab lets you control the amount of data displayed:

- **Show Global Functions** toggles the display of all global function definitions.
- **Show Object Methods** toggles the display of all functions that are attached to objects. Most often, the interesting data in an object are its callable methods.
- **Show JavaScript Language Elements** toggles the display of all data that is part of the JavaScript language standard, such as the Array constructor or the Math object. An interesting property is the __proto__ property, which reveals the JavaScript object prototype chain.

Each variable has a small icon that indicates the data type. An invalid object is a reference to an object that has been deleted. If a variable is undefined, it does not have an icon.

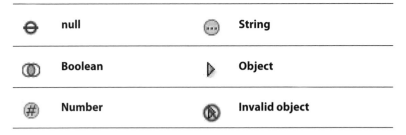

⊖	null	💬	String
⓪	Boolean	▷	Object
#	Number	🚫	Invalid object

You can inspect the contents of an object by clicking its icon. The list expands to show the object's properties (and methods, if **Show Object Methods** is enabled), and the triangle points down to indicate that the object is open.

Note: In Photoshop® CS2 the Data Browser pane is populated only during the debugging of a JavaScript program within Photoshop.

The JavaScript console

The JavaScript console is a command shell and output window for the currently selected JavaScript engine. The console connects you to the global namespace of that engine.

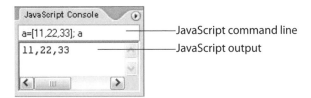

JavaScript command line

JavaScript output

The command line entry field accepts any JavaScript code, and you can use it to evaluate expressions or call functions. Enter any JavaScript statement on the command line and execute it by pressing ENTER. The statement executes within the stack scope of the line highlighted in the Call Stack tab, and the result appears in the output field.

- The command-line input field keeps a command history of 32 lines. Use the Up and Down Arrow keys to scroll through the previous entries.
- Commands entered in this field execute with a timeout of one second. If a command takes longer than one second to execute, the Toolkit generates a timeout error and terminates the attempt.

The output field is standard output for JavaScript execution. If any script generates a syntax error, the error is displayed here along with the file name and the line number. The Toolkit displays errors here during its own startup phase. The tab's flyout menu allows you to clear the contents of the output field and change the size of the font used for output.

The call stack

The Call Stack tab is active while debugging a program. When an executing program stops because of a breakpoint or run-time error, the tab displays the sequence of function calls that led to the current execution point. The Call Stack tab shows the names of the active functions, along with the actual arguments passed in to that function.

For example, this stack pane shows a break occurring at a breakpoint in a function `dayOfWeek`:

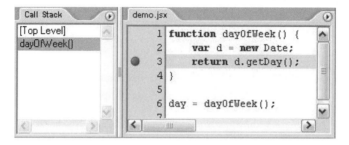

The function containing the breakpoint is highlighted in both the Call Stack and the Editor tabs.

You can click any function in the call hierarchy to inspect it. In the Editor, the line containing the function call that led to that point of execution is marked with a green background. In the example, when you select the line `[Top Level]` in the call stack, the Editor highlights the line where the `dayOfWeek` function was called.

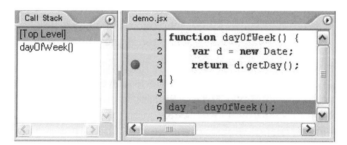

Switching between the functions in the call hierarchy allows you to trace how the current function was called. The Console and Data Browser tabs coordinate with the Call Stack pane. When you select a function in the call stack:

- The Console pane switches its scope to the execution context of that function, so you can inspect and modify its local variables. These would otherwise be inaccessible to the running JavaScript program from within a called function.

- The Data Browser pane displays all data defined in the selected context.

The Script Editor

You can open any number of Script Editor tabs; each displays one Unicode source code document. The editor supports JavaScript syntax highlighting,

JavaScript syntax checking, multiple undo and redo operations, and advanced search and replace functionality.

You can use the mouse or special keyboard shortcuts to move the insertion point or to select text in the editor.

Mouse navigation and selection

Click the left mouse button in the editor to move the position caret.

To select text with the mouse, click in unselected text, then drag over the text to be selected. If you drag above or below the currently displayed text, the text scrolls, continuing to select while scrolling. You can also double-click to select a word, or triple-click to select a line.

To initiate a drag-and-drop of selected text, click in the block of selected text, then drag to the destination. You can drag text from one editor pane to another. You can also drag text out of the Toolkit into another application that accepts dragged text, and drag text from another application into a Toolkit editor.

You can drop files from the Explorer or the Finder onto the Toolkit to open them in an editor.

Keyboard navigation and selection

In addition to the usual keyboard input, the editor accepts these special movement keys. You can also select text by using a movement key while pressing SHIFT.

Enter	Insert a Line Feed character
Backspace	Delete character to the left
Delete	Delete character to the right
Left arrow	Move insertion point left one character
Right arrow	Move insertion point right one character
Up arrow	Move insertion point up one line; stay in column if possible
Down arrow	Move insertion point down one line; stay in column if possible
Page up	Move insertion point one page up
Page down	Move insertion point one page down
CTRL + up arrow	Scroll up one line without moving the insertion point
CTRL + down arrow	Scroll down one line without moving the insertion point
CTRL + page up	Scroll one page up without moving the insertion point

CTRL + page down	Scroll one page down without moving the insertion point
CTRL + left arrow	Move insertion point one word to the left
CTRL + right arrow	Move insertion point one word to the right
Home	Move insertion point to start of line
End	Move insertion point to end of line
CTRL + Home	Move insertion point to start of text
CTRL + End	Move insertion point to end of text

The editor supports extended keyboard input via IME (Windows®) or TMS (Mac OS®). This is especially important for Far Eastern characters.

Syntax checking

Before running the new script or saving the text as a script file, you can check whether the text contains JavaScript syntax errors. Choose **Check Syntax** from the **Edit** menu or from the Editor's right-click context menu.

- If the script is syntactically correct, the status line shows "No syntax errors."
- If the Toolkit finds a syntax error, such as a missing quote, it highlights the affected text, plays a sound, and shows the error message in the status line so you can fix the error.

Debugging in the Toolkit

You can debug the code in the currently active Editor tab. Select one of the debugging commands to either run or to single-step through the program.

When you run code from the Editor, it runs in the current target application's selected JavaScript engine. The Toolkit itself runs an independent JavaScript engine, so you can quickly edit and run a script without connecting to a target application.

Evaluation in help tips

If you let your mouse pointer rest over a variable or function in an Editor tab, the result of evaluating that variable or function is displayed as a help tip. When you are not debugging the program, this is helpful only if the variables and functions are already known to the JavaScript engine. During debugging, however, this is an extremely useful way to display the current value of a variable, along with its current data type.

You can turn off the display of help tips using the **Display JavaScript variables** and **Enable UI help tips** options on the Help Options page of the Preferences dialog.

Controlling code execution

The debugging commands are available from the **Debug** menu, from the Editor's right-click context menu, through keyboard shortcuts, and from the toolbar buttons. Use these menu commands and buttons to control the execution of code when the JavaScript Debugger is active.

▶	**Run Continue**	**F5** (Windows) **Control R** (Mac OS)	Starts or resumes execution of a script. Disabled when script is executing.
‖	**Break**	**Ctrl F5** (Windows) **Cmd .** (Mac OS)	Halts the currently executing script temporarily and reactivates the JavaScript Debugger. Enabled when a script is executing.
■	**Stop**	**Shift F5** (Windows) **Control K** (Mac OS)	Stops execution of the script and generates a run-time error. Enabled when a script is executing.
▶	**Step Over**	**F10** (Windows) **Control S** (Mac OS)	Halts after executing a single JavaScript line in the script. If the statement calls a JavaScript function, executes the function in its entirety before stopping (do not step into the function).
▼	**Step Into**	**F11** (Windows) **Control T** (Mac OS)	Halts after executing a single JavaScript line statement in the script or after executing a single statement in any JavaScript function that the script calls.
▲	**Step Out**	**Shift F11** (Windows) **Control U** (Mac OS)	When paused within the body of a JavaScript function, resumes script execution until the function returns. When paused outside the body of a function, resumes script execution until the script terminates.

Visual indication of execution states

While the engine is running, an icon ⟳ in the upper right corner of the Toolkit window indicates that the script is active.

When the execution of a script halts because the script reaches a breakpoint, or when the script reaches the next line when stepping line by line, the Editor displays the current script with the current line highlighted in yellow.

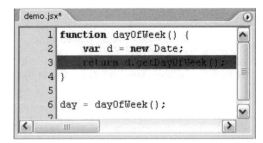

```
demo.jsx
    1  function dayOfWeek() {
    2      var d = new Date;
    3      var day;
    4      try { // test dayOfWeek
    5          day = d.getDayOfWeek();
    6      }
    7      catch (error) { // no dayOfWeek
●   8          day = -1;
    9      }
   10      return day;
   11  }
```

If the script encounters a run-time error, the Toolkit halts the execution of the script, displays the current script with the current line highlighted in red, displays the error message in the status line, and plays a sound.

```
demo.jsx*
    1  function dayOfWeek() {
    2      var d = new Date;
    3          return d.getDayOfWeek();
    4  }
    5
    6  day = dayOfWeek();
    7
```

Scripts often use a `try`/`catch` clause to execute code that might cause a run-time error, to catch the error programmatically rather than have the script terminate. You can choose to allow regular processing of such errors using the `catch` clause, rather than breaking into the debugger. To set this behavior, choose **Debug** > **Don't Break On Guarded Exceptions**. Some run-time errors, such as `Out Of Memory`, always cause the termination of the script, regardless of this setting.

Setting breakpoints

When debugging a script, it is often helpful to make it stop at certain lines so that you can inspect the state of the environment, whether function calls are nested properly, or whether all variables contain the expected data.

- To stop execution of a script at a given line, click to the left of the line number to set a breakpoint. A filled dot indicates the breakpoint.
- Click a second time to temporarily disable the breakpoint; the icon changes to an outline.
- Click a third time to delete the breakpoint. The icon is removed.

Some breakpoints need to be conditional. For example, if you set a breakpoint in a loop that is executed several thousand times, you would not want to have the program stop each time through the loop, but only on each 1000th iteration.

You can attach a condition to a breakpoint, in the form of a JavaScript expression. Every time execution reaches the breakpoint, it runs the JavaScript expression. If the expression evaluates to a nonzero number or `true`, execution stops.

To set a conditional breakpoint in a loop, for example, the conditional expression could be `"i >= 1000"`, which means that the program execution halts if the value of the iteration variable `i` is equal to or greater than 1000.

You can set breakpoints on lines that do not contain any code, such as comment lines. When the Toolkit runs the program, it automatically moves such a breakpoint down to the next line that actually contains code.

Breakpoint icons

Each breakpoint is indicated by an icon to the left of the line number. The icon for a conditional breakpoint is a diamond, while the icon for an unconditional breakpoint is round. Disabled breakpoints are indicated by an outline icon, while active ones are filled.

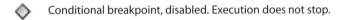 Unconditional breakpoint. Execution stops here.

Unconditional breakpoint, disabled. Execution does not stop.

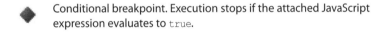 Conditional breakpoint. Execution stops if the attached JavaScript expression evaluates to `true`.

Conditional breakpoint, disabled. Execution does not stop.

The Breakpoints tab

The Breakpoints tab displays all breakpoints set in the current Editor tab. You can use the tab's flyout menu to add, change, or remove a breakpoint.

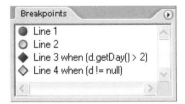

You can edit a breakpoint by double-clicking it, or by selecting it and choosing **Add** or **Change** from the context menu. A dialog allows you to change the line number, the breakpoint's enabled state, and the condition statement.

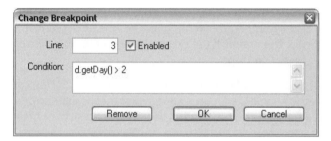

Whenever execution reaches this breakpoint, the debugger evaluates this condition. If it does not evaluate to `true`, the breakpoint is ignored and execution continues. This allows you to break only when certain conditions are met, such as a variable having a particular value.

Profiling

The Profiling tool helps you to optimize program execution. When you turn profiling on, the JavaScript engine collects information about a program while it is running. The tool counts how often the program executes a line or function, or how long it takes to execute a line or function. You can choose exactly which profiling data to display.

Because profiling significantly slows execution time, the **Profile** menu offers these profiling options.

Off	Profiling turned off. This is the default.
Functions	The profiler counts each function call. At the end of execution, displays the total to the left of the line number where the function header is defined.
Lines	The profiler counts each time each line is executed. At the end of execution, displays the total to the left of the line number. Consumes more execution time, but delivers more detailed information.
Add Timing Info	Instead of counting the functions or lines, records the time taken to execute each function or line. At the end of execution, displays the total number of microseconds spent in the function or line, to the left of the line number. This is the most time-consuming form of profiling.
No Profiler Data	When selected, do not display profiler data.
Show Hit Count	When selected, display hit counts.
Show Timing	When selected, display timing data.

Erase Profiler Data	Clear all profiling data.
Save Data As	Save profiling data as comma-separated values in a CSV file that can be loaded into a spreadsheet program such as Excel.

When execution halts (at termination, at a breakpoint, or due to a run-time error), the Toolkit displays this information in the Editor, line by line. The profiling data is color coded:

- Green indicates the lowest number of hits, or the fastest execution time.
- Red indicates trouble spots, such as a line that has been executed many times, or which line took the most time to execute.

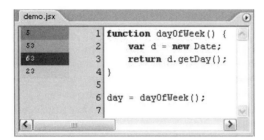

This example displays timing information for the program, where the fastest line took 4 microseconds to execute, and the slowest line took 29 microseconds. The timing might not be accurate down to the microsecond; it depends on the resolution and accuracy of the hardware timers built into your computer.

Dollar ($) Object

This global ExtendScript object provides a number of debugging facilities and informational methods. The properties of the $ object allow you to get global information such as the most recent run-time error, and set flags that control debugging and localization behavior. The methods allow you to output text to the JavaScript Console during script execution, control execution and other ExtendScript behavior programmatically, and gather statistics on object use.

Dollar ($) object properties

build	Number	The ExtendScript build number. Read only.
buildDate	Date	The date ExtendScript was built. Read only.
error	Error String	The most recent run-time error information, contained in a JavaScript Error object.
		Assigning error text to this property generates a run-time error; however, the preferred way to generate a run-time error is to throw an Error object.
flags	Number	Gets or sets low-level debug output flags. A logical AND of the following bit flag values:
		0x0002 (2): Displays each line with its line number as it is executed.
		0x0040 (64): Enables excessive garbage collection. Usually, garbage collection starts when the number of objects has increased by a certain amount since the last garbage collection. This flag causes ExtendScript to garbage collect after almost every statement. This impairs performance severely, but is useful when you suspect that an object gets released too soon.
		0x0080 (128): Displays all calls with their arguments and the return value.
		0x0100 (256): Enables extended error handling. See strict (page 425).
		0x0200 (512): Enables the localization feature of the toString method. Equivalent to the localize property (page 425).
global	Object	Provides access to the global object, which contains the JavaScript global namespace.
level	Number	Enables or disables the JavaScript debugger. One of:
		0: No debugging
		1: Break on run-time errors
		2: Full debug mode

locale	String	Gets or sets the current locale. The string contains five characters in the form *LL_RR*, where *LL* is an ISO 639 language specifier, and *RR* is an ISO 3166 region specifier. Initially, this is the value that the application or the platform returns for the current user. You can set it to temporarily change the locale for testing. To return to the application or platform setting, set to `undefined`, `null`, or the empty string.
localize	Boolean	Enable or disable the extended localization features of the built-in `toString` method. See "Localizing ExtendScript Strings" on page 431.
memCache	Number	Gets or sets the ExtendScript memory cache size in bytes.
objects	Number	The total count of all JavaScript objects defined so far. Read only.
os	String	The current operating system version. Read only.
screens	Array	An array of objects containing information about the display screens attached to your computer. Each object has the properties `left`, `top`, `right`, and `bottom`, which contain the four corners of each screen in global coordinates. A property `primary` is `true` if that object describes the primary display.
strict	Boolean	When `true`, any attempt to write to a read-only property causes a run-time error. Some objects do not permit the creation of new properties when `true`.
version	String	The version number of the ExtendScript engine as a three-part number and description; for example: "3.6.5 (debug)" Read only.

Dollar ($) object functions

about `$.about ()`	Displays the About box for the ExtendScript component, and returns the text of the About box as a string.
bp `$.bp ([condition])`	Executes a breakpoint at the current position. Returns `undefined`. If no condition is needed, it is recommended that you use the JavaScript `debugger` statement in the script, rather than this method.
condition	Optional. A string containing a JavaScript statement to be used as a condition. If the statement evaluates to `true` or nonzero when this point is reached, execution stops.
clearbp `$.clearbp ([line])`	Removes a breakpoint from the current script. Returns `undefined`.
line	Optional. The line at which to clear the breakpoint. If 0 or not supplied, clears the breakpoint at the current line number.
gc `$.gc ()`	Initiates garbage collection. Returns `undefined`.

getenv `$.getenv (envname)`	Returns the value of the specified environment variable, or `null` if no such variable is defined.
envname	The name of the environment variable.
list `$.list ([classname])`	Collects object information into a table and returns this table as a string. See "Object statistics" on page 427.
classname	Optional. The type of object about which to collect information. If not supplied, collects information about all objects currently defined.

setbp
`$.setbp`
`([line, condition])`
	Sets a breakpoint in the current script. Returns `undefined`.
	If no arguments are needed, it is recommended that you use the JavaScript `debugger` statement in the script, rather than this method.

line	Optional. The line at which to stop execution. If 0 or not supplied, sets the breakpoint at the current line number.
condition	Optional. A string containing a JavaScript statement to be used for a conditional breakpoint. If the statement evaluates to `true` or nonzero when the line is reached, execution stops.
sleep `$.sleep (milliseconds)`	Suspends the calling thread for the given number of milliseconds. Returns `undefined`. During a sleep period, checks at 100 millisecond intervals to see whether the sleep should be terminated. This can happen if there is a break request, or if the script timeout has expired.
milliseconds	The number of milliseconds to wait.

summary
`$.summary ([classname])`
	Collects a summary of object counts into a table and returns this table as a string. The table shows the number of objects in each specified class. For example:
	`3 Array`
	`5 String`

classname	Optional. The type of object to count. If not supplied, counts all objects currently defined.

write
`$.write`
`(text[, text...]...)`
	Writes the specified text to the JavaScript Console. Returns `undefined`.

text	One or more strings to write, which are concatenated to form a single string.

writeln
`$.writeln`
`(text[, text...]...)`
	Writes the specified text to the JavaScript Console and appends a linefeed sequence. Returns `undefined`.

text	One or more strings to write, which are concatenated to form a single string.

Object statistics

The output from $.list() is formatted as in the following example.

Address	L	Refs	Prop	Class	Name
0092196c	4	0	Function	[toplevel]	
00976c8c	2	1	Object	Object	
00991bc4L	1	1	LOTest	LOTest	
0099142cL	2	2	Function	LOTest	
00991294	1	0	Object	Object	workspace

The columns show the following object information.

Address	The physical address of the object in memory.
L	This column contains the letter "L" if the object is a LiveObject (which is an internal data type).
Refs	The reference count of the object.
Prop	A second reference count for the number of properties that reference the object. The garbage collector uses this count to break circular references. If the reference count is not equal to the number of JavaScript properties that reference it, the object is considered to be used elsewhere and is not garbage collected.
Class	The class name of the object.
Name	The name of the object. This name does not reflect the name of the property the object has been stored into. The name is mostly relevant to Function objects, where it is the name of the function or method. Names in brackets are internal names of scripts. If the object has an ID, the last column displays that ID.

ExtendScript Reflection Interface

ExtendScript provides a reflection interface that allows you to find out everything about an object, including its name, a description, the expected data type for properties, the arguments and return value for methods, and any default values or limitations to the input values.

Reflection Object

Every object has a `reflect` property that returns a `reflection` object that reports the contents of the object. For example, you can show the values of all the properties of an object with code like this:

```
var f= new File ("myfile");
var props = f.reflect.properties;
for (var i = 0; i < props.length; i++) {
    $.writeln('this property ' + props[i].name + ' is ' +
f[props[i].name]);
}
```

Reflection object properties

All properties are read only.

`description`	String	Short text describing the reflected object, or undefined if no description is available.
`help`	String	Longer text describing the reflected object more completely, or undefined if no description is available.
`methods`	Array of ReflectionInfo	An Array of ReflectionInfo Objects (page 429) containing all methods of the reflected object, defined in the class or in the specific instance.
`name`	String	The class name of the reflected object.
`properties`	Array of ReflectionInfo	An Array of ReflectionInfo Objects (page 429) containing all properties of the reflected object, defined in the class or in the specific instance. For objects with dynamic properties (defined at runtime) the list contains only those dynamic properties that have already been accessed by the script. For example, in an object wrapping an HTML tag, the names of the HTML attributes are determined at run time.

Reflection object functions

find *reflectionObj*.find (*name*)	Returns the ReflectionInfo Object (page 429) for the named property of the reflected object, or `null` if no such property exists. Use this method to get information about dynamic properties that have not yet been accessed, but that are known to exist.
name	The property for which to retrieve information.

➤ Examples

This code determines the class name of an object:

```
obj = new String ("hi");
obj.reflect.name; // => String
```

This code gets a list of all methods:

```
obj = new String ("hi");
obj.reflect.methods; //=> indexOf,slice,...
obj.reflect.find ("indexOf"); // => the method info
```

This code gets a list of properties:

```
Math.reflect.properties; //=> PI,LOG10,...
```

This code gets the data type of a property:

```
Math.reflect.find ("PI").type; // => number
```

ReflectionInfo Object

This object contains information about a property, a method, or a method argument.

- You can access `ReflectionInfo` objects in a Reflection Object's `properties` and `methods` arrays (page 428), by name or index:

```
obj = new String ("hi");
obj.reflect.methods[0];
obj.reflect.methods["indexOf"];
```

- You can access the `ReflectionInfo` objects for the arguments of a method in the `arguments` array of the `ReflectionInfo` object for the method, by index:

```
obj.reflect.methods["indexOf"].arguments[0];
```

ReflectionInfo object properties

arguments	Array of ReflectionInfo	For a reflected method, an array of ReflectionInfo Objects (page 429) describing each method argument.

dataType	String	The data type of the reflected element. One of:
		    `boolean`
		    `number`
		    `string`
		    Classname: The class name of an object.
		Note: Class names start with a capital letter. Thus, the value `string` stands for a JavaScript string, while `String` is a JavaScript `String` wrapper object.
		    `*`: Any type. This is the default.
		    `null`
		    `undefined`: Return data type for a function that does not return any value.
		    `unknown`

defaultValue	any	The default value for a reflected property or method argument, or `undefined` if there is no default value, if the property is undefined, or if the element is a method.
description	String	Short text describing the reflected object, or `undefined` if no description is available.
help	String	Longer text describing the reflected object more completely, or `undefined` if no description is available.
isCollection	Boolean	When `true`, the reflected property or method returns a collection; otherwise, `false`.
max	Number	The maximum numeric value for the reflected element, or `undefined` if there is no maximum or if the element is a method.
min	Number	The minimum numeric value for the reflected element, or `undefined` if there is no minimum or if the element is a method.
name	String Number	The name of the reflected element. A string, or a number for an array index.

type	String	The type of the reflected element. One of:
		    `readonly`: A read-only property.
		    `readwrite`: A read-write property.
		    `createonly`: A property that is valid only during creation of an object.
		    `method`: A method.

Localizing ExtendScript Strings

Localization is the process of translating and otherwise manipulating an interface so that it looks as if it had been originally designed for a particular language. ExtendScript gives you the ability to localize the strings in your script's user interface. The language is chosen by the application at startup, according to the current locale provided by the operating system.

For portions of your user interface that are displayed on the screen, you might want to localize the displayed text. You can localize any string explicitly using the Global localize function (page 434), which takes as its argument a *localization object* containing the localized versions of a string.

A localization object is a JavaScript object literal whose property names are locale names, and whose property values are the localized text strings. The locale name is a standard language code with an optional region identifier. For details of the syntax, see "Locale names" on page 432.

In this example, a `msg` object contains localized text strings for two locales. This object supplies the text for an alert dialog.

```
msg = { en: "Hello, world", de: "Hallo Welt" };
alert (msg);
```

ExtendScript matches the current locale and platform to one of the object's properties and uses the associated string. On a German system, for example, the property `de: "Hallo Welt"` is converted to the string `"Hallo Welt"`.

Variable values in localized strings

Some localization strings need to contain additional data whose position and order might change according to the language used.

You can include variables in the string values of the localization object, in the form `%n`. The variables are replaced in the returned string with the results of JavaScript expressions, supplied as additional arguments to the `localize` function. The variable `%1` corresponds to the first additional argument, `%2` to the second, and so on.

Because the replacement occurs after the localized string is chosen, the variable values are inserted in the correct position. For example:

```
today = {
   en: "Today is %1/%2.",
   de: "Heute ist der %2.%1."
   };
d = new Date();
alert (localize (today, d.getMonth()+1, d.getDate()));
```

Enabling automatic localization

ExtendScript offers an automatic localization feature. When it is enabled, you can specify a localization object directly as the value of any property that takes a localizable string, without using the `localize` function. For example:

```
msg = { en: "Yes", de: "Ja", fr: "Oui" };
alert (msg);
```

To use automatic translation of localization objects, you must enable localization in your script with this statement:

```
$.localize = true;
```

The `localize` function always performs its translation, regardless of the setting of the `$.localize` variable. For example:

```
msg = { en: "Yes", de: "Ja", fr: "Oui" };
//Only works if the $.localize=true
alert (msg);
//Always works, regardless of $.localize value
alert ( localize (msg));
```

If you need to include variables in the localized strings, use the `localize` function.

Locale names

A locale name is an identifier string in that contains an ISO 639 language specifier, and optionally an ISO 3166 region specifier, separated from the language specifier by an underscore.

- The ISO 639 standard defines a set of two-letter language abbreviations, such as `en` for English and `de` for German.
- The ISO 3166 standard defines a region code, another two-letter identifier, which you can optionally append to the language identifier with an underscore. For example, `en_US` identifies U.S. English, while `en_GB` identifies British English.

This object defines one message for British English, another for all other flavors of English, and another for all flavors of German:

```
message = {
   en_GB: "Please select a colour."
   en: "Please select a color."
   de: "Bitte wählen Sie eine Farbe."
};
```

If you need to specify different messages for different platforms, you can append another underline character and the name of the platform, one of `Win`, `Mac`, or `Unix`. For example, this object defines one message in British

English to be displayed in Mac OS, one for all other flavors of English in Mac OS, and one for all other flavors of English on all other platforms:

```
pressMsg = {
    en_GB_Mac: "Press Cmd-S to select a colour.",
    en_Mac: "Press Cmd-S to select a color.",
    en: "Press Ctrl-S to select a color."
};
```

All of these identifiers are case sensitive. For example, `EN_US` is not valid.

➤ How locale names are resolved

1. ExtendScript gets the hosting application's locale; for example, `en_US`.

2. It appends the platform identifier; for example, `en_US_Win`.

3. It looks for a matching property, and if found, returns the value string.

4. If not found, it removes the platform identifier (for example, `en_US`) and retries.

5. If not found, it removes the region identifier (for example, `en`) and retries.

6. If not found, it tries the identifier `en` (that is, the default language is English).

7. If not found, it returns the entire localizer object.

Testing localization

ExtendScript stores the current locale in the variable `$.locale`. This variable is updated whenever the locale of the hosting application changes.

To test your localized strings, you can temporarily reset the locale. To restore the original behavior, set the variable to `null`, `false`, 0, or the empty string. An example:

```
$.locale = "ru"; // try your Russian messages
$.locale = null; // restore to the locale of the app
```

Global localize function

The globally available `localize` function can be used to provide localized strings anywhere a displayed text value is specified.

`localize`
`localize (localization_obj[, args])`
`localize (ZString)`
	Returns the localized string for the current locale.

`localization_obj`	A JavaScript object literal whose property names are locale names, and whose property values are the localized text strings. The locale name is an identifier as specified in the ISO 3166 standard, a set of two-letter language abbreviations, such as "en" for English and "de" for German.
	
	For example:
	
	`btnText = { en: "Yes", de: "Ja", fr: "Oui" };`
	`b1 = w.add ("button", undefined, localize (btnText));`
	
	The string value of each property can contain variables in the form %1, %2, and so on, corresponding to additional arguments. The variable is replaced with the result of evaluating the corresponding argument in the returned string.

`args`	Optional. Additional JavaScript expressions matching variables in the string values supplied in the localization object. The first argument corresponds to the variable %1, the second to %2, and so on. Each expression is evaluated and the result inserted in the variable's position in the returned string.

➤ Example

```
today = {
   en: "Today is %1/%2",
   de: "Heute ist der %2.%1."
   };
d = new Date();
alert (localize (today, d.getMonth()+1, d.getDate()));
```

`ZString`	Internal use only. A ZString is an internal Adobe format for localized strings, which you might see in Adobe scripts. A ZString begins with $$$ and contains a path to the localized string in an installed ZString dictionary. For example: `w = new Window ("dialog", localize ("$$$/UI/title1=Sample"));`

User Notification Helper Functions

ExtendScript provides a set of globally available functions that allow you to display short messages to the user in platform-standard dialog boxes. There are three types of message dialogs:

- **Alert**: Displays a dialog containing a short message and an **OK** button.
- **Confirm**: Displays a dialog containing a short message and two buttons, **Yes** and **No**, allowing the user to accept or reject an action.
- **Prompt**: Displays a dialog containing a short message, a text entry field, and **OK** and **Cancel** buttons, allowing the user to supply a value to the script.

These dialogs are customizable to a small degree. The appearance is platform specific.

Global alert function

`alert` `alert (message[, title, errorIcon]);`	Displays a platform-standard dialog containing a short message and an **OK** button. Returns `undefined`.
`message`	The string for the displayed message.
`title`	Optional. A string to appear as the title of the dialog, if the platform supports a title. Mac OS does not support titles for alert dialogs. The default title string is "Script Alert".
`errorIcon`	Optional. When `true`, the platform-standard alert icon is replaced by the platform-standard error icon in the dialog. Default is `false`.

➤ Examples

This figure shows simple alert dialogs in Windows and Mac OS.

This figure shows alert dialogs with error icons.

Global confirm function

confirm confirm (message[,noAsDflt ,title]);	Displays a platform-standard dialog containing a short message and two buttons labeled **Yes** and **No**. Returns true if the user clicked **Yes**, false if the user clicked **No**.
message	The string for the displayed message.
noAsDflt	Optional. When true, the **No** button is the default choice, selected when the user types ENTER. Default is false, meaning that **Yes** is the default choice.
title	Optional. A string to appear as the title of the dialog, if the platform supports a title. Mac OS does not support titles for confirmation dialogs. The default title string is "Script Alert".

➤ **Examples**

This figure shows simple confirmation dialogs in Windows and Mac OS.

This figure shows confirmation dialogs with **No** as the default button.

Global prompt function

prompt prompt (*message, preset*[, *title*]);	Displays a platform-standard dialog containing a short message, a text edit field, and two buttons labeled **OK** and **Cancel**. Returns the value of the text edit field if the user clicked **OK**, null if the user clicked **Cancel**.
message	The string for the displayed message.
preset	The initial value to be displayed in the text edit field.
title	Optional. A string to appear as the title of the dialog. In Windows, this appears in the window's frame, while in Mac OS it appears above the message. The default title string is "Script Prompt".

> **Examples**

This figure shows simple prompt dialogs in Windows and Mac OS.

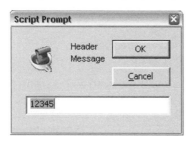 

This figure shows confirmation dialogs with a `title` value specified.

Specifying Measurement Values

ExtendScript provides the UnitValue Object (page 438) to represent measurement values. The properties and methods of the `UnitValue` object make it easy to change the value, the unit, or both, or to perform conversions from one unit to another.

UnitValue Object

Represents measurement values that contain both the numeric magnitude and the unit of measurement.

UnitValue object constructor

The `UnitValue` constructor creates a new `UnitValue` object. The keyword `new` is optional:

```
myVal = new UnitValue (value, unit);
myVal = new UnitValue ("value unit");
myVal = new UnitValue (value, "unit");
```

The *value* is a number, and the *unit* is specified with a string in abbreviated, singular, or plural form, as shown in the following table.

Abbreviation	Singular	Plural	Comments
in	inch	inches	2.54 cm
ft	foot	feet	30.48 cm
yd	yard	yards	91.44 cm
mi	mile	miles	1609.344 m
mm	millimeter	millimeters	
cm	centimeter	centimeters	
m	meter	meters	

Abbreviation	Singular	Plural	Comments
km	kilometer	kilometers	
pt	point	points	inches / 72
pc	pica	picas	points * 12
tpt	traditional point	traditional points	inches / 72.27
tpc	traditional pica	traditional picas	12 tpt
ci	cicero	ciceros	12.7872 pt
px	pixel	pixels	baseless (see below)
%	percent	percent	baseless (see below)

If an unknown unit type is supplied, the type is set to "?", and the `UnitValue` object prints as "UnitValue 0.00000".

For example, all of the following formats are equivalent:

```
myVal = new UnitValue (12, "cm");
myVal = new UnitValue ("12 cm");
myVal = UnitValue ("12 centimeters");
```

UnitValue object properties

baseUnit	UnitValue	A UnitValue Object (page 438) that defines the size of one pixel, or a total size to use as a base for percentage values. This is used as the base conversion unit for pixels and percentages; see "Converting pixel and percentage values" on page 440. Default is 0.013889 inches (1/72 in), which is the base conversion unit for pixels at 72 dpi. Set to null to restore the default.
type	String	The unit type in abbreviated form; for example, "cm" or "in".
value	Number	The numeric measurement value.

UnitValue object functions

as unitValueObj.as (unit)	Returns the numeric value of this object in the given unit. If the unit is unknown or cannot be computed, generates a run-time error.
unit	The unit type in abbreviated form; for example, "cm" or "in".

convert	Converts this object to the given unit, resetting the `type` and
`unitValueObj.convert (unit)`	`value` accordingly. Returns `true` if the conversion is successful. If the unit is unknown or the object cannot be converted, generates a run-time error and returns `false`.
`unit`	The unit type in abbreviated form; for example, "cm" or "in".

Converting pixel and percentage values

Converting measurements among different units requires a common base unit. For example, for length, the meter is the base unit. All length units can be converted into meters, which makes it possible to convert any length unit into any other length unit.

Pixels and percentages do not have a standard common base unit. Pixel measurements are relative to display resolution, and percentages are relative to an absolute total size.

- To convert pixels into length units, you must know the size of a single pixel. The size of a pixel depends on the display resolution. A common resolution measurement is 72 dpi, which means that there are 72 pixels to the inch. The conversion base for pixels at 72 dpi is 0.013889 inches (1/72 inch).

- Percentage values are relative to a total measurement. For example, 10% of 100 inches is 10 inches, while 10% of 1 meter is 0.1 meters. The conversion base of a percentage is the unit value corresponding to 100%.

The default `baseUnit` of a `unitValue` object is 0.013889 inches, the base for pixels at 72 dpi. If the `unitValue` is for pixels at any other dpi, or for a percentage value, you must set the `baseUnit` value accordingly. The `baseUnit` value is itself a `unitValue` object, containing both a magnitude and a unit.

For a system using a different dpi, you can change the `baseUnit` value in the `UnitValue` class, thus changing the default for all new `unitValue` objects. For example, to double the resolution of pixels:

```
UnitValue.baseUnit = UnitValue (1/144, "in"); //144 dpi
```

To restore the default, assign `null` to the class property:

```
UnitValue.baseUnit = null; //restore default
```

You can override the default value for any particular `unitValue` object by setting the property in that object. For example, to create a unitValue object for pixels with 96 dpi:

```
pixels = UnitValue (10, "px");
myPixBase = UnitValue (1/96, "in");
pixels.baseUnit = myPixBase;
```

For percentage measurements, set the `baseUnit` property to the measurement value for 100%. For example, to create a `unitValue` object for 40% of 10 feet:

```
myPctVal = UnitValue (40, "%");
myBase = UnitValue (10, "ft")
myPctVal.baseUnit = myBase;
```

Use the `as` method (page 439) to get to a percentage value as a unit value:

```
myFootVal = myPctVal.as ("ft"); // => 4
myInchVal = myPctVal.as ("in"); // => 36
```

You can convert a `unitValue` from an absolute measurement to pixels or percents in the same way:

```
myMeterVal = UnitValue (10, "m"); // 10 meters
myBase = UnitValue (1, "km");
myMeterVal.baseUnit = myBase; //as a percentage of 1
kilometer
pctOfKm = myMeterVal.as ('%'); // => 1

myVal = UnitValue ("1 in"); // Define measurement in
inches
// convert to pixels using default base
myVal.convert ("px"); // => value=72 type=px
```

Computing with unit values

`UnitValue` objects can be used in computational JavaScript expressions. The way the value is used depends on the type of operator.

- Unary operators (~, !, +, -)

~unitValue	The numeric value is converted to a 32-bit integer with inverted bits.
!unitValue	Result is `true` if the numeric value is nonzero, `false` if it is not.
+unitValue	Result is the numeric value.
-unitValue	Result is the negated numeric value.

- Binary operators (+, -, *, /, %)

  If one operand is `unitValue` object and the other is a number, the operation is applied to the number and the numeric value of the object.

The expression returns a new `unitValue` object with the result as its `value`. For example:

```
val = new UnitValue ("10 cm");
res = val * 20;
// res is a UnitValue (200, "cm");
```

If both operands are `unitValue` objects, JavaScript converts the right operand to the same unit as the left operand and applies the operation to the resulting values. The expression returns a new `unitValue` object with the unit of the left operand, and the result `value`. For example:

```
a = new UnitValue ("1 m");
b = new UnitValue ("10 cm");
a + b;
// res is a UnitValue (1.1, "m");
b + a;
// res is a UnitValue (110, "cm");
```

- Comparisons (=, ==, <, >, <=, >=)

  If one operand is a `unitValue` object and the other is a number, JavaScript compares the number with the `unitValue`'s numeric value.

  If both operands are `unitValue` objects, JavaScript converts both objects to the same unit, and compares the converted numeric values.

  For example:

```
a = new UnitValue ("98 cm");
b = new UnitValue ("1 m");
a < b;    // => true
a < 1;    // => false
a == 98; // => true
```

Modular Programming Support

ExtendScript provides support for a modular approach to scripting by allowing you to include one script in another as a resource, and allowing a script to export definitions that can be imported and used in another script.

Preprocessor directives

ExtendScript provides preprocessor directives for including external scripts, naming scripts, specifying an ExtendScript engine, and setting certain flags. You can specify these in two ways:

- With a C-style statement starting with the # character:

    ```
    #include "file.jsxinc"
    ```

- In a comment whose text starts with the @ character:

    ```
    // @include "file.jsxinc"
    ```

When a directive takes one or more arguments, and an argument contains any nonalphanumeric characters, the argument must be enclosed in single or double quotes. This is generally the case with paths and file names, for example, which contain dots and slashes.

`#engine name`	Identifies the ExtendScript engine that runs this script. This allows other engines to refer to the scripts in this engine by importing the exported functions and variables. See "Importing and exporting between scripts" on page 444.
	Use JavaScript identifier syntax for the name. Enclosing quotes are optional. For example:
	`#engine library` `#engine "$lib"`
`#include file`	Includes a JavaScript source file from another location. Inserts the contents of the named file into this file at the location of this statement. The `file` argument is an Adobe portable file specification. See "Specifying Paths" on page 447.
	As a convention, use the file extension `.jsxinc` for JavaScript include files. For example:
	`#include "../include/lib.jsxinc"` To set one or more paths for the `#include` statement to scan, use the `#includepath` preprocessor directive.
	If the file to be included cannot be found, ExtendScript throws a run-time error.
	Included source code is not shown in the debugger, so you cannot set breakpoints in it.

#includepath path	One or more paths that the #include statement should use to locate the files to be included. The semicolon (;) separates path names. If a #include file name starts with a slash (/), it is an absolute path name, and the include paths are ignored. Otherwise, ExtendScript attempts to find the file by prefixing the file with each path set by the #includepath statement. For example: ``` #includepath "include;../include" #include "file.jsxinc" ``` Multiple #includepath statements are allowed; the list of paths changes each time an #includepath statement is executed. As a fallback, ExtendScript also uses the contents of the environment variable JSINCLUDE as a list of include paths. Some engines can have a predefined set of include paths. If so, the path provided by #includepath is tried before the predefined paths. If, for example, the engine has a predefined path set to predef;predef/include, the preceding example causes the following lookup sequence: file.jsxinc: literal lookup include/file.jsxinc: first #includepath path ../include/file.jsxinc: second #includepath path predef/file.jsxinc: first predefined engine path predef/include/file.jsxinc: second predefined engine path
#script name	Names a script. Enclosing quotes are optional, but required for names that include spaces or special characters. For example: ``` #script SetupPalette #script "Load image file" ``` The *name* value is displayed in the Toolkit Editor tab. An unnamed script is assigned a unique name generated from a number.
#strict on	Turns on strict error checking. See the Dollar ($) Object's strict property (page 425).
#target name	Defines the target application of this JSX file. The *name* value is an application specifier; see "Application and Namespace Specifiers" on page 451. Enclosing quotes are optional. If the Toolkit is registered as the handler for files with the .jsx extension (as it is by default), opening the file opens the target application to run the script. If this directive is not present, the Toolkit loads and displays the script. A user can open a file by double-clicking it in a file browser, and a script can open a file using a File object's execute method.

Importing and exporting between scripts

The ExtendScript JavaScript language has been extended to support function calls and variable access across various source code modules and ExtendScript engines. A script can use the export statement to make its definitions available to other scripts, which use the `import` statement to access those definitions.

To use this feature, the exporting script must name its ExtendScript engine using the `#engine` preprocessor statement. The name must follow JavaScript naming syntax; it cannot be an expression.

For example, the following script could serve as a library or resource file. It defines and exports a constant and a function:

```
#engine library
export random, libVersion;
const libVersion = "Library 1.0";
function random (max) {
   return Math.floor (Math.random() * max);
}
```

A script running in a different engine can import the exported elements. The import statement identifies the resource script that exported the variables using the engine name:

```
import library.random, library.libVersion;
print (random (100));
```

You can use the asterisk wildcard (*) to import all symbols exported by a library:

```
import library.*
```

Objects cannot be transferred between engines. You cannot retrieve or store objects, and you cannot call functions with objects as arguments. However, you can use the JavaScript `toSource` function to serialize objects into strings before passing them. You can then use the JavaScript `eval` function to reconstruct the object from the string.

For example, this function takes as its argument a serialized string and constructs an object from it:

```
function myFn (serialized) {
   var obj = eval (serialized);
   // continue working…
}
```

In calling the function, you deconstruct the object you want to pass into a serialized string:

```
myFn (myObject.toSource()); // pass a serialized object
```

Operator Overloading

ExtendScript allows you to extend or override the behavior of a math or a Boolean operator for a specific class by defining a method in that class with same name as the operator. For example, this code defines the addition (+) operator for the class `MyClass`. In this case, the addition operator simply adds the operand to the property value:

```
// define the constructor method
function MyClass (initialValue) {
   this.value = initialValue;
}
// define the addition operator
MyClass.prototype ["+"] = function (operand) {
   return this.value + operand;
}
```

This allows you to perform the "+" operation with any object of this class:

```
var obj = new MyClass (5);
Result: [object Object]
obj + 10;
Result: 15
```

You can override the following operators:

Unary	+, - ~
Binary	+, - *, /, %, ^ <, <=, == <<, >>, >>> &, |, ===

- The operators `>` and `>=` are implemented by executing NOT operator `<=` and NOT operator `<`.
- Combined assignment operators such as `*=` are not supported.

All operator overload implementations must return the result of the operation. To perform the default operation, return `undefined`.

Unary operator functions work on the `this` object, while binary operators work on the `this` object and the first argument. The + and - operators have both unary and binary implementations. If the first argument is undefined, the operator is unary; if it is supplied, the operator is binary.

For binary operators, a second argument indicates the order of operands. For noncommutative operators, either implement both order variants in your function or return `undefined` for combinations that you do not support. For example:

```
this ["/"] = function (operand, rev) {
    if (rev) {
        // do not resolve operand / this
        return;
    } else {
        // resolve this / operand
        return this.value / operand;
    }
}
```

Specifying Paths

When creating a `File` or `Folder` object, you can specify a platform-specific path name, or an absolute or relative path in a platform-independent format known as *universal resource identifier* (*URI*) notation. The path stored in the object is always an absolute, full path name that points to a fixed location on the disk.

- Use the `toString` method to obtain the name of the file or folder as string containing an absolute path name in URI notation.

Absolute and relative path names

An absolute path name in URI notation describes the full path from a root directory down to a specific file or folder. It starts with one or two slashes (/), and a slash separates path elements. For example, the following describes an absolute location for the file `myFile.jsx`:

```
/dir1/dir2/mydir/myFile.jsx
```

A relative path name in URI notation is appended to the path of the current directory, as stored in the globally available `current` property of the `Folder` class. It starts with a folder or file name, or with one of the special names dot (.) for the current directory, or dot dot (..) for the parent of the current directory. A slash (/) separates path elements. For example, the following paths describe various relative locations for the file `myFile.jsx`:

`myFile.jsx` `./myFile.jsx`	In the current directory.
`../myFile.jsx`	In the parent of the current directory.
`../../myFile.jsx`	In the grandparent of the current directory.
`../dir1/myFile.jsx`	In `dir1`, which is parallel to the current directory.

Relative path names are independent of different volume names on different machines and operating systems, and therefore make your code considerably more portable. You can, for example, use an absolute path for a single operation, to set the current directory in the `Folder.current` property, and use relative paths for all other operations. You would then need only a single code change to update to a new platform or file location.

Character interpretation in paths

There are some platform differences in how pathnames are interpreted:

- In Windows and Mac OS, path names are not case sensitive. In UNIX, paths are case sensitive.
- In Windows, both the slash (/) and the backslash (\) are valid path element separators.
- In Mac OS, both the slash (/) and the colon (:) are valid path element separators.

If a path name starts with two slashes (or backslashes in Windows), the first element refers to a remote server. For example, `//myhost/mydir/myfile` refers to the path `/mydir/myfile` on the server `myhost`.

URI notation allows special characters in pathnames, but they must specified with an escape character (%) followed by a hexadecimal character code. Special characters are those which are not alphanumeric and not one of the characters:

```
/ - _ . ! ~ * ' ( )
```

A space, for example, is encoded as `%20`, so the file name `"my file"` is specified as `"my%20file"`. Similarly, the character ä is encoded as `%E4`, so the file name `"Bräun"` is specified as `"Br%E4un"`.

This encoding scheme is compatible with the global JavaScript functions `encodeURI` and `decodeURI`.

The home directory

A path name can start with a tilde (~) to indicate the user's home directory. It corresponds to the platform's HOME environment variable.

UNIX and Mac OS assign the HOME environment variable according to the user login. In Mac OS, the default home directory is `/Users/username`. In UNIX, it is typically `/home/username` or `/users/username`. Extend Script assigns the home directory value directly from the platform value.

In Windows, the HOME environment variable is optional. If it is assigned, its value must be a Windows path name or a path name referring to a remote server (such as `\\myhost\mydir`). If the HOME environment variable is undefined, the Extend Script default is the user's home directory, usually the `C:\Documents and Settings\username` folder.

Adobe® GoLive® CS2 Official JavaScript Reference

Volume and drive names

A volume or drive name can be the first part of an absolute path in URI notation. The values are interpreted according to the platform.

Mac OS volumes

When Mac OS X starts, the startup volume is the root directory of the file system. All other volumes, including remote volumes, are part of the `/Volumes` directory. The `File` and `Folder` objects use these rules to interpret the first element of a path name:

- If the name is the name of the startup volume, discard it.
- If the name is a volume name, prepend `/Volumes`.
- Otherwise, leave the path as is.

Mac OS 9 is not supported as an operating system, but the use of the colon as a path separator is still supported and corresponds to URI and to Mac OS X paths as shown in the following table. These examples assume that the startup volume is `MacOSX`, and that there is a mounted volume `Remote`.

URI path name	Mac OS 9 path name	Mac OS X path name
/MacOSX/dir/file	MacOSX:dir:file	/dir/file
/Remote/dir/file	Remote:dir:file	/Volumes/Remote/dir/file
/root/dir/file	Root:dir:file	/root/dir/file
~/dir/file		/Users/jdoe/dir/file

Windows drives

In Windows, volume names correspond to drive letters. The URI path `/c/temp/file` normally translates to the Windows path `C:\temp\file`.

If a drive exists with a name matching the first part of the path, that part is always interpreted as that drive. It is possible for there to be a folder in the root that has the same name as the drive; imagine, for example, a folder `C:\C` in Windows. A path starting with `/c` always addresses the drive `C:`, so in this case, to access the folder by name, you must use both the drive name and the folder name, for example `/c/c` for `C:\C`.

If the current drive contains a root folder with the same name as another drive letter, that name is considered to be a folder. That is, if there is a folder `D:\C`, and if the current drive is `D:`, the URI path `/c/temp/file` translates to the Windows path `D:\c\temp\file`. In this case, to access drive C, you would have to use the Windows path name conventions.

To access a remote volume, use a uniform naming convention (UNC) path name of the form `//servername/sharename`. These path names are portable, because both Max OS X and UNIX ignore multiple slash characters. Note that in Windows, UNC names do *not* work for local volumes.

These examples assume that the current drive is `D:`

URI path name	Windows path name
`/c/dir/file`	`c:\dir\file`
`/remote/dir/file`	`D:\remote\dir\file`
`/root/dir/file`	`D:\root\dir\file`
`~/dir/file`	`C:\Documents and Settings\jdoe\dir\file`

Aliases

When you access an alias, the operation is transparently forwarded to the real file. The only operations that affect the alias are calls to `rename` and `remove`, and setting properties `readonly` and `hidden`. When a `File` object represents an alias, the `alias` property of the object returns `true`, and the `resolve` method returns the `File` or `Folder` object for the target of the alias.

In Windows, all file system aliases (called *shortcuts*) are actual files whose names end with the extension `.lnk`. Never use this extension directly; the `File` and `Folder` objects work without it.

For example, suppose there is a shortcut to the file `/folder1/some.txt` in the folder `/folder2`. The full Windows file name of the shortcut file is `\folder2\some.txt.lnk`.

To access the shortcut from a `File` object, specify the path `/folder2/some.txt`. Calling that `File` object's `open` method opens the linked file (in `/folder1`). Calling the `File` object's `rename` method renames the shortcut file itself (leaving the `.lnk` extension intact).

However, Windows permits a file and its shortcut to reside in the same folder. In this case, the `File` object always accesses the original file. You cannot create a `File` object to access the shortcut when it is in the same folder as its linked file.

Portability issues

If your application will run on multiple platforms, use relative path names, or try to originate path names from the home directory. If that is not possible, work with Mac OS X and UNIX aliases, and store your files on a machine that is remote to your Windows machine so that you can use UNC names.

As an example, suppose you use the UNIX machine `myServer` for data storage. If you set up an alias share in the root directory of `myServer`, and if you set up a Windows-accessible share at `share` pointing to the same data location, the path name `//myServer/share/file` would work for all three platforms.

Application and Namespace Specifiers

All forms of interapplication communication use *Application specifiers* (page 451) to identify Adobe applications.

- In all ExtendScript scripts, the `#target` directive can use an specifier to identify the application that should run that script. See "Preprocessor directives" on page 443.

- In interapplication messages, the specifier is used as the value of the `target` property of the message object, to identify the target application for the message.

- Bridge (which is integrated with all Adobe Creative Suite 2 applications) uses an application specifier as the value of the `document.owner` property, to identify another Creative Suite 2 application that created or opened a Bridge browser window.

When a script for one application invokes Cross-DOM or exported functions, it identifies the exporting application using Namespace specifiers (page 452).

Application specifiers

Application specifiers are strings that encode the application name, a version number and a language code. They take the following form:

```
appname[-version[-locale]]
```

appname	An Adobe application name. One of:
	
	`acrobat`
	`aftereffects`
	`atmosphere`
	`audition`
	`bridge`
	`encore`
	`golive`
	`illustrator`
	`incopy`
	`indesign`
	`photoshop`
	`premiere`

version	Optional. A number indicating at least a major version. If not supplied, the most recent version is assumed. The number can include a minor version separated from the major version number by a dot; for example, `1.5`.
locale	Optional. An Adobe locale code, consisting of a 2-letter ISO-639 language code and an optional 2-letter ISO 3166 country code separated by an underscore. Case is significant. For example, `en_US`, `en_UK`, `ja_JP`, `de_DE`, `fr_FR`. If not supplied, ExtendScript uses the current platform locale. Do not specify a locale for a multilingual application, such as Bridge, that has all locale versions included in a single installation.

The following are examples of legal specifiers:

```
photoshop
bridge-1
bridge-1.0
illustrator-12.2
bridge-1-en_us
golive-8-de_de
```

Namespace specifiers

When calling Cross-DOM and exported functions from other applications, a namespace specifier qualifies the function call, directing it to the appropriate application.

Namespace specifiers consist of an application name, as used in an application specifier, with an optional major version number. Use it as a prefix to an exported function name, with the JavaScript dot notation.

```
appname[majorVersion].functionName(args)
```

For example:

- To call the Cross-DOM function `quit` in Photoshop CS2, use `photoshop.quit()`, and to call it in GoLive CS2, use `golive.quit()`.

- To call the exported function `place`, defined for Illustrator® CS2 (version 12), call `illustrator12.place(myFiles)`.

Script Locations and Checking Application Installation

On startup, all Adobe Creative Suite 2 applications execute all JSX files that they find in the user startup folder:

- In Windows®, the startup folder is:

      %APPDATA%\Adobe\StartupScripts

- In Mac OS®, the startup folder is

      ~/Library/Application
      Support/Adobe/StartupScripts/

A script in the startup directory is executed on startup by all applications. If you place a script here, it must contain code to check whether it is being run by the intended application. You can do this using the `appName` static property of the `BridgeTalk` class. For example:

```
if( BridgeTalk.appName == "bridge" ) {
      //continue executing script
    }
```

In addition, individual applications might look for application-specific scripts in a subfolder named with that application's specifier and version, in the form:

```
%APPDATA%\Adobe\StartupScripts\appname\version
~/Library/Application
Support/Adobe/StartupScripts/appname/version/
```

The name and version in these folder names are specified in the form required for Application specifiers (page 451). For example, in Windows, GoLive CS2 version 8.2 would look for scripts in the directory:

```
%APPDATA%\Adobe\StartupScripts\golive\8.2
```

The *version* portion of the Bridge-specific folder path is an exact version number. That is, scripts in the folder `bridge/1.5` are executed only by Bridge version 1.5, and so on.

Individual applications might also implement a path in the installation directory for application-specific startup scripts. For example:

```
IllustratorCS2_install_dir\Startup Scripts
IllustratorCS2_install_dir/Startup Scripts/
```

If a script that is run by one application communicates with another application, or adds functionality that depends on another application, it

---

must first check whether that application and version is installed. You can do this using the `BridgeTalk.getSpecifier` static function. For example:

```
if( BridgeTalk.appName == "bridge" ) {
// Check that PS CS2 is installed
    if( BridgeTalk.getSpecifier("photoshop",9)){
        // add PS automate menu to Bridge UI
    }
}
```

A | Object Palette Sort Order

This appendix lists the values GoLive uses to sort items in the Objects palette.

The objects in the Objects palette are sorted into tabs, and further sorted into icon groups within a tab. The higher the value is, the further to the right the tab icon appears. When an extension creates a new tab or icon group using the `<jsxpalettegroup>` (page 343) tag, it gets a tab number from the `taborder` attribute to either select an existing tab or determine a new tab's placement with respect to existing tabs. If the tag is adding an entry to an existing tab, it must provide an `order` number for the entry to place its icons with respect to the tab's existing icon groups.

- You cannot add items to the Custom or Library tab of the Objects palette.
- Some built-in modules install more than one icon in a tab group. You cannot place your entries' icons between icons for built-in modules, only to the left or right of them.

This table lists the values used to sort predefined Objects palette entries:.

Entry Name	taborder	order
Basic	0	
Layout Grid		10 (2 icons in this group)
Floating Box		15
Table		20
Image		30
Plugin		40 (5 icons in this group)
Java Applet		50
Object		60
Line		70
Horizontal Spacer		80
JavaScript		90
Marquee		100
Comment		110
Anchor		120
Line Break		130
Tag		140

Entry Name	taborder	order
Smart	1	
Smart items		200 (all icons in this group)
Forms	2	
Form items		10 (all icons in this group)
Head	3	
Head items		20000 (all icons in this group)
Frames	4	
Frame items		20000 (all icons in this group)
Site	50	
Site items		1 (all icons in this group)
Site Extras	51	
Site extras items		2 (all icons in this group)
QuickTime	5000	
QuickTime items		1 (all icons in this group)
Extensions (default)	30000	
Extension items (default)		30000

B | Menu Names

This appendix lists the JavaScript names of GoLive menu items and submenus. You can use these names to add items to GoLive menus and submenus in locations relative to existing items.

The names of the predefined menus (accessible by name through the global menubar array, page 48) are:

```
file
edit
type
special
view
window
help
site
diagram
movie
```

File Menu

File menu items	JavaScript name
New Document	NEDC
Open	OPDC
Close	CLDC
Save	SVDC
Save As	SADC
Print	PRNT
Quit	QUIT
separators 1-5	dfi1 - dfi5

File submenus	JavaScript name
Import	Impo
Export	Expo
Server	SrvM
separator 1, 2	dse1, dse2
Line Breaks	LINB

File submenus	JavaScript name
separator	dfi6
Preview In	PRIV
separator	dfi7

Edit Menu

Edit menu items	JavaScript name
Undo	UNDO
Redo	REDO
Cut	CUTT
Copy	COPY
Paste	PAST
Delete	DELE
separators 1-7	ded1 - ded7

Edit submenus	JavaScript name
Find	FIND

Type Menu

Type items and submenus	JavaScript name
CSSStyle	CSSs
Font	+fnt
Size	+siz
Style	+sty
Paragraph Format	+hdr
Alignment	+aln
separators 1-2	al-1, al-2
List	+lst
separators 1-3	dty1 - dty7

Special Menu

Special items and submenus	JavaScript name
Insert	INSR
Convert	CONV
separators 1-2	CON5, CON9
CSS	CSSs
New	CSSn
Edit	CSSe
separator 1	css1
Table	TABs
separators 1-7	dsp6 - ds12
Forms	FRMs
Component	COMP
Template	TMPL
JavaScript	JAVS
separator	jav1
Source Code	SOUR
separators 1-5	dsp1 - dsp5

Window Menu

Window items and submenus	JavaScript name
Workspace	wPSP
separators 1, 2	dwi2, dwi3
Cascade and Tile	CaTi
separator 1	dwi1

Help Menu

Help items	JavaScript name
separator 1	dhe1

Site Menu

Site items	JavaScript name
New	SiNw
separator 1	dsi4
Explorer	SiFi
Publish Server	FTPS
separator 1	dsi5
separator 2	SBEP
separator 3-4	dsi7, dsi8
Version Control System	SiVC
separator 1-2	dsi9, ds10
View	NoSC
separator 1-3	dsi1, dsi2, dsi3

View Menu

Site items and submenus	JavaScript name
Zoom To	ZOOM
Document Mode	SDOC
Status	DSTA
View Configuration	VCon
Source View	SOvi
separator	sov1
Source Theme	SOth
CSS	CSSV
Info Column	CSIC
separator 1-5	dcs1 –dcs5
separator 1-6	viw1 - viw6

Diagram Menu

Diagram items and submenus	JavaScript name
Diagrams	DiDI
Staging	DiSg
separator	dDi1
New	DiNw
separators 1-3	dDi1 - dDi3

Movie Menu

Movie items and submenus	JavaScript name
Track	MoTr
separators 1-7	dMo1 - dMo7

C | Managed Layout Tags

This appendix lists the markup items that you can manipulate with functions of the layout Object (page 191), layout.grid Object (page 193), and textArea Object (page 278) without causing GoLive to reparse the document.

- The textArea Object's insertBox (page 280) function can insert supported elements in a document's main text area.

  ```
  document.mainTextArea.insertBox("table");
  ```

- The layout.grid Object's insertBox (page 194) function can place supported elements on a layout grid in Layout view.

  ```
  var bod = document.documentElement.getSubElement("body");
  var result = bod.layout.grid.insertBox("hr");
  ```

- The layout Object's `getAttribute`, `setAttribute`, and `hasAttribute` functions (page 191) can edit the attributes of supported elements.

  The values these methods accept and return vary according to the kind of element the `layout` object manages. For each supported markup item, this appendix specifies:

  - Attribute names that are valid arguments to these methods
  - The read-only or write-only status of each attribute that is not read/write
  - Any special values the `getAttribute` method returns. Standard HTML values of text strings, numbers, and so on are not listed.

Note: Be sure to enter all attribute values in quotes, except the Boolean values `true` and `false`. The string "`false`" is a non-empty string, which evaluates to `true`.

Elements the Layout Object Manages

This table lists the elements whose appearance is managed by a `layout` object. For the list of attributes in each element that the `layout` object can modify without reparsing, see the corresponding section in "Attributes the Layout Object Manages" on page 465.

Element	Tag
Extra Space	`<spacer>` (page 481)
Line Break	` ` (page 466)
Horizontal Rule	`<hr>` (page 471)
Image	`<img>` (page 471)

Element	Tag
Image	`<img>` (page 471)
Java Applet	`<applet>` (page 465)
Anchor	`<a>` (page 465)
User Input Form	`<form>` (page 471)
Form Label	`<label>` (page 478)
Form Button	`<button>` (page 467)
Form Submit Button	`<input type="submit">` (page 476)
Form Reset Button	`<input type="reset">` (page 476)
Form Input Button	`<input type="button">` (page 476)
Form Text Input Field	`<input type="text">` (page 477)
Form Password Input Field	`<input type="checkbox">` (page 473)
Form File Input Field	`<input type="file">` (page 473)
Form Checkbox	`<input type="checkbox">` (page 473)
Form Radio Button	`<input type="radio">` (page 476)
Form Hidden Button	`<input type="hidden">` (page 474)
Form Image Input Field	`<input type="image">` (page 474)
Text Field	`<textarea>` (page 482)
Form Selection List	`<select>` (page 480)
Key Generator	`<keygen>` (page 477)
Form Field Set	`<fieldset>` (page 470)
RealAudio Embedded Object	`<embed type="audio/x-pn-realaudio-plugin">` (page 469)
SWF Embedded Object	`<embed type="application/x-shockwave-flash">` (page 468)
QuickTime Embedded Object	`<embed type="video/quicktime">` (page 470)
SVG Embedded Object	`<embed type="image/svg-xml">` (page 470)
Embedded Audio Object	`<embed type="audio/">` (page 469)
Embedded Object	`<marquee>` (page 478)
Marquee Display	`<marquee>` (page 478)
Body of Document	`<table>` (page 481)
Table	`<table>` (page 481)
Table Data	`<td>` (page 482)

Element	Tag
Table Heading	`<th>` (page 483)
Table Row	`<tr>` (page 484)
Scripts	`<script>` (page 479)
Meta-Information	`<link>` (page 478)
Index Prompt	`<link>` (page 478)
Base URL	`<link>` (page 478)
Link to External Resource	`<link>` (page 478)

Attributes the Layout Object Manages

GoLive creates a `Layout` object to manage the Layout view appearance of each of the markup items this section lists. The supported tags are listed alphabetically.

a

Attribute	Values	Notes
name		

applet

Attribute	Values	Notes
align		
alt		
code		
codebase		
height		
heightmode	pixel %	Measurement unit for `height`.
hspace		
name		
vspace		
width		
widthmode	pixel %	Measurement unit for `width`.

base

Attribute	Values	Notes
href		
target		

body

Attribute	Values	Notes
alink		
background		
bgcolor		
link		
text		
usealink	true false	Switches `alink` on or off.
usebackground	true false	Switches `background` on or off.
usebgcolor	true false	Switches `bgcolor` on or off.
uselink	true false	Switches `link`. on or off.
usetext	true false	Switches `text` on or off.
usevlink	true false	Switches `vlink` on or off.
vlink		

br

Attribute	Values	Notes
clear	none false left right all	

button

Attribute	Values	Notes
accesskey		
disable	true false	
name		
tabindex		
tabindexmode	true false	Switches `tabindex` on or off.
type	normal submit reset	
value		

embed

These attributes are supported for all types.

Attribute	Values	Notes
align	top middle bottom left right absmiddle absbottom texttop baseline	

chgparametername		Write only. Changes the name of a newly inserted parameter. For example, this changes the name of the attribute `mypara` to `yourpara`:
		
		``
		layoutObject.setAttribute
		    ("newparameter", "mypara");
		layoutObject.setAttribute
		    ("chgparametername", "mypara",
		    "yourpara");
		``

chgparametervalue		Write only. Changes the value of a newly inserted parameter.
delparameter		Write only. Deletes a newly inserted parameter.
height		
heightmode	percent % pixel	Measurement unit for `height`.

Attribute	Values	Notes
hidden	true false	
hspace		
name		

newparameter		Write only. Adds a new attribute to the element. For example:
		
		`call layoutObject.setAttribute`
		`   ("newparameter", "newparametername")`

nolabels	true false	
palette	default foreground background	
type		
usefile	true false	Switches `src` on or off.
usemime	true false	Switches `type` on or off.
usepagelink	true false	Switches `pluginspage` on or off.
vspave		
width		
widthmode	percent % pixel	Measurement unit for `width`.

embed type="application/x-shockwave-flash"

These additional attributes are supported for this type:

Attribute	Values	Notes
loop		
play		
quality		
scale		

embed type="audio/"

These additional attributes are supported for this type:

Attribute	Values	Notes
autostart		
controls		
endtime		
loop		
mastersound	true false	
starttime		
volume		

embed type="audio/x-pn-realaudio-plugin"

These additional attributes are supported for this type:

Attribute	Values	Notes
autostart	true false	
console	default _master _unique	
controls	imagewindow controlpanel playbutton playonlybutton pausebutton stopbutton rwctrl mutectrl volumeslider tacctrl homectrl infovolumepanel infopanel statusbar statusfield positionfield	

embed type="image/svg-xml"

These additional attributes are supported for this type:

Attribute	Values	Notes
use_svgz	true false	

embed type="video/quicktime"

These additional attributes are supported for this type:

Attribute	Values	Notes
autoplay		
bgcolor		
cache		
controler		
loop		
playeveryframe		
scale		
target		
usehref	true false	Switches href on or off.
volume		

fieldset

Attribute	Values	Notes
accesskey		
align	default top bottom left right center	
legend	true false	Write only.

form

Attribute	Values	Notes
action		
enctype		
method	default get post	
name		
target		

hr

Attribute	Values	Notes
height	none false	
heightmode	full false percent % pixel	Measurement unit for `height`.
noshade	false true	
width		
widthmode	full false percent % pixel	Measurement unit for `width`.

img

Attribute	Values	Notes
align	top middle bottom left right absmiddle absbottom texttop baseline	
alt		
border		

Attribute	Values	Notes
bordermode	true false	Switches `border` on or off.
height		
heightmode	pixel percent % image	Measurement unit for `height`.
hspace		
iccprofile		
lowsrc		
mapname		Sets the corresponding attributes of the `<img usemap=#>` and `<map name=>` tags.
name		
orgsize	true	Write only. Set `width` and `height` to the original values of the image.
src		
uselowsrc	true false	Switches `lowsrc` on or off.
usemap	false true	Adds or removes the `usemap` attribute. If a `<map>` does not immediately follow the `<img>`, a new `<map>` is created with a generated name attribute.
vspace		
width		
widthmode	pixel percent % image	Measurement unit for `width`.

input type="button"

Attribute	Values	Notes
accesskey		
disable	true false	
name		
tabindex		
tabindexmode	true false	Switches `tabindex` on or off.

Attribute	Values	Notes
type	normal submit reset	
value		
valuemode	true false	Switches value on or off.

input type="checkbox"

Attribute	Values	Notes
accesskey		
checked	true false	
disable	true false	
name		
tabindex		
tabindexmode	true false	Switches tabindex on or off.
value		

input type="file"

Attribute	Values	Notes
accesskey		
disable	true false	
name		
size		
tabindex		
tabindexmode	true false	Switches tabindex on or off.

input type="hidden"

Attribute	Values	Notes
disable	true false	
name		
value		

input type="image"

Attribute	Values	Notes
align	top middle bottom left right absmiddle absbottom texttop baseline	
alt		
border		
bordermode	true false	Switches `border` on or off.
height		
heightmode	pixel percent % image	Measurement unit for `height`.
hspace		
iccprofile		
lowsrc		
mapname		Sets the corresponding attributes of the `<img usemap=#>` and `<map name=>` tags.
name		
orgsize		Write only. Set `width` and `height` to the original values of the image.
src		
uselowsrc	true false	Switches `lowsrc` on or off.

Attribute	Values	Notes
usemap	false true	Adds or removes the `usemap` attribute. If a `<map>` does not immediately follow the `<img>`, a new `<map>` is created with a generated name attribute.
vspace		
width		
widthmode	pixel percent % image	Measurement unit for `width`.

input type="password"

Attribute	Values	Notes
accesskey		
disable	true false	
maxlength		
name		
password	true false	Write only.
readonly	true false	
size		
tabindex		
tabindexmode	true false	Switches `tabindex` on or off.
value		

input type="radio"

Attribute	Values	Notes
accesskey		
checked	true false	
disable	true false	
name		
tabindex		
tabindexmode	true false	Switches `tabindex` on or off.
value		

input type="reset"

Attribute	Values	Notes
accesskey		
disable	true false	
name		
tabindex		
tabindexmode	true false	Switches `tabindex` on or off.
type	normal submit reset	
value		
valuemode	true false	Switches `value` on or off.

input type="submit"

Attribute	Values	Notes
accesskey		
disable	true false	
name		
tabindex		

Attribute	Values	Notes
tabindexmode	true false	Switches `tabindex` on or off.
type	normal submit reset	
value		
valuemode	true false	Switches `value` on or off.

input type="text"

Attribute	Values	Notes
accesskey		
disable	true false	
maxlength		
name		
password	true false	Write only.
readonly	true false	
size		
tabindex		
tabindexmode	true false	Switches `tabindex` on or off.
value		

isIndex

Attribute	Values	Notes
prompt		

keygen

Attribute	Values	Notes
accesskey		
challenge		

Attribute	Values	Notes
disable	true false	
name		
tabindex		
tabindexmode	true false	Switches `tabindex` on or off.

label

Attribute	Values	Notes
accesskey		
for		
tabindex		
tabindexmode	true false	Switches `tabindex` on or off.

link

Attribute	Values	Notes
href		
methods		
name		
rel		
rev		
title		
urn		

marquee

Attribute	Values	Notes
behavior	default scroll slide alternate	
color		
direction	left right	

Attribute	Values	Notes
height		
heightmode	pixel percent %	Measurement unit for height.
hspace		
loop		
loopforever	false true	
scrollamount		
scrolldelay		
text		Write only.
vspace		
width		
widthmode	pixel percent %	Measurement unit for width.

meta

Attribute	Values	Notes
content		
http-equiv		
mode	http http-equivalent name	

script

Attribute	Values	Notes
language		
name		
src		

select

Attribute	Values	Notes
disable	true false	
itemlabel		Write only. Sets the label of the `<option...>` element. For example, consider this HTML source: <pre><code><select name="selectName" size="4" multiple>
<option value="one">hello</option>
<option selected value="three">
mylabel</option>
</select></code></pre>Change this value to change `mylabel` to another value. For example: <pre><code>call layoutObject.setAttribute
("itemlabel", 1, "newlabel");</code></pre>The result is: <pre><code><select name="selectName" size="4" multiple>
<option value="one">hello</option>
<option selected value="three">
newlabel</option>
</select></code></pre>
itemvalue		Write only. Sets the value of the `<option...>` element. For example, in the code given for `itemlabel`, this changes the value `three` to `test`: <pre><code>call layoutObject.setAttribute
("itemvalue", 1, "test");</code></pre>The result is: <pre><code><select name="selectName" size="4" multiple>
<option value="one">hello</option>
<option selected value="test">
mylabel</option>
</select></code></pre>
multiple	true false	
newitem		Write only. Inserts a new `<option>` element with this value after the select element: <pre><code><option value="value">item</option></code></pre>
rows		
selectitem		Write only. The index of the `<option...>` element. Switches `selected` on or off in the corresponding element.
tabindex		
tabindexmode	true false	Switches `tabindex` on or off.

spacer

Attribute	Values	Notes
align	top middle bottom left right absmiddle absbottom texttop baseline	
height		
size		Read only.
type	horizontal vertical block	
width		

table

Attribute	Values	Notes
align	left right center	
background		
bgcolor		
border		
cellpadding		
cellspacing		
height		
heightmode	pixel percent % auto	Measurement unit of height.
usebackground	true false	Switches background on or off.
usebgcolor	true false	Switches bgcolor on or off.

Attribute	Values	Notes
width		
widthmode	pixel percent % auto	Measurement unit of width.

td

Attribute	Values	Notes
background		
bgcolor		
halign	default left right center	
height		
heightmode	pixel percent % auto	Measurement unit of height.
nowrap	true false	
usebackground	true false	Switches background on or off.
usebgcolor	true false	Switches bgcolor on or off.
valign	default top bottom middle	
width		
widthmode	pixel percent % auto	Measurement unit of width.

textarea

Attribute	Values	Notes
accesskey		
cols		

Attribute	Values	Notes
content		Write only.
disable	true false	
name		
readonly	true false	
rows		
tabindex		
tabindexmode	true false	Switches tabindex on or off.
wrap	default off virtual physical	

th

Attribute	Values	Notes
background		
bgcolor		
halign	default left right center	
height		
heightmode	pixel percent % auto	Set value of height to given measurement unit.
nowrap	true false	
usebackground	true false	Switches background on or off.
usebgcolor	true false	Switches bgcolor on or off.
valign	default top bottom middle	

Attribute	Values	Notes
width		
widthmode	pixel percent % auto	Set value of width to given measurement unit.

tr

Attribute	Values	Notes
bgcolor		
halign	default left right center	
height		
heightmode	pixel percent % auto	Measurement unit for height.
usebgcolor	true false	Switches bgcolor on or off.
valign	default top bottom middle	

D | C API for External Binary Libraries

This appendix describes C-language macro functions defined in the `JSA.h` header file. The functions in a compiled external library call these functions to obtain arguments from the GoLive environment and to pass return values back to GoLive.

For a guide to the use of these functions, see Appendix A, "Using External Libraries," in the full written version of the reference on the Adobe GoLive CS2 CD.

Installing the C Interface to Extend Script

The `JSA.h` file required to access the functions and data types this chapter describes is available in the
`Adobe_GoLive_SDK_dir/C Library Samples/include/` folder the SDK provides. Before beginning development of your external binary library, you'll need to copy this file into your development directory or configure your development environment to include files residing in this folder.

Determining Whether an External Library Is In Memory

The SDK makes currently running modules available by name in the JavaScript global namespace. Thus, the JavaScript name of a module that has not been loaded is undefined. You can test this condition as the following line of JavaScript does.

```
If (typeof moduleName == "undefined")
    alert ("Cannot find external library.");
```

For example, if your function were built into an external file named `JSASample`, this test would look like the following line of JavaScript.

```
if (typeof JSASample == "undefined")
```

C API Synopsis

This section summarizes use of the C API.

```
// you must include the JSA.h header
#include "JSA.h"

// include any other libs your extension requires
#include <math.h>

// include platform-specific drawing support
#ifdef WIN32
   #include <windows.h>
#else
   #include <QuickDraw.h>
#endif

// Call this macro once to initialize the JavaScript
environment.
JSA_INIT

// define your functions
// use argc/argv pairs to pass args
// use returnValue to return this fn's result
static void power(int argc, JSValue *argv, JSValue
returnValue)
{
   double a, b, c;
   // call JSAXxx fns to extract args passed by JavaScript
callers
   a = JSAValueToDouble(argv[0]);
   b = JSAValueToDouble(argv[1]);

   c = pow (a, b);

   // call JSAXxx fns to pass values back to JavaScript
callers
   JSADoubleToValue(returnValue, c);
}

// you must implement this fn, which registers your lib's
fns with GoLive
void JSAMain() {
   JSARegisterFunction ("power", power);

}
/***********************************************************
****************/
```

```
/* Assuming you've built this fn into a library named
JSASample.dll (or */
/* just JSASample in Mac OS) which resides in
the          */
/* "Modules/Extend Scripts/Common" folder, your
JavaScript code calls    */
/* the external library function as
follows:                        */
/************************************************************
******************/
JSASample.power (2,3);
```

Data Types

This section describes the C-language data types GoLive provides for use by external binaries.

JSValue pointer

The `JSValue` type is an opaque `void` pointer that is a data element in the *argv* vector GoLive passes to an externally defined binary function. Internally, GoLive casts this pointer's type as necessary to hold each element's data.

```
typedef void *JSValue;
```

JSAValueType scalar types

The following macros define `JSAValueType` scalar data types as returned by the `JSAGetValueType` function.

Type	Macro	Description
Undefined	JSA_UNDEFINED	The undefined or empty value.
Boolean	JSA_BOOL	A Boolean value expressed as an integer. 0 is `false`, and 1 is `true`.
Integer	JSA_INTEGER	A 32-bit signed integer quantity.
Floating Point	JSA_DOUBLE	An 8-byte, double-precision, floating-point value.
String	JSA_STRING	A `null`-terminated ASCII string.

JSANativeMethod type

The GoLive external binary API encodes your library's function definitions as `JSANativeMethod` structures. This data type implements the following data structures, which your functions use to implement their parameters.

argc	Integer	Number of array elements in the *argv* vector.
*argv	JSValue	Vector of argument values.
return	JSValue	Empty pointer passed to your function by GoLive when it is called. C functions call the appropriate JSA*Xx*ToValue function to store a return value in this pointer.

JSADrawInfo struct

Use the JSADrawInfo struct to implement C-language drawing functions you can call from JavaScript.

```
typedef struct _JSADrawInfo {
    long context; // a DC (Windows) or a GrafPort (Mac OS)
    long left, top;// upper left corner of the drawing rect
    long right, bottom;// lower right corner of the
drawing rect
} JSADrawInfo;
```

Initialization and Termination Functions

This section describes functions that initialize or terminate an external binary library.

JSA_INIT JSA_INIT // macro	The initialization function. The JSA_INIT macro must appear exactly once in the implementation of a binary extension. This macro call must appear after the JSA.h include statement and before the required call to the JSAMain function. The JSA_INIT macro inlines the JSAEntry function. GoLive tests for the presence of the JSAEntry function to determine whether an external binary is intended for use by Extend Script extensions. Thus, if the external binary does not call the JSA_INIT macro, GoLive does not make the external binary available to Extend Script extensions. The JSAEntry function: ● Sets an environment pointer containing references to the various JSA*Xx* functions this appendix describes. ● Calls the JSAMain function.
JSAMain JSAMain()	The main function. Every external binary must implement the JSAMain function. Your implementation of this function must register your external binary's functions with the GoLive JavaScript engine. To do so, it calls the JSARegisterFunction function once for each function it registers. Optionally, your implementation of the JSAMain function can perform any additional initialization tasks your external binary requires.

JSARegisterFunction JSARegisterFunction (`name`, `fn`[, `return`])	Registers a C-language function under a JavaScript name. Registration makes an external binary function available under the specified JavaScript name. Only registered JSANativeMethod functions are available to extension modules. To register a function, call the JSARegisterFunction function from within the body of the external library's JSAMain function. You must call JSARegisterFunction function once for each function to be registered.
`name`	The JavaScript name for the function. This name must observe JavaScript naming conventions.
`fn`	The token that the function definition associates with the function's implementation. For example: myFun() {return;} This associates the myFun token with the {return;} implementation.
`return`	Optional. An integer value to return instead of the result of the function call.
JSAExit JSAExit()	GoLive calls each external binary's JSAExit function before it unloads that library. Your implementation of this optional method performs any housekeeping tasks required to exit your extension, such as setting the values of your own C-language pointers and variables to null. Returns void.

Accessor Functions

The SDK provides C-language functions that use the `JSValue` pointer to extract arguments from GoLive and return values to GoLive:

- Functions that extract values from the JavaScript environment in GoLive accept a `JSValue` pointer and return another data type, such as integer or string
- Functions that export values from the C language environment to the JavaScript environment accept a fundamental data type like string or integer and return it as a `JSValue` pointer your external binary function can pass back to GoLive

JSABoolToValue JSABoolToValue(*arg*, *val*)	Converts an integer value to a JavaScript value.
arg	The `JSValue` pointer to the converted value.
val	32-bit integer value to convert. Non-zero values specify a Boolean value of `true`.
JSACreateEmptyValue JSACreateEmptyValue()	Creates a new empty JavaScript value. The returned `JSValue` must be released after use with JSARelease (page 491). (Introduced in 7.0)
JSADoubleToValue JSADoubleToValue(*arg*, *val*)	Converts a double value to a JavaScript value.
arg	The `JSValue` pointer to the converted value.
val	Double-precision floating-point value to convert.
JSAEncodedStringToValue JSAEncodedStringToValue (*value*, *string*, *charSetName*)	Converts a `null`-terminated ASCII string to a JavaScript unicode value. Returns `void`. (Introduced in 7.0)
value	The `JSValue` pointer to the converted value.
string	The `null`-terminated ASCII string to convert. (`char*`)
charSetName	The encoding to use to convert the string to JavaScript unicode. (`char*`)

JSAGetValueType
JSAGetValueType(*arg*)
	Gets an integer value that indicates the type of a JavaScript value. Returns one of the following integer values indicating the type of the object.
	    0: `Undefined`
	    1: `Boolean`
	    2: `Integer`
	    3: `Double`
	    4: `Text`

arg	A pointer to the value to test.

```
static void myFn(int argc, JSValue *argv, JSValue returnValue)
{
   int a, b, c;
   a = JSAGetValueType(argv[0]);
   JSAIntToValue(returnValue, a);
}
void JSAMain() {
   JSARegisterFunction ("myFn", myFn);
```

JSAIntToValue JSAIntToValue(*arg*, *val*)	Converts a long value to a JavaScript value.
arg	The JSValue pointer to the converted value.
val	32-bit integer value to convert.
JSARelease JSARelease(*value*)	Releases a created value. Returns void.
val	A void* pointer to the JSValue to release.
JSAStringToValue JSAStringToValue(*arg*, *val*)	Converts a null-terminated ASCII string to a JavaScript value.
value	The JSValue pointer to the converted value.
string	The null-terminated ASCII string (char*) to convert.
JSAUndefinedToValue JSAUndefinedToValue(*arg*)	Sets a JavaScript value to undefined.
arg	A pointer to the JSValue to set.
JSAValueToBool JSAValueToBool(*arg*)	Converts a JavaScript value to a Boolean (0 or 1).
arg	A pointer to the JSValue to convert.
JSAValueToDouble JSAValueToDouble(*arg*)	Converts a JavaScript value to an eight-byte floating point value.
arg	A pointer to the JSValue to convert.
JSAValueToEncodedString JSAValueToEncodedString (*value*, *charSetName*)	Creates a new char buffer and fills it with the ASCII string from the value. If the string of value contains non-ASCII characters the encoding for the given charset name is used. The returned buffer should be released after use with JSARelease (page 491).
value	A pointer to the JSValue to convert.
charSetName	An encoding character set name (char*).
JSAValueToInt JSAValueToInt(*arg*)	Converts a JavaScript value to a 32-bit integer.
arg	A pointer to the JSValue to convert.

CJSAValueToNewString JSAValueToNewString(*value*)	Converts a JavaScript value to an ASCII `null`-terminated string in a new buffer. If the string contains non-ASCII characters, uses the system encoding. The returned buffer should be released after use with JSARelease (page 491).
value	A pointer to the `JSValue` to convert.
JSAValueToString JSAValueToString(*arg*)	Converts a JavaScript value to a `null`-terminated ASCII string in an internal string buffer, which can be overwritten at any time. Copy the string for further use.
arg	A pointer to the `JSValue` to convert.
JSAValueToWString JSAValueToWString(*value*)	Converts a JavaScript value to an ASCII `null`-terminated string in a new buffer. Returns An `unsigned short*` (also known as `wchar_t`). The returned buffer should be released after use with JSARelease (page 491).
value	A pointer to the `JSValue` to convert.
JSAWStringToValue JSAWStringToValue(*value*, *string*)	Converts a null-terminated wide character string (`unsigned short*` or `wchar_t`) to a JavaScript value. Returns `void`.
value	The `JSValue` pointer to the converted value.
string	A string value to convert (`unsigned-short*`).

Execution functions

This section describes functions that an external C function can call to:

- Evaluate JavaScript expressions in the JavaScript scope of the calling extension.
- Provide processor time to other extensions during lengthy operations.
- Generate its own JavaScript runtime errors.

JSAEval JSAEval (*scriptlet*, *returnValue*, *timeout*)	Evaluates a specified JavaScript scriptlet in the current execution context (inside the JavaScript function that called the external C function that calls the `JSAEval` function). See "Notes on evaluation" on page 493.
scriptlet	The expression the JavaScript engine is to interpret. String.
returnValue	A `JSValue` pointer that can hold a value to return to the caller. When `null`, discards the result of scriptlet evaluation.
timeout	The number of milliseconds to wait for the call to complete. If the timeout elapses, the engine generates a runtime error. Integer. A value of 0 causes the engine to run the scriptlet asynchronously—that is, the call returns immediately, regardless of whether the scriptlet completes execution successfully. A negative value causes the caller to wait unconditionally.

JSAPoll JSAPoll()	Polls all scriptlets scheduled for timed execution and executes those that are ready for execution. An external C function that carries out a lengthy procedure must call this function regularly to prevent timed scriptlets from timing out. Returns void.	
JSASetError JSASetError(text)	Generates a JavaScript runtime error with a specified message.	
text	The text of the error message. (String)	

Notes on evaluation

Typically, the JSAEval function is built into a function (myFn) in an external binary. When an extension calls myFn, GoLive supplies a valid *returnValue* pointer to the function. The body of the function can pass on this pointer as the *returnValue* to JSAEval. When the evaluation completes, the pointer contains the result of evaluating the scriptlet. The body of the calling function (myFn) can then extract this data using one of the utility conversion functions.

If you do not intend the result of scriptlet evaluation to be the calling function's return value, the calling function must clear the *returnValue* pointer before it exits. It can set some other return value by passing the *returnValue* pointer to another utility accessor function. For example, pass the *returnValue* pointer to JSAUndefinedToValue (page 491) to return an undefined result.

External library functions use the JSAEval function to evaluate a text string as a JavaScript expression. The SDK evaluates the expression in the execution scope of the JavaScript module that calls the external library. For a discussion of scope, see "JavaScript Scope of Name Attribute Values" on page 495.

C functions in external libraries can use the JSAEval function to:

- Retrieve the values of JavaScript properties from within the scope of the calling module.
- Execute a JavaScript function call within the scope of the calling module.
- You cannot pass arguments of any kind, but the scriptlet is evaluated in the context of the JavaScript variables and properties available to the extension module that called the external binary library.
- Retrieve or discard the results of the script evaluation.

➤ Example

The following example function myFn uses the JSAEval function to call the getOuterHTML method of the markup object that represents the <mytag> custom element in the current document's markup tree,

---

This function would be defined in an external library, and called by a function defined in the extension.

```
static void myFn(int argc, JSValue *argv, JSValue
returnValue)
{
    char* pTheSource;


    JSAEval("document.documentElement.getSubElement("mytag")
    .getOuterHTML()",
                returnValue, -1);
    // convert the extracted HTML result to a string and
save it
    pTheSource = JSAValueToString(returnValue);
    // return undefined from this call (instead of the
result of eval)
    JSAUndefinedToValue(returnValue);
}
```

E | Scoping in JavaScript

This appendix provides details on the scoping rules for shared JavaScript control names.

JavaScript Scope of Name Attribute Values

A module is the object that a `Main.html` file defines. In general, `name` attributes are defined within the scope of the module that defines them, except for the special cases this section describes.

The following figure summarizes the rules of JavaScript name scope that prevent clashes between extensions in the GoLive environment:

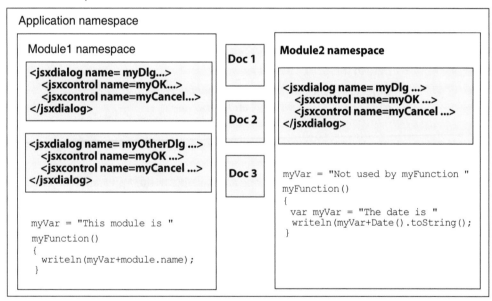

- In general, any object or function an extension module creates is visible only to that extension module, so its name attribute need only be unique within its module's namespace. Thus, both modules can define a `myFunction` function and a `myVar` variable, and a couple of the exact same `<jsxdialog>` elements without concern about accidentally calling each other's functions, using each others' variables, and so on.
- When the object is one that the SDK adds to one of its global collections, such as the `menus []` array, a name clash can interfere with name-based

retrieval of the object from the global collection. However, it causes no other difficulties.

- Control names can be reused by different windows within the same extension. In the figure, both `<jsxdialog>` elements in module 1 can use the same `<jsxcontrol>` element names. Note, however, that controls having non-unique names cannot be retrieved by name reliably from collections such as the `controls` global collection.

- When the name attribute of a `<jsxmenu>` or `<jsxpalettegroup>` tag is non-unique, the SDK appends the non-unique entries to the current instance of the element, if it exists. For example, when a `<jsxmenu>` element's name attribute matches one the SDK has already loaded, the SDK appends the new menu's items to the menu that already uses the same `name` attribute.

Global Scope

Items that are global in scope are available to all modules via properties in the global JavaScript namespace. Such items include:

- Data in the `common` object
- Data in the `prefs` object
- Objects in SDK-provided global collections such as `menus[]`, `dialogs[]`, `controls[]`, and so on

Application Scope

Items of application-wide scope are available to the Application object (`app`). For example, extension modules themselves are application-wide in scope. In many cases, the GoLive application makes such items available to all modules, so the only practical difference between application scope and global scope is in the way they are accessed. You must use properties or methods of the global Application object to obtain application-scope items. In contrast, a global item's JavaScript name appears directly in the global JavaScript namespace.

Items of application-wide scope include the following:

- Menu names

      `<jsxmenu name="xxxx">`

  When a menu's `name` attribute is not unique among the `name` attributes defined by previously loaded menus, the non-unique menu's items are appended to the previously loaded menu having the same JavaScript name.

- Object palette tab names

  ```
  <jsxpalettegroup name="xxxx">
  ```

  A non-unique name attribute causes this palette's items to be added to the already-defined palette. Although palettegroup names are shared application-wide, data belonging to an individual palette entry is local to that palette entry.

- Tag names

  ```
  <jsxelement tagname="xxxx">
  ```

  The value of your custom element's `tagname` attribute must be unique among all `<jsxelement>` elements that all currently running extensions define.

- `classid` attributes

  ```
  <jsxelement ... classid="uniqueIdentifier">
  <jsxinspector ... classid="uniqueIdentifier">
  <jsxpaletteentry ... classid="uniqueIdentifier">
  ```

  An individual `classid` value must be unique among all currently running extensions, and must be used by one extension only.

- Data in the Global Preferences object

- Documents: HTML (web pages), Non-HTML (site documents, text documents)

Module Scope

An item of module-wide scope is visible only to the module that defines it. As a result, different modules can reuse the same `name` attribute values for such items. This feature simplifies the creation of windows because their JavaScript names need only be unique within the extension that defines them. For example, no JavaScript naming conflict results when two different modules can define a `<jsxdialog name=myDlg ...>` element.

Items of module-wide scope include the following:

- Module names

  ```
  <jsxmodule name="xxxx">
  ```

  The value of your module's `name` attribute must be unique among all `name` attributes defined by all currently running extensions.

- Dialogs names

  ```
  <jsxdialog name="xxxx">
  ```

  The value of your dialog's `name` attribute must be unique among all `name` attributes defined by the extension that defines this dialog. Other extensions can reuse this `name` attribute value without conflict.

- Inspector names

  ```
  <jsxinspector name="xxxx">
  ```

  The value of your Inspector's `name` attribute must be unique among all `name` attributes defined by the extension that defines this palette. Other extensions can reuse this `name` attribute value without conflict.

- Palette names

  ```
  <jsxpalette name="xxxx">
  ```

  The value of your palette's `name` attribute must be unique among all `name` attributes defined by the extension that defines this palette. Other extensions can reuse this `name` attribute value without conflict.

- All other JavaScript `name` attribute values except those which name controls

  Controls are local to their containing window. Although different windows in the same extension can reuse control names, the usefulness of such architecture is somewhat limited by the fact that the `controlSignal` method typically uses the passed control's `name` property to identify it.

- Boxes

  GoLive creates box objects on demand and names them dynamically. These names are local to the module that creates them, but you never set a Box object's name yourself or retrieve box objects by name.

- Pictures

  The name attribute of an `<img>` element or that of a picture created by the `createPicture` method is local to the module that creates the picture.

- Global variables and functions defined by this extension module

  When an extension declares a variable outside the body of a function, the variable appears as global to the module that defines it; however, it is not visible outside this module. Functions follow similar rules of scope: a function appears as global only within the module that defines it.

  An extension cannot define a true global variable—one that is defined in all extensions. The only truly global variables are those which the SDK provides, such as the `app` global. An extension module makes data available globally by storing it in the Common object or by using the broadcast mechanism to pass string data to other extensions.

Container-wide Scope

The JavaScript names of controls and palette entries are local to their containing entity. In the case of a control, the containing entity is a window or panel. In the case of a palette entry, the containing entity is the palette group (if provided) or palette in which the entry is installed.

- Controls

  Control names must be unique within their containing window; different dialogs can reuse control names without causing naming conflicts.

- Palette Entries

  A `paletteentry` element's name must be unique within the palette or palette group that contains it. A `paletteentry` element's content is always local to the `paletteentry` element that provides it.

Local Scope

Variables declared as `var` in the body of a function are available only within that function. All other variables and functions the extension defines are available in the module's namespace.
